CW01082979

Robespierre

Two centuries after the French Revolution, Maximilien Robespierre is still regarded as its towering figure – for good or ill. Perceived by some as the champion, indeed the incarnation, of the Revolution's purest and noblest ideals, among others he will always be remembered as the reasoned advocate of the Terror, the defender of mass killing during the Revolution's darkest and most tragic phase. It is still almost impossible to be neutral about a man whose memory has been so consistently revered or reviled.

This volume comprises essays by an international array of scholars and examines Robespierre's life and work from three main perspectives. First, it explores Robespierre's ideology and his vision of the Revolution. Secondly, it investigates his rôle in the period's tumultuous politics, culminating in his year on the Committee of Public Safety in 1793–4. Lastly, much space is devoted to nineteenth- and twentieth-century representations of the Incorruptible – not only by historians, but also by dramatists and writers of fiction.

Individually, these essays illuminate many facets of Robespierre's career, thought and reputation. Collectively, they provide a balanced and up-to-date appraisal of one of the great figures of European history, still capable of arousing the fiercest of passions over two hundred years after his death.

COLIN HAYDON is Principal Lecturer in History at King Alfred's College, Winchester.

WILLIAM DOYLE is Professor of History at the University of Bristol.

Robespierre

Edited by

Colin Haydon

and

William Doyle

PUBLISHED BY THE PRESS SYNDICATE OF THE UNIVERSITY OF CAMBRIDGE
The Pitt Building, Trumpington Street, Cambridge CB2 1RP, United Kingdom

CAMBRIDGE UNIVERSITY PRESS
The Edinburgh Building, Cambridge, CB2 2RU, United Kingdom
http://www.cup.cam.ac.uk
40 West 20th Street, New York, NY 10011–4211, USA http://www.cup.org
10 Stamford Road, Oakleigh, Melbourne 3166, Australia

First published 1999

Printed in the United Kingdom at the University Press, Cambridge

Typeset in Plantin 10/12 pt [CE]

A catalogue record for this book is available from the British Library

Library of Congress Cataloguing in Publication data

Robespierre / edited by Colin Haydon and William Doyle.
p. cm.
Includes bibliographical references.
ISBN 0 521 59116 3
1. Robespierre, Maximilien, 1758–1794 – Political and social views.
2. Revolutionaries – France – History and criticism.
3. France – History – Revolution, 1789–1799 – Biography.
4. France. Convention nationale. Comité de salut public.
I. Haydon, Colin, 1955– . II. Doyle, William, 1942– .
DC146.R6R53 1999 944.04′092–dc21 98–38090 CIP

ISBN 0 521 59116 3 hardback

Contents

Contributors

MALCOLM COOK is Professor of Eighteenth-Century French Studies at the University of Exeter

FRANÇOIS CROUZET is Emeritus Professor of Modern History at the Université de Paris-IV-Sorbonne

GEOFFREY CUBITT is Lecturer in History at the University of York

MARK CUMMING is Associate Professor of English Language and Literature at Memorial University of Newfoundland

WILLIAM DOYLE is Professor of History at the University of Bristol

ALAN FORREST is Professor of Modern History at the University of York

JAMES FRIGUGLIETTI is Professor of History at Montana State University-Billings

HUGH GOUGH is Associate Professor of Modern History at University College Dublin

NORMAN HAMPSON is Emeritus Professor of History at the University of York

COLIN HAYDON is Principal Lecturer in History at King Alfred's College, Winchester

WILLIAM D. HOWARTH is Emeritus Professor of French at the University of Bristol

DAVID P. JORDAN is Professor of History at the University of Illinois at Chicago

A. JOURDAN is Lecturer in European Studies at the University of Amsterdam

GWYNNE LEWIS is Honorary Visiting Fellow at the University of Southampton

MARISA LINTON is Senior Lecturer in the School of Humanities at Kingston University

MORRIS SLAVIN is Professor Emeritus of History at Youngstown State University

FRANK TALLETT is Senior Lecturer in History at the University of Reading

Acknowledgements

Most of the essays in this collection were originally delivered as papers at a conference on 'Robespierre: history, historiography and literature' held at King Alfred's College, Winchester, in July 1994. We are grateful to the College for hosting the event and also to the Council of the Royal Historical Society and the Research Committee, King Alfred's College, for the award of grants which helped to defray the conference's costs. The occasion was a very stimulating and enjoyable one and we should like to thank all those who participated in it. The contributors to the volume have greatly assisted our task as editors by adhering to deadlines and promptly answering our various queries. We should like to thank Mrs Jean Richards and Mr Geoff Couling for their help with the word-processing of the volume. Lastly, we have incurred many debts at Cambridge University Press. In particular, we wish to record our gratitude to Richard Fisher for initially supporting the project, and to Vicky Cuthill, Carol Fellingham Webb, Elizabeth Howard and Caroline Murray for their exemplary work at the various stages of the book's production.

C. M. H.
W. D.

Abbreviations

AHRF	*Annales historiques de la Révolution française*
AN	Archives Nationales, Paris
BN	Bibliothèque Nationale, Paris
Robespierre, *Œuvres*	*Œuvres complètes de Maximilien Robespierre*, ed. E. Déprez *et al.*, 10 vols. (Paris, 1910–67)

Part I

Introduction

1 Robespierre: after two hundred years

William Doyle and Colin Haydon

The seagreen incomprehensible?

Even two centuries after his death, Robespierre can still inspire deep unease or revulsion in France. This is perhaps best shown by the paucity of monuments to the man who was the towering figure of the Revolution. Unlike Danton, whose statue in the Latin Quarter rallies the *patrie*'s youth against the enemy, Robespierre has no statue in the capital. One has to go to Saint-Denis for that – or rather for a large, rather ugly bust, provocatively near the royal basilica. In Paris, there is a Métro station named after him in a working-class district long dominated by the communists; a plaque – recently smashed, but now restored[1] – outside his lodgings in the rue Saint-Honoré; and another in the Conciergerie, erected by the Société des Etudes robespierristes. Even in Arras, his birth-place, the plaque on the house where he lived as a young lawyer is set high up, to prevent vandalism. Unlike Condorcet or Desmoulins, he did not appear on the bicentenary's commemorative stamps. None the less, he was selected for inclusion in a recent poll as one of the figures personifying an epoch in French history. The poll's results revealed that, although controversial, he had a better image than both Louis XIV and Napoleon.[2]

Other polls, in fact, reveal widespread popular ignorance about Robespierre in France (in one conducted in 1988, 29 per cent of those questioned thought he was a Girondin, with only 21 per cent knowing he was a Montagnard).[3] But what is more alarming is the degree to which historians can arrive at diametrically opposed positions on the subject of the Incorruptible. Ernest Hamel, whose hagiographical *Histoire de Robespierre* was published between 1865 and 1867, concluded

1 Personal observations by W. Doyle, July 1996 and August 1997.

2 *Le Monde*, 19 September 1996, supplément, p. iv. We owe this reference to Professor Edward James.

3 F. Crouzet, *Historians and the French Revolution: the Case of Maximilien Robespierre* (Swansea, 1989), p. 26.

that his hero was 'un des plus grands hommes de bien qui aient paru sur la terre'.[4] Lord Acton, in his magisterial summing-up of his career, famously declared: 'Only this is certain, that he remains the most hateful character in the forefront of history since Machiavelli reduced to a code the wickedness of public men.'[5] In the twentieth century, he was 'this great democrat' and 'the immovable and incorruptible head of revolutionary Resistance' in the eyes, respectively, of Albert Mathiez and Georges Lefebvre,[6] whereas Richard Cobb reduced him to 'a fumbling, prissy, routinal, comfort-loving, vaguely ridiculous, prickly little man'.[7] It was in 1974 that Norman Hampson, in his *Life and Opinions of Maximilien Robespierre*, came clean about the problem, with a frankness that is unusual among historians. Such, on occasions, are the inadequacies or the complexities of the evidence, that the book's three fictional commentators – a clergyman who takes Robespierre's side, a party member, uninterested in the individual, and a civil servant, who remorselessly scrutinises the Incorruptible's deeds – frequently find it impossible to reach a mutually satisfying conclusion. That historians' own convictions can colour their interpretations, despite their professional ideals, is plainly a truism. It is the extent of the difficulty respecting Robespierre that is abnormal, and hence peculiarly disconcerting.

Politics provides part of the explanation for this. That the Incorruptible would be a political totem in France after Thermidor or under the Restoration was inevitable; but, as François Crouzet details, he has remained one right up to our own times. In the nineteenth century, left-wing republicans and early socialists took up his cause (though it is worth noting that Hamel was only an unsuccessful republican politician). In England too, as Gwynne Lewis describes in chapter 12, he was greatly admired by the Chartist Bronterre O'Brien. His stock continued to rise in the twentieth century with the triumph of Bolshevism in Russia and the growth of communist parties in western Europe. Mathiez was a member of the French communist party in the early 1920s, Lefebvre was a convinced socialist, and both men were profoundly influenced by Marxism. The impact of these influences can be seen in specific as well as general interpretations. In chapter 6 Frank Tallett, for instance, highlights the strength of Robespierre's religious beliefs; but, for Mathiez, the cult of the Supreme Being was simply a social programme,

4 E. Hamel, *Histoire de Robespierre*, 3 vols. (Paris, 1865–7), vol. III, p. 807.

5 Lord Acton, *Lectures on the French Revolution*, ed. J. N. Figgis and R. V. Laurence (London, 1910), p. 300.

6 A. Mathiez, 'Robespierre jeune en Franche-Comté (Pluviôse, An II)', in his *Autour de Robespierre* (Paris, 1925, repr. 1926), p. 13; G. Lefebvre, 'Remarks on Robespierre', *French Historical Studies* 1 (1958), 10.

7 R. Cobb, 'Robespierre', in his *Tour de France* (London, 1976), p. 53.

a means of unifying the nation.[8] All this is not to say that historians sympathetic to Marxism might not be critical of some of Robespierre's policies; Albert Soboul was. Even so, it is the new 'revisionist school', invigorated by increasing disenchantment with communism and revulsion at the Gulag, and by the collapse of the USSR and the Soviet bloc, that has once more cut Robespierre down to size.

For historians, there are major problems with sources. Very little is known about five-sixths of Robespierre's life, the two principal authorities for his early years contradict each other, and one can only speculate on what made him generally or psychologically the man he was. The Thermidorians not only blackened his memory but possibly also exaggerated his importance for posterity. Many of his papers were destroyed in 1815, whilst proper records were not taken of the Committee of Public Safety's meetings. Above all, in his speeches and publications, designed to persuade his hearers and readers, was Robespierre always convinced of his stance, and did he always mean what he said? Certainly he always appeared to believe everything he said, but how far, in 1793–4, was he fronting the collective stance of the government, and how far was he speaking for himself? His closest associates died with him at Thermidor, so we lack the testimonies which, with most politicians, help to clarify issues of this kind. We also lack any kind of useful table-talk (no doubt it would have been exceedingly dull, interspersed with long silences). All too often, historians are obliged to interpret the evidence without adequate guides – so that the results may say as much about them as about the subject. This is, very appropriately, a particularly horrible case of 'the death of the author'.

Robespierre's speeches elicit a variety of responses from readers. At one level, they display the highest ideals of the Revolution, with their emphasis on liberty, happiness, peace, respect for the people, virtue and love of the *patrie*. But there is the darker rhetoric of plots, enemies disguised as friends, 'fripons', the dangers of calumny, the persecution of the people's defenders, military treachery, the need for purges, the necessity of terror. They can be probing and far-sighted, notably when describing the dangers posed to the Revolution by war, but, especially towards the end, they can display, alarmingly, a slackening grasp of reality.[9] Besides the speeches' content, there is their general character. Sophisticated and erudite, employing classical and historical allusions, they can also, notoriously, be verbose and tedious. The repeated use of the first person singular and the suffocating self-pity – 'A slave of liberty,

[8] A. Mathiez, 'Robespierre et le culte de l'Etre suprême', in *Autour de Robespierre*, pp. 94–129.

[9] See chapter 10.

a living martyr of the Republic ... I am the most wretched of men'[10] – are disconcerting. Still more so are the prophecies of his approaching martyrdom and the self-deceiving circumlocutions, veiling the reality of the Terror. The chapters in this volume dealing with Robespierre's outlook and politics make considerable use of his own words; and readers will gather a great deal about the man from them.

A further bar to assessing Robespierre is that his personality excites an intensity of admiration, or loathing and contempt, which is most unusual for a figure long dead. Acton's 'hateful' is significant: it applies to the man himself, not his political actions. Ardent and energetic himself, Mathiez revered his strength of principle and purpose, his perspicacity and commitment. The austere republican Georges Lefebvre admired his integrity, hard work and frugality. By contrast, Richard Cobb, anarchic, fun-loving and generous, revealed, both in his writings and conversation, an utter hatred of Robespierre, 'not only for what he did, what he, so boringly, so labouredly, said, but for what he represented in the form of self-righteousness, unctuousness, obstinacy, lack of understanding of others, and puritanism'.[11] Moreover, his cold-blooded inflexibility and reasoned advocacy of terror have established him as a monstrous archetype of the visionary fanatic, zealous for some fantastic Utopia, prepared to liquidate to achieve it and quite indifferent to human suffering. It is difficult to believe that, in his Identikit picture of Heinrich Himmler's precursors (containing as it does glances towards the Terror, the Republic of Virtue, the lifestyle of the Maison Duplay, even the dog, Brount), Hugh Trevor-Roper was not thinking of Robespierre:

> if we look back at the cataclysmic periods of society, at periods of revolution and violent social change ... [Himmler's] prototype is there. It is the Grand Inquisitor, the mystic in politics, the man who is prepared to sacrifice humanity to an abstract ideal. The Grand Inquisitors of history were not cruel or self-indulgent men. They were often painfully conscientious and austere in their personal lives. They were often scrupulously kind to animals.[12]

Even so, it was perhaps J. M. Thompson who, in human terms, hit the bull's-eye. Throughout his biography, he wrestled valiantly to be fair to his subject, and, when he reached the abandonment of Desmoulins, he meticulously explained Robespierre's point of view. 'It would be surprising', he concluded, 'if, under the circumstances, Robespierre had acted otherwise.' 'But', he added, 'who would not like him better, if he had?'[13]

[10] Robespierre, *Œuvres*, vol. X, p. 556.
[11] R. Cobb, *Reactions to the French Revolution* (London, 1972), p. 5.
[12] H. R. Trevor-Roper, *The Last Days of Hitler* (London, 1947), p. 21.
[13] J. M. Thompson, *Robespierre*, 3rd edition (Oxford, 1988), p. 445.

François Furet maintained that Robespierre's personal psychology was irrelevant to an understanding of his significance in the Revolution. At a superficial level, the description of Robespierre as the incarnation of the Revolution is awkward. Whilst he projected himself as its embodiment in his speeches, there is a glaring asymmetry between the tumultuous, titanic events and the small, fastidious, bespectacled lawyer, lacking the hideous passion of Marat or the volcanic personality of Danton. 'O unhappiest Advocate of Arras, wert thou worse than other Advocates?',[14] wrote Carlyle, always anxious to belittle him. His orderly life in the Maison Duplay – one thinks of the cakes and the oranges – had nothing in common with the toil, dirt and suffering of 'the people' whom he venerated; given his protected, though modest, lifestyle, his pronouncements on virtuous poverty – 'The people can bear hunger, but not crime'[15] – appear grotesque. Whilst he claimed to represent the people, his dress and manners proclaimed the chasm; and, when in government, he supported the limitation of the sections' meetings and the clamp-down on their politics.

Robespierre's relation to the Revolution as a whole remains the most perennially fascinating issue. How far did *he* make a difference? Was his oratory largely a retrospective justification of events that tidal factors, or other people, had initiated? How far was he the plaything of social forces that he could not comprehend, let alone control? Was his justification of the Terror whilst in power always implicit in the espousal of the Manichaean discourse of the early Revolution, in which the politics of the righteous could not tolerate dissent? Was his political genius simply to let himself be carried to power by the irresistible revolutionary flood? The number of occasions when he initiated policy appears small: the self-denying ordinance of 1791; the establishment of the cult of the Supreme Being; and, one presumes, the passing of the law of 22 Prairial. On the great issue of the war, he was out of step with majority opinion. When in power, he held no departmental brief, assumed no responsibility for practical imperatives such as the organisation of war and provisioning, and remained in Paris. But, precisely because of this, he had time to ponder events and their meaning and, as the government's spokesman, was able not only to annunciate and vindicate policy but also to invest it with an ideological coherence and moral justification. No one else could have undertaken this rôle so successfully, given Robespierre's prestige in both the Convention and the Jacobin club and his reputation for sincerity. Capable of adapting tactically to the

[14] T. Carlyle, *The French Revolution*, 3 vols. (London: George Routledge and Sons, 1888), vol. III, p. 198.

[15] Robespierre, *Œuvres*, vol. X, p. 560.

changing circumstances of the Revolution whilst retaining his fundamental principles, he was able to provide later generations of the left with a seemingly consistent inspiration. It was in this way, for Furet, writing in 1978, that he had, irrespective of his personal shortcomings or strengths, 'the strange privilege' of incarnating the Revolution. More than any other politician, he was able to articulate its language. When he died at Thermidor, the Revolution died with him.[16]

It is, of course, for the discourse of terror and the novel linking of terror and virtue that Robespierre is, above all, remembered. Here, problems abound. How did the man who, in the Constituent, had argued against the death penalty's retention become the Terror's principal proponent? Why is he chiefly associated with it, when Carrier, responsible for the *noyades* at Nantes, and Collot d'Herbois and Fouché, overseers of the *mitraillades* at Lyon, had so much blood on their hands? Why did he not, after the victories over the counter-revolution and Fleurus, seek, like Lincoln, 'to bind up the nation's wounds', instead of continuing to denounce the 'fripons' and 'scélérats' to the end? A number of the chapters in this volume are concerned with these questions. Marisa Linton examines Robespierre's justification of terror in the context of his wider political thought, whilst Geoffrey Cubitt describes the hold which conspiracy theories exerted on his mind. Norman Hampson charts how Robespierre's attitude to the Terror was often rooted in characteristics which were evident in 1789, or earlier, and how these developed, moving towards a ghastly crescendo, as he had to come to terms with the ever-changing revolutionary situation. And, as David Jordan argues, it is his neat, reasoned formulae, justifying terror as an emanation of virtue, rather than the deeds of the ultra-terrorists, that are remembered, making Robespierre, like Machiavelli, an immortal apologist for political ruthlessness. Once adopted, these formulae prevented him changing tack as the republican armies triumphed and, applicable in so many contexts, they have an especially appalling resonance in the twentieth century.

As the archetypal revolutionary terrorist, Robespierre has repeatedly been depicted in literary works – a subject which Malcolm Cook and William Howarth investigate. In the greatest drama depicting the Revolution, Büchner's *Dantons Tod*, he is less interesting as an individual than as the embodiment of the historical forces against which the tragic Danton finds himself pitted.[17] None the less, it is as the single-minded, ruthless, calculating puritan in power, dyspeptic, unattractive, but very dangerous, that Robespierre has most to offer the modern playwright.

[16] F. Furet, *Penser la Révolution française* (Paris, 1978), pp. 82, 87.
[17] See chapter 15.

In this guise, he is reborn in Anouilh's *Pauvre Bitos*, set in the 1950s, as the persecutor of wartime collaborators and right-wing profiteers. Again, in Andrzej Wajda's film *Danton* (1982), the parallels between revolutionary France and communist Poland – with bread queues, show trials and the language of liberty masking repression – and between Robespierre and Jaruzelski are wonderfully effective (it was a lucky coincidence that the general, like the Incorruptible, so often wore tinted glasses). In French novels, too, it is the repellent aspects of Robespierre that are to the fore. It is noticeable that Hilary Mantel's *A Place of Greater Safety* (1992) portrays a more human Robespierre than any French novelist has yet dared depict.

After news of Robespierre's death had reached Oxford, a fellow of Brasenose wrote: 'Glad the infamous Robespierre is gone at last. Gone to hell as sure as he's born, and Barrere [*sic*] and all the Tribe of them. I only wish that all the French Convention were gone with 'em – Aye, and the French nation too.'[18] Since 1794, the influence of partisanship – both hostile and adulatory – has suffused studies of Robespierre and the Revolution – if less forcefully expressed. However, by 1935, another Oxford don, J. M. Thompson, thought such distorting bias was at an end among professional historians. Accepting the methodology of 'scientific history' and optimistic that its ideal of impartiality was attainable, he observed:

> for 140 years, historical opinion about Robespierre and the Revolution has swung to and fro, under the impulse of personal predilection, or political passion. But two steadying influences have gradually come into action – the publication of orginal sources, and freedom of historical study. The first of these cannot be taken away; the second may be withdrawn, but only for a time . . . There is a growing consensus of informed opinion, establishing conclusions which will not easily be upset.[19]

Yet, despite such high hopes, Thompson's pendulum has, inevitably, not stopped swinging. In 1978, Furet had to insist that 'the French Revolution is over' and could therefore be studied dispassionately,[20] whilst, with the approach of the bicentenary and during the celebrations, political divisions among French historians, and their impact on their interpretations, were glaringly in evidence. The debate about Robespierre and his rôle in the Revolution will go on. None the less, the current state of play is worth describing as a prelude to the detailed chapters in this volume.

[18] Quoted in L. G. Mitchell, 'Politics and revolution 1772–1800', in *The History of the University of Oxford V: the Eighteenth Century*, ed. L. S. Sutherland and L. G. Mitchell (Oxford, 1986), p. 185.

[19] Thompson, *Robespierre*, p. 633.

[20] Furet, *Penser la Révolution française*, pp. 13–109.

Robespierre today

That Robespierre remains as controversial as ever, two centuries after his death, is an embarrassment to most historians. At the time of the bicentennial celebrations of the Revolution in and around 1989, hundreds of scholarly gatherings were devoted to it all over the world, and the number of publications ran into thousands. Inevitably Robespierre figured in many of these; but he was not the main focus of any. Despite general agreement that, for better or worse, the Incorruptible was the outstanding figure of the Revolution, no important publication commemorated the fact. Only one French conference was eventually organised around him, in his native Arras.[21] It was planned before the bicentenary and eventually met fully four years after it. Participation was international, and ran to 200 attenders, but a suspiciously large number of the leading French authorities on the Revolution contrived to miss it. Two other, much smaller gatherings in 1994 marked the bicentenary of Robespierre's death in Thermidor. Both were organised outside France. One, held in England, produced the present volume; the other met in the Netherlands and later published proceedings of its own.[22] What these belated, scattered and diffuse conferences on Robespierre's historical importance had in common was a resolute determination to avoid the central issue.

There were sound grounds for doing so. From a scholarly point of view the question of Robespierre and the Terror had been debated to death, and there was no new evidence. Any attempt to address it afresh risked degeneration into sterile polemics. Besides, obsession with this problem had diverted attention from other aspects of the man about which there was more to be said. And so the Arras conference consciously dwelt on the evolution of Robespierre's idea of the Nation, his economic views and instincts, and his attitudes to international questions. The Amsterdam colloquium concentrated on his character, his discourse and contemporary perceptions of him. The present collection devotes considerable space to later perceptions, fictional as well as historical, while attempting to review the full range of his ideas. In the event, it proved impossible to avoid the unmentionable entirely. At Arras, an open call for papers brought the attendance of substantial numbers of the old intellectual left, led by the redoubtable Claude Mazauric, who had criss-crossed the country throughout 1989 extolling

21 J.-P. Jessenne, G. Deregnaucourt, J.-P. Hirsch and H. Leuwers (eds.), *Robespierre: De la Nation artésienne à la République et aux Nations* (Lille, 1994).

22 A. Jourdan (ed.), *Robespierre: figure-réputation*, Yearbook of European Studies IX (Amsterdam and Atlanta, 1996).

the merits of the Incorruptible against a background of official silence.[23] Mazauric, it is true, confined himself to admiring the purity and inflexibility of Robespierre's principles, leaving his audience to draw any conclusions;[24] but one at least of his fellow participants insisted on interpreting the notorious law of 22 Prairial as a humanitarian measure.[25] At Amsterdam, a much less partisan Bronislaw Baczko admitted that there was nothing new to be said about Robespierre and the Terror, but offered his reflections anyway since the question was too important to ignore.[26]

He was right; and paradoxically, while conferences devoted entirely to Robespierre could skirt around the issue, works on the Revolution in general could not. The point at which they chose to end was a judgement in itself. A scholarly concern not to be mesmerised by the drama of Thermidor led two of the more successful recent general surveys to bury the fall of the Incorruptible in a longer continuum of events. Though bound by the demands of a series to take his story down to 1815, D. M. G. Sutherland roundly declared that the Revolution was not over in July 1794, as the continued vitality of counter-revolution showed. And Robespierre had been overthrown by 'a cabal of ultra-terrorists', implying that responsibility for the Terror was at least shared.[27] Four years later, one of the present authors chose to end *The Oxford History of the French Revolution* in 1802, and not even to make a chapter break with Robespierre's overthrow. His so-called dictatorship, it was argued, was not so much a reality as a political insult, and became a retrospective justification propagated by those who had destroyed him.[28] Neither Sutherland's study nor the *Oxford History* denied his importance in the Revolution, both before and after his death. He was not blamed above others for the Terror that he was far from alone in defending; nor were the Terror and the Republic of the Year II presented as the inevitable climax of all that had occurred since 1789, much less the essence of the entire Revolution.

These perceptions were not shared by most of the other general works appearing around the time of the bicentenary. The classic interpretation, going back to Jaurès and Mathiez, had presented the coup of Thermidor

23 S. L. Kaplan, *Farewell, Revolution. Disputed Legacies, France 1789–1989* (Ithaca and London, 1995), pp. 447–8.

24 Jessenne *et al.* (eds.), *Robespierre*, p. 232.

25 L. Abdoul-Mellek, 'D'un choix politique de Robespierre: la Terreur', in Jessenne *et al.* (eds.), *Robespierre*, pp. 191–203.

26 B. Baczko, 'Robespierre et la Terreur', in Jourdan (ed.), *Robespierre*, pp. 153–67.

27 D. M. G. Sutherland, *France 1789–1815. Revolution and Counterrevolution* (London, 1985), pp. 248–9.

28 W. Doyle, *The Oxford History of the French Revolution* (Oxford, 1989), p. 281.

as the end of the Revolution, aborting both its social promise and the resolute elimination of those who threatened it. This tradition lost much of its pugnacious vigour after the death of Albert Soboul in 1982. In English, its final twitch came from George Rudé, an earlier biographer of Robespierre,[29] whose last book was a general history of the Revolution. Although it did not stop in 1794, Rudé's account rapidly petered out after that date. Thermidor was the end of 'not only a man or a group but a system', when the Revolution turned sharply off course into 'something of an anti-climax'.[30] The fullest recent statement in French of the classic viewpoint came in a dictionary of over a thousand pages published under the posthumous editorship of Soboul.[31] The entry on Robespierre was the work of Mazauric, who described him as the central figure of the Revolution, the very incarnation of its 'profoundly levelling [*roturière*] and democratic essence'. He was a man of humanity, yet 'naturally the theoretician of terror as a legal terror, the substitute for popular violence whose fragility and disorder divided more than it brought together'. Mazauric also wrote the article on the Terror. Here, after much equivocation, the essential point eventually emerged. 'Whether we like it or not, the episode of the Terror is all of a piece [*fait 'bloc'*] with the whole movement of the democratic and liberal Revolution of 1789.'[32]

Mazauric did like it: but ironically, apart from that, his judgement on Robespierre and the Terror differed little from the verdict of his bitterest opponents. They too thought 1789 and 1794 were all of a piece, and that Robespierre epitomised the whole frightful episode. Theirs proved the dominant perception of the Revolution in 1989, and they were led from the front by François Furet. He had once thought differently. When, in tandem with Denis Richet, he had made his first foray into revolutionary historiography in 1965,[33] it had been to depict the period 1791–4 as an aberration, the Revolution skidding off course. Tellingly, they did not end the story at Thermidor, because Robespierre's fall simply represented a return to the original script. Over the next few years, however, Furet's perceptions changed. By 1978 he saw the Revolution as locked from the start into a discourse of popular sovereignty whose only possible and logical outcome was terror, since it did not recognise the legitimacy of political dissent.[34] And 'what makes Robespierre an immortal figure is not that he ruled for some months

[29] G. Rudé, *Robespierre. Portrait of a Revolutionary Democrat* (London, 1975).
[30] G. Rudé, *The French Revolution* (New York and London, 1988), pp. 111–12.
[31] A. Soboul (ed.), *Dictionnaire historique de la Révolution française* (Paris, 1989).
[32] 'Terreur', in *ibid.*, p. 1025.
[33] F. Furet and D. Richet, *La Révolution*, 2 vols. (Paris, 1965).
[34] Furet, *Penser la Révolution française*.

over the Revolution; it is that the Revolution speaks through him its most tragic and purest discourse'.[35] When he fell it ended, in the sense at least that this Jacobin discourse was abandoned, along with the limitless ambitions which it articulated.

Ten years on, Furet's later views had not changed. The requirements of the general history of France between 1770 and 1880, which he published the year before the bicentenary,[36] precluded him ending in 1794; but his appraisal of Robespierre[37] echoed often word for word what he had said before: 'the Incorruptible ended up as the Revolution incarnate', and in Thermidor 'the Revolution left the shores of Utopia' and 'real life resumed its rights'.[38] A fuller articulation of his viewpoint came in the critical dictionary of the Revolution which he orchestrated the next year, in a conscious challenge to that of Soboul.[39] Entries were chosen on interpretative rather than inclusive grounds, but Robespierre could not be omitted on either. Furet, while reserving the Terror for himself, left the entry on the Incorruptible to a young acolyte. Patrice Gueniffey did what was expected of him. There was terror, he argued, in Robespierre's very rhetorical strategies, admitting no sincere disagreement with his own conception of the truth.[40] Like Furet, Gueniffey emphasised that after 1789 Robespierre had no private life. Politics was everything, and he made no distinction between his personal ambitions and the public welfare. His genius was to go with the flow, never leading but following, at least until he attained supreme power. By then that meant acquiescing willingly in the Terror from which his name is inseparable. At the Amsterdam colloquium five years later, Gueniffey substantially repeated this appraisal.[41]

In the English-speaking world, meanwhile, the publishing sensation of the bicentennial year was Simon Schama's *Citizens*, a self-proclaimed 'chronicle' of the Revolution whose unifying theme was its bestial violence. Schama evidently saw the Terror as the first step on the road to the Holocaust. The law of 22 Prairial was 'the founding charter of totalitarian justice';[42] and extermination was 'the logical outcome of an ideology that dehumanised its adversaries, and that had become incapable of seeing any middle ground between total triumph and utter

[35] *Ibid.*, p. 87.
[36] F. Furet, *La Révolution 1770–1880. De Turgot à Jules Ferry* (Paris, 1988), vol. IV of the *Histoire de France Hachette*, published in five volumes.
[37] *Ibid.*, pp. 150–7.
[38] *Ibid.*, p. 162.
[39] F. Furet and M. Ozouf (eds.), *Dictionnaire critique de la Révolution française* (Paris, 1989).
[40] 'Robespierre', in *ibid.*, p. 324.
[41] Jourdan (ed.), *Robespierre*, pp. 1–18.
[42] S. Schama, *Citizens. A Chronicle of the French Revolution* (New York and London, 1989), p. 836.

eclipse'.[43] The book ended when the Terror did, in Thermidor. A studied, though far from ingenuous, essay in letting the story speak for itself, it offered no final explicit judgement on Robespierre, apart from passing asides. A denunciation was 'crazy enough to be credible' to him;[44] 'in the end, he saw himself as a messianic schoolmaster, wielding a very big stick to inculcate virtue'.[45] The only weapon against which he was helpless was laughter.[46] Nevertheless the story as told by Schama is no laughing matter. Although, in the book's most famous phrase, the Terror was merely 1789 with a higher body count,[47] Robespierre was one of the architects of its last great, Parisian, phase. He had to die to end it.

Astonishment has often been expressed that Schama's epic was never translated into French. Did it advance truths that the French found too painful to contemplate? On the contrary, it offered them nothing that they had not already heard from Furet and his cohorts. They claimed to have won the bicentennial argument. President François Mitterrand and the state-sponsored commission for celebrating the bicentenary wished to make its theme the Rights of Man, the Revolution of '89 but not of '94. The Furet school (and outside France, Schama) argued that they were inseparable. The issue surfaced whenever the commemoration escaped the official grip. Paradoxically, the only question that transcended the division was that of Robespierre. There was a good case, repeatedly made by writers in the classic tradition, for regarding the provincial lawyer from Arras, who bored his fellow deputies to distraction, as the most faithful and persistent defender of the Rights of Man under the Constituent. It was often heard from the left in 1989.[48] But for the purposes of the official bicentenary celebrations, his later association with the Terror tainted him beyond redemption. And if, as was now being argued, terror and the terroristic frame of mind were present in 1789 itself, there was no place for even partial recognition of terror's most notorious defender.

In these circumstances, the embarrassment of most professional historians was understandable. Any attempt to focus attention on Robespierre, at any stage in his revolutionary career, risked appearing to condone mass-murder. The embarrassment was compounded by the identity of those still prepared to defend the man of blood as a man of principle. The most vocal, like Mazauric, were professed communists, committed not just to vindicating Robespierre but to an ideology that, by an ironic coincidence, was collapsing or being challenged throughout

[43] *Ibid.*, p. 792. [44] *Ibid.*, p. 808. [45] *Ibid.*, pp. 828–9.
[46] *Ibid.*, p. 844. [47] *Ibid.*, p. 447.
[48] See Kaplan, *Disputed Legacies*, pp. 444–50, 456–63.

the world in the very year of the bicentenary. Communist régimes, whether national or local, had always been the only authorities to venerate Robespierre's memory with plaques, shrines or street names. Their discredit now stained his reputation even further (if that were possible) with the sort of guilt by association which he himself had found so persuasive in 1794. The judgements of Furet on Robespierre were certainly influenced by the fact that he had once been a party member himself, now expiating his youthful credulity with the zeal of a convert.[49] And Furet's arguments, though no longer new, gained authority as they emanated from a historian who had seen the error of his ways long before the system which had once deluded him collapsed.

For all the intellectual success of Furet (in French) or Schama (in English), it remains true that the general public knows little or nothing about Robespierre.[50] What it knows about the entire Revolution, indeed, is largely confined to grisly images of the guillotine and the Terror. These perceptions were reinforced rather than modified by the publicity of the bicentennial year, as the press, instinctively drawn to reporting the lurid and sensational, happily confirmed its readers in what they thought they knew already. The link to the horrors of the twentieth century was repeatedly emphasised. And in so far as Robespierre was perceived as the architect and perpetrator of terror, he found himself more reviled than ever, and stigmatised as responsible in some sense for political bloodshed long after he himself had fallen victim to it.

Even in Arras his memory is contentious. A bust commissioned by the local council in the 1920s remains securely locked away in the town hall. A much-publicised attempt to erect a statue to him in the communist-run Lorraine town of Thionville failed to raise adequate funds from the public, and received none from the state,[51] even though warmly supported by vocal left-wing groups, including the Arras-founded 'Amis de Robespierre pour le Bicentenaire de la Révolution'.[52] This body's activities bore more fruit in the 1993 colloquium in his birth-place. But so far from his remains (supposing that any could be identified) being transferred, as Mazauric advocated, to the Pantheon, Robespierre remained without a monument of any significance in France. The triumph of the Bolsheviks in 1917 ensured that he received fuller public commemoration in Russia than in his native country.[53] But how long,

49 S. L. Kaplan, *Farewell, Revolution. The Historians' Feud 1789/1989* (Ithaca and London, 1995), chapter 6.

50 For the depth of French ignorance, see Crouzet, *Historians*, pp. 25–6; Kaplan, *Disputed Legacies*, p. 48.

51 Kaplan, *Disputed Legacies*, pp. 463–9.

52 *Ibid.*, pp. 456–9.

53 See E. J. Hobsbawm, *Echoes of the Marseillaise. Two Centuries Look Back on the French Revolution* (London, 1990), pp. 70–1.

now that the Soviet Union has gone, will he retain his honoured slot in the Kremlin wall?

In less public scholarly circles, the leading, indeed the only, learned journal devoted entirely to the Revolution, the *Annales historiques de la Révolution française*, is still published under the auspices of Mathiez's Société des Etudes robespierristes. But it remains sectarian in spirit. Little work by foreigners, and none by associates of Furet, ever appears or is noticed in its pages. And so, although the publication of the present volume and others shows that it is possible with careful planning to discuss Robespierre on more-or-less neutral ground, what seems as absent as ever is middle ground. The closest recent writing has come to that is in fiction. The Robespierre of Hilary Mantel's *A Place of Greater Safety* is neither a bloodless calculator nor a bloodthirsty tyrant. The novel ends, it is true, with the fall of Danton, who is abandoned by 'Max' after betraying his trust. But throughout the story Robespierre is portrayed as honest, humane, a loyal friend, almost amiable. He is progressively caught up by colleagues and circumstances that he cannot control, and his growing anguish is emphasised. The novel is obviously grounded in wide and detailed historical reading; and although there is plenty of artistic licence, the anguish is not pure invention. One of the sources that Mantel clearly used was Norman Hampson's *The Life and Opinions of Maximilien Robespierre*. Hailed by Richard Cobb on its first appearance as brilliant, dramatic, a formidable achievement which made its subject human[54] (praise indeed, given his loathing of 'His Holiness'), it never made the impact it deserved among historians. No doubt its literary approach, the conversation between the characters, disconcerted them. The appeal for a novelist was more obvious. It brought out the ambiguities, uncertainties and genuine difficulties of interpretation thrown up by all the evidence about the man. Historians, perhaps, cannot forgive Hampson for refusing to take a final position on these complexities. Novelists must be allowed that privilege. Robespierre himself once said that the Revolution had taught him the truth of the axiom that history is fiction.[55] The time may have come when fiction contributes as much to our understanding of him as the disagreements of historians, most of them still unable to see him as anything other than a symbol or precursor of things he never intended or even dreamed.

[54] *New Statesman*, 13 September 1974, pp. 349–51.

[55] Quoted in N. Hampson, *The Life and Opinions of Maximilien Robespierre* (London, 1974), p. viii.

2 The Robespierre problem

David P. Jordan

'The Revolution', François Furet reminded us, 'is an epoch without great men.' Robespierre, with all his flaws and shortcomings as a man, fits the pronouncement perfectly. He was unworldly, resentful, vain, egotistical, susceptible to flattery, contemptuous of or indifferent to all the social pleasures except conversation, guarded and suspicious, his innermost self carefully shielded by ancien régime manners. As a politician he was equally compromised, being inflexible, unforgiving, ill at ease in public, secretive, stiff and pedantic as a speaker (with an unpleasing and not very powerful voice), lacking the common touch, preoccupied. As a political and social thinker he was annoyingly fastidious, adroit and closely focused rather than original, prone to substitute Jacobin rhetorical formulae for logical steps, obsessively self-regarding, too tied to circumstances to formulate general principles (or disentangle those he held from the personalities and issues of the moment), enthralled by abstractions. Yet he imposed, then imprinted, himself on the Revolution. No other figure of the Revolution (save the special case of Napoleon) could provide the focus and the fulcrum for so many aspects of that tremendous event. He remains fascinating partly because he was (and is) so controversial, partly because he was (and is) so elusive, at least to the biographer, but mostly because he managed for a few short but significant years to convince his contemporaries that his life, his words, his very self were indistinguishable from the Revolution. He was its embodiment. He somehow *was* the Revolution incarnate, an act of faith that lay at the very centre of his thought and effectiveness. As he once told his listeners, 'I am the people myself!'[1]

This kind of insistence on political embodiment as an instrument of authority or an assertion of destiny has been brilliantly analysed by Pierre Nora.[2] Robespierre, of course, left no memoirs, but the ten

[1] Robespierre, *Œuvres*, vol. VIII, p. 311.

[2] Pierre Nora, 'Les mémoires d'état, de Commynes à de Gaulle', *Les lieux de mémoire*, sous la direction de Pierre Nora, 7 vols. (Paris, 1984–92), vol. II, 2, pp. 355–400. See especially the discussion of Sully, Richelieu, de Retz, Louis XIV and Napoleon,

volumes of his *Œuvres complètes*, especially volumes IV–X which contain his journalism and oratory, are a kind of *mémoire d'état*, a history of the Revolution's ideology by one of its creators, self-consciously and publicly presented by a man unable to distinguish himself from the events of which he was a part. From his first to his final speeches he both defined a new historical man, the revolutionary, and reminded his listeners that he was the exemplar. 'Who am I?', he rhetorically interrogated the Convention on 8 Thermidor. 'A slave of the *patrie*, a living martyr of the Republic, the victim and the scourge of crime ... The faults of others will be pardoned: my zeal for the *patrie* is made into a crime.'[3] This constant celebration of self – sometimes as the Revolution, sometimes as the people, sometimes as patriotism – was seen by his contemporaries as the essence of his influence. 'If you ask me', wrote Billaud-Varenne, an enemy and rival, 'how he was able to have so much ascendance over public opinion, I would answer that it is because he ostentatiously showed the most austere virtues, the most absolute dedication and the purest principles.'[4]

For historians, his self-conscious embodiment of the Revolution has led us to use Robespierre as a cryptogram: if we can crack the code, we can understand the Revolution. Put another way, our view of Robespierre reveals our view of the Revolution. But here the difficulties begin. His biography, rather than revealing the great events of the day, is scant, suggestive rather than obvious. He held power for only a year, albeit the most tumultuous and bloody year of the Revolution, very little of the legislation he proposed or supported was adopted, and none of it has endured. In traditional political terms he was a failure. He remains as elusive today as he was during the Revolution, and the swings of the pendulum of judgement remain as extreme.

First a brief sketch of his early life. The lives of almost all the revolutionaries are obscure, and give little hint, before 1789, of future greatness or notoriety (let alone revolutionary tendencies, potential or ambitions). None of the revolutionaries, and certainly not the Jacobins, wanted to recall their lives before the Revolution. At best embarrassment and humiliation lay in their past. Robespierre was no exception. It was tacitly understood that what happened before 1789 was a part of the detested ancien régime.

Maximilien Marie Isidore Robespierre was born on 6 May 1758, in

pp. 379–91. *Mémoires d'état* is Nora's neologism, and he is careful to include a wide variety of texts, among them Napoleon's memoirs, monologues dictated to Las Casas rather than written.

3 Robespierre, *Œuvres*, vol. X, p. 555.

4 Quoted from Louis Jacob, *Robespierre vu par ses contemporains* (Paris, 1938), pp. 200–1.

Arras, the small capital of the province of Artois, four months after the marriage of his parents. His father was Maximilien Barthélemy François, a lawyer and the son and grandson of local lawyers; his mother, Jacqueline-Marguerite Carraut, was the daughter of a successful brewer and innkeeper of the town. The boy was born into comfortable bourgeois surroundings. Fortune and his father's temperament soon changed all that. In 1764, Robespierre's mother died giving birth to her fifth child, who also perished – only three children would survive. His father allowed his law practice to deteriorate and two years later he abandoned his young family to relatives. Their childhood, Robespierre's sister Charlotte later wrote, was 'filled with tears, and each of our early years was marked by the death of some cherished character; it made him [Maximilien] sad and melancholy.'[5]

At the age of eleven Robespierre received a coveted scholarship to Louis-le-Grand in Paris. He was a brilliantly successful student, his name regularly on the prize lists in Latin and Greek, and he was considered the best Latinist in the school, earning the sobriquet 'The Roman', the earliest of his embodiments. In 1775, he was chosen to deliver a Latin address welcoming Louis XVI and Marie-Antoinette, who briefly visited the school on their return from the coronation ceremonies at Reims cathedral.

Upon graduation Robespierre received a prize of 600 *livres*, which he used to set up a law practice in Arras, and was permitted to pass his scholarship on to his brother, Augustin. His law practice was respectable if not flourishing and his *plaidoyers* reveal a conscientious lawyer in command of a studied, stiff eloquence, and holding conventional if 'enlightened' ideas. He was sociable yet serious, looking after his brother and sister as he had since childhood. He seems to have had no serious love affairs or encounters, he was careful, even finicky, about his appearance – especially his hair – and was fond of animals. He wrote mediocre light verse, entered a few provincial essay contests with modest success, and was in all ways unremarkable. Hardly the stuff of greatness.

The Revolution made Robespierre. He fought hard for his seat in the Third Estate, climbing the hustings in every little town and burgh around Arras, and, although his earliest recorded political opinions and utterances are undistinguished and not very radical, they inaugurated a life obsessed with democratic, revolutionary politics. Almost from the time of his election he was at the centre of events, constantly in the

[5] Quoted from Jules Michelet, *Histoire de la Révolution française*, ed. Gérard Walter, 2 vols. (Paris, 1952), vol. I, p. 102.

public eye, making his opinions known, yet he remains as elusive a personality as he had been in pre-revolutionary obscurity.

He quickly learned, or knew intuitively, that his presentation of self, his oratorical *mémoire d'état*, was the instrument of his hold on public opinion, and that his ideas were inextricably tied to his being. Others knew this as well:

> Learn [Marat lectured Robespierre] that my reputation with the people rests, not on my ideas, but upon my boldness, upon the impetuous outbursts of my soul, upon my cries of rage, of despair and of fury against the rascals who impede the action of the Revolution. I am the anger, the just anger, of the people, and that is why they listen to me and believe in me.[6]

The Robespierre of the Revolution is a made-up creature, whose creator would spend the five years remaining to him elaborating this new being.

Even the text of Robespierre's ongoing *mémoire d'état* is problematical. Despite wielding a fluent pen, he himself saw but six of his speeches through the press. Only in these instances do we know precisely what he said. The overwhelming majority of his orations exist in approximate or variant versions. Glimpses of his private life are few, and testimony about both his public and private doings is tainted. Louis Jacob has usefully collected the contemporary evidence and separated it into pre- and post-Thermidor testimony – the former mixed, the latter venomous.[7]

The sparse and ambiguous biographical information has, ironically, helped make Robespierre an attractive (or a monstrous) figure. The bareness of his personal narrative, punctuated by pregnant details, lends itself to invention or elaboration. Since the abbé Proyart's fulminations, his sparse biography has been teased or tormented to fit the changing contours, and views, of the Revolution.[8] His loneliness, for example, provided Robespierre's most successful psycho-biographer, Max Gallo, with the key to his hero's character.[9] Almost alone among the revolutionaries, Robespierre has fascinated novelists and playwrights.

It is perfectly clear that there are several Robespierres. One does not want to make one of the many by some alchemy here. Rather, a way of looking at Robespierre can be suggested that combines a biographical approach with close attention to what he said. In his case, *faute de mieux*,

6 Quoted from Louis R. Gottschalk, *Jean Paul Marat: a Study in Radicalism* (Chicago, 1927, repr. 1967), p. 178.
7 Jacob, *Robespierre*.
8 Published under the name of Le Blond de Neuvéglise as *La vie et les crimes de Maximilien Robespierre* (Augsburg, 1795), this is almost certainly by the abbé Proyart. See the discussion by Norman Hampson, *The Life and Opinions of Maximilien Robespierre* (London, 1974), esp. pp. 2–7.
9 Max Gallo, *Robespierre, histoire d'une solitude* (Paris, 1968).

we have to heed what he said (and when he said it), rather than import meaning from outside the circumscribed circle of the available evidence.

The crucial moment (and problem) is the Terror, to which Robespierre's self and reputation are inseparably linked. He does not appear to have been a born terrorist nor a man hopelessly enthralled by ideological formulae of his own fabrication which he followed to his doom. Nor was he an abstraction, a Hegelian category through whom history worked its tortuous way. He was both a terrorist and an ideologue but these are existential not abstract categories. He was given to abrupt or extreme solutions – as men of ideas who wander into politics often are – but he was also that rarest of political beings: an ideologue with exquisite political reflexes. He could be patient and tactically almost unerring, simultaneously ideologue and floor manager, as he proved himself in the months of the king's trial; and he could be peremptory, vindictive, reckless and impatient, as he was on Danton's destruction. He became a terrorist, or more precisely the philosophical apologist for terror, only in late 1793, it will be argued, but once embarked on that course, he never looked back, steering thenceforth by the logic of his ideas. As his stark, Manichaean ideology gradually and then sharply diverged from the course of the Revolution – and, certainly by Germinal Year II, the divergence was clear to all but the most ardent *robespierristes* – he held stubbornly to his ideas until he was destroyed.

Patrice Gueniffey, perhaps the most persuasive advocate of the thesis that the Incorruptible was a pure ideologue whose revolutionary trajectory was apparent from his first utterances until 8 Thermidor, whose revolutionary career was an unfolding, a gradual and grim becoming, is unambiguous in his assessment: 'Robespierre perfected ideological discourse in the highest degree, because he was himself ideology incarnate.' And again: 'In him immobility became action, and he stood as a fixed point in the tumult of the Revolution, which turned everything upside down and swept men away.'[10] The argument which follows is different.

Robespierre was, until the early winter of 1794, mobile, to use Gueniffey's imagery. The politics of virtue, so central to and characteristic of Robespierre's ideology in 1794, rising in a long crescendo to 8 Thermidor, was a process of evolution and growth rather than revelation and exposure. The politics of virtue was not always at the centre of Robespierre's ideological discourse. If we read his life and ideas backwards, from 8 Thermidor, it seems only some *idée fixe* can explain his trajectory. But this is to confuse, as several of his biographers – whether

[10] Patrice Gueniffey, 'Robespierre', in François Furet and Mona Ozouf (eds.), *A Critical Dictionary of the French Revolution*, trans. Arthur Goldhammer (Cambridge, Mass. and London, 1989), pp. 299, 301.

sympathetic or hostile – have done, the set aspects of his character and *la force des choses*. He indeed had a puritanical streak, was a lonely, self-absorbed man deeply partial to Rousseau's moral fervour – in politics, as in his personal life, the *Confessions* had made an indelible mark on his mind and sensibility – and from his first revolutionary utterances he set himself apart from what he saw as the self-serving, egotistical politicians who battened on the Revolution. He identified himself with an abstract, mythic and virtuous 'people' whom he imagined and whose will he insisted he embodied, incarnated: 'I am not the courtier, nor the moderator, nor the tribune, nor the defender of the people, I am the people myself!', he proudly declared.[11] But these tendencies received full ideological elaboration and became obsessive (and immobile) only in response to the Revolution. He indeed had innate tendencies that turned him in disgust from Danton's voluptuousness, Mirabeau's cynicism, Brissot's enthusiasm, Custine's arrogance, Lafayette's ambition. He was austere, self-righteous and priggish, his rectitude and reserve, shamelessly and regularly proclaimed in his oratory and used as political weapons, made him the Incorruptible. His tenacity and discipline, often mistaken for mediocrity, kept him doggedly at the mundane tasks involved in parliamentary politics and misled his enemies to underrate his abilities, while he diligently honed his tactical and strategic skills. Even his Manichaean cast of mind proved useful. The Revolution was a dangerous time: suspicion was prudent, patriotic, and made him appear prophetic. Marat, even more suspicious, was also a beneficiary of universal distrust and a readiness to believe in plots. But these characteristics did not, necessarily, make Robespierre a terrorist, nor did they provide all the ingredients for the politics of virtue. Robespierre's personality proved a fertile soil for the growth of the politics of virtue; but it was the course of the Revolution itself, working on his special nature, that slowly, and even insensibly, moved virtue from the foreground of his many political concerns – where it served as a kind of ready metaphor for all that he valued – to the absolute centre of his politics – where it became a murderous and blinding principle.

Robespierre in Year II, Robespierre the terrorist, has riveted the attention of all students of the Revolution, determining how his early life would be seen and judged. We look for every precocious hint of future fanaticism in his early career. This obsession is inherited from the Thermidorian tradition that first vilified and then demonised the Incor-

[11] Robespierre, *Œuvres*, vol. VIII, p. 311. 'Je suis peuple moi-même' is the French. This is from the same speech quoted above, n.1. It was delivered on 27 April 1792 at the Jacobins in the midst of a stormy session and was Robespierre's response to the speeches of Brissot and Guadet on 25 April.

ruptible. After 1917 (and again after 1933), Thermidorian vengeance was enhanced by the needs of twentieth-century politics and polemics. Let us imagine – and it is not so far-fetched, for Charlotte Corday was determined to kill either Robespierre or Marat – that Robespierre had been assassinated in July 1793. He would be remembered as an admirable yet minor political figure, the hammer of privilege, a fearless and untainted democrat, the prophet of the disasters of war and, already, the Incorruptible. He would be ranked as less significant than Mirabeau and Danton, more important than Brissot or Vergniaud, but not a terrorist, let alone the heartless, cruel fanatic who has passed into legend (and historical remembrance). It was Year II that fixed Robespierre's reputation and underlined moral, ideological and political ambiguities.

He was never squeamish about violence in the course of the Revolution, but he never called for blood. The violent rhetoric of Marat and Hébert, with their chilling proscription lists, is absent from Robespierre's speeches: so too is the cynicism of Barnave ('Is this blood so pure?'). He was a peculiar kind of terrorist.

Robespierre held no elected position in the National Convention until he became its president from 22 August to 5 September 1793.[12] He was thus in the chair during the 'Hébertist' uprising, which forced terror to the top of the agenda, yet he played a relatively small rôle in the flurry of parliamentary activity that followed the latest Paris uprising, and, as always, he took no part in the extraordinary revolutionary tumult of September to October. He made no major speech between 29 July (when he presented Lepeletier's education plan in the name of his assassinated colleague) and 17 November (when he delivered, in the name of the Committee of Public Safety, the important 'Rapport sur la situation politique de la République'). The ideologue of the Revolution was oddly silent in the weeks when terror was made the order of the day. He confined himself to specific interventions without formulating a general theory. On 28 July, the day after his nomination to the Committee of Public Safety, that body was authorised to issue arrest warrants; on 2 August, it was given unconditional grants of secret service money; on 13 September, it nominated members of other committees; and, on 10 October, it was entrusted with supervising ministers, generals and public authorities.[13] We may presume Robespierre supported this accumulation of power in the hands of the Committee, but there is no evidence he worked for these measures.

Robespierre took no part publicly in the debates on the legislation of

[12] He would again be president at an equally momentous time: 4–18 June 1794, when the festival of the Supreme Being was celebrated.

[13] J. M. Thompson, *Robespierre*, 2 vols. (Oxford, 1935), vol. II, pp. 73–4.

the Terror and the accompanying empowering of the Committee of Public Safety. He did not participate in the debates on the law of Suspects (17 September), or the second maximum (29 September), and it was Saint-Just who delivered, for the Committee, the notorious 'Rapport sur la nécessité de déclarer le gouvernment révolutionnaire jusqu'à la paix' (10 October). Robespierre's fingerprints are not visible on the legislation initiating the Terror, nor on many of its most shrill acts. One could, of course, argue that silence is not definitive evidence of opposition or indifference any more than it is evidence of support, and he could well have done his most effective political work behind the scenes – yet another of the many lacunae in the public (as well as the private) record. But if the record is scant, the pattern of Robespierre's interventions during this period is revealing.[14] Virtually all were concerned with repression, purification and reorganising the government. The themes, or rather the atmosphere, surrounding the beginnings of the Terror interested Robespierre, but not the practicalities of policy or implementation; he was still months away from formulating the ideology of terror. His attendance at the meetings of the Committee of Public Safety, incidentally, was regular throughout this period.[15]

It is the events of October that are crucial in Robespierre's emerging ideology of virtue, with terror as its major component. Early in the month, the Revolutionary Tribunal had been reorganised and brought under the direct control of the Committee. The trials of the queen and the Girondins, apparently related although there is no clear evidence of a *quid pro quo*, now became possible, without the endless legal wrangling that had preceded and then accompanied the trial of the king a year

[14] There were eleven interventions in September, fairly equally divided between the Jacobins and the Convention, and ten in October (three at the Jacobins). Robespierre spoke against General Kellermann and the journalist Prudhomme on 8 September, and for Hanriot and Bourdon de l'Oise on 11 September. He spoke against Briez, an old political ally, on 25 September, and opposed 'l'organisation constitutionelle du pouvoir exécutif' that night at the Jacobins. On 18 September, he did not support a motion by Collot d'Hérbois. He made three substantial interventions on 3 October concerning the trial of the Girondins, and, on 7 October, two rather long interventions at the Jacobins against generals and aristocrats. The next day, he spoke on the Compagnie des Indes and supported the continued suspension of the constitution. Only at the end of the month – 24 and 29 October – do we unmistakably hear the voice of terror, which will become familiar: on the former day, he opposed communicating the reasons for an arrest to suspects, and he proposed to have the first four *jours sans-culottides* devoted to virtue; on the latter, he proposed the closure of arguments before the Revolutionary Tribunal after three days.

[15] Thompson, *Robespierre*, vol. II, p. 74, wrote: 'between July 26 and September 26 ... Robespierre only missed fourteen [of sixty-two meetings of the Committee] ... In October Robespierre missed only two meetings out of the twenty-eight for which lists of attendance are available: in November, December, and January he was present at every meeting.'

earlier. The parliamentary politics of this important month are murky. Despite elaborate political and procedural precautions, despite the extraordinary example of the king's trial, and the long-familiar detestation of the queen – dating from the diamond necklace affair and renewed periodically, most recently by Hébert in his *Père Duchesne* – there was unexpected sympathy for Marie-Antoinette. Even further tampering with procedures was necessary to send the Girondins to the guillotine. Neither trial ran smoothly. Robespierre took no particular interest in the trial of Marie-Antoinette, quietly yielding to *hébertiste* hysteria. He is reported to have snapped angrily at the stupidity of Hébert's accusations of incest against the queen when he declared: 'That idiot Hébert! ... It's not enough that she should be a Messalina; he must make her Agrippina.'[16]

When it came, however, to an act of Jacobin vengeance, the destruction of the Girondin deputies, Robespierre took an active rôle, but only behind the scenes. He was set on their destruction, although unwilling (or unprepared) to make it a part of some grand ideological scheme. His personal animus, as it would again at Danton's trial, perverted his political judgement. It was probably some sixth political sense that kept him out of the spotlight, for he might well have blundered seriously. The cool detachment and masterful generalship he showed during the king's trial were missing in October 1793, as they would be the following April. His public interventions in October were few but pointed. On 3 October, the day forty-four deputies were accused, he spoke against having a roll-call vote (*appel nominal*), hoping to make it easier for the Convention to send their colleagues before the Revolutionary Tribunal. He had been one of those who had insisted upon a roll call in the king's trial. He also opposed including the seventy-three signatories of the protest against the purge of deputies of 2 June, thus limiting the proscription. Those who were thus spared, however, showed no gratitude and never forgave him for the ruin of their colleagues (or the attack on the National Convention). The destruction of the Girondins was to be focused; his decision – and it was not his alone – seems to have been tactical rather than ideological. He also proposed, on 29 October, his

[16] Quoted in Thompson, *Robespierre*, vol. II, p. 99. Some recent books are now important: Lynn Hunt (ed.), *Eroticism and the Body Politic* (Baltimore, 1991), especially the essays by Sarah Maza, 'The diamond necklace affair revisited (1785–1786): the case of the missing queen', pp. 63–89, and Lynn Hunt, 'The many bodies of Marie Antoinette: political pornography and the problem of the feminine in the French Revolution', pp. 108–30; Chantel Thomas, *La reine scélérate: Marie-Antoinette dans les pamphlets* (Paris, 1989); and Madame de Staël, *Réflexions sur le procès de la reine par une femme*, présentation Monique Cottret (Montpellier, 1994).

infamous formula: the trial could be stopped after three days if the jury thought it had enough evidence to deliver a verdict.[17]

There was one additional spur to Robespierre's new politics of virtue. Around 12 October, Fabre d'Eglantine began denouncing the 'foreign plot' in an escalating series of accusations and fabrications that would only end with his own arrest on 12 January. Fabre's startling revelations fed the ongoing obsession with *scrutins épuratoires* of candidates for command of the *Armée révolutionnaire* decreed by the Committee of Public Safety on 9 September and extended to the Jacobins by Robespierre himself, who was the first to present his credentials of political and civic virtue at the society.[18] Henceforth at the meetings of the Jacobins, one after another, both renowned and obscure, both national and local militants, would stand before the society, recite their revolutionary biographies – nothing before 1789 was included – explain, if necessary, how their personal wealth had grown during the Revolution, and ask their comrades for revolutionary absolution.

Purification presupposes pollution and, as Fabre's fictive powers unfolded plots within plots, exposing the revolutionary élite's betrayal by profiting from the Revolution, it became more and more apparent that the domestic enemies of the Revolution, the counter-revolution, constituted an enemy within the very nerve-centre of patriotism. 'Citizens', Saint-Just announced on 10 October, 'all the enemies of the Republic are in the government.' It is 'not only the traitors who have to be punished, but the indifferent as well ... whoever is passive in the Republic and does nothing to support it ...'[19]

Saint-Just's speech was rhetorically brilliant and intellectually flawed. There is no single thread of analysis relentlessly followed and elaborated. Rather he reiterated the view, first declared in his maiden speech during the king's trial (13 November 1792), that what was alien must be cut from the body politic, and the guarantees and delays of legal procedures were in themselves criminal. He shone his dazzling light, in breathless spurts, on government corruption, bureaucratic ineptitude, inflation, trafficking in *assignats* and the army. Saint-Just identified the symptoms,

[17] '[S]i leur conscience est assez éclairée' is how he put it.

[18] See Robespierre, *Œuvres*, vol. X, pp. 129–30, for the part of the debate at the Jacobins on 28 September 1793 involving Robespierre. The catechism used for these autobiographies of revolutionary purity had been proposed on 26 November by Merlin de Thionville (quoted from Gérard Walter, *Histoire des Jacobins* (Paris, 1946), p. 330): 'Where were you in 1789? What had you done till 1793? What was your fortune in 1789? What is it now? If your fortune has increased, how do you explain it? What have you done for the Revolution? Have you ever signed a counter-revolutionary petition? If you are an administrator, journalist or representative of the people, have you devoted your efforts only to the service of liberty?'

[19] A. Saint-Just, *Œuvres choisies*, intro. J. Gratien (Paris, 1968), pp. 171, 169.

diagnosed the disease, warned of an epidemic, and called for radical surgery: he did not provide an ideology of terror. It was to this task that Robespierre turned his attention after the traumas of September and October. His ideological fastidiousness was as obsessive as his sartorial. He needed to have reasons for what he was doing. His success in making an ideology for repression tied him inextricably to the Terror, fixed his historical reputation and provided the central problematic of his personality and revolutionary career.

It is not violent fulminations that characterise Robespierre's speeches on the Terror. It is the language of unmasking, unveiling, revealing, discovering, exposing the enemy within, the enemy hidden behind patriotic posturings, the language of suspicion. The idea of terror as necessary self-defence imposed upon the Revolution by circumstances beyond its control, which would become the official Jacobin view and the view taken up by first Jacobin, then republican and eventually Marxist posterity and historiography, was not part of Robespierre's ideology of terror. He was not concerned with defence. The Terror was for him an instrument of assault: first discovery, then punishment resulting in education. The people 'must keep the enemy under surveillance, discover him beneath a false façade ... and mark with the seal of condemnation those who, to avoid the punishment due their crime, seek to overthrow the Republic and annihilate liberty'.[20] Robespierre's incessant depiction of a dangerous and deadly universe, filled with enemies who could not be seen because they appeared to be friends, was the Incorruptible's authentic rhetorical violence. The revolutionary world itself was violent: death was the order of the day. He was obsessed with discovering counter-revolutionaries: the laws would do the rest. The enemies of the Revolution, he told the Convention in a striking image on 27 Brumaire (17 November 1793), have travestied 'august liberty' as 'a vile prostitute'.[21] The punishment for those who travestied the Revolution, camouflaged themselves and their designs, did not need to be spelled out.

Robespierre's world, during the final year of his life, was a fearful and fatal place, inhabited by the enemy without and within. It was not a fantasy world of the speaker's making, or, if it was his lurid fiction, it was widely shared, to judge from the debates in the Convention and the reception of his speeches. If the seeds of his universal suspicion were long present, they had not previously taken so stark a form, and his was

[20] Robespierre, *Œuvres*, vol. X, p. 377.

[21] *Ibid.*, vol. X, p. 172: 'Le despotisme et la trahison présentoient le peuple français à tous les peuples comme une faction éphémère et méprisable, le berceau de la République comme le repaire du crime; l'auguste liberté étoit travestie en un vile prostituée.'

only one of many near-hysterical voices in the last months of 1793. Fabre was rejected and guillotined for his denunciations, but his feverish world of plots and corruption was accepted as authentic, and Marat had been proclaimed a martyr for similar denunciations. Robespierre gave voice to the very real revolutionary crisis at the end of 1793 and during the first months of 1794, and perpetuated the fear engendered by crisis long after the acute threat of military defeat was gone. He was enveloped in a culture of fear to which he regularly, and eloquently, gave voice. He enunciated the dualisms of good and evil, light and darkness, patriots and counter-revolutionaries: 'there can only be two groups in the Convention,' he declared, 'the good and the wicked, the patriots and the counter-revolutionary hypocrites'.[22] 'In the shadows crime conspires the destruction of liberty,'[23] he warned the Jacobins. The historic mission of the Revolution, as he now saw it, was no longer the creation of political freedom through laws, representative government and a constitution, but the destruction of evil and the enshrinement of virtue. By some unspecified alchemy, democracy would follow virtue.

In the spring and early summer of 1794 he vacillated between attacking the counter-revolution and submission to a cruel destiny. The Revolution must have a united front: 'Every representative of the people who sincerely loves liberty, every representative of the people who is determined to die for the *patrie*, is a Montagnard.'[24] There can be no partial measures against 'the fury of the most dangerous factions'. Only 'in attacking them head-on ... in plunging the dagger of liberty into their hearts, can we rescue liberty from all the scoundrels who want to destroy it',[25] he triumphantly told the Jacobins on the day of Danton's fall. His pompous line, 'plunging the dagger of liberty into their hearts', reminds us that he loved to read Corneille and Racine aloud to his friends.

The enemy is a vast host and the weapons available to the patriots are few and even feeble. 'Truth is the only weapon that remains in the hands of the intrepid defenders of liberty,' he said at the beginning of the Terror, and reiterated throughout: 'Against the minions of the tyrants and their friends, we have no other resource than truth at the tribunal of public opinion, and no other support than that of good men.'[26] The

[22] *Ibid.*, vol. X, p. 493: 'Mais du moment que les intrigues furent dévoilées; du moment que le scélérats qui les tramaient sont tombés sous le glaive de la loi; du moment que la probité, la justice, les moeurs sont mises à l'ordre du jour; du moment que chaque membre de cette Assemblée veut se dévouer pour la Patrie, il ne peut y avoir que deux partis dans la Convention, les bons et les méchans, les patriotes et les contre-révolutionnaires hypocrites.'

[23] *Ibid.*, vol. X, p. 512. [24] *Ibid.*, vol. X, p. 492. [25] *Ibid.*, vol. X, p. 424.

[26] *Ibid.*, vol. X, p. 512.

work is risky, perhaps fatal: 'By combating such fury, armed with the blade of patriotism, we have consented to die for our country if necessary, provided that we have been able to raise a corner of the veil that hid the abyss where they were leading us.'[27] Had Robespierre been content to remain on this rhetorical level, which satisfied the majority of his contemporary Jacobin orators, he would only have continued to repeat the formulae of Year II. But, with his passion for ideological comprehension and clarity, he developed a theory of terror as an instrument not only of national self-defence, but also of purification, beyond whose flames lay the Utopia of virtuous democracy.

The goal of the Revolution is simple enough, he told the Convention on 17 Pluviôse: '... the peaceful enjoyment of liberty and equality. The reign of eternal justice whose laws have been engraved not in marble or stone, but in the hearts of all men, even in those of the slave who forgets them and the tyrant who denies them.'[28] The fundamental principle of the new government is virtue, which 'is nothing else but the love of one's country and its laws'. In the Revolution, 'what is immoral is impolitic, what corrupts is counter-revolutionary'. With a stunning juxtaposition he identified terror with virtue: 'If the appeal of the popular government in peace is virtue, its appeal in revolution is simultaneously to *virtue and terror* ... Terror is nothing else but prompt, severe, inflexible justice. It is, consequently, an emanation of virtue.'[29] Amending one of Montesquieu's political axioms – virtue as the spring of popular governments – and yoking it to terror – for Montesquieu the spring of despotism – Robespierre created a new (and dangerous) synthesis. He was aware of the novelty and moral ambiguity of his juxtaposition, and immediately explained that terror was used by tyrants to maintain their despotism, whereas 'The government of the Revolution is the despotism of liberty against tyranny.' Terror would be used only against royalists and aliens who were not a part of the Republic: 'Protection is owed only to peaceful citizens: there are only republican citizens in a republic.'[30] The juxtaposition is more clever than convincing. Robespierre had, in fact, shifted categories. It was now the purpose of terror that determined its morality. He had distinguished a 'good' and a 'bad' terror, depending upon its

[27] *Ibid.*, vol. X, p. 394. [28] *Ibid.*, vol. X, p. 352.

[29] *Ibid.*, vol. X, p. 357. The entire passage is: 'Si le ressort du gouvernement populaire dans la paix est la vertu, le ressort du gouvernement populaire en révolution est à la fois *la vertu et la terreur*: la vertu, sans laquelle la terreur est funeste; la terreur, sans laquelle la vertu est impuissante. La terreur n'est autre chose que la justice prompte, sévère, inflexible; elle est donc une émanation de la vertu; elle est moins un principle particulier, qu'une conséquence du principe général de la démocratie, appliqué aux plus pressans besoins de la patrie.'

[30] *Ibid.*

goal and the government resorting to terror. Siéyès's seminal idea that the Third Estate alone constituted the nation and the privileged orders had to be cast out is here tacitly invoked, given a moral dimension and made to fit the circumstances of Year II. Those without virtue, by definition the enemies of the Revolution, deserved terror: 'To punish the oppressors of humanity is clemency, to pardon them is barbarity. The rigour of tyrants has only rigour for its principle. That of the republican government derives from the social good.'[31]

Robespierre gave terror a philosophical pedigree on 17 Pluviôse, linking it to familiar eighteenth-century notions. The linkages are original and ingenious, and their implications are deadly. He might have made a practical argument for terror: circumstances imposed harshness upon us, we are fighting for the very survival of the Revolution, we have no choice but to save the Republic, whatever the cost, whatever the weapons. The foreigners, the monarchs, the counter-revolutionaries imposed the need for terror upon France. This is essentially the apologia made by the members of the Committee of Public Safety who survived Robespierre's fall (especially Barère and Billaud-Varenne) or other Jacobins (René Levasseur or Dr Baudot) and in recollections left behind. It was the view taken up by later historians sympathetic to the Jacobins. Such a defence, by throwing himself on the mercy of the court of posterity and appealing simultaneously to the humanity of his contemporaries, might well have spared the Incorruptible's reputation. Billaud-Varenne, for example, a far more blood-thirsty character than Robespierre, has not been demonised. But an argument from circumstance, from expediency, from necessity, was impossible for Robespierre. Actions, political and personal, had to spring from a pure heart and be clothed in the robes of truth. Robespierre's entire revolutionary career turned on his ability to project sincerity, attachment to principles, while his rivals were excoriated as opportunists. His was the politics of authenticity, of passionate personal conviction whatever the consequences. Here, even more than in his ideas, he was enthralled by Rousseau. True to form to the very end, he neither retracted nor modified his philosophical justification of terror. On 8 Thermidor, when so many were looking for a way to end the Terror, Robespierre thundered the murderous logic of the politics of virtue. It then cost him his life; it has subsequently cost him his reputation.

[31] *Ibid.*, vol. X, p. 359. I have translated 'bienfaisance' freely as 'social good' to get the sense of its social implications. It is worth recalling that in Saint-Just's maiden speech, delivered on 13 November 1792, during the king's trial, he made this same argument: Louis did not deserve the protection of the laws for he was not and had never been a citizen. See the speech in Saint-Just, *Œuvres choisies*, pp. 74–83, and the discussion in David P. Jordan, *The King's Trial* (Berkeley, 1979), pp. 67–8.

Robespierre's tragedy, which he himself chronicled, was Greek. The irony that the great democrat shared with Oedipus the king a complete lack of self-awareness is more than bitter. At the end Robespierre's blindness was ideological, his vanity self-righteousness, and both had been burnished to a stunning lustre by the Revolution. Having enunciated the politics of virtue and tied it to terror in early 1794, he pursued its course tenaciously, logically, relentlessly, dimly aware of the doom that awaited, unable or unwilling to change course. In his ambition to control the Revolution by articulating it, he lost what had sustained his long climb to power, his hold on mundane politics. He became increasingly enveloped in, even intoxicated by, the imaginative world he had made. During the long years of his political obscurity, then isolation, then recognition, crowned by his first months of membership of the Committee of Public Safety, his analyses of the Revolution, his ideology, struck profound resonances in the hearts and minds of his listeners. He had, for a brief historical moment – extending approximately from the *journée* of 10 August 1792 to early February 1793 – the gift of transforming the mundane events of the Revolution into intricate and compelling ideological patterns, whose logic seemed irresistible and whose contemplation proved satisfying. The speeches at the festival of the Supreme Being, despite the disturbing voices of criticism and the smoking guillotine only momentarily stilled, briefly recaptured the magic. But the next day (9 June 1794), the executions resumed and Robespierre was again out of touch, back with his formulae of virtue and terror, purification and democracy, all in the name of a people now become abstract and mythic.

He had inklings of his end, and perhaps these were also inklings of the growing gap between his ideas and the living Revolution, but he stumbled on in darkness, repeating the old phrases about calumny and undeclared enemies lurking. On 13 Messidor (1 July), he lamented that he could not 'entirely discover this huge system of conspiracy' but could only 'paint a faint picture' of it.[32] Three weeks later, in his final speech, he first presented virtue not as terror but as the 'egoism of men not degraded, who find a heavenly voluptuousness in the repose of a pure conscience and in the ravishing spectacle of public happiness'. It was a 'tender passion, imperious and irresistible, the torment and delight of

[32] Robespierre, *Œuvres*, vol. X, p. 508: 'L'orateur regrette ensuite de ne pouvoir découvrir entièrement ce système de conspiration trop vaste, et qui tient à des fils trop nombreux pour pouvoir être dévoilé par la voix d'un homme; cependant il essaie d'en tracer un foible tableau, et prouve que les armes de ces monstres sont le poison, la calomnie et l'assassinat.'

magnanimous hearts'.[33] Virtue now had two forms, terror and love, the former expressed in the cult of the Supreme Being. 'Your decree of 18 Floréal [7 May] is in itself a revolution,' he told the Convention. 'You have struck atheism and priestly despotism with a single blow. You have advanced by a half-century the final hour of tyrants. You have reattached all pure and generous hearts to the Revolution . . .'[34]

On 8 Thermidor, a bewildered Robespierre struggled to make sense of his career and the Revolution. Terror had apparently failed, but he could not see it. Rather he called for more. The cult of the Supreme Being was a joke to many a veteran Jacobin. There are clear signs of change or confusion in this last and oddest of Robespierre's speeches, but they are not easily read. The speech of 8 Thermidor is long, rambling, repetitive and filled with self-pity.[35]

Intellectually Robespierre could not extricate himself from the policies of the Terror, for he had made it an instrument not for punishing the Revolution's enemies, but of purification, simultaneously the creation and the emanation of virtue. Precisely because the Terror was not, for him, an expedient forced upon the Revolution by circumstances, it could not stop when circumstances changed. The Terror had to run its course until France was peopled only with the virtuous. He could not follow the path of moderation proposed by Danton, who linked the Terror to the war. The failure of the cult of the Supreme Being meant he had nothing else to offer.

It is a melancholy observation that it is better for one's reputation to do the deed than to justify it. Politics as the art of force and fraud existed long before Machiavelli wrote *The Prince*. But it is the Florentine republican whose name became synonymous with double-dealing, perfidy and political violence, rather than Ferdinand of Spain or Cesare Borgia, who actually did evil deeds. To echo Machiavelli: men will more easily forget the death of their fathers than the public justification of their murder. Collot d'Herbois, Fouché, Billaud-Varenne, men with much blood on their hands, men who enjoyed their work, would live on. So too would supple apologists – like Bertrand Barère – but the man who gave terror political principles and a philosophic pedigree had to die. Only his death, it now seems, could end the Terror. 'The cowards!', Robespierre cried out to the Convention on 8 Thermidor. 'They want to

33 *Ibid.*, vol. X, p. 554. The sexual imagery of the passage is noteworthy.

34 *Ibid.*, vol. X, pp. 560–1.

35 There is an especially striking repetition (*ibid.*, vol. X, pp. 567, 574). The two passages in question, beginning 'En voyant la multitude des vices que le torrent de la révolution . . .' are virtually identical. In addition, in the numerous phrases crossed out in the manuscript, there are a number of other repetitions.

send me to my grave with ignominy! And I would have left behind me on earth only the memory of a tyrant!'[36]

Robespierre's *cri de cœur* has proved only partly true. His reputation has oscillated radically in the two centuries since his death. But if there is no single Robespierre to remember, he has become the most representative figure of the French Revolution. The very ambiguities of his life, complemented by the sparseness of evidence, have made him a malleable historical figure, moulded to the changing contours of interpretations of the Revolution itself. Not only do his public utterances on virtually every major issue in the Revolution make him an indispensable witness to his own times, but they also form the most extensive repository of the ideology of the age.

In addition, his life has mythic qualities, of which two have proved especially enduring. The clash of personalities between Robespierre and Danton has intrigued for two centuries. Georg Büchner was the first to see the dramatic possibilities in the contrast between the two men, and Andrzej Wajda has recently followed him closely, brilliantly casting Gérard Depardieu as a lusty, energetic, intelligent, exaggerated and compelling Danton. The best scenes in the film are historical fictions: the dinner, with Danton-Depardieu gluttonously sampling all the dishes while a shocked, puritanical Robespierre looks on, never took place. Much has been made of the themes of betrayal and treachery, the cold-blooded puritan determined to destroy the passionate (and vulgar) voluptuary. The two men have been used to signify opposite views of revolution. Danton has become a kind of Trotsky to Robespierre's Stalin. Yet the actual confrontation was never this dramatic, nor is it clear that Robespierre was chiefly responsible for Danton's fall. Danton, after all, made a fatal political error, especially in revolution: his timing was off by nearly two months. The battle of Fleurus was not won until 26 June. We might usefully ask another hypothetical question: had Danton, rather than Robespierre, survived, would the Revolution have been markedly different? Perhaps more the work of Saint-Just than Robespierre, Danton's arrest, trial and execution, with their inherent drama, have been used to focus the debate on the Terror in a way otherwise impossible. But how soon, or how effectively, could Danton and his friends have stopped the killing?

The other aspect of Robespierre's life that has made him so useful a figure for historians, and literature generally, is his fall. There are tragic elements in 9 Thermidor that have been exploited by all shades of opinion. In addition to the traditional characteristics of Greek tragedy

[36] *Ibid.*, vol. X, p. 565.

already mentioned, there are mythic properties befitting the Revolution: greatness achieved from obscurity, only to be lost by the abandonment of the people of Paris and their sections, bitter ironies of an unrealised revolutionary vision literally cut off, leaving posterity to speculate on Robespierre's true legacy.

One should not suggest that, had there been no Robespierre, it would have been necessary to invent him. But rather that the narrative of the life and career of the historical Robespierre, for all its ambiguities and lacunae – and sometimes because of them – is the most satisfactory vehicle for conceptualising and symbolising the Revolution as a transcendant event with human proportions. His life, or rather his revolutionary life, has served so well precisely because he was able to embody the Revolution for so long and so well, despite the protean forms it assumed. He was 'ideology incarnate' but, as with everything else in the Revolution, ideology was in a constant state of becoming. Robespierre's ideology was not fixed from the outset, but was itself the work of the Revolution. Robespierre himself sensed this, and it is the quality that makes him unique among French revolutionaries. He felt and often said the Revolution had made him its voice. He was misled when he failed to realise that he and the Revolution had ceased to speak with a single voice. In theoretical terms it has been said that 9 Thermidor was the reclaiming of the Revolution by the state, the reassertion of the National Assembly. Respecting Robespierre, 9 Thermidor was the realisation and conviction that his was no longer the voice of the people, that he was no longer the Revolution made flesh. The fine yet durable thread that bound the man and events had broken. Robespierre never realised what had happened. He could only see his fall as the perfidy of men, the rejection of virtue.

Part II

Robespierre's outlook

3 Robespierre's political principles

Marisa Linton

Robespierre's politics have often been seen as synonymous with the Revolution itself. He encapsulated what was best – and worst – about the Revolution. He was a tireless advocate for liberty and equality, yet, to defend these principles, he was prepared to adopt the Terror. Nevertheless, he was only one man amongst many, and we may ask why it is that revolutionary ideology as a whole has so often been identified with this one individual. The reasons for this are complex and manifold. For one thing, Robespierre held a place at the centre of revolutionary events longer than any of his contemporaries, successfully negotiating the turbulent seas of rapidly changing politics. In the years from 1789 to 1794, he became adept as a political tactician, surviving many changes of fortune and seeing off a number of political opponents. Almost from the very outset, he was a focus for radical opposition. At times, he was a lone critic of government policy. When the political coup of June 1793 brought the Montagnards to government, Robespierre's moment came and he took his place at the heart of policy-making during the Revolution's most critical period. Although he never dominated executive power to the extent that has often been credited, as a member of the Committee of Public Safety he was the most articulate spokesman of the politics of the revolutionary government, both in the Convention and at the Jacobin club. He preferred, whenever possible, to speak about general political principles, leaving the details of organisation to others, and his speeches offer some of the most powerful expositions of Jacobin ideology.

If we see him now almost as the living embodiment of the Revolution, it is partly because this is what he wanted us to think. He saw himself as the Revolution's watch-dog, its very conscience. In his speeches, he consistently suggested that it was he who spoke for the Revolution – whilst his political opponents were not 'true revolutionaries'. Of course, we do not have to agree with him in this respect. But he does give us an insight into some of the more radical directions in revolutionary thought. Despite his many tactical shifts, his political principles remained remarkably consistent. He was a radical political democrat from first to last. His steadfast political principles earned him both respect and loathing in his lifetime. They still command the attention of anyone who seeks to understand the meaning of the Revolution.

Much could be, and indeed has been, said about Robespierre's political ideas, and, in order to examine them properly, we would have to look at the entire context of revolutionary politics. This brief essay will focus on the general principles that underlay his conception of politics and will use this issue to focus on two particular questions. The first concerns the derivation of Robespierre's conception of politics. The French Revolution was the first of its kind ever to take place. Where, then, did he get his ideas of what it should be about? The second question concerns the paradoxical inconsistency of his ideas: that is, how was it possible for Robespierre, self-vaunted 'man of virtue', political democrat and one-time opponent of the death penalty, to reconcile his libertarian political ideals with the Terror? This latter question is, of course, the fundamental problem about Robespierre. And yet it is not an easy question to answer, for there is so much about Robespierre both as a man and as a politician that we simply do not know.[1] It would be too easy to say that Robespierre was a hypocrite and leave it at that. This may be true, but it leaves so much unexplained. Some historians, primarily those on the political left and influenced by Mathiez, took the opposite viewpoint. They exonerated the man and claimed that what made him a terrorist was circumstances, not personality. From 1792 onwards, they argued, war, civil war and the precarious legitimacy of the Montagnard government forced Robespierre and other Montagnards to adopt brutal methods in defence of a just cause.

Post-modernism – and the resurgence of the political right – have changed all that. More recent historians, following François Furet, will have no truck with the contextual explanation. Instead, they have looked to the language or discourse of revolution as a crucial determining factor in its own right. Furet argued that the revolutionaries tried 'to found a new society through a new language' invented in 1789: that is, a new language that conflated politics with morality, the language of political virtue.[2] This political language in itself led inevitably to the Terror. According to Furet, Robespierre's significance lies in his having been 'the mouthpiece' of the purest revolutionary discourse in which the

[1] The two biographies of Robespierre which offer the most thoughtful evaluations of the conflicting and often fragmentary evidence are J. M. Thompson, *Robespierre*, 3rd edition (Oxford, 1988) and Norman Hampson, *The Life and Opinions of Maximilien Robespierre* (London, 1974).

[2] François Furet, *Interpreting the French Revolution*, trans. E. Forster (Cambridge, 1981), pp. 25–7.

libertarian and egalitarian principles of 1789 were already sowing the seeds of 1793.[3] Neither Robespierre's own personality, nor the decisions that he made, nor the political context in which he acted, it is now implied, had a significant effect on the transformation from man of virtue to terrorist: the link was already there in the rhetoric of moral politics. Such an approach is obliging historians to look again, and with renewed care, at the actual rhetoric which Robespierre used and the ways in which the idea of revolution was constructed through language, but it still leaves much about his politics unanswered.

If, as Furet claimed, the language of moral politics was new in 1789, why was much of what Robespierre included in his conception of politics so familiar? This brings us back to the first question, regarding the derivation of Robespierre's political ideas. As Alfred Cobban put it, 'Robespierre belonged to the past, rather than to the future, in holding that the application of fundamental moral principles in government was the only cure for political evils.'[4] It seems, then, that the two questions, about the origins of Robespierre's political ideas and the way in which he arrived at a 'justification' of terror, can be explored in relation to each other and it is the link between these two problems that concerns us here.

I

Robespierre's political thought was firmly in the broad tradition of natural rights, whose principles were believed to be engraved in the human heart and were discernible through the application of reason and conscience. He shared with the Enlightenment *philosophes* the basic conviction that it was possible for human society to be improved and consequently for people's lives to be made happier.

In terms of specific theorists, and in common with most revolutionaries, Robespierre owed most to Rousseau and Montesquieu. His debt to Rousseau has been discussed at length by a number of commentators.[5] What is not always clear is the extent to which many of the ideas often attributed to Rousseau had a long provenance and were by no

[3] *Ibid.*, pp. 60–1.

[4] Alfred Cobban, 'The fundamental ideas of Robespierre', in his *Aspects of the French Revolution* (St Albans, 1971), p. 138. Also in this volume, see Cobban's essay on 'The political ideas of Maximilien Robespierre during the period of the Convention', pp. 159–91.

[5] Such studies include Norman Hampson, *Will and Circumstance: Montesquieu, Rousseau and the French Revolution* (London, 1983) and Carol Blum, *Rousseau and the Republic of Virtue: the Language of Politics in the French Revolution* (Ithaca, 1986).

means exclusive to him.[6] Possibly Rousseau's most original quality was the eloquence with which he wrote. This had won him a cult following and an audience which identified with him emotionally to a degree which no other writer of his generation could rival.[7] Like so many of his generation, Robespierre felt a fierce personal attachment to Rousseau. The *philosophe*'s influence on Robespierre was at least as emotional as it was political: indeed, for both men, politics and emotion were often intermingled. In addition to this general affinity for Rousseau, three key themes in his ideas had a particularly profound effect on Robespierre's political development. The first was the idea of the virtuous self: that is, the man (or woman) who stands alone, sustained only by private conscience. Rousseau was by no means the inventor of this concept, but he gave it an emphasis all his own. He had frequently declared how much he loved virtue and wanted to dedicate his life to it (although, in his later years, this feeling was to turn into a form of paranoia as he believed former friends to be conspiring to undermine his virtue). In similar fashion, Robespierre saw himself as the defender of virtue in a hostile universe. A second belief which was fundamental to Robespierre was that virtue was most likely to be found amongst ordinary people. The rich and privileged were more likely to have been corrupted by the false values of a society obsessed by social status and material wealth, whereas the ordinary people were closer to nature. Again, this idea was not exclusive to Rousseau. For example, the moralist La Bruyère had unfavourably contrasted the corruption and vice which he observed at first hand at the court of Louis XIV with the simple good-heartedness of the common people. The idea also owed much to the rhetoric of Jansenist thinkers such as Père Nicole and their strictures on the moral corruption that was endemic in a grasping and materialist society. But Rousseau brought out the political dimensions of the idea of the virtuous people, using this as a moral justification for a theory of popular sovereignty, whereby the single and all-powerful authority of the monarch was replaced by the single and all-powerful rule of the people. This in turn led to the formulation of the third major area of Rousseau's political influence on Robespierre, the theory of the 'general will'. This

6 For example, the concept of virtue should not be seen as essentially Rousseauist, but has a much wider and more complex history. See Marisa Linton, 'Concepts of virtue in eighteenth-century France 1745–1788', D.Phil. thesis, University of Sussex, 1993 and forthcoming book.

7 On the power of Rousseau's writing see, for example, Robert Darnton, 'Readers respond to Rousseau', in his *The Great Cat Massacre and Other Episodes in French Cultural History* (Harmondsworth, 1985), pp. 209–49. On the religious origins of the concept of the general will, see Patrick Riley, *The General Will before Rousseau: the Transformation of the Divine into the Civic* (Princeton, 1986).

phrase, made famous in the *Social Contract*, meant something more than an amalgam of the will of every person in the body politic: it was a right-thinking will – an idea which in turn owed much to contemporary religious, particularly Jansenist, rhetoric. All these ideas occupied a vital place in Robespierre's political thought, although it is not always easy to be certain whether he took these themes exclusively from Rousseau rather than from other writers with similar preoccupations.

In terms of specifically political ideas, particularly about the nature and basis of the different forms of government, Robespierre owed a much greater debt to Montesquieu than to Rousseau. Montesquieu's political framework in turn was based upon the broad tradition of classical republicanism which he helped to popularise in France. Montesquieu's own political loyalties were to the nobility. Robespierre, like other radical revolutionaries, was careful to distance himself from Montesquieu the man, who was seen as tainted by his noble status and support for the caste and its privileges. But Montesquieu's political framework – particularly his conception of the republic as expressed in *De l'esprit des lois* – proved indispensable to the republicans of 1792.

In addition to these specific writers, Robespierre's political thinking also drew on broader intellectual traditions. Like all the revolutionary leaders, and in common with all educated men of his time, Robespierre had received a grounding in the classical republican tradition during his time at college. Classical republicanism provided the most important language for conceptualising politics in the eighteenth century. It was familiar to all those who had attained any education beyond the basic levels and formed part of a world view for radicals and conservatives alike.[8] Republicanism as it was taught in the schools entailed a thorough study of such writers as Livy, Tacitus, Cicero and Plutarch, all of whom idealised the early Roman republic as a time when men of heroic virtue walked the earth. Robespierre's speeches contained many allusions to this period, although his love of antiquity was more restrained and measured than that of some of his younger contemporaries. Unlike Saint-Just, he refused to see Sparta as an appropriate model for France.[9]

As well as the secular morality of classical republicanism, religious conceptions of politics also appear to have affected Robespierre pro-

[8] Amongst the many books on this subject, one can consult J. G. A. Pocock, *The Machiavellian Moment: Florentine Political Thought and the Atlantic Republican Tradition* (Princeton, 1975); J. G. A. Pocock, *Virtue, Commerce and History* (Cambridge, 1985); Anthony Pagden (ed.), *The Languages of Political Theory in Early Modern Europe* (Cambridge, 1987). The best study of the classical culture of the revolutionary generation remains Harold T. Parker's *The Cult of Antiquity and the French Revolutionaries* (Chicago, 1937; repr. New York, 1965).

[9] See Robespierre, *Œuvres*, vol. X, p. 354.

foundly, although the precise impact of such influences is hard to gauge.[10] He had long since abandoned the tenets of orthodox Catholicism: as he said himself, since his college days he had been 'a pretty poor Catholic'.[11] But the spiritual dimension in his political thought, which culminated in his organisation of the festival of the Supreme Being, has been widely recognised, and was acknowledged by his political contemporaries and enemies, many of whom deeply resented it. Some of them spoke maliciously about the Supreme Being as though it was Robespierre's particular obsession, but in this respect again he was drawing on a fairly broad basis of ideas, those concerned with natural religion and deism. However, there was also a puritanical note running through Robespierre's thought. Time and again (and, towards the end of his life, almost incessantly), he voiced the belief that politicians could be divided into a small band of virtuous (or righteous) men, of whom he himself was a member, and those who opposed virtue and embraced deceit. There are echoes of this idea also in Rousseau's writings, but, whereas Rousseau's conception may have owed much to his youthful immersion in the Calvinist culture of his native Geneva, this had not been Robespierre's experience. The messianic note in some of Robespierre's key speeches probably owes more to the Catholic version of a puritanical discourse – that of Jansenism. It is notable also that, for much of the eighteenth century, there had been links between Jansenist and 'patriotic' rhetoric in French political culture.[12]

All these themes – natural law theory, Montesquieu, Rousseau, classical republicanism, deism and Christian discourses – fed into Robespierre's conception of politics. These ideas diverged from each other in a number of important ways but they also had many elements in common. This makes it difficult to isolate and identify the impact of specific political ideologies in Robespierre's thinking. He appears to have drawn on what he wanted as the need arose, picking and discarding from the political conceptions available to him.

II

How then did Robespierre employ these influences to develop political theories for the Revolution? His fundamental conception of radical democratic politics can be understood in terms of three general princi-

[10] On this subject, see chapter 6. [11] Cited in Thompson, *Robespierre*, p. 11.

[12] On the continuing importance of religious, particularly Jansenist, rhetoric in patriotic and republican discourse in the 1780s and the early stages of the Revolution, see Dale Van Kley, *The Religious Origins of the French Revolution: from Calvin to the Civil Constitution 1560–1791* (New Haven, 1996), chapter 6.

ples or beliefs. The first was the belief that the basis of politics was morality. The second was the belief that the people were fundamentally good. The third was the idea that sovereignty was one and indivisible and that it should be popular, that is, it belonged collectively to the people.[13] These three principles in turn all derived their justification from the notion of political virtue. It was virtue which gave validity and legitimacy to radical and republican conceptions of democratic politics. Unless the citizens were virtuous, true democracy could not function and the Republic could not exist. Since it was the corner-stone of his thought, we need to look more closely at what Robespierre meant by political virtue. It was defined as an active moral force which sought out the public good. Robespierre believed that those people who were responsible for the public good must be guided only by virtue. In a monarchy, it was the responsibility of the king to have political virtue, but, in a republic, all the citizens had to exercise it. Virtue derived from the highest form of love – that selfless love which all citizens should have for their fellows and the *patrie*. This love for the community was more important than love of oneself and even love for one's particular friends and family. Thus it was the duty of those who held public office to act for the public good and for the benefit of all – not for personal profit. They must hold aloof from any political faction, interest group or personal allegiance. This idea was by no means exclusive to Robespierre: it was a commonplace of eighteenth-century political theory. It acted as an ideological counterpoint to the realities of politics under the old régime, to the institutionalised systems of patronage, clientage and venality of office. Behind its seemingly simple definition, virtue was one of the most complex ideas of the eighteenth century, carrying a great deal of ideological baggage in its train – much of it conflicting. It was a key word for Enlightenment thinkers, Christian theologians and theorists of classical republicanism alike – although its meaning was subtly varied in the hands of each.

Robespierre was the supreme exponent of this rhetoric of political virtue during the revolutionary period. His conception of political virtue was based closely on that of Montesquieu in *De l'esprit des lois* almost half a century before, which Montesquieu in turn had adapted from the classical republican tradition of civic virtue. When Robespierre spoke in February 1794 'sur les principes de morale politique qui doivent guider la Convention Nationale dans l'administration intérieure de la République', he almost paraphrased Montesquieu:

13 For a discussion of these principles and the centrality of virtue to them, see Cobban, 'Fundamental ideas', pp. 138–41.

What is the fundamental principle of democratic or popular government, that is to say, the essential spring that supports it and makes it work? It is virtue; I speak of that public virtue that worked so many wonders in Greece and Rome, and which should produce even more astonishing ones in the French Republic; of that virtue that is no other thing than love of the *patrie* and of its laws.[14]

Although Robespierre made this speech at the very height of Jacobin rule and the Terror, after several years of dramatic political transformations his conception of political virtue here showed remarkably few changes from the account he had given of it long before the Revolution in his *Discours sur les peines infamantes* (1785):

The essential mainspring of republics is virtue, as the author of the *Spirit of the Laws* has proved, that is to say political virtue, which is no other thing than love of the laws and of the *patrie*; their very constitution requires that all particular interests, all personal ties, unceasingly give way to the general good.[15]

The paradox about Robespierre's conception of the republic of virtue was that all the authors from whom he might have derived it agreed that it was beautiful but unworkable. The ideal was based on a nostalgic view of the ancient republics of Greece and Rome that had little basis in historical fact. Classical writers agreed that the best form of political organisation was an egalitarian republic of citizens sustained by their virtue, but such republics were doomed to decline. For Montesquieu, Rousseau and others of their generation, the republic of virtue appeared simultaneously both as the highest political ideal and as the most unattainable one, for it depended upon its citizens achieving a level of integrity and selflessness difficult to attain and impossible to sustain. This was the conclusion of Montesquieu's story of the virtuous Troglodytes in the *Lettres persanes*. The Troglodytes eventually abandoned their egalitarian republic and asked the oldest of their number to take on the responsibility of kingship. Tearfully and despairingly, he felt obliged to accept, while lamenting the decline of their virtue. The point of the tale was that virtue was altogether too exalted and too exhausting to be maintained indefinitely. Most people did not want to be virtuous

14 Robespierre, *Œuvres*, vol. X, pp. 353–4. Compare this with the account of virtue given in Montesquieu's *De l'esprit des lois*, in his *Œuvres complètes*, ed. Roger Caillois, 2 vols. (Paris, 1949–51), vol. II, book III, p. 251. On the extent to which Robespierre's concept of political virtue derived from Montesquieu rather than from Rousseau, see Cobban, 'Fundamental ideas', pp. 137–58, esp. pp. 141, 152.

15 Robespierre, *Discours sur les peines infamantes* (Amsterdam, 1785), p. 9. Like so many writings on virtue before the Revolution, this work originated in response to one of the periodic academic competitions in which so many intelligent and ambitious would-be writers participated: it was based upon his inaugural address to the Academy of Arras, and further developed for a competition held by the Société royale des arts et des sciences de Metz. See Thompson, *Robespierre*, pp. 22–4.

citizens, but would prefer to delegate their sovereignty, give up their political liberty and so escape responsibility.

For Montesquieu – and Rousseau – the purest form of democracy was not representative but direct – where all citizens had the opportunity to make their voices heard. Their conception was based on the classical political form of the city state. Seen from this perspective, it was agreed that France was simply too big to be able to function as a direct democracy. Therefore some kind of political compromise, avoiding the extremes of a democratic republic and of despotism, was the best that could be hoped for. This view was generally accepted by the revolutionaries during the early years of the Revolution.[16] Robespierre put aside his radical idealism and agreed that the fully-fledged republican ideal was unsuitable for France. He endorsed the notion of a limited republic, a compromise which retained a constitutional monarchy.

It was the flight to Varennes in June 1791 which finally made it apparent that Louis XVI and the Revolution were incompatible with each other. According to Madame Roland on the afternoon of that day, whilst others, such as Brissot, had already made the mental leap into envisioning France without a monarchy, Robespierre still hesitated, biting his nails and saying, 'What is a republic?'[17] For some time afterwards, he continued to hesitate. He showed himself to be no slave to words, continuing to maintain that it was possible for a limited and compromised form of republic to co-exist with monarchy. What mattered, he said, was not so much the form of government, as what existed in men's hearts.

> I have been accused, in the midst of the Assembly, of being republican – too great an honour, for I am not. If I had been accused of being monarchist, I would have been dishonoured, for I am not that either. I would first like to point out that for many people the words 'republic' and 'monarchy' are entirely without meaning. The word 'republic' does not signify any particular form of government, it belongs to any government of free men who have a *patrie*. Now, one may be free with a monarch, as with a senate. What is the present French constitution? It is a republic with a monarch. It is therefore neither monarchy nor republic, it is both one and the other.[18]

But the political fallout of the flight to Varennes and the massacre of the Champ de Mars made it clear that such compromise was no longer

[16] Montesquieu, *De l'esprit des lois*, book VIII, chapter 16; Jean-Jacques Rousseau, *Du contrat social* (Paris: Garnier Flammarian, 1966), book III, chapter 8. On the revolutionaries' acceptance of this view, see Parker, *The Cult of Antiquity*, pp. 63, 89–102.

[17] Marie-Jeanne Roland (née Phlipon), *The Memoirs of Madame Roland*, ed. and trans. Evelyn Shuckburgh (London, 1989), p. 82.

[18] Robespierre, *Œuvres*, vol. VII, p. 552.

possible. The revolutionaries were obliged to choose between a monarchy and a republic. It was only at this point that Robespierre, in common with other radicals, turned to the concept of the virtuous republic as an active goal. This republic of virtue was more than a form of government, it was also a way of life for its citizens who would form a moral community: the *patrie*. When Robespierre spoke of the *patrie*, he was invoking one of the most powerful and widespread ideas of the eighteenth century.[19] The *patrie* was more than a physical or geographical community brought together by expediency and self-interest. It was also a spiritual and emotional community where people were bonded by fellow-feeling and mutual sympathy. The basis of the *patrie* was virtue, both private and public, and on that basis was placed the justification for popular sovereignty. It was because 'la vertu est naturelle au peuple' that the people had the right to be sovereign. But corrupt government (i.e. monarchical or aristocratic government) was a threat to the virtue of the people, by encouraging vice and irresponsibility.[20] The people's virtue could only be threatened by corrupt government, so that private and public virtue were interdependent. The morality of the people and their form of government were intimately connected. This was a constant theme of Robespierre's political thought.

> Not only is virtue the soul of democracy; but it can only exist under this form of government. In a monarchy, I know of only one person who can love the *patrie*, and who does not even need virtue to do it: it is the monarch. The reason for this is that of all the inhabitants of all his lands, the monarch is the only one who has a *patrie*.[21]

Returning to the theme at a later date, he concluded 'that immorality is the basis of despotism, as virtue is the essence of the Republic'.[22] The question, of course, was whether the people really were virtuous – and therefore could be left to themselves to form a *patrie* in accordance with nature – or whether centuries of monarchical government had so corrupted them that the government would have to intervene and make the people virtuous, and if so by what means: regeneration, education or republican institutions?[23] This question, of course, presented the Jacobins with a profound dilemma and it was one which they never resolved and arguably could not resolve, for they were dealing, not with abstract

[19] Cobban, 'Fundamental ideas', p. 141.
[20] Robespierre, *Œuvres*, vol. X, p. 355.
[21] *Ibid.*, vol. X, p. 353. [22] *Ibid.*, vol. X, p. 447.
[23] For Saint-Just's ideas on republican institutions, see his *Fragments sur les institutions républicaines*, republished in L.-A. Saint-Just, *Théorie politique*, ed. A. Liénard (Paris, 1976). On the idea of regeneration, one can consult Mona Ozouf, 'La Révolution française et l'idée de l'homme nouveau', in Colin Lucas (ed.), *The Political Culture of the French Revolution* (Oxford, 1988), pp. 213–32.

ideas, but with the realities of a recalcitrant population who proved often to be unwilling to adopt the theoretical position intended for them.

'Happiness is a new idea in Europe,' Saint-Just had defiantly declared.[24] He meant by this that the revolutionary government would take it upon itself to promote human happiness. It was an audacious idea and one which needs further explanation. This belief was a key theme of eighteenth-century thought long before Robespierre, Saint-Just and other revolutionaries took it up and gave it a more political application.[25] It had its roots in the belief that individuals could not be happy alone, that humanity was interconnected through natural feelings of *sensibilité*, and that it was only through helping each other, especially the poorer and weaker members of the community, that true happiness could be obtained. Such feelings could find expression through active virtue or *bienfaisance*, that is acts of philanthropy to secure the well-being of others. For the revolutionaries, these acts of *bienfaisance* would go beyond the actions of private individuals in the private sphere to become a principle of government. In the *patrie*, each member of the community would feel for his or her fellows and accept responsibility for the happiness and well-being of all.

III

In opposition, Robespierre was a political libertarian. He doggedly defended revolutionary principles and denounced the hypocrisies and half-measures of more moderate revolutionaries even though this often made him unpopular with the men who had come to power in 1789. Thus, he spoke out consistently against the decision of the Constituent Assembly to make distinctions between citizens based on property, denying the franchise to the poor and obscure. He defended the rights of all men to participate in political sovereignty: 'I believed that the nation included the labouring classes, and everyone without distinctions of wealth.'[26] He also spoke in defence of the civic rights of Jews and was one of the most forceful speakers to denounce the hypocrisy of revolutionaries who spoke glibly of 'the rights of man' and then denied those

[24] A. Saint-Just, *Discours et rapports*, ed. Albert Soboul (Paris, 1957), p. 150.

[25] On social virtue and *bienfaisance* before the Revolution and the link with the *patrie*, see Daniel Mornet, *Les origines intellectuelles de la Révolution française: 1715–1787*, new edition (Paris, 1938; repr. 1954), pp. 258–66; Robert Mauzi, *L'idée du bonheur dans la littérature et la pensée française au XVIIIe siècle* (Paris, 1960); and Catherine Duprat, *Le temps des philanthropes* (Paris, 1993).

[26] Robespierre, 'Adresse aux français' (July 1791), cited in Cobban, 'Fundamental ideas', p. 147.

rights to slaves in the French colonies. At the time of the Constituent Assembly, he made no distinction between the rights of the individual and the right of the people to collective sovereignty. He considered the latter to be the logical extension and conclusion of the former.[27]

But the gap between the revolutionary ideal of participatory democracy and the reality of a deeply divided French nation became increasingly apparent. A large section of the population would never be reconciled to republican government – and certainly not to the Jacobin version of it. A significant section of the population actively opposed the Revolution, and many more were passively resentful and hostile. The majority of these opponents were not from the old privileged orders but from 'the people' themselves. If the theory of popular sovereignty broke down, what then was to be the basis of revolutionary government? For Robespierre, once he accepted political power in the summer of 1793, the gap between theory and exigency widened into an unbridgeable gulf. Previously, he had expressed hostility to the idea that elected government could sufficiently represent the will of the people. Now his views began to shift. In principle, he continued throughout his political career to defend the rights of individuals, but in practice the political ideals to which he clung were increasingly at variance with the political expedients which he adopted as a member of the Committee of Public Safety. He changed his views also on the status of direct democracy. His position on the relationship between the people and the people's representatives was placed under considerable strain. As the forces of the *sans-culottes* and the Hébertists threatened to outflank the National Convention, Robespierre came to the position that the Convention could indeed represent the general will, thus obviating the need for the people to exercise direct democracy on their own behalf and to intervene in the political process. He continued to defend in principle individual rights and civil liberties, but, when these came into conflict with the collective good as an abstraction, he sided with the latter. 'No doubt it is necessary to protect individual liberty; but does it follow that it is necessary, in subtle ways, to let public liberty perish?'[28]

It is perhaps hardly surprising that the political radical of 1789 should have become a political authoritarian by 1793, justifying his actions in the name of the people but with consequences which were not so very different from the most autocratic of despotisms. Such transformations have not been a rare occurrence in the world of politics. What is so singular about Robespierre is that he appears to have tried to hold his

[27] See Cobban, 'Fundamental ideas', pp. 145–8.
[28] From an intervention of Robespierre in the Convention, 26 October 1793, *Réimpression de l'ancien Moniteur* (Paris, 1847), vol. XVIII, p. 215.

principles with sincerity, clinging to his beliefs even though he tied himself in ideological knots and thoroughly compromised himself in so doing. He struggled to maintain consistency in a world in which consistency was no longer possible. Thus, he retained his belief in political virtue and he never swerved from the theoretical conviction that the people were sovereign. He attempted to keep faith with the principle that the people as a whole were naturally virtuous, but this position was difficult to reconcile with the fact that not all the people were supporters of himself or of the Revolution. He maintained therefore that, whilst the people were naturally virtuous, they must have been either corrupted by the previous régime or misled by unscrupulous persons who manipulated public opinion and deceived the people, so that it was hard to be sure who had pure intentions and who was a deceiver. In this manner, the political libertarian began to justify the reimposition of political censorship, the ending of which had been one of the earliest triumphs of the revolutionaries of 1789. More and more, he saw the course of the Revolution in messianic terms, a cataclysmic struggle between good and evil. 'Vice and virtue forge the destiny of this earth; these two opposing spirits fight each other for it.'[29]

In practical terms, this meant that he saw himself, and the rapidly dwindling group of 'patriots' in whom he trusted, as the defenders of virtue, whilst his political opponents became 'scoundrels' ('fripons') and opponents also of the Revolution. He brought a puritanical religious fervour to his politics, although he did not invoke God, but the republic of virtue itself. Desmoulins mocked this self-righteousness in the last edition of the *Vieux Cordelier*, terming it 'le jansénisme de républicain' and thus attacking Robespierre's belief that he was a true defender of virtue in an apostate republican church.[30] Indeed, for Robespierre, private moral 'failings' were also political ones, sins against the Republic. He justified the destruction of those who had once been his friends but had now become his political enemies on the grounds that their revolutionary fervour had always been assumed and hypocritical. The notes with which he provided Saint-Just for the accusation of Danton sought to show that Danton had never been on the side of the angels, but had been a dissembler since the beginning of the Revolution. The irony was that Robespierre was able to provide such detailed notes on Danton's words and behaviour over several years precisely because the two men had been friends fighting the same battles. Amongst Danton's many iniquities, according to Robespierre, was the fact that he had laughed at

[29] Robespierre, *Œuvres*, vol. X, p. 446.
[30] *Vieux Cordelier* 7, republished in Camille Desmoulins, *Le Vieux Cordelier*, ed. Albert Mathiez and Henri Calvet (Paris, 1936), p. 202.

the idea of virtue, and used to say, as though it were a joke, that there was no sounder virtue than that which he practised every night with his wife.[31] The worst crime was to lack faith, to laugh at virtue.

The underlying problem with secular virtue, the problem which none of the *philosophes* had ever been able to resolve satisfactorily, was that it might not be rewarded this side of the grave. Vice might be stronger and most people might find it the more attractive option. In the murky sea of revolutionary politics and beset by political opponents, the Jacobins in 1793 were politically isolated, their hold on power precarious. It was not enough in such circumstances for revolutionaries to be virtuous – they had also to be strong and impose their will by force. The logic of this was inexorable and obvious. Most revolutionaries simply went about the business of imposing the Revolution without troubling themselves over-much about the inconsistencies of their position. But for a man like Robespierre, this was unthinkable. It was not enough for the Revolution to win; it had to be morally in the right. Without this, he said, revolution was nothing but crime. Virtue and force must be theoretically joined. He therefore set about redefining virtue, linking it with terror in a sudden and traumatic move which owed nothing to the established meaning of virtue and everything to the dilemmas of revolutionary government. In the same speech of February 1794 in which he had defined virtue in Montesquieu's terms, Robespierre went on to state that:

> If the mainspring of popular government in peacetime is virtue, the mainspring of popular government during a revolution is both virtue and terror: virtue, without which terror is baneful; terror, without which virtue is powerless. Terror is nothing more than speedy, severe and inflexible justice; it is thus an emanation of virtue; it is less a principle in itself than a consequence of the general principle of democracy, applied to the most pressing needs of the *patrie*.[32]

Unlike the conflation of morality and politics, the linking of virtue and terror appears to have been without precedent. It first appeared in the autumn of 1793, at a time when the Montagnard government was attempting to shore up the shaky legitimacy of its authority.[33] Indeed, as Robespierre's contemporaries well knew, to link virtue and terror was to juxtapose two principles which Montesquieu had considered incompatible: the virtue of republics with the terror (*la crainte*) of despotisms.[34]

[31] These notes are reprinted in Albert Mathiez, *Etudes sur Robespierre (1758–1794)* (Paris, 1958), pp. 121–56, with Danton's views on virtue, p. 138.

[32] Robespierre, *Œuvres*, vol. X, p. 357.

[33] See G. A. Kelly, 'Conceptual sources of the Terror', *Eighteenth-Century Studies* 14 (1980), 18–36.

[34] Strictly speaking, *la terreur* and *la crainte* did not have identical meanings, for the former in this context meant the process of making people afraid, whilst *la crainte* had the passive sense of the fear thus engendered by *la terreur*.

Robespierre's juxtaposition of virtue and terror was a traumatic shift, but it followed rather than led events. By the autumn of 1793, terror was already taking place on a significant scale – led by the anarchic terror of the *sans-culottes*. Robespierre's argument was indicative of the Montagnards' attempt to rationalise theoretically their centralisation and legitimation of the spontaneous and anarchic terror. Rather than having *caused* the Terror, the stated connection between virtue and terror was part of a belated attempt by the Montagnards to justify and explain – even to themselves – a process which was already happening.

Distorted though it was, Montesquieu's theoretical framework remained at the heart of this conception of politics. Terror was necessary to defend virtue, and virtue must be defended because without it the Republic would fail. Recognising this fact, Desmoulins, in the final edition of the *Vieux Cordelier*, challenged Robespierre's political position by a direct attack on its philosophical derivations. Desmoulins claimed that Montesquieu had been palpably wrong to state that virtue was the basis of republics – on the contrary, said Desmoulins, the basis of republics was liberty of the press.[35] He had a fair point, but it did him little good. The Committee of Public Safety was not prepared to tolerate criticism of its policy. This last edition of Desmoulins's journal remained unpublished, whilst he himself was to be hustled off to the guillotine.

Faced, as the *philosophes* had been, with the problem of how to ensure that people were virtuous, Robespierre maintained his belief in the need for a spiritual power over and beyond humanity: the Supreme Being. Speaking of the idea of the immortality of the soul and of eternal justice which would reward the virtuous and punish the wicked, he said:

> I cannot think in the least how Nature could have suggested to man any fictions more useful than all these truths; and, if the existence of God, if the immortality of the soul, were only dreams, they would still be the most beautiful of all the conceptions of the human mind.[36]

Yet one has the impression that he was speaking here in desperation. The last time Robespierre spoke before the Convention, he appeared almost to be courting his own martyrdom, as though he could no longer stand the strain of trying to bring about his virtuous republic: 'My reason, not my heart, is on the point of doubting this virtuous republic whose image I had traced for myself.'[37] In the unprecedented circumstances of 1793–4, the language of virtue helped to articulate Robespierre's sense of the rightness of what had been done in the name of the Revolution, to construct a truth and to make sense of what had become senseless. Rather than concentrate on the fight for his political – and

[35] *Vieux Cordelier* 7, pp. 237–8. [36] Robespierre, *Œuvres*, vol. X, p. 452.
[37] *Ibid.*, vol. X, p. 566.

personal – survival, he chose that moment to reaffirm his belief in the existence of virtue.

[Virtue] is a natural passion, no doubt; but how will they know it, these venal souls who will never open themselves to any but cowardly and ferocious passions; these wretched schemers who never associate patriotism with any moral idea, who trot in the Revolution in the train of some ambitious and important personage, of I know not which despised prince, just as lackeys once did in the footsteps of their masters? But it does exist, I can vouch for it, you pure and feeling souls; this tender, imperious and irresistible passion, the torment and delight of magnanimous hearts does exist; this profound horror of tyranny, this sympathetic zeal for the oppressed, this sacred love of the *patrie*, this most sublime and most holy love of humanity, without which a great revolution is only an illustrious crime that destroys another crime, it does exist; this generous desire to found on this earth the first republic in the world, it does exist; that egoism of men not degraded, that finds a heavenly pleasure in the calm of a pure conscience, and in the ravishing spectacle of public happiness – you can feel it at this moment burning in your souls; I feel it in mine.[38]

IV

If so many of Robespierre's ideas derived from mainstream political thought in the eighteenth century, why then did he stand out amongst his contemporaries? In large part this seems to be attributable to his personality and the single-mindedness with which he pursued his political convictions. Robespierre's conception of politics amounted to far more than the passive adoption of a rhetoric. He was a supreme tactician and manipulator. He was prepared, on many occasions, to reject the easy rhetorical path, to make up his own mind and to go against popular revolutionary opinion – most famously in his opposition to war in 1792. It is given to very few politicians to win the accolade of 'incorruptible'. Robespierre tried to oppose corruption and self-interest in his life as well as in his rhetoric: it was this which made him so effective. For observers, such as J.-V. Delacroix, for example, Robespierre was the most eloquent man of the Revolution precisely because he was the most virtuous.[39] The Revolution made things which had formerly seemed abstractions suddenly realisable. In such circumstances, the scene was set for the ascendancy of a man like Robespierre who combined the attributes of a tactical politician with those of an idealistic visionary. For Robespierre, the only limits to the Revolution lay in humanity's capacity to envisage a better future. Thus its bound-

[38] *Ibid.*, vol. X, p. 554.

[39] J.-V. Delacroix, *L'intrigue dévoilée ou Robespierre vengé des outrages et des calomnies des ambitieux*, cited in Louis Jacob, *Robespierre vu par ses contemporains* (Paris, 1938), p. 110.

aries could be pushed back by a combination of imagination and will: 'it is the imagination that usually sets the limits of the possible and the impossible; but when one has the will to do good, one must have the courage to go beyond these limits'.[40]

The difference between Robespierre and many of his contemporaries on the left lay not so much in the nature of his political principles as in the lengths to which he was prepared to go to defend them – so far indeed as to compromise those very ideals on which he had based his political life. His conception of politics was characterised both by fixed principles and by striking inconsistencies and changes of tactical position. In many cases, the inconsistencies themselves stemmed from the very rigidity of his principles as he sought to adapt general theoretical principles to the tortuous complexities of revolutionary politics. He wanted to be certain that he was in the right. This mattered to him more than anything else. In the cause of the Revolution and the *patrie* he lied, signed death warrants and betrayed his former friends. He was not alone in this: many other revolutionaries were similarly compromised. But Robespierre found it harder than most to live with the contradiction, and he has often been judged more harshly for the same reason – because, having set himself up on the pedestal of his own virtue, he had further to fall. It is not, then, enough to look at his political perspective in isolation – we have to look also at him as a man together with the circumstances of the Revolution in order to understand why Robespierre, who wanted to be remembered by posterity as a 'man of virtue', will also be remembered as a man of terror.

[40] From an intervention made in the Convention on the plan for national education by Lepeletier, 13 August 1793, in Robespierre, *Œuvres*, vol. X, p. 70.

4 Robespierre and revolutionary heroism

A. Jourdan
translated by William Doyle

> I may choose either many years without glory, or a few days followed by long memories.
>
> (Diderot (on Achilles))

No revolution can ever occur without, in Danton's words, 'this vast demolition of the existing order of things being harmful to somebody'. The reign of liberty, justice and virtue cannot come about without problems. The damage will be commensurate with the upheaval, and revolutionaries quickly become aware of the fact. Initially, absorbed in marking victory over the old order, they do not notice the scale of the dangers and the sacrifices that will be required of them, but as the clashes and troubles accumulate, and the number of victims mounts up, the revolutionary outlook changes from triumphalist pride to an attitude of heroic, patriotic sacrifice.

Alongside the cult of great men which the Revolution carried to extremes, it borrowed ideas from the Enlightenment more closely tied to the cult of the hero; because, for all its emphasis on genius, talent and merit, the Enlightenment had also retained a great admiration for heroism. Not aristocratic, warlike heroism, seeking personal glory, but the heroism of the courageous, just man, 'the fruit of whose death', as Diderot maintained, 'will be his country's freedom, and the survival of all those for whom he lays down his life'. The spiritual strength of such a man, said Rousseau, lights up all minds, and lends energy and vigour to all virtues. A hero, for Rousseau, would show a burning love for the *patrie* and unconquerable firmness in adversity. Such civic and patriotic heroism, as typified by Socrates, would inspire the men of the Revolution repeatedly to assume the mantle of the heroes of antiquity.

In the Revolution, heroism and patriotism would walk truly hand in hand. Patriotism would beget heroism, without which patriotism itself would seem pale indeed. The greater the dangers, the more excited men became, seeing themselves bringing about an exceptional, inimitable achievement. The national fever which took hold in 1789, said Danton, 'worked miracles that will amaze posterity'. The issues at stake, and the scale of the task, inspired patriots to efforts undreamed of, and persuaded them that their achievement would be as sublime as that of Jesus, or Brutus. Aware of the glorious destiny awaiting them, they also faced death from day to day, for that is often true heroism's sanction, nearer to Christian martyrdom than to Roman heroism and the triumphal march of the victorious general to the Capitol. Revolutionary heroism would be tragic, or it would be nothing; but it would be followed by honours and the nation's gratitude, self-sacrifice rewarded by posthumous glory.

This concern for immortality, faith in posterity's recognition and certainty of working for the happiness of future generations, explains why so many devoted themselves body and soul to the Revolution. In sacrificing all private interests to public ones, revolutionary heroism went beyond the cult of talent and genius. Unlike that of great men, this heroism was in principle open to anyone. And this momentary heroism also contrasted with warlike heroics, because it required courage above all, limitless self-sacrifice, great strength of character, unconditional patriotism. Earlier, the *Encyclopédie* had already drawn a distinction between the perfect and the classical hero. The former, in addition to military courage, had a sincere desire for public happiness. And in this he was not entirely dissimilar to the eighteenth-century ideal of the great man.[1] So it is not altogether surprising to find Rousseau blending the hero and the great man to endow both with spiritual strength, and absolute energy, virtue and commitment.

Thus it was possible for all the men of 1789, who had defied 'armed despotism' and risen up against the Crown to form a National Assembly, to regard themselves as great men and heroes. They had shown themselves 'beyond fear' and demonstrated all sorts of courage as they undertook their glorious mission, even when, in Mirabeau's words, 'beset by cruel alarms'. They had, he claimed, 'everything to fear, everything to brave'. The Constituents were well aware of it, and responded to Mounier's call to 'confront every peril to serve their country'. And to this courage in facing untold danger would soon be added an inexhaustible energy, essential for the nation's 'regeneration'.

With the dramatisation of the Revolution that began with the massacres at Nancy, a more pathetic tone began to be heard. On 29

[1] In *Essai sur les éloges* (Paris, 1771), A.-L. Thomas defined a great man as the benefactor and, as it were, the legislator of society whose goal was the perfection of the human race. Here, too, his fate was scarcely enviable. Persecuted and eclipsed, his only solace would be the knowledge that 'in dying his name at least would be avenged'. Saint Pierre, in his *Discours sur les différences du grand homme et de l'homme célèbre* (Paris, 1734), had a similar definition.

January 1791, the deputy Gouy launched the debate when he suggested commemorating the tragic death of the officer Desilles and offered a definition of what distinguished a modern hero from one of the old régime: 'Until now this apotheosis conferred by gratitude and admiration had been reserved for another sort of hero. Figures sanctified by the fury of conquest were granted these honours . . .; it would be worthy of humanity and of liberty to give them as well to martyrs to patriotism.' To create heroes was not so difficult; all it needed was to celebrate them. And yet this time the Assembly refused to do so, and chose only to honour great men such as Mirabeau and Voltaire. But the fact that it was they who were installed in the Pantheon, with the promise of Rousseau to follow, should not let us forget that the problem of the hero was often discussed, and became central from 1792 onwards. Robespierre's views on the matter were eloquent. They set out a whole theory of civic heroism; and they also reveal their proponent's patriotic longings.

Robespierre's heroes: the divine legislator

The young deputy from Arras quickly convinced himself that the legislators chosen by the nation would be swift to imitate the ancients. His view of the legislator was then quite close to that offered by Rousseau. A man of action working for human happiness, hoping for nothing more than gratitude, a legislator worthy of his mission would be 'superior, pure and unflinching', in the mould of Lycurgus or Cato, and not Alexander or Antony. Like Jean-Jacques, Robespierre drew no real distinction between great men and heroes.[2] The legislator was both. A great man in his work of regeneration, he became a hero in overcoming obstacles. Superior men, as the nation's deputies would be, had 'sublime destinies' to fulfil and much to do. For not only had they to 'rise up, and raise up the souls of their fellow citizens' so as to regenerate the French people, they had also to be the 'saviours' of France and 'models' for Europe.[3] The hero-deputy would be firm and generous, unflinching in the face of tyrants and intrigues, and know how to thwart the king's attempts to seize general sovereignty for himself alone. He would work for the happiness of the French people and of humanity, and would defend only principles. In fact, the whole duty of the citizen, whether private or as elected representative, would be 'the wish to serve his country, and the love of true glory'; his ambitions would seek not

[2] Jean-Jacques Rousseau, *Discours sur la vertu du héros*, in Rousseau, *Œuvres complètes*, 5 vols. (Paris, 1955–95), vol. II, pp. 1262–74.

[3] Robespierre, *Œuvres*, vol. VI, p. 95.

dignities but 'the happiness of deserving the love of others by his talents and virtues'. Fundamental among these virtues were justice and humanity, sympathy, love and respect for the people. That meant taking the side of the poor and weak against the rich and powerful. Throughout the Constituent, Robespierre the patriot kept up this argument, urging the Assembly to accomplish its 'sacred mission' and bring to a conclusion its 'immortal struggle', making itself the 'protector of human rights' and winning respect for its character and disinterestedness.

Yet Robespierre's great expectations for an assembly of demigods were disappointed. Despite his interventions, the Assembly took few steps to aid ordinary people. It preferred the 'law of blood' to giving the people bread, balked at granting Jews unequivocal citizenship, and refused to abolish the silver mark or reduce other voting qualifications. Instead of conferring the dignity of men and citizens on all Frenchmen, it supported privilege and perpetuated injustice. Robespierre was almost alone in opposing these iniquities. Against him, he now saw not Rousseau's legislator but intriguers who would not give up their power – whether the king, the court, ministers or deputies. These, ultimately, were people who were either working 'to keep absolute power for themselves or people like them' or 'struggling less for the cause of the Revolution than to achieve dominant power under the king's name'.[4] And then, there were all those who, from weakness or blindness, were working without realising it to put the Revolution into reverse. As time went by, Robespierre increasingly dreaded a return to the abuses of the old order: 'Unhappy the day when the legislator of a people passing from servitude into liberty infects its institutions with traces of prejudices and vicious habits born of despotism.'[5] The 'transient enthusiasm' released after 14 July had flagged. Without vigilance, ancient prejudices and frivolous habits would resurface, 'miserable, vain pretensions' would re-emerge, charlatanism and intrigue reappear. Living up to the Revolution's ambitions could never be taken for granted; it was a permanent struggle. Two years' experience had taught Robespierre that. Weakness and greed were undermining the foundations of liberty and equality. Partisanship was poisoning wise and just opinions, and blinding men to the true benefits that the people had a right to expect. Yet on 29 September 1791, Robespierre refused to believe the Revolution was over. Even then, he was aware that the newborn constitution had much to fear from external and internal enemies. 'Every petty means has been employed by those petty men who are the shame and

[4] *Ibid.*, vol. VI, p. 641, vol. VII, p. 124. [5] *Ibid.*, vol. VII, p. 632.

the scourge of revolutions.' Instead of breeding the expected giants, the Constituent had given birth to 'dwarfs'.

The Assembly which had 'held the destiny of France and the universe in its hands', which 'could at one blow have raised the French people to the summit of happiness, glory and freedom ... had fallen short of its sublime mission'.[6] It had failed to be firm, pure and enlightened.[7] Nor had the Legislative which followed it amid so much promise shown the great character, genius and energy necessary to smash plots and intrigues. It 'appeared humbly self-restrained in the mere shadow of the Constituent Assembly'. Humble it was not, since it soon trespassed on the prerogatives of the executive, but the legislator of 1792 was once more confronted by court intrigues and by discord between Feuillants and Jacobins, not to mention discord among Jacobins themselves, between those in power and their Robespierrist opponents. Disillusionment was compounded when the Brissotins took over ministries and committees, neglected the people's interests in favour of their own, traduced the true defenders of liberty and refused to make way for the public interest. This at least was Robespierre's viewpoint. The Convention, where he hoped to keep the leading rôle he played at the Jacobins, filled him with more hope – provided that it showed 'great character' and adopted 'purer and more popular principles'.

By now, Robespierre was explicitly citing the *Contrat social*; but he was forced to reduce Rousseau's idealisation of a divine legislator to its true dimensions. He was describing him as an intrepid philosopher without vanity, envy or ambition, who would seek neither court favour nor the joys of power, but the nation's esteem.[8] He would be a philosopher, animated by 'unalterable zeal for humanity', who would forget his own interests in the service of principles and who would fight for justice and equality. He certainly did not discern such a philosopher among his opponents, even if Roland, his wife and Brissot in the last analysis held the same ideal. Madame Roland, indeed, also described the true hero as a man whose 'spiritual strength, sustained by a sense of what is correct ... and a breadth of vision which sees into the future', would make possible the regeneration of France. In 1792–3, however, she could not see such a great character anywhere. Robespierre, by contrast, seemed to have found such a man, 'a single man, just and brave, who would continually thwart their schemes, and, contemptuous of life, would fear neither steel nor poison and be but too happy if his death could be of service to liberty and his country'. Of course, he meant himself. As the

[6] *Défenseur de la constitution* (repr. Paris, 1939), p. 6. [7] *Ibid.*, p. 319.

[8] Robespierre, *Œuvres*, vol. VIII, p. 143. For his definition of the ideal legislator, see *Lettres à ses commettans* (repr. Gap, 1961), p. 19.

months went by, he would urge the Assembly to improve itself, to give up ambition and deceit and 'sacrifice itself for the people'. Was this not its true mission? And the Convention, torn apart by murderous conflicts, after much reluctance, would indeed finally sacrifice its 'faithless' representatives to the people of Paris.[9]

The fall of the Girondins brought back the hope that a purged Assembly would prove worthy of its task. Once again Robespierre reminded it that, to save the country, what was needed was 'great character, great virtues; men with the energy and courage to propose strong measures, even ones that dare attack the self-regard of individuals'. Increasingly courage and energy became the key words of the republican creed. Reading the various speeches of the Incorruptible, the dominant impression is that he wanted nothing less than to resurrect and surpass the virtues of antiquity. And the idea of sacrifice was always implied. Themistocles, Scipio, Cato, Brutus and a host of others were the models offered by classical history. Since the French Republic was founded on purer and more generous principles, its legislators owed it to themselves to measure up to these Herculean figures of patriotism. The Committee of Public Safety of the Year II would partially fulfil these hopes. Absorbed day and night by the country's interests, defending liberty and the people's rights at the peril of life itself, constantly threatened on all sides by daggers, the Committee gave 'one character to one government'. It had restored strength through unity, bound the nation back together. Inflexible, severe, vigilant, virtuous and heroic, revolutionary government for one fleeting moment fulfilled Robespierre's hopes. It trod 'with rapid and firm steps towards public happiness', and felled all factions with a sweep of its mighty arm. Speed compounded its energy, its courage, its strength, its unity. What the critical young deputy had called 'precipitation' in 1790, when the Constituent passed decrees without thinking them through, was now that swiftness so necessary if revolutionary government were to destroy internal and external enemies, and make laws without debates and 'endless qualifications'. Now that the Convention had decimated the 'last' factions, the way was open for the 'reign of understanding, unity and concord'.[10] Speed of decision seemed proof of it. But it was at this very moment that the 'poison of calumny' began to seep in. Instead of supporting the Committee, the Convention became divided, and began to plot. The reign of wisdom, justice and virtue of which Robespierre dreamed did not attract all its members; to many the ancient heroism

[9] See also A. Jourdan, 'La guerre des dieux ou l'héroïsme révolutionnaire chez Madame Roland et Robespierre', *Romantisme* 85 (1994), 19–26.

[10] Robespierre, *Œuvres*, vol. X, p. 486.

that he wished to revive seemed beyond recovery, or too Spartan. There were new slanders, and corrupt men struck fear into the pure majority, to the shame of the Republic. Instead of pressing on towards its goal of 'the peaceful enjoyment of liberty and equality', the Revolution was turning in criminal directions. Robespierre became convinced that there were intrigues afoot, and that conspirators were shaming the Republic. Before 'making every effort of genius to bring the Republic back to the gentle order of nature', the 'last heads of the hydra' must be struck off.[11] But these last heads would resist as those before never had.

On the eve of his downfall, the Incorruptible would one last time express his wish to see 'great figures' who might alone bring this wayward revolution into port. But these dying professions marked the defeat of the Terror, the end of 'the heroism of virtue'.[12] Despite repeated urgings, none of the successive assemblies had made the heroes of antiquity live again. Instead of Hercules or Atlas, there had only been pygmies, 'puppets' even,[13] who could never match up to the stature required by the 'finest' of all revolutions.

Robespierre's heroes: the collective hero – the people

In Robespierre's eyes the real hero, unnoticed in an assembly where no legislator was able to forget himself for long, was the collective body of the people. The people 'good, great and generous' often want what is good but do not always see it, whereas their representatives often see it but do not always want it. The people were heroic, because the Revolution was ultimately their work; a mass uprising had brought about 'countless recent heroic deeds'. The problem was that the people were 'too good and too credulous', and sometimes unable to unmask those intriguing against them. No sooner were their first demands satisfied, than they sank back into lethargic slumber, trusting too much in the patriotism of their representatives. It was the duty of patriotic societies to dispel this *naïveté* by enlightening, educating and exhorting. Robespierre was always encouraging the emergence of good citizens whose sole desire was to 'serve their country', to show 'an imperious zeal' for the defence of liberty and a willingness to give up 'not only their lives

[11] *Ibid.*, vol. X, p. 538.

[12] *Ibid.*, vol. X, p. 531. Yet by 8 Thermidor he was losing hope that the virtuous republic of which he dreamed would ever last: *ibid.*, vol. X, pp. 542–76.

[13] It was L.-S. Mercier who wrote (in *Le nouveau Paris* (repr. Paris, 1990), pp. 377, 383) that 'competition between talents held them all back and no giant emerged among them'; 'all the villains and even the men of decency were puppets on strings'. Of course, Mercier was thinking of them as victims of a plot.

but their attachments and their prejudices'.[14] This divine mission was to be carried out by the Jacobin club.

From the outset, Robespierre set himself up as a defender of the popular cause, of the unfortunate, the poor, the persecuted. It is true that in his frequently proclaimed compassion and thirst for justice there was an important element of popularity seeking.[15] Soon, however, his speeches were directed not just at winning the attention of the Parisian public, but at arousing its energy and courage. For the king and his court were dissimulating, backtracking and deceiving the nation. Deputies either too weak or too corrupt were not taking adequate steps to avoid the executive power's deceptions. Only the people could now save the Revolution, a people 'energetic and wise, formidable and just, rushing to arms to defend the magnificent work of its courage and its virtue'.[16] Compassion would produce action. More than ever Robespierre had come to believe that what makes revolutions is opinion. It would be moulded by the Jacobin club, the patriotic press and correspondence with the provinces, in a Robespierrist direction, just as the Brissotins often tried to bend it in their own.

A first step down the path of patriotic exaltation came in January 1792, when Robespierre emphasised the rôle played by ordinary people in the Revolution, celebrating popular heroes who usually ended up as martyrs: the heroes of 14 July (whom the Assembly initially refused to honour), the heroes of Châteauvieux, soldiers persecuted for having too much civic sense, patriots massacred under bloody laws, women and children butchered by all-powerful criminals.[17] The people had been the Revolution's first victims, everywhere despised, outraged, oppressed. The Incorruptible saw it as his mission to show the people their rights, bring out their strength and character, and work to unite the scattered members of this sublime body. During the troubled times of the Legislative, Robespierre's dream was to form an 'immortal legion' comprising all the victims of despotism. It would bring together soldiers, National Guardsmen and French guards who 'suffered under oppression like the rest of the people': for all this time, the only patriotic army he could envisage was one made up of soldiers persecuted for their public spirit. Already we can see the dawning conviction that sufferings undergone would be commensurate with degrees of patriotism, and vice versa.

[14] Robespierre, *Œuvres*, vol. VII, pp. 408, 483.

[15] *Ibid.*, vol. VII, pp. 366, 385.

[16] *Ibid.*, vol. X, p. 230. The urge to action was particularly felt on the eve of 10 August 1792 and in May 1793.

[17] *Ibid.*, vol. VIII, p. 107.

This tirelessly invoked hero took the particular form, in July 1792, of the Marseille *fédérés*. As Robespierre wrote to Couthon, they were 'French Brutuses' coming to save the country. The Jacobins spared nothing to propel them into action. Even though Robespierre, following his usual tactic, urged them to show wisdom and prudence, he was relying on their steadiness and bravery to carry along the patriots of Paris when the moment came. His address on 20 July showed the heights to which he urged them: the French Brutuses should leave Paris only after victory or death; here they would triumph or go to their graves.[18] And yet, on the eve of 10 August, Robespierre was still unsure of the support they would receive from an Assembly which, instead of acting against the true villains, 'was only taking steps to punish the people'; 'abandoned thus, we shall have to find all our resources within ourselves. The French people must take on the whole weight of the world, and vanquish all its monsters; it will need to be among peoples what Hercules was among heroes.'[19] Atlas or Hercules, the people had a delicate task and no alternative but to perish or conquer. And Robespierre now renewed his praise of Marseille's immortal legion, whose 'sacred fire should spread to all the French'. He saw in them a new sort of energy, harmoniously blending patriotic enthusiasm, Roman pride and Spartan heroism. Such superior men exceeded these distant forebears in generosity, since they had won liberty not only in their own interests, as the Athenians and Spartans had, but in those of all the French.[20] Following the fall of the Tuileries, Robespierre attributed the victory to the whole of the French people and vaunted 'the finest revolution ever to honour humanity'. In this final struggle, the mighty and sublime people had performed miracles of heroism far beyond anything in history. And now, the need was for an assembly that was 'new, pure, incorruptible' and worthy of this 'great people struggling [alone] against all the oppressors of nations'.

The victory had been sealed with blood. There had been victims. 'Heroes from Marseille have perished, and unspeakable, dangerous intriguers who have laid their country waste since the Revolution began are now panting to tear it apart once again.' But the tone was far from despairing. Robespierre noted how every soul was filled with 'sublime sentiments'. 'Victims heaped up by court savagery were before the eyes of citizens on all sides . . .; citizens had fathers, friends, brothers, to weep for; but love of country and enthusiasm for liberty overcame all other attachments.'[21] The dead were as nothing beside the results. The Republic would be built and strengthened on piles of corpses.

18 *Défenseur de la constitution*, p. 308.
19 *Ibid.*, p. 330. 20 *Ibid.*, p. 334. 21 *Ibid.*, p. 364.

Robespierre would hymn the French people until his downfall, but his initial enthusiasm was not unaffected by his rise to power. Little by little he distanced himself from the people, and in his turn he followed Madame Roland and Brissot, despite having never wished to split this seamless whole, in dividing the people into two. And so in Prairial Year II, bitter and disillusioned as factions and calumny re-emerged, he came to discern two peoples in France: 'One is the mass of citizens, pure, simple, thirsting for justice and in love with liberty . . . the other is that clutch of ambitious schemers, false and insinuating prattlers whom we see everywhere persecuting patriotism, self-promoting and often too in public office': rogues, foreigners and two-faced counter-revolutionaries. And the *sans-culottes*, the very people who had supported Robespierre, seemingly belonged to the latter category. Robespierre, member of the Committee of Public Safety, no longer saw them as 'his' people; the restless *sans-culottes* who revered the holy image of Marat, made fun of the Supreme Being, and rose up not for the Republic but for sugar, coffee, butter or soap[22] had nothing now to do with the idyllic people, the Rousseauistic abstraction that he had celebrated since 1789. Even as he encouraged them still to 'show relentless energy in strangling every monster',[23] Robespierre would now, just like his Girondin predecessors, appeal more and more to respectable folk and men of purity to back him in rooting out scoundrels. Alas, 'the time has not yet come when decent folk can serve their country without fear'.[24] Thermidor would sound their final defeat.

Robespierre's heroes: martyrs of liberty

Since death reigned supreme, more and more heroes took the form of martyrs. But a republican martyr was not the same as a Christian one. His tireless energy made him different. The republican was a ferocious defender of the new and entirely secular faith, and he was required not only to know how to suffer and to die, but to carry on the armed fight until exhaustion, and to devote his last breath to the sacred cause of the *patrie*. The Christian martyr was entirely passive, his eyes on heaven alone, indifferent to his fellow citizens. The revolutionary martyr, by contrast, worked for the public good, for humanity and for this life, to

[22] Robespierre, *Œuvres*, vol. IX, p. 275. In June 1793, he refused to allow the people to be present at the sittings of the Committee of Public Safety (*ibid.*, vol. IX, p. 573); and, in September, he demanded that the sections should not assemble more than twice a week (*ibid.*, vol. X, p. 110).

[23] *Ibid.*, vol. X, p. 477.

[24] M. Robespierre, *Discours* (Paris, 1965), p. 308. See also Madame Roland, *Lettres à Bancal* (Paris, 1835), p. 447.

bring about liberty, equality and fraternity for the happiness of all. All this brought him much nearer to the heroes of antiquity than to the saints of Catholicism, even though, like the latter, he stood for a new faith, gave up his life for his beliefs, and obstinately spurned the most awful dangers.

It is true that there had been martyrs for liberty from the start of the Revolution, such as the soldiers of Châteauvieux, the victims of the Champ de Mars massacre and of 10 August. But, little by little, they became not only those who fell in battle but also victims of a personal fate. Martyrs became named individuals, and this had the advantage of serving the revolutionary cause more durably. Anonymous martyrs, or martyrs of antiquity, were too abstract a category for those to whom the cult appealed, those who had to be persuaded that death and sacrifice were not annihilation and that freedom's defenders would be gloriously rewarded by the nation. The first such martyr would be Lepeletier, murdered for voting for the death of the king. Robespierre was quick to praise his civic heroism, his virtues, his gentle and courageous soul, the fervent patriotism that would dictate his last words – sublime ones, of course. The martyr with a name was all the more prized if he could speak until his last breath, loquacious in his agony. His words would guarantee him immortality, a place in the Revolution's memory. Bourdon and Thibaudeau would distribute a *Collection of Heroic Acts* (*Recueil des actes héroïques*) throughout the departments relating the sublime actions and lapidary phrases of these new republican saints. A 'divine religion', this cult of martyrs, to be spread by its own 'missionaries'.[25] Robespierre would be one of them, asking the Jacobins to accord supreme honours to Lazowski, the father of the people, who helped the poor with the soul of a hero and rare sensitivity. The first two martyrs celebrated by Robespierre had this in common, too, that their devotion to the cause of the people could not have been predicted. Despite their wealth and their origins (one a nobleman, the other a foreigner), they had both chosen nevertheless to defend popular and egalitarian principles. Indeed, Robespierre's heroes had private virtues – sensitivity and generosity – which bolstered their patriotism. And so, among the great men invoked by him, alongside profound writers (such as the model for them all, Rousseau), there was a place for rich men who loved liberty enough 'to devote part of their fortunes to spreading Enlightenment ideas and public spirit'. For the Incorruptible, Lepeletier and Lazowsky were men of this sort.[26]

[25] Robespierre, *Œuvres*, vol. IX, p. 257 (on the death of Lepeletier).

[26] Relieving misfortune was important for Robespierre. Lepeletier, Lazowski and even Barra gave up their wealth (or rather their pittance in Barra's case) to help the

The cult of martyrs fostered by the authorities aimed, as Robespierre poetically put it, 'to resurrect millions of avengers from their own ashes'. The counter-revolutionary hydra would be confronted by the revolutionary phoenix and, in the Year II, the crop of revolutionary heroes would be particularly heavy. The members of the Convention made it their duty to seek them out and produce relics relating to them. Such was the case with Chalier, whose remains were laid before the Convention, his undecayed body disinterred and his head carried in triumph. Other no less macabre spectacles followed. Victims came to the tribune to display gaping wounds and mutilated limbs. Legislators vied with each other in detailed and sometimes distasteful descriptions, such as Lakanal on the fate of Joseph Sauveur.[27] Terror and horror became synonymous, with livid, butchered corpses, like that of Marat, sanctified in funeral rites. Showing off the bodies stirred the emotions and a sense of sacrifice. It bore witness to the Republic's vitality, and to the patriotism of the French people. It bore witness, too, to the fact that this patriotism was an equal commitment of body and soul.

And Robespierre, if he did not always relish such overblown ostentation,[28] shared fully in the invocation of sacrifices made. One, even two hundred thousand heroes had given up their lives,[29] and women were not spared, having sacrificed brothers, children, husbands. The whole of France had become a land of heroes, striking down the satellites of tyranny 'with the thunderbolt of their invincible courage'.[30] Every day, marvels of heroism confronted 'excesses of cowardice and wickedness'. It was all thanks to the Convention, which had succeeded in elevating the people to the highest standards of the Revolution. 'By bringing fine deeds before her eyes, France will see them repeated; and by rewarding them we show ourselves worthy to represent the French people.'[31] The Convention had done all this, and for charlatanism and self-serving talents had substituted 'the virtues of modesty and service to the country'. Victims maimed or murdered by counter-revolution also

wretched. Barra supported his mother. But this (almost Christian) charity had to go with constancy and modesty.

[27] *Moniteur*, vol. XVI, p. 603: 'Joseph Sauveur fell into the hands of rebels . . . who made him undergo all the cruelties that aristocracy can think up. They cut off his fingers and toes, shot out his eyes and into his mouth, and threw him into a blazing pyre where he died, with his civic medallion pressed to his lips.'

[28] For example, he opposed the reading of a letter about a young soldier of nineteen, who wished to make a knife sheath from a bone of the arm he had lost in combat. Robespierre, *Œuvres*, vol. X, p. 538: 'These words are so appalling, they could never have come from the mouth of a republican hero.'

[29] Robespierre, *Discours*, p. 224 (5 February 1794).

[30] Robespierre, *Œuvres*, vol. IX, p. 309.

[31] *Moniteur*, vol. XIX, p. 169 (Barère's speech of 9 Nivôse Year II).

served as a metaphor for the Convention's own sufferings. It, too, had faced death and braved the rage of all tyrants,[32] as was shown by the violent deaths of Lepeletier, Marat, Fabre and Chalier, and attempts on the lives of Bourdon, Collot and Robespierre himself.

Heroism would soon become contagious, and spread to the younger generation. The child-hero Barra would be joined by a Decius of just thirteen. The annals of Greece and Rome offered no heroes as young and generous as Barra or Viala, who brought together all the patriotic virtues of heroism, courage and love of country.[33] Revolutionary exaltation was even spreading to the families of the poor; and this democratisation of heroism would entail a democratisation of the nation's glory and honours. To attain them, all it would take would be to live a virtuous life and die like a hero. In his famous report of 18 Floréal, Robespierre came back to the problem and offered a typology of heroism which took in defenders of their country, heroes of liberty as well as martyrs, unknown heroes 'buried in the obscurity' of history, or great men 'of whatever time or place who have freed their country of tyrants or set up liberty through wise laws'. Thus Robespierre did not forget great men but he reserved his veneration for those who combined patriotic heroism with the virtues of the legislator – not for him those who merely had great talents, like Voltaire. The truly great man, the preceptor of the human race and benefactor of humanity, could be found above all in Rousseau, or in ancient lawgivers. Robespierre's great men did not keep the Jacobin Pantheon for themselves. They kept pride of place for liberty's martyrs: those unknown and unnamed citizens, obscure and persecuted soldiers, children fired by patriotic fervour and those French women who 'had nothing to envy in the wives of Sparta, having given birth like them to heroes'. This wide typology was far from the élitist pantheon of Diderot, where only a select few entered, and the rest 'perished like brutes'. On the contrary, the boast of the Year II Pantheon was that it welcomed within its walls the most diverse representatives of national self-sacrifice. The meaning of this for the Montagnard republic was summed up by Couthon in a lapidary phrase: 'Forget the living, honour the dead, that is how to give the Republic a solid foundation.'[34] This was what the cult of martyrs meant. To honour the Republic's dead would be to endow it with a past in the expectation of a more radiant future. Its temple would be the Pantheon.

32 Robespierre, *Discours*, p. 183.

33 Robespierre, *Œuvres*, vol. X, pp. 292–3. For Robespierre these were 'the sum of all virtues'. The only private virtue that seemed important to him in this context was filial love, which lent some humanity to these extraordinary young heroes.

34 *Moniteur*, vol. XIX, p. 16.

Generous though Robespierre's distribution of the palms of martyrdom was, he none the less made a distinction between Lazowsky's death and Marat's. Whereas no words were too much for praising the ashes of the 'leader of the most vigorous group of freedom's friends', who had been in the forefront of the conquerors of the Tuileries, on Marat his tone was more measured. In the case of Marat, the People's Friend, the most zealous of his country's defenders, the Incorruptible sought to check enthusiasm and direct it towards a more specific object: defence of the *patrie*. Robespierre's enemies would impute this to his morbid jealousy. But although the tone had changed, so had the situation, with a people's deputy murdered, the fall of the Girondins, internal and foreign wars and defeated armies. Instead of using Marat's murder in his struggle against the 'factions' as he had in the cases of Lepeletier and Lazowski, whose tragic ends helped to swell distrust of the Girondin enemy, Robespierre wished to use this death to urge the French on to battle and to victory, and to sketch out the first elements of economic, social and military policies.[35] Besides, Marat was scarcely in the image of the republic that Robespierre hoped to establish. To men who knew how to work for posterity, Barra and Viala, those symbols of innocence and purity cut down in the flower of their youth, were much more fitting, for what the Robespierrist republic sought was dignity and respectability.[36] Marat was more a caricature than the symbol of a virtuous republican that Robespierre dreamed of; Barra, by contrast, epitomised a virtuous revolution's dream of murdered purity.[37]

Robespierre as hero

The hero of Robespierre's dreams was never a reality. Neither in the legislator nor in the people was he really discovered. Barra, it is true, was the incarnation of the Republic of which Robespierre dreamed. But the Republic also needed flesh-and-blood heroes who would act out their heroism. Robespierre's true hero, inflexible, incorruptible, imperturbable, was without any doubt himself. Even before praising himself as a new Cato or Brutus, Robespierre was treated as such by his contempor-

[35] Robespierre, *Œuvres*, vol. IX, p. 624. Now that the Girondins had been eliminated, it really seemed possible to think about 'governing'. Thus Robespierre demanded not only the raising of a revolutionary army but also policies to 'gently bring the people back to their duties', to make justice more rigorous, food more readily available, laws wiser, and to make the murderers of Marat and Lepeletier pay for their crimes.

[36] This is the general argument of A. Jourdan, *Les monuments de la Révolution: une histoire de représentation* (Paris, 1997).

[37] On this subject, see A. de Baecque, 'Le sang des héros: figures du corps dans l'imaginaire politique de la Révolution française', *Revue d'histoire moderne et contemporaine* 34 (1987), 575.

aries from the time of the Constituent Assembly onwards. Then there was no shortage of praise from Brissot, Carra, Gorsas, Barère, Desmoulins or Madame Roland. The last regarded him as 'the most vigorous defender of liberty'. Until the split between the two factions who would become Girondins (or rather Brissotins) and Jacobins, Robespierre was endlessly called energetic, courageous, the sole incarnation of a hero in the Roland mould.[38]

In so far as the Incorruptible had a messianic vision of the hero, it was not dissimilar to Madame Roland's and Rousseau's conception of someone with the strength of mind necessary to be 'capable of any sacrifice'. He, too, saw the hero as a man of virtue, energy and courage. But Robespierre's heroes always had something about them of the martyr, the persecuted sufferer. Liberty's true hero was quite often its martyr, much like the people, always good, always victimised, with whom Robespierre tended to identify very quickly. Convinced of his messianic, prophetic vocation, 'this impassioned soul' would mark out the high road to happiness and liberty with his own blood. Viewed in this way, the career of one who had so often urged the people and the Assembly to 'lift up your souls' to the heights of their 'sublime destiny' has many elements recalling Christian self-sacrifice[39] and antique heroism at the same time.

What made Robespierre heroic above all was the stubbornness which enabled him to face down aristocratic sarcasm when addressing the Assembly, or which made him persist in voicing views that went against the general opinion. He risked his popularity with such stands, but later on they were powerful evidence of how sincere he had always been and, when his warnings were borne out, how far-sighted. He would turn his stubbornness to advantage when he spoke of great legislators who strove alone 'against the torrents of prejudice and faction',[40] following the voice of their conscience over everything and against everyone. A case in point was when, all alone, he protested that the king had gone unpunished for the flight to Varennes. And there were many others. This early isolation helped to give him a sense of a rare 'stormy destiny'. 'I must follow it', he exclaimed to Buissart, 'until the last sacrifice that I can make for my country.'[41] Of course, the argument from sacrifice was not Robespierre's monopoly. From Madame Roland to Vergniaud, from Marat to Danton, all the revolutionaries quickly foresaw that the high

[38] Jourdan, 'La guerre des dieux', 19–26.

[39] He admitted, like Rousseau, to an admiration for 'the sublime doctrine of the son of Mary' (*Lettres à ses commettans*, p. 117).

[40] Robespierre, *Œuvres*, vol. VIII, p. 64.

[41] *Correspondance de Maximilien et d'Augustin Robespierre*, ed. G. Michon (Paris, 1926), p. 110.

road to freedom would not be without hazards. All would declare themselves ready to die rather than cease defending their principles, to die without regret and to follow wherever liberty led, 'even through a sea of blood',[42] to save the Revolution or perish. With others, however, the thirst for sacrifice was put in less moving terms. Where Robespierre excelled in depicting torments and persecutions endured, there were often somewhat triumphalist echoes in Girondin heroism. Girondins were not given to melancholy: no words of despair, no apocalyptic visions for them. While Robespierre lamented, Madame Roland on the eve of her death would invoke 'the energy born of great courage', which made her like the martyred saints going proudly to their deaths, in all the 'joy of innocence which despised death and knew that their own would be avenged'. Such a death would be the ultimate example.

Before perishing, it was important to act, and so be heard. Robespierre was no less stubborn about this. Whether in the Constituent, at the Jacobins or in the Convention, opponents were always trying to prevent him from speaking. It was all the easier since his weak voice was already hard to hear. In the Tuileries, the terrible acoustics caused him even more problems. He had, then, all the more need of 'spiritual strength' to overcome attempts to obstruct him, and raise his feeble voice above the catcalls. As G. Walter observed, the hall of the Jacobins suited him much better from this point of view.[43] It was here that he would make his true gains with public opinion, and through this public that he would take his first steps in preparing for power. And Robespierre's constancy and stubbornness had other, more dangerous, repercussions. In October 1790, for example, he was challenged to a duel by an officer of the King's Regiment, and refused to fight on the grounds that he did not believe 'that honour was a matter of killing for mere words'. On this occasion, the Incorruptible set civic heroism above the warlike sort.[44] But civic heroism also had many dangers, since at any moment someone might attempt an assassination. When the king fled, and Robespierre once more did not fear to say aloud what many were quietly thinking, he expressed his first forebodings from the rostrum of the Jacobins. In denouncing almost the entire Assembly, he knew he was 'sharpening countless daggers, and inviting hatred of all sorts'. And it

42 Roland, *Lettres à Bancal*, p. 243.

43 G. Walter, *Robespierre* (Paris, 1946), p. 132. See also A. Jourdan, 'Les discours de Robespierre. La parole au pouvoir', in Jourdan (ed.), *Robespierre: figure-réputation*, Yearbook of European Studies IX (Amsterdam and Atlanta, 1996).

44 Robespierre played down aristocratic honour, which he saw only as 'gothic prejudice' (*Œuvres*, vol. VII, pp. 5, 6, 492). He also declared that the greatest heroes were 'those who die to free their country from tyranny's yoke'. Those who gave their lives fighting foreign enemies came only after them (*Défenseur de la constitution*, p. 367).

was then that he revealed his 'profession of faith': he knew the fate awaiting him; from the very start of the Revolution, as a young unknown, lost in the mass of deputies, he had 'sacrificed his life to truth, to liberty, to his country'. This first declaration had its intended effect. The Jacobins were moved to tears and swore to follow him even unto death. From then on he was regularly prepared to argue for the need for sacrifice. And it was true that the time seemed ripe. There were rumours of a price on the head of this most faithful of patriots. Yet despite the danger, he was soon on his feet again to defy 'the daggers of crime and the snares of intrigue', as Gorsas put it. Thenceforth, Robespierre could set himself up as a model. He would be the man of patriotism. He would be the man of justice and courage, who, 'scorning life, fears neither steel nor poison'. Indifferent to his fate, so long as the country survived, Robespierre would know how to die, not like the ancients 'to save expiring liberty but for the salvation of a sensitive and generous people'.[45] The Marseillais would even come to compare him to the Roman Fabricius 'whose virtues were praised by the despot Pyrrhus in these celebrated words: it is easier to turn the sun from his course than to sway Fabricius from the path of honour'.

The first talk of sacrifice had come from the platform at the Jacobins. On 29 September 1791, as the Constituent came to an end, Robespierre, worried at the turn of events, took up the sacrificial theme in his attempts to defend the patriotic societies. Whatever moderates might say, the Revolution was not over and the suppression of the societies would damage the propagation of revolutionary principles. 'If I must cease declaiming against the scheming of the country's enemies, if I must applaud the ruin of the land of my birth, order me to do as you will, let me perish before liberty is lost.'[46] Perish rather than cease to defend good principles, perish rather than see the rule of knaves and fools! Such unwavering commitment and tireless labours would lead at the end of September 1791 to a triumphant climax. Pétion and Robespierre were crowned as great men and heroes of the Assembly. Even for Brissot, still only a journalist, the Incorruptible was nothing less than the Assembly's Cato.

With the rise of Brissot and his friends in the Legislative, Robespierre fell into the background, but he secured a leading position in the Jacobins. From this platform, he could once again declare his commitment and show that a true friend of freedom must be firm in his principles. His unwavering opposition to war showed this particularly. The intrigues of Lafayette and Narbonne and the growing conflicts with

[45] Robespierre, *Œuvres*, vol. VII, p. 588. [46] *Ibid.*, vol. VII, p. 747.

Brissot and his supporters would exacerbate his sense of the dangers besetting one who was becoming the leader of the Jacobins. In April 1792, threatened by a supporter of Lafayette, Robespierre once more brought up the picture of his own death: he had long been ready for assassins,[47] but that would not deter him from doing what he had to do. For 'you do not abandon your country; you do not fly from it, you save it, or die in the attempt'. Sacrifice demanded everything, and more. And so, under attack from Brissot and Guadet on 25 April, Robespierre would declare himself ready to give up not only his life but even his reputation, his renown, his name. Even though, just like Rousseau (steeped as he was in the *Confessions*),[48] the Incorruptible was deeply anxious that the name he would leave should not be besmirched. Had not history taught him that the benefactors of humanity had become martyrs to it?[49] The only remedy against the perfidy of history was the 'belated help of time which will surely avenge betrayed humanity and oppressed peoples'.[50]

Heroism was not just the sacrifice of a life and a reputation. In this time of troubles, legislators and patriots would also give up their rest, their strength, their health. As Madame Roland put it: 'in such times, there is scarcely time to live and do everything that every day demands'. Ten years of life could pass in twenty-four hours. 'Never to sleep and be more than human in deed' would be the patriot's fate. For five long years Robespierre would be among them, not sparing his strength. Like some Atlas,[51] he would carry an immense, superhuman burden. Exhausted by all this (his enemies in the Year II would say 'worn out'), sometimes he simply had to rest. But it was so as to return with all the more energy to the battlefield. Reinvigorated, he could resume his endless labours.[52] It was no easy thing to create a republic, as Robespierre never ceased to emphasise in warning of the pitfalls.

Always ready to model himself on the ancients, the Incorruptible's civic heroism brought him in some ways closer to the Christian martyrs. For all his desire to personify courage and energy as a man of feeling, he found it hard to hide what he called his melancholia and his contemporaries dubbed his 'evil temper'. Robespierre tended to identify compul-

47 *Ibid.*, vol. VIII, p. 260.
48 See N. Hampson, '"Je veux suivre ta trace vénérée." Robespierre as a reincarnation of Rousseau', in Jourdan, *Robespierre: figure-réputation*, pp. 19–36.
49 *Lettres à ses commettans*, p. 157.
50 Robespierre, *Œuvres*, vol. VIII, p. 316.
51 Atlas could be seen as a symbol of the statesman, with his huge burden, and Hercules as symbolising the terrorist, exterminating monsters. Yet, from the start, Hercules was the preferred metaphor for Mirabeau, Desmoulins, Barère and Robespierre.
52 It is perhaps worth reflecting on how far the strategic errors of the Year II derived from the accumulated exhaustion of five years of ceaseless work.

sively with victims rather than victorious heroes. He seemed to feel every blow against patriots personally. Every death seemed to presage his own, Marat's more than any, because it showed danger growing ever closer and the necessity of taking implacable measures to survive. Janus-like, the murdered hero would become a murdering one, Robespierre would have two faces, martyr and executioner at the same time. He would suffer, be persecuted, and exhaust himself physically and morally for the country's safety. But he would also demand the extermination of all traitors, bring down the 'national blade' on all of the guilty, and call for individuals whose vices stained the Assembly to be sent to the scaffold.[53] And he gloried in this severity. But the man of feeling, believing in and inclined towards virtue, must also hearken to the voice of his conscience. And what did it tell him if not that abuses must be sought out, good citizens defended, useless annoyance punished? The problem would be to distinguish between good and evil, between virtuous citizens and rogues. Nor was this a simple business, since hypocrites, schemers and intriguers themselves also wore the mask of patriotism. Robespierre would therefore come to work out some delicate distinctions, subtle gradations in republicanism. Thus any excess – whether in language, appearance or behaviour – would be condemned as a sign of hypocrisy and false zeal. And if there was a touchstone for recognising the wicked, it would be

> when a man is silent at a moment when he should speak out . . . When he lurks in the shadows or shows a fleeting energy soon gone; when he confines himself to empty tirades against tyrants, paying no heed to public morality and the happiness of all his fellow citizens.[54]

Also suspect would be those who dreaded public notice, those who only sacrificed aristocrats for form's sake, who mouthed commonplaces against Pitt and Coburg or who covertly attacked revolutionary government; those who were moderate and extreme by turns in order to oppose useful courses of action; and those who made treacherous insinuations so as to alarm members of the Convention. It was not only looks (as in Fouché's case) that concealed souls of villainy. Rogues would flaunt private virtues to conceal their contempt for public ones. And yet what the Republic most needed in order to strengthen itself was these very public virtues, consisting of 'generous devotion to the cause of the people', the only 'heroism of virtue'. To identify these rare and true republicans, the Incorruptible would be reduced to relying on his agents and his own infallible intuition.[55]

Did the repeated failure to bring about an impossible unity lie behind

[53] Robespierre, *Œuvres*, vol. X, p. 381. [54] *Ibid.*, vol. X, pp. 522, 528, 531.

[55] In the *Papiers inédits trouvés chez Robespierre*, 3 vols. (Paris, 1828), there are lists of good

the despair which led Robespierre to identify with Lepeletier and Marat? All that divided them from him in his eyes was death.[56] And Robespierre sensed that it was near. Only chance had made Marat the first to go. Soon enough, he would be proved right by the assassination attempts made by Admiral (or 'Admirat') and Cécile Renault. Then he confessed that he no longer believed in 'the necessity of living',[57] already he had reached 'the new order of things' to which would-be assassins wished to consign him, in so far as the result of plots and the misfortunes of the Republic had made this 'profoundly sensitive man' 'insensitive to everything, seeing the certain and precious refuge reserved by Providence for virtue only in the tomb'.[58] Robespierre gave up his fleeting life for the vision of an eternal one; the Terror severed his worldly ties; he had already become (as A. de Baecque has put it)[59] a living corpse. It was this that made the Terror almost sublime, because henceforth neither life nor death was really important. Robespierre the individual was long dead. Now he was only a personified essence, his will sublimated – and so all the more inflexible.

Seeing this, the prophet 'with the experience of the past and a vision of the future' was more muted on the eve of his downfall. He saw immortality slipping away, glory eclipsed by ignominy, and felt the onset of despair. He had become 'the most wretched of men'. On 8 Thermidor, Robespierre the Great described himself as now only 'my country's slave, a living martyr to the Republic, the victim and scourge of crime'. The Girondins had been galvanised by their downfall, but Robespierre was petrified by the prospect of his own.[60] The 'morose' man he had been had overcome his melancholia by an absolute revolutionary commitment. Defeat, in destroying his ambitions and hopes, finally annihilated his whole being and sealed the failure of a life and a reputation. In contrast with Madame Roland's pride and the Girondins' final challenge, Robespierre could only offer an ominous despair.

It was this melancholia and obsessive sense of persecution, this certainty that 'pure and proven virtue' would go unrecognised,[61] which was closest in Robespierre to Rousseau and which underlay the legend of the brooding tyrant. He was made to be persecuted, he declared, and

and bad behaviour, indeed a catechism of virtue. And one spy, Guérin, closely observed suspected deputies such as Legendre, Bourdon, Thuriot, Tallien, Coupé and Fouché.

56 Robespierre, *Œuvres*, vol. X, p. 269.

57 *Ibid.*, vol. X, pp. 471, 475.

58 *Ibid.*, vol. IX, p. 623.

59 A. de Baecque, 'Le cadavre de Robespierre', in Jourdan, *Robespierre: figure-réputation*, pp. 169–202. Rhetorical though these terms obviously were, they are too frequent and too pathetic to be entirely insincere.

60 As seen in the awkwardness of his behaviour on 8 and 9 Thermidor, his silence in the face of sudden attacks and his inertia throughout the hours preceding his death.

61 *Défenseur de la constitution*, p. 68.

only death could fulfil him, whether that of others or his own. For as we have seen, Robespierrist heroism had its grim side, as when he did not hesitate to shed blood in the service of his cause. But to shed blood was to run the risk of eternal condemnation.[62] In 1790, nothing in his eyes justified the taking of human life, or setting before the popular gaze scenes of cruelty and the corpses of the slain; the drift of the Revolution persuaded him otherwise. Early indulgence gave way to severity; no pardon was possible for all those monsters. When founding and saving the Republic was at issue, there was only one way to achieve the ends – the way of the scaffold. So it was not only from its works but from the blood it shed, founding blood, that the Republic derived its legitimacy.[63]

Robespierre longed to believe in the immortality of the soul, but, like his contemporaries, he had no less faith in the immortality of memory, in posthumous glory. The whole eighteenth century had come back to this secular immortality, taken from the ancients to make up in some way for the retreat of religious feeling. The certainty of living on in the memory of ages to come lay behind many sacrifices and deeds. Rousseau was intensely preoccupied by it. Yet Robespierre, the living martyr of the Republic, was uncertain on the eve of his death about his own fame. He saw immortality obscured by calumny, intrigue rampant again, vice triumphant over virtue, and the people's abuse falling on a memory that should have been dear to the human race.[64] Robespierre seemed confused as he faced the final sacrifice, the greatest a man can make. Conscience alone lent him true solace. The moment of his death was more martyrdom than heroism. It confirmed what he himself had endlessly foreseen – the path to happiness would be stained with his own blood. He met his fate on 10 Thermidor impassively, through seventeen hours of agony.

[62] It is true that this point is impossible to document definitively. Robespierre condemned abuses that might discredit the Republic, but pursued his adversaries inflexibly. He seemed to see no way out but death, the only difference being that some reached it through the way of virtue, and others through crime.

[63] Robespierre, *Œuvres*, vol. X, p. 231. See also his speech of 3 December 1792 (*ibid.*, vol. IX, p. 129): 'In general, the death penalty is a crime . . . it can only be justified when it is necessary for the security of individuals and the social body.'

[64] More precisely, Robespierre envisaged two solutions, depending on whether he won or lost. In the event of vanquishing the 'last' factions, he wished to eliminate adversaries (Cambon among others), remodel the committees, simplify justice (by activating the law of 22 Prairial), and restore all authority to the Convention (*ibid.*, vol. X, pp. 543–76). On his acceptance of sacrifice, see the speeches of 27 April and 10 May 1792 as well as that of 8 Thermidor.

5 Robespierre and conspiracy theories

Geoffrey Cubitt

'M. de Robespierre a, comme à son ordinaire, parlé de complots, de conspiration, etc. etc.' ('M. de Robesp]ierre, as is his wont, spoke of plots, of conspiracy, etc. etc.')[1] Thus, in January 1790, did Adrien Duquesnoy summarise Robespierre's intervention in the National Assembly's debate on the recent incident in Toulon, which had culminated in the arrest of officers of the naval garrison by the National Guard. Another commentator on the debate supplied further detail: Robespierre, who sided with the National Guard, 'regarded the events of Toulon as a continuation of the plots formed from one end of the kingdom to the other against public liberty'. He had listed the circumstances which led him to this conclusion, speaking for example of the suspect attitudes of the *prévôt* of Marseille 'as of a fact which must form one of the links in the chain of oppressive systems against a nation which has regained its freedom'.[2]

Already, by this relatively early stage in the Revolution, the denunciation of conspiracy had become part of Robespierre's recognised stock in trade, and a central element in the persona conferred on him by unsympathetic caricature. Already, also, the conspiracies he claimed to detect embraced the length and breadth of France and the highest objects of national politics. His mind linked them in a chain, whose connections the next four and a half years would gradually tighten. For few themes were to be more consistently and obsessively present in Robespierre's political rhetoric than that of conspiratorial intrigue. Each crisis, each wave of factional conflict, moved him to fresh formulations of this central theme. The faces of conspiracy were various, as were its limited objects – the corruption of public opinion, treason in the face of the enemy, the fomenting of civil war, the ruination of the finances, the assassination of patriots, the old *complot de famine* and that characteristi-

1 Robespierre, *Œuvres*, vol. VI, p. 184. Except where the reference is to an indirect journalistic report of the speech, the original source from which the editors of the *Œuvres* drew the text is not cited.

2 *Journal de Versailles*, cited in Robespierre, *Œuvres*, vol. VI, p. 188.

cally French Revolutionary complaint, the 'avilissement de la représentation nationale'. Each of these limited objectives, however, was taken by Robespierre to be a means to a more general and consistent end: the defeat of the Revolution, the destruction of liberty. Grammatically, he might talk of conspiracies in the plural, as if each had a certain specificity; analytically, he became increasingly convinced of the essential similarity and connectedness of all the conspiracies he denounced. To use Marcel Gauchet's terminology, he moved in the end, and began to move almost from the beginning, from 'le complot imaginaire' to 'l'imaginaire du complot' – from the imagining of conspiracies to the sense of conspiracy as a perpetual presence, constantly unfolding and repeating itself.[3] By March 1794, certainly, a unitary vision had emerged, trenchantly expressed and retrospectively applied in the draft of a speech he did not pronounce: 'When did this conspiracy first appear? At the very beginning of the Revolution. What were its prime movers? The courts leagued against us. Its aim? The ruin of France. The victims? The people and yourselves [the Convention]. The means? Every crime.' If the detailed means had varied according to circumstances, 'the mind and the hand which directed it were always the same'.[4]

The purpose of this chapter is not to trace the evolution of Robespierre's conspiratorial obsession step by step, but to explore its salient characteristics, to examine some of the shifts and oscillations that took place within it, and to suggest ways of relating it to other aspects of his political understanding and historical context. The investigation is concerned more with the general forms of conspiracy theories than with their detailed content, and the consideration of that content is not essentially geared to the discovery of how much or how little truth there was in any of Robespierre's specific allegations. Such a methodological stance does not imply that Robespierre's vision of conspiracy was a hermetically sealed system of fantasy, a kind of complex hallucination into which no shred of evidence or reality intruded. Rather it is founded simply on the assumption that the structures and larger themes of highly developed conspiracy theories, such as those enunciated by Robespierre, have expressive functions and psychological resonances that cannot be grasped unless we treat them as something other than fumbling exercises in empirical detection. To focus on these expressive functions is not to deny that Robespierre's denunciations had a strong pragmatic purpose. His declamations about conspiracy did not take place in a kind of philosophical echo-chamber, but in a political arena that was public and

[3] See M. Gauchet, 'Le démon du soupçon', *L'Histoire* 84 (1985), 49–56.
[4] Robespierre, *Œuvres*, vol. X, p. 398.

dangerous and concerned with real power. What he said was meant to destroy opponents, to justify his own actions and positions, to persuade people of the necessity of particular courses of political action. This political context can scarcely be ignored. But the motives of politicians do not perfectly control the significance of their verbal actions for historians. By focusing on the quirks and tensions and obsessive repetitions of their rhetoric we can hope to learn things about their political imagination – about their latent anxieties, their cultural assumptions and the broader mental world in which they operated.

In Robespierre's case, we can hope not only to shed light on the mental peculiarities of one of the Revolution's foremost political actors, but also to say something of broader relevance both to the study of French Revolutionary political culture and to the comparative study of conspiracy theories in different historical contexts. For, if Robespierre's emphasis on conspiracy was striking in its relentlessness and intensity, it was scarcely something that removed him from the mainstream of French Revolutionary political discourse. That discourse, as Lynn Hunt has pointed out, was 'permeated ... at every political level' by the 'rhetoric of conspiracy'.[5] Robespierre's own declamations were matched by those of his enemies – both Girondin like Louvet and royalist like Montjoie[6] – accusing him of conspiracies as vile as those he denounced in others; his own fall prompted Fréron to declare that 'the leader of a great conspiracy has been struck down'.[7] The language of conspiracy, in short, was common currency during the Revolution, an idiom of mutual and general recrimination.

The consolidation and rampant extension of a conspiracy theory over time that we find in Robespierre's thinking also conformed to a common pattern during the Revolution. The present author has argued elsewhere[8] that the conspiracy rhetoric of the Revolution marked a distinctive transitional moment in the long-term evolution of what American historians have labelled the 'paranoid style' in politics.[9] The transition in

5 L. Hunt, *Politics, Culture and Class in the French Revolution* (London, 1986), p. 41. For another influential discussion of the rhetoric of conspiracy during the Revolution, see F. Furet, *Interpreting the French Revolution*, trans. E. Forster (Cambridge, 1981), especially pp. 53–5; see also G. Cubitt, 'Denouncing conspiracy in the French Revolution', *Renaissance and Modern Studies* 33 (1989), 144–58.

6 See, for example, Louvet's 'A Maximilien Robespierre et à ses royalistes' (1792), in *Mémoires de Louvet de Couvrai sur la Révolution française*, ed. F.-A. Aulard (Paris, 1989) and G. de Montjoie, *Histoire de la conspiration de Maximilien Robespierre* (1795).

7 Fréron cited in Robespierre, *Œuvres*, vol. X, p. 594.

8 The line of argument summarised in this paragraph is developed at greater length in my 'Denouncing conspiracy', especially 144–6, 151–2.

9 The term was coined by Richard Hofstadter in the title essay of his *The Paranoid Style in American Politics, and Other Essays* (New York, 1965).

question was one from the ubiquitous but relatively small-scale conspiracy theories that were characteristic of eighteenth-century political culture on both sides of the Atlantic towards the much more grandiose and sprawling visions of global conspiracy by Jesuits or Freemasons that were to haunt the nineteenth and early twentieth centuries.[10] By conflating a whole succession of imagined conspiracies of the older type (court intrigues and *complots de famine*), the men of the Revolution arrived, in the space of half a decade, at a consolidated conspiracy theory closer in scale and in explanatory pretension to those of the following century. It still, however, differed from these later visions in one very important respect. The nineteenth-century theories about Jesuits or Freemasons sustained their lavish dimensions by being, essentially, theories of occult power. They claimed, in other words, to expose the activities of hidden political actors, grouped in some kind of secret society directing events from behind the scenes. The conspiracy theories of the Revolution were still, like those of the eighteenth century, largely theories of occult *intention*. The conspirators they denounced were not shadowy figures behind the scenes; they were known and often prominent public figures – men like Lafayette and Danton and Dumouriez. What was hidden and had to be exposed was not their personal identity but their secret motivation. It was this combination of a constantly extended vision of conspiracy with a relentless focus on the inner treachery of public figures and the deceptiveness of public faces that distinguished the conspiracy theories of the Revolution (as it was later to do those of Stalinist Russia). The case of Robespierre supplies a good opportunity to explore it.

Perhaps the most basic formal characteristic of Robespierre's vision of conspiracy, as it emerged from his speeches and published writings in the course of his political career, was the tendency to conflate conspiratorial intrigues detected at different points in time. The essential mechanism here was the gradual establishment of a line of succession between different waves of conspiracy. Thus, Robespierre declared in October 1792 that the fall of Lafayette and of the monarchy had not been decisive: 'he [Lafayette] has left the heirs to his ambition and to his intrigues'. Indeed nothing but the name of the régime had changed: 'Everywhere, I see the same vices, the same cabals, the same methods and calumny above all.'[11] Lafayette and the Feuillants had merely given way to Brissot and the Girondins, he repeated in April 1793: the aims

[10] For general discussion of these later conspiracy theory traditions, see J. M. Roberts, *The Mythology of the Secret Societies*, 2nd edition (St Albans, 1974); G. T. Cubitt, *The Jesuit Myth: Conspiracy Theory and Politics in Nineteenth-Century France* (Oxford, 1993).

[11] Robespierre, *Œuvres*, vol. IX, p. 51.

and means were the same, though the conspirators' resources and support had grown.[12] It was the same with the fall of Dumouriez: 'consider that the faction of Dumouriez still exists . . .; the thread of the conspiracies has not been broken, or at least has almost immediately been joined again'.[13] A year later: 'There is Hébertism; it was believed to be dead, but it lives on; it is there in the conspiracy of plotters made up of the debris of the Orléans faction'.[14] The whole line of succession was finally strung together in Robespierre's attack on the 'indulgents' a few weeks before Thermidor:

> This faction, swollen with the debris of all the others, gathers in one bond everything that has conspired since the beginning of the Revolution: it has profited from experience, to weave its plots with greater perfidy: today it sets in motion the same methods that formerly were used by the Brissots, the Dantons, the Héberts, the Chabots and so many other rascals.[15]

The rhetoric of such denunciations was remarkably consistent. What was implied was not, on the whole, a continuity of personnel between successive waves of conspiracy, but a continuity of spirit, of aim and of tactics. The successive prima donnas of alleged conspiracy – Lafayette, Brissot, Dumouriez, Danton, Hébert (and lesser stars like Fabre d'Eglantine) – appeared as the successive tenants, not of a stable conspiratorial organisation, but of a durable system of methods and intentions, a kind of spiritual framework to which conspiracy unerringly conformed.

This way of establishing and invoking conspiratorial continuity was gradually reinforced by another one: the invocation of foreign direction. In the last year of his life, 'la faction anglaise' became a kind of synonym in Robespierre's lexicon for 'la faction conspiratrice'. The activity of this faction, he told the Jacobins in August 1793, had dominated the whole history of the Revolution.[16] The theme was developed further in a report to the Convention on behalf of the Committee of Public Safety in November, in which the whole crocodile of leading intriguers – Necker, d'Orléans, Lafayette, Lameth, Dumouriez, Custine, Brissot, with 'tous les pygmées de la Gironde' bringing up the tail – were revealed as instruments of English policy.[17] 'Le célèbre et méprisable Pitt'[18] became the grand continuity man of counter-revolutionary conspiracy.

This served to tighten the sinews of the Robespierrist vision of conspiracy. It also represented a shift of emphasis within it. One of the more established commonplaces of Robespierre's political thinking (as of that of many other politicians during the Revolution) was the idea

12 *Ibid.*, vol. IX, p. 377.
13 *Ibid.*, vol. IX, p. 521.
14 *Ibid.*, vol. X, p. 510.
15 *Ibid.*, vol. X, p. 513.
16 *Ibid.*, vol. X, p. 62.
17 *Ibid.*, vol. X, p. 169.
18 *Ibid.*, vol. V, p. 284.

that there was an organic link between the 'ennemis du dehors' and the 'ennemis du dedans'.[19] France's involvement in war was the product of a joint intrigue by these two categories of enemy, designed to deliver the Revolution to destruction; as Robespierre put it in January 1792, 'the rebels across the Rhine, the foreign princes, your ambassadors, your court, all freedom's internal enemies, must be considered, in this regard, to be a single power'.[20] At this stage, Robespierre's priority was to warn of treason within: his tendency was therefore to focus on the internal pole of the conspiratorial axis, to imagine a conspiracy driven by the intrigues of the French court and its ministerial accomplices, rather than by the *émigrés* or the foreign powers. 'The real Coblenz is in France', he declared; the *émigré* headquarters on the Rhine was but 'one of the springs of a deep conspiracy against liberty, whose focus, whose centre, whose leaders are in our midst'.[21] This vision of a conspiracy driven from within required adjustment with the fall of the monarchy,[22] and lost its appeal when the fall of the Girondins brought Robespierre himself and his associates to the centre of power in France. In the second half of 1793, the emphasis was firmly on Pitt – Pitt whose guineas funded the anti-Jacobin press, Pitt whose agents were everywhere, staging bread-riots, corrupting the *sans-culotte* sections, generally driving the Revolution to excess and compromising it by disorder.[23] The earlier influence of the 'faction anglaise' was now retrospectively discovered, and the word 'étranger' became part of the standard anti-conspiratorial vocabulary. 'Je me méfie indistinctement de tous ces étrangers dont le visage est couvert du masque de patriotisme' ('I mistrust, without distinction, all these foreigners whose faces are covered with the mask of patriotism'),[24] Robespierre told the Convention in October, and the following month, reversing the implicit emphasis of two years before, he told the Jacobins that the foreign courts were 'the true authors of our ills and internal discords'.[25] The real danger to France still came from within her own borders (rather than from the 'satellites féroces' whom the despots of Europe let loose from outside), but this internal danger was the work of 'émissaires étrangers'.[26] Despotism was now a foreign force; the discord and intrigue to which it gave rise were surreptitious imports.

The shift in Robespierre's own political vantage-point that helped to produce this adjustment in his vision of conspiracy also modified that vision in another way. Here again, the modification was underpinned by

[19] See, for example, *ibid.*, vol. X, p. 357. [20] *Ibid.*, vol. VIII, p. 134.
[21] *Ibid.*, vol. VIII, p. 86. [22] See, for example, *ibid.*, vol. V, p. 244.
[23] See, for example, *ibid.*, vol. X, pp. 71, 73, 193, 278–9.
[24] *Ibid.*, vol. X, p. 155. [25] *Ibid.*, vol. X, p. 193. [26] *Ibid.*, vol. X, pp. 279–80.

a significant degree of imaginative continuity. This continuity was supplied, in this case, by the fear of political false pretences, and, more specifically, by the suspicion that the appearance of revolutionary virtue or zeal might serve as the ultimate counter-revolutionary weapon. Already in February 1790, Robespierre was warning of the threat to the Revolution posed by 'des aristocrates déguisés sous le masque du civisme' ('aristocrats disguised beneath the mask of civic virtue').[27] From then until his death, the figure of the 'faux patriote' – the cynical exploiter of revolutionary appearances – remained one of the central motifs in his analysis of French politics. The framework within which the 'faux patriote' was assumed to operate, however, underwent a significant change. Up until the fall of the Girondins, the dominant pattern was essentially that which Robespierre himself sketched out in a speech to the Jacobins in December 1791. The nation was divided into three parties: the 'aristocrates' and the 'patriotes', facing each other in mutual and recognised antipathy, and between them, 'this middling, hypocritical party, which is called ministerial', composed of 'intriguers ... hidden under the mask of patriotism', pursuing 'an aristocratic system in conformity with their personal interests'.[28] The identity of this falsely patriotic middle group changed over time – the Feuillants giving way, for example, to the Girondins – but their rôle in the dynamics of French politics remained essentially the same. In each case, they were prepared to court the 'patriotes' to get into power; once there, their self-interest and their corrupted character bound them secretly to the cause of 'aristocracy', turning their patriotic pretences into a deadly trap for the nation. Using the mask of patriotism to undermine patriotism and the language of the laws to overthrow the laws,[29] theirs was the stealthiest of treasons.

The establishment of Jacobin ascendancy in the Republic, and the declaration of a revolutionary government, altered the scenario, in ways which anxieties about the provocational activities of Pitt's agents served to reinforce. The 'patriotes' (identified increasingly narrowly as those who thought like Robespierre himself) now stood at the centre of the picture, besieged and affronted by two different kinds of false patriot, whose conflicting appearances concealed their joint participation in the counter-revolutionary design co-ordinated and funded by Pitt: the *Modérés* on the one hand, who criticised the Terror and revolutionary government for going too far; the *Exagérés* on the other (men like Roux and later Hébert), who sought to push them further still. This basic picture, to which Robespierre returned repeatedly in the final months of

[27] *Ibid.*, vol. VI, p. 239. [28] *Ibid.*, vol. VIII, pp. 57–8.
[29] *Ibid.*, vol. VIII, pp. 436–7.

his life, was well set out in his great speech on the principles of domestic policy, delivered to the Convention on 5 February 1794. 'The internal enemies of the French people', he declared,

> have divided themselves into two factions, like two corps of an army. They march under banners of different colours and along different routes, but they march towards the same end; this end is the disorganisation of popular government, the ruination of the Convention, in short the triumph of tyranny. One of these factions pushes us towards weakness, the other towards excess.

The leaders of the two parties were 'servants employed by the same master, or, if you prefer, accomplices who pretend to fall out with each other the better to conceal their crimes. Judge them, not by the difference of their language, but by the identity of the results.'[30]

This, then, was the vision of conspiracy that Robespierre's conspiracy theory in its mature form had to offer – a vision that bound together factions and conspiracies across time and across the political spectrum to generate a sense of conspiratorial ubiquity and consistency that played a central rôle in Robespierre's ideological system. Pitt and the 'faux patriote' were the two symbolic points around which this vision was ultimately spun: the first, the counter-revolutionary as foreigner; the second, the counter-revolutionary within the Revolution. And Pitt, too, the symbol of continuity and fixity of counter-revolutionary purpose; the 'faux patriote', the symbol of tactical flexibility, of the treachery of appearance, of the interchangeability of counter-revolutionary rôles.

Robespierre's increasing tendency to regard 'faux patriotes' as Pitt's agents imposed an intermittent neatness of design on what was otherwise a highly fluid conception of conspiracy. One reason why it was fluid was that conspirators were not, in Robespierre's imagination, what they would be for the anti-masonic and anti-Jesuit conspiracy theorists of the nineteenth century – a tightly disciplined group of men marshalled under the auspices of a particular organisation. With him, the imputation or suspicion of conspiracy tended to cling, not to organisations, but to social milieux (the court, the aristocracy), to political rôles (ministerial office) and, above all, to moral character types: 'intrigans', 'ambitieux', 'scélérats', 'corrompus' and the seemingly ever-increasing race of 'fripons'. In fact, Robespierre's developments of the theme of conspiracy characteristically proceeded on two levels. On one, networks of political influence and links between different factions were established, the names of notorious figures like Lafayette or Dumouriez or Fabre d'Eglantine serving as markers of the progress and dimensions of the conspiracy; on the other, such political complexities were collapsed

30 *Ibid.*, vol. X, pp. 359–60.

through an exercise in invective into the politico-moral opposition between the 'fripons' and the 'gens de bien'. The situation in July 1792 was summarised thus: 'On one side the people, humanity, all the virtues; on the other, the perfidies, the cowardice, the treason, in short the court and all its vices.'[31] The same point was made in more desperate tones in May 1794:

> there are two peoples in France: one is the mass of citizens, pure, simple, thirsty for justice and friend to liberty . . .; the other is this bunch of ambitious men and intriguers – this babbling, charlatan, artificious people which crops up everywhere, which takes over the tribunes and often the public offices; . . . this people of scoundrels, of foreigners, of hypocritical counter-revolutionaries, which imposes itself between the French people and its representatives, to deceive the one and to calumny the others . . .[32]

Something more was involved here than the merely polemical application of terms of moral opprobrium to political enemies. At the core of Robespierre's conspiratorial obsession lay a more complex entanglement of political and moral analyses that must now be explored further by examining some of the mental ingredients that helped to nourish and to mould the concept of conspiracy whose salient features have just been described. That vision of conspiracy was underpinned, it may be suggested, by three interacting patterns or habits of thought and expression – discourses, for convenience – each of which contributed something distinctive to the mental matrix within which conspiracy was imagined and described.

The first of these three discourses, and in some ways the most obvious, was Rousseauism.[33] From Rousseau, directly or indirectly, the men of the Revolution, Robespierre included, acquired the habit of thinking of the public interest as embodied in a general will. This will, it was supposed, was graven and readable in the hearts of all who sincerely sought it. Conflict and dissension in the body politic were to be understood as the products of obstinate selfishness and egoism – deliberate deviation from and resistance to the general will. This way of thinking gave selfishness a dramatically enhanced political significance, as an effective denial of sovereignty. It did not, of course, automatically commit those who followed it to an obsessive concern with conspiracy, but it certainly supplied a mental framework that could readily accommodate and nurture one. By implying, firstly, that the general will was

[31] *Ibid.*, vol. VIII, p. 388. [32] *Ibid.*, vol. X, pp. 476–7.

[33] For discussions of Rousseau's influence on French Revolutionary political mentalities, see N. Hampson, *Will and Circumstance: Montesquieu, Rousseau and the French Revolution* (London, 1983); C. Blum, *Rousseau and the Republic of Virtue: the Language of Politics in the French Revolution* (Ithaca, 1986); J. McDonald, *Rousseau and the French Revolution 1762–1791* (London, 1965).

continuous, coherent and accessible, and, secondly, that the precise content of any obstinately particular will was less important than the overwhelming fact of its formal opposition to the will which encapsulated the general interest, Rousseauism encouraged the kind of blurring or undermining of distinctions between different factional aims and interests that was a feature of Robespierre's denunciations of conspiracy. It may also have encouraged the paradoxical elevation of selfish egoism into a kind of politically significant group identity, traces of which can be found in Robespierre's diatribes against the scheming hordes of 'ambitieux' and 'intrigans'. Certainly, the ideas of counter-revolutionary conspiracy and of self-interest (explicitly contrasted with the general interest expressed as a will) were closely and suggestively coupled in Robespierre's rhetoric: 'The French people wills liberty, and it cannot will anything else,' he told the Jacobins in May 1793. 'Its enemies are the corrupted men who prefer their own interest to the general interest', and who must be exterminated to prevent them conspiring eternally against the rights of man and the happiness of peoples.[34]

Rousseauism's other notable contribution was to focus a suspicious gaze on government, by contrasting the automatic collective purity of the sovereign people with the inherently individual, and therefore perpetually suspect, character of the tenants of executive power. As Robespierre himself put it in his speech to the Convention in May 1793: 'The ills of society never come from the people, but from government. How could it be otherwise? The interest of the people is the public good; the interest of the man in office is a private interest.' The government was charged with securing respect for the general will, yet only the austerest virtue in the magistrates themselves, and the utmost vigilance on the part of others, could prevent them from conspiring to frustrate it.[35] The implications of this insight were clear in Robespierre's denunciations of successive governmental factions.

If Rousseauism connected the conspiratorial theme to a larger realm of political theory, the second of the discursive patterns that can be traced in Robespierre's rhetoric related this theme more precisely to the dramatic tensions and uncertainties of politics under revolutionary conditions. It focused on the Revolution as a period of attempted transition, but also of continuing and all-absorbing tension, between despotism (or 'aristocracy') and liberty. Such an analysis was most obviously applicable during the period of constitutional monarchy – that 'monstrous mixture of the old and the new régimes' as Robespierre called it[36] – when the court supplied an obvious focus for suspicions of

[34] Robespierre, *Œuvres*, vol. IX, p. 487.
[35] *Ibid.*, vol. IX, p. 496.
[36] *Ibid.*, vol. VIII, p. 418.

resurgent despotism or aristocratism, but its basic terms were by no means abandoned with the advent of the Republic. In January 1793, for example, Robespierre invited the readers of his *Lettres à ses commettans* to consider whether the principal cause of current troubles did not lie in the perfidious efforts of public functionaries to deprave public opinion 'by dragging it down from the height of the principles of liberty to the spirit of royalism and aristocracy'.[37]

Monarchy and aristocracy were thought of here, not primarily as constitutional forms, but as systems of moral corruption, characterised by intrigue and ambition; the Republic, by contrast, was the régime of virtue. 'Despotism has produced the corruption of morals, and the corruption of morals has sustained despotism.'[38] It was therefore not surprising that the counter-revolution was the revenge of the 'fripons', that 'all the perfidious and corrupted beings are of your tyrants' faction'.[39] Corruption and self-interested intrigue, in other words, were not incidental hazards of politics under revolutionary conditions: they were the poisonous legacy of the old régime to the new. 'We – unfortunate wretches! – we are building the temple of liberty with hands still branded with the irons of servitude. What was our former education, but a continual lesson in egoism and foolish vanity?'[40]

France's political troubles, according to this view, stemmed essentially from the initial failure of the Revolution to make a complete break with the ancien régime. Robespierre was already warning of this in February 1790: 'Nations have but one moment to become free . . .; once this moment has passed, if despotism is given the time to recover, the warning cries of good citizens are denounced as acts of sedition, freedom vanishes, and servitude remains.'[41] In January 1792, in a speech to the Jacobins, he developed the theme in far greater detail. Speaking in general terms, but with current French conditions clearly in mind, he evoked an unfolding semi-hypothetical scenario. 'Despotism' feigns death in the moment of popular revolution, only to revive once immediate danger has receded: 'soon it raises itself again; it approaches the people in an affectionate manner; it substitutes ruse for force; people think it is converted; the word liberty is heard to issue from its mouth'. Lulled into a false sense of security, the people entrust it with wealth and power, and it is then that the real work of *liberticide* begins. Despotism draws to itself 'whoever combines vice with talent', and launches them on a general campaign of intrigue, seduction and corruption: 'it exerts itself above all to corrupt public opinion; it revives the old prejudices and old habits which have not yet been effaced; it encourages the

[37] *Ibid.*, vol. V, p. 210. [38] *Ibid.*, vol. IX, p. 496. [39] *Ibid.*, vol. X, p. 230.
[40] *Ibid.*, vol. IX, p. 497. [41] *Ibid.*, vol. VI, p. 239.

depravation of morals which have not yet been regenerated; it smothers the seed of the new virtues'. Public tranquillity and confidence in government – rather than public vigilance – become the catchwords of the moment. Liberty becomes a dirty word, its defenders are abused and persecuted, the delegates of the people are duped or corrupted, 'intriguers and parties press upon each other like the waves of the sea', while all the time the people are gulled with acts of illusory patriotism. 'The moment arrives when division reigns everywhere, when all the snares of the tyrants are set, when the league of all the enemies of equality is fully formed, when those in public authority are its leaders . . .' Placed between civil war and servitude, the people are in no position to resist.[42]

This speech affords a remarkable example of the ways in which an implicit meta-narrative can be used to blur the distinctions between observation and speculation, blending recognisable past, suspected present and imagined future into a seamless and imaginatively compelling narrative progression, artfully poised on the unstable boundary between certainty and hypothesis. Robespierre admitted, in fact, that France was still some way from the fulfilment of the sinister scenario he depicted;[43] he refrained from saying how far. What his speech provided (and itself drew upon) was a kind of template of expectation, into which events could be fitted. The perception that despotism played a long and complex game, in which temporary setbacks could be accommodated, was one which would inform some of his own most notable exercises in detective foresight – his argument in July 1792, for example, that proposals to suspend the power of the king were part of yet another conspiratorial manoeuvre by the court to keep the nation asleep while its chains were being forged.[44]

This, then, was an imaginative model that treated despotism as the self-reconstituting serpent of legend. Despotism's various legacies of thought, of social habit, of moral degeneracy, were turned from the apparent debris of its ruin into the materials and instruments of its ingeniously managed reconstruction. This way of thinking about despotism supplied the basis for a kind of evolutionary account of conspiracy which interacted with the more formalistic account of it that could be derived from a certain understanding of Rousseau. Just as Rousseauism might encourage the imaginative conflation of different particular wills into a conspiracy to frustrate the general interest, so this way of imagining a renascent despotism encouraged the imaginative linking

[42] *Ibid.*, vol. VIII, pp. 90–2. [43] *Ibid.*, vol. VIII, p. 92.
[44] *Ibid.*, vol. VIII, p. 411.

of disparate petty intrigues and acts of arbitrary authority into a regular conspiratorial progression.

The third body of discourse in which Robespierre's concern with conspiracy was embedded revolved around the issues of opinion and reputation. It can be approached by focusing on a theme to which he returned with obsessive regularity: the theme of calumny. Calumny, according to Robespierre, was the most redoubtable of counter-revolutionary weapons. 'Follow the progress of calumny since the beginning of the Revolution,' he urged the Jacobins in October 1792, 'and you will see that all the unhappy events which have bloodied its [the Revolution's] course are due to this.'[45] In his last speech to the Convention, he declared his belief in 'the detestable influence of intrigue', but above all in 'the sinister power of calumny'.[46] More specific references abound in his speeches and writings. In September 1792, for example, he warned the newly arriving members of the Convention against

> the criminal coalition which, for so long, has not ceased to circulate error and imposture ... through the channel of the periodical papers which it controls ... It is this coalition that seeks to tear the Republic apart, by ceaselessly calumnying the people of Paris and all the representatives whom it has honoured with its trust ...[47]

The political significance of calumny was related, of course, to the power of opinion. As Robespierre wrote in November 1792: 'Opinion is the queen of the world; like all queens, she is courted and often deceived.'[48] It was calumny that explained the tiresome disjuncture between public opinion and revolutionary logic – to put it more contentiously, between the general will and what people actually seemed to think and believe. Hence, for example, the disappointing failure to capitalise on the fall of the monarchy: 'The public spirit has lagged behind the Revolution, for since that time all the scoundrels have joined together [under Girondin auspices] to lead public opinion astray.'[49]

Calumny, in essence, was the point of intersection between intrigue and opinion. If the disposition to intrigue was, in Robespierre's view, a fatal legacy from the old régime, he knew well enough that the political significance of opinion had been dramatically enhanced by the Revolution. The overwhelming power of calumny, in other words, was related to specific and novel historical conditions. Robespierre's most notable recognition of this came in a speech entirely devoted to the influence of calumny on the Revolution, delivered to the Jacobins on 28 October 1792. Under the old régime, he explained, calumny (along with other vices and virtues) had been petty in character and limited in scope – a

[45] *Ibid.*, vol. IX, p. 45.
[46] *Ibid.*, vol. X, p. 551.
[47] *Ibid.*, vol. IX, p. 15.
[48] *Ibid.*, vol. V, p. 75.
[49] *Ibid.*, vol. IX, p. 297.

vehicle for family jealousies, social rivalries and small-scale court intrigue. The Revolution had given it far wider horizons. Now the victims of calumny were not just individuals, but humanity; allied to intrigue, 'it has embraced ... the universe in its plots'. Opinion had given the impetus to the Revolution, and opinion alone could stop it; corruption of opinion had become the necessary tactic of despotism and counter-revolution.[50]

If calumny, in particular, had become the crucial vehicle by which opinion might be corrupted, it was because reputation had become the key to politics. Robespierre spelt this out: 'The intriguers well knew that the ignorant multitude is inclined to link political principles to the names of those who defend them; they applied themselves above all to defaming the most zealous partisans of the popular cause.'[51] The vulnerability of reputation – the ease with which it could be falsified or fabricated – was, for Robespierre, the Achilles heel of the Revolution. Hence his increasingly frequent and embittered denunciations of the press as a tool in the hands of his enemies: how was one to struggle against a foe whose orchestra contained 'all the trumpets of renown'?[52]

Viewed from outside, Robespierre's attitude to calumny and to reputation involved the most brazen of double standards. Few men were more insistent, when in opposition, on the need to protect the vigilant citizen from prosecution for allegations – however unsubstantiated – against public figures;[53] few were more loudly convinced, when their own motives and conduct were questioned, that calumny was the greatest of moral atrocities and the conspiracy of 'libellistes' the direst threat to liberty.[54] To Robespierre's own mind, of course, the cases were not the same. Freedom of denunciation was the only safeguard against ministers and courtiers who otherwise held all the cards, including that of secrecy and that of mercenary publicity, and whose motives were inherently suspect by virtue of their backgrounds and positions. Calumny against patriots was a wanton persecution of individuals whose conduct was open and whose reputation was unprotected.

Odious as it was in itself, calumny in the strict sense – the destruction or denial of the virtuous reputation of individuals through the propagation of falsehood – was, in Robespierre's view, part of a broader strategy of corruption played out across the whole field of public reputation. This strategy aimed to inflate the deceptive reputation of corrupted intriguers – 'le vertueux Roland', the untouchable Danton – and to sully the good name of 'patriotisme' at both an individual and a collective

50 *Ibid.*, vol. IX, p. 44. 51 *Ibid.* 52 *Ibid.*, vol. IX, p. 60.
53 See, for example, *ibid.*, vol. VII, pp. 328–31, 655–6.
54 *Ibid.*, vol. IX, p. 559.

level. The tactics of the defaming 'libellistes' dovetailed with those of the 'faux patriotes'[55] who used their patriotic credentials, acquired under false pretences in the *sociétés populaires*, to render the cause ridiculous by exaggerated behaviour and to load it down with their own infamy.[56] False patriotism, in fact, was defamation by deed rather than by word – an extension of calumny by other means.

Like other features of his conspiracy theory, Robespierre's obsessive concerns with calumny and with false patriotism offer an extreme and personal instance of anxieties that were probably widespread. There was ample reason, in France in the 1790s, to be uneasy about the insecurity of reputation and the fluidity of opinion. Before the Revolution, reputation had been pre-eminently a facet of social position in a society that was still essentially hierarchical and corporate in structure. By destroying the legal framework of that society, and postulating instead a society of free and theoretically interchangeable individuals, the Revolution had created conditions in which reputation was a matter of opinion, and a facet of political rather than of social identity. In the political instability of the revolutionary years, however, political identities were scarcely rigidly fixed: there was no stable framework of political alignments in which reputations of a solid but limited kind, analogous to the socially based reputations of the old régime, could be rooted. Instead, and thanks in part to the influence of Rousseauistic habits of mind, reputation became a matter of all-or-nothing: either one was a man of virtue and a pure 'patriote', comprehensively attuned to the general will, or one was a base intriguer and enemy of the people. It was within such an ideological context that men like Robespierre (and Marat, the quintessential 'Ami du Peuple') framed, with deep self-consciousness, their public personae. At the same time, however, reputation became closely and problematically linked to appearances. In the frequent absence of other indicators, to be a 'patriote' was to speak and dress in certain ways, to frequent certain societies, above all to use a certain kind of political language. Enemies of the people, if they knew their place (which of course they did not), would use a different language and adopt different external signs. To the untutored eye, the intelligibility of revolutionary politics seemed to depend on the stability of this system of signs, and on the integrity of the assumed relationship between outward form and inner content on which public reputations were founded. Robespierre's profound sense of the insecurity of that relationship, of the ease with which it could be subverted by calumny and imposture, led him into desperate rhetorical efforts to establish more reliable

[55] *Ibid.*, vol. X, p. 227 (Convention, 5 December 1793) makes this clear.
[56] *Ibid.*, vol. X, p. 400 (unpronounced speech of late March 1794).

foundations for judgements of moral and political character in the shifting world of revolutionary politics. He did this by affirming the basic unchangeability of political character (founded on that of moral character) and the revealing coherence of lines of conduct over time. Repeatedly in Robespierre's speeches – and in those of many other revolutionaries[57] – the warning of a disparity between patriotic exterior and blackness of heart within was coupled with the insistence that the villainy would be uncovered if the underlying patterns of past and present behaviour (and its consequences) were revealed. 'One begins to judge people not by the maxims which they publicly profess, but by their fidelity in following them,' he declared in December 1791, before launching his attack with the words, 'Tremble, perfidious administrators, lest your present conduct enlighten us on your past conduct . . .'[58] The reasoning was similar on a slightly earlier occasion: 'I see that the speeches and external signs have changed, but that the actions are still the same, and that it will be a miracle if the hearts have changed . . .'[59] In practice, of course, these principles of detection opened up vast areas of arbitrary judgement, providing ample opportunity to incriminate almost anyone. The insecurities of reputation were not to be so easily overcome.

Robespierre's complaint that the Revolution 'was destined to demonstrate to the universe the power of calumny'[60] thus conveyed something more than the routine disgruntlement of a politician upset by a bad press: it expressed a deeper and more generalised sense of the Revolution's vulnerability. The rhetoric in which his denunciations of conspiracy were couched issued from an imperfectly submerged awareness of the ways in which the logic of the Revolution as historical process might work to frustrate the Revolution as glorious cause. Something more runs through that rhetoric, especially in the final months of his life, than the conspiracy theorist's standard alarmist vision of a *patrie* always 'en danger' and conspirators spinning their plots on the perpetual verge of success. There is also a sense of frustration, almost at times of impotence, a conception of revolutionary purity as something that is constantly being sullied and undermined. It is there in his report of 17 May 1794, moving the establishment of the cult of the Supreme Being, which slides from an assertion of how the French people have leapt two thousand years ahead of the rest of humanity to a more anguished diatribe against the conspirators who 'were going to sully everything, to confound everything, by an odious mixing of the purity of our principles

[57] See Cubitt, 'Denouncing conspiracy', 150–8.
[58] Robespierre, *Œuvres*, vol. VIII, p. 32. [59] *Ibid.*, vol. VII, p. 746.
[60] *Ibid.*, vol. IX, p. 570.

with the corruption of their hearts'.[61] Gloomier still, coming as they do in a speech meant to set out the principles of political morality that would guide the nation into the future, are the pronouncements of 5 February:

> It is thus that intrigue always mixes the baseness of its criminal plots with the continual miracles operated through the virtue of a great people . . . In perfidious hands, all the remedies for our ills become poisons; everything you can do, everything you can say, they will turn against you, even the truths I have just developed.[62]

It is true that such remarks were interspersed with more confident suggestions that liberty would triumph in the end, but the tension is obvious. The rhetoric of conspiracy was not simply a rhetoric of alarm that could be used to mobilise revolutionary energies: it was a rhetoric of frustration, drawing deeply on the bad dreams of revolutionary Messianism – dreams in which the corrupting spirit of the old régime reached out beyond the grave, in which the Revolution became indistinguishable from its own parody, and in which each bold stride towards liberty lost its footing in the mud of history.

[61] *Ibid.*, vol. X, pp. 444, 449.
[62] *Ibid.*, vol. X, p. 363.

6 Robespierre and religion

Frank Tallett

The purpose of this essay is to elucidate the personal religious views of Maximilien Robespierre and to see how these interlocked with the formation of religious policy during the Revolution, particularly with the establishment of the cult of the Supreme Being. It is not special pleading to say at the outset that this is not a straightforward task. Robespierre has always been a controversial figure, and in no area has historical opinion been more divided than with respect to religion.[1] Academic debate came to a peak in the bitter arguments between Alphonse Aulard and his one-time disciple, Albert Mathiez. 'The person of Robespierre has been so grossly misrepresented during the last twenty years, even by republican historians,' wrote the latter in 1910, with Aulard in mind, 'that to talk now of the "Incorruptible's" religious ideas would appear a rash undertaking.'[2] Although less fierce than hitherto, disagreement between historians over Robespierre and religion persists. Indeed, it is unlikely ever to be finally resolved. The reason for this lies in the nature and availability of the surviving evidence. We lack the diaries, private papers, letters, reminiscences and epistolatory confidences that might clarify once and for all Robespierre's religious opinions and the motives behind the formation of revolutionary religious policies. To be sure, we have his public writings and speeches, although these, with their dense thickets of prose, can be as wearying to read now as they were to hear two centuries ago.[3] They were, of course, drafted with the aim of

[1] There are useful historiographical summaries in G. Rudé, *Robespierre: Portrait of a Revolutionary Democrat* (London, 1975), pp. 55–92; J. M. Thompson, *Robespierre*, 3rd edition (Oxford, 1988), pp. 595–633; C. Lucas, 'Bibliographical note', in *ibid.*, pp. 635–40.

[2] A. Mathiez, 'Robespierre and the cult of the Supreme Being', in his *The Fall of Robespierre and Other Essays* (London, 1927), p. 84. The article appeared originally in *Annales révolutionnaires* 3 (1910). For the two men's points of view (which, with hindsight, were not as different as they appeared at the time) see, in addition to the above, Mathiez, *Les origines des cultes révolutionnaires* (Paris, 1904), and A. Aulard, *Le culte de la raison et le culte de l'Etre suprême (1793–1794): essai historique* (Paris, 1892).

[3] 'He is too verbose; he does not know when to stop,' commented Reybaz after one of his speeches to the National Assembly: E. Dumont, *Souvenirs sur Mirabeau*, ed. J. Bénétruy

influencing others rather than with the intention of revealing the author's innermost feelings. But, if we accept that Robespierre said what he meant and meant what he said – and we probably can – we may use them to infer what he thought. However, his elliptical mode of discourse can lead to varying interpretations of his words.[4]

There are three textual landmarks on which we must above all rely when seeking to chart Robespierre's religious experiences. The first, and arguably most crucial, is the *mémoire* produced in 1789 as part of his conduct of a legal case at Arras. The second is his spontaneous defence at the Jacobin club in March 1792 of a belief in Providence. Thirdly, there are his speeches in 1793–4 leading up to and including the establishment of the cult of the Supreme Being. To these may be added his contributions to debates on church affairs in the Constituent Assembly in 1790–1. Taken together, these sources indicate some limited evolution of Robespierre's opinions with respect to the church and the clergy. However, much more striking is the consistency of his core religious beliefs, which remained essentially unchanged between 1789 and 1794.[5] His sense of a universal morality, grounded upon the existence of a Supreme Being, already existed at the outbreak of the Revolution and provided the underpinning for his political ideas and principles until his death.

We do not know much in detail about Robespierre's early years, but he cannot have escaped the influence of religion. Within the domestic sphere his aunts, who played a large part in his upbringing even before his father's death, maintained a conventionally pious routine. His home town, Arras, was an important ecclesiastical city whose streets were frequently thronged with processions and festivals celebrating the passing of the liturgical year. Robespierre is reputed to have served as an altar boy at mass in its cathedral. At both the Collège d'Arras, a former Jesuit institution, and at the Oratorian Louis-le-Grand in Paris, to which he moved in October 1769 with the help of a scholarship obtained through the patronage of one of the family's clerical friends, the teaching

(Paris, 1951), p. 64. See also the comments in N. Hampson, *The Life and Opinions of Maximilien Robespierre* (London, 1974), pp. 55–6. Overall, one might conclude that his discourses were characterised by a deadening compulsiveness.

[4] Richard Cobb made a different but cognate point when he noted that Robespierre 'seldom *appeared* either to be saying what he meant or meaning what he said' (my italics): *Tour de France* (London, 1976), p. 45.

[5] E. Hamel, *Histoire de Robespierre*, 3 vols. (Paris, 1865–7), vol. I, p. 175, agreed: 'As we see him in the Constituent Assembly, so we find him in the Convention.' On the other hand, D. P. Jordan in his excellent *The Revolutionary Career of Maximilien Robespierre* (New York, 1985), p. 197, maintains that Robespierre's deism underwent 'enormous transformation during the Revolution'. This merely illustrates the extent of disagreement between historians over the man and his religious opinions.

was conducted against a background of regular and compulsory religious services. It is impossible to judge how deeply Robespierre was affected by the religious influences of his early years. But something seems to have rubbed off, for it was while he was at Louis-le-Grand that he lost such faith as he had acquired. The abbé Proyart, *sous-principal* at the College, tells us that religious celebrations became odious to him. He went through the motions at the services 'like an automaton', and ceased to receive even Easter communion as soon as he could avoid it.[6] There is no need to take all this at face value: Proyart never lost an opportunity to blacken his former pupil's character. But Robespierre's own later testimony at the Jacobin club in November 1793 that 'he had been quite a poor Catholic since his time at College'[7] suggests that it was indeed around this time that habits of, and sympathy for, routine religious observance were lost. Why Robespierre ceased to be a conventional, if not especially fervent, Catholic is not clear. Perhaps it was as a result of his contact with the religious life as it was expressed by his teachers at Louis-le-Grand. Whether he thought much about the whole business or simply allowed religious sentiments to which he had never been strongly attached to slide, we do not know. Nor do we know whether he subsequently entertained atheistic or agnostic ideas or merely slipped into the vague theism characteristic of so many of his class in the late eighteenth century.

The only detailed statement of his religious attitudes before the outbreak of the Revolution is the *mémoire* that Robespierre had printed in 1789 for the Dupond case, the last he was to conduct before the bar at Arras.[8] We have to be cautious in using the document since it was clearly intended as a commentary on the ideas of 1789, and this may have led Robespierre to slant what he had to say. Nevertheless, the *mémoire* confirms that by the late 1780s Robespierre had, by whatever route,[9] come to embrace a set of deist beliefs, and provides a clear

6 M. Le Blond de Neuvéglise, *La vie et les crimes de Robespierre, surnommé le tyran, depuis sa naissance jusqu'à sa mort* (Augsburg, 1795), pp. 30–2, 35–6. The author was almost certainly Proyart. He reported that Robespierre established a tannery at Meudon to turn the skin of victims of the guillotine into shoes for *sans-culottes*, the first member of the Convention to wear such boots being Barère (*ibid.*, pp. 279–80).

7 Robespierre, *Œuvres*, vol. X, p. 197.

8 An outline of the case together with the *mémoire* are in V. Barbier and C. Vellay (eds.), *Œuvres complètes de Maximilien Robespierre*, supplement to vol. I of *Revue historique de la Révolution française* (Paris, 1910), pp. 573–682.

9 Most biographers suggest that Robespierre derived his religious ideas from Rousseau. If this were so, then they were certainly taken from the *Contrat social* and not the *Vicaire savoyard*; and, unlike Rousseau, the evolution of Robespierre's sentiments did not involve a long and anguished journey of discovery. There are equally signs of Aristotelian influences in Robespierre's thought, perhaps derived from his schooling. The source of his religious ideas is a matter for speculation, and I have preferred to avoid this.

indication of the nature of the deity in whom he believed. The document began with a lengthy rehearsal of the facts of the case. Robespierre then moved on to territory where he was always happiest: a discussion of fundamental issues and first principles. God was the creator of all. His intention was that man should be happy. Happiness would only be found by living within society, and man's God-given faculties were purposely designed to fit him for life as a social animal. The proper ordering of society was contingent upon adhesion to divinely ordained principles of justice and morality. Only then would society reflect God's purpose, allowing man to exercise and perfect his God-given faculties and thereby attain happiness. It followed from this, Robespierre argued, that any form of government or society was good only insofar as it conformed to this divine aim. If it did not, then it was not only 'vicious and useless' but stood under divine condemnation.

> Here is the basis of that social contract about which men talk so much, which is not a free and voluntary agreement made by men. Rather, its fundamental terms, written in heaven, were established for all time by that supreme legislator who is the source of all order, of all happiness and of all justice.[10]

Robespierre asked rhetorically whether such a divinely sanctioned social and governmental system had existed in the past, and answered with a resounding 'No'. But Providence watched over the destiny of France and had worked through history to bring about the current opportunity to establish it. The providentially designated agent of change was the king. His mission was to produce a *moral* regeneration of France that would then serve as a beacon to the rest of the world. 'Another sovereign might have limited himself to restoring the old laws protecting property; he would have thought he had completed his task by renewing the sources of national wealth,' Robespierre told the king.

> But this is not the most crucial part of the august mission entrusted to you by God and your own conscience. Rather, it is to lead men to happiness through *vertu* and to *vertu* through laws founded on the unchanging principles of universal morality . . . to renew the immortal chain that should link man to God and to his fellow men, by destroying all sources of oppression and tyranny which sow fear, mistrust, pride, baseness, egoism, hatred, covetousness and all the vices that turn men away from the purpose that the eternal legislator has ascribed to society.[11]

If this unique, providentially ordained, opportunity for change were squandered, Robespierre continued in apocalyptic vein, then it was perhaps decreed that God would inflict trouble, desolation and calamity on France.

Having thus established the nature of divine rewards and punishments

[10] Barbier and Vellay, *Œuvres*, p. 662. [11] *Ibid.*, pp. 669–70.

in the here-and-now, Robespierre did not concern himself much with the life to come. But he did hint that there was such a thing: it provided consolation for those who suffered in this world. Those who bore the brunt of earthly suffering were the people. Robespierre lamented their poverty, but on the unusual grounds that it came close to extinguishing those 'divine principles of morality' which were innate in them. The theme of the people as the repository of *vertu* was one that would be repeated on many subsequent occasions. Overall, the performance in the *mémoire* would have done credit to an Old Testament prophet, and most of the future Robespierre was to be found within it: the perception of the French as a divinely chosen people; the apocalyptic vision of history; the moral absolutism; the Manichaean perspective.

Following his election to the Estates General, Robespierre's writings and speeches continued to be littered with references to a divinity. These ought not to be dismissed as mere commonplaces or figures of speech, given what he had said in the *mémoire* of 1789. Such references usually appeared in the context of his frequent warnings that the enemies of the Revolution were plotting its overthrow, and would have succeeded but for the intervention of Providence. He did not elaborate upon this until his outburst at the Jacobin club on 26 March 1792. On this occasion he sought the adoption of a circular he had drafted expressing opposition to the war policy on which the government and most politicians, including many within the Jacobin club, seemed determined. In his speech he rehearsed arguments that had become tediously familiar to his listeners. But when he got to an apparently innocuous passage in which he referred to Providence delivering the Revolution from disaster by striking down the Emperor Leopold,[12] and warned against exhausting the patience of heaven, he was interrupted by Guadet, the Bordeaux lawyer and associate of Brissot, who accused him of propagating superstition. Robespierre might easily have passed this off by indicating that he had merely used a conventional formula, especially as Guadet himself had claimed the previous year, in language that might have come from Robespierre's own lips, that Providence had delivered France from the intrigues of the court.[13] Instead, Robespierre launched into a passionate and unprepared defence of his deist beliefs. He detested superstition, he declared, which was a prop for despotism. He abhorred those religious sects which used the name of the eternal

[12] Died 1 March 1792.

[13] 'Providence, which watches over the destinies of France, caused this execrable conspiracy to fail': speech to the Jacobin club at Bordeaux, 27 February 1791, quoted in Hamel, *Histoire de Robespierre*, vol. II, p. 47.

being to propagate ambition and fanaticism. Refusing to be silenced by the murmurs from his audience, he continued:

> To invoke the name of Providence and to put forward the idea of an eternal being who influences the destiny of nations and who has watched over the French Revolution in particular, this is not speculation, but a belief that springs from my heart, a belief that is necessary to me.[14]

How could it be otherwise, he went on, lapsing into a familiar self-pitying tone, since only this belief in God had sustained him, surrounded as he was by vile intrigues and numberless enemies? 'How could I have accomplished tasks which were beyond human power if I had not lifted up my soul? . . . This sense of the divine has more than compensated me for the advantages otherwise gained by those who are prepared to betray the people.'[15]

All this suggests that Robespierre's deist beliefs had not substantially altered since 1789 and the writing of the *mémoire*. God was still the Revolution's divine patron and defender. The experiences of two years of revolution, during which time Robespierre had often felt himself disregarded, may have led him to acquire a more personal sense of God who was now a 'consolation in trouble and the inspiration of a work-a-day life', as J. M. Thompson put it.[16] Yet we should be careful not to take this aspect of his religious belief too far. Robespierre was not implying that he communicated with the divine through prayer or that he brought particular problems before God for solution. Rather, as he himself put it, God was an inspiration, the source of 'those eternal principles in which human weakness can find the strength it needs to make the leap to virtue'.[17]

Apart from his deism, the other aspect of Robespierre's religious beliefs in the earlier stages of his revolutionary career that merits comment is his attitude towards the clergy and the church. As a lapsed Catholic and a deist, Robespierre was sceptical of established religion. Yet he was tolerant of popular religiosity. While on a visit to Arras in 1791, for example, he heard reports of the miraculous cure of a lame man during a refractory priest's mass. His reaction was to note that the clergy would increase its sale of votive candles, and he sardonically remarked, 'I don't intend to stay long in this Holy Land; I am not worthy of it.'[18] In the same year, during debates at the Jacobin club, he argued that it was a tactical error to mount a frontal attack upon popular beliefs and practices: these should be left to wither away.[19] However, he was contemptuous of those exponents of revealed religion who were

14 Robespierre, *Œuvres*, vol. VIII, p. 234.
15 *Ibid.*, vol. VIII, p. 235.
16 Thompson, *Robespierre*, p. 217.
17 Robespierre, *Œuvres*, vol. VIII, p. 233.
18 Thompson, *Robespierre*, p. 192.
19 Robespierre, *Œuvres*, vol. VIII, p. 26.

drawn from among the higher clergy and the regulars. There is some evidence of this from quite early on. In 1783, Robespierre acted in a libel suit on behalf of Deteuf, a rope maker. The man had been falsely accused of theft by a Benedictine monk, Dom Brogniard, who was seeking to cover up his own criminal and sexual misdeeds. During the case Robespierre issued a *mémoire* that sharply criticised the lifestyle and scandalous morals of Brogniard's own community, the Abbey of Anchin, and of monks in general.[20] He subsequently made some play of the same theme in his election pamphlet, *A la nation artésienne*, referring to the regulars as 'idle and wealthy', a stock eighteenth-century characterisation.[21] This did not stop him defending the local Oratorians in the case of Berbizotte versus Gillet in 1784, nor from accepting a post of judge in the bishop's court. Nevertheless, he appears decisively to have turned his back on his ecclesiastical patrons by 1789 and had gained a sufficient reputation as an anti-clerical for Beaumetz, an opponent in the election campaign, to accuse him of attacking religion.[22]

After his election to the Assembly Robespierre remained hostile towards the upper clergy, suspicious right from the outset of their political motives and censorious of their wealth. Both sentiments led to his heated outburst on 6 June 1789. The Archbishop of Nîmes appeared before the Third Estate to ask for a joint meeting of all three orders to establish measures to relieve the plight of the poor. Suspecting a trick designed to undermine the independence of the Third Estate, Robespierre jumped up to reject the request, declaring to wide applause that bishops and dignitaries should renounce their luxurious lifestyles, sell one quarter of church property and give it to the poor.[23] There were echoes of this one year later in the debates on clerical salaries, when he argued that, 'The poor and beneficent author of religion advised the rich young man to share his wealth with the needy; it was his intention that his ministers should be poor men.'[24]

Robespierre was no crude anti-clerical, however. He spoke frequently on ecclesiastical matters in 1790. Yet it is significant that, in an Assembly that was becoming polarised between a pro-clerical right and an anti-clerical left, his speeches were notably free of cheap and vituperative

20 Barbier and Vellay, *Œuvres*, pp. 120–66 for details of the case; *ibid.*, pp. 120–46 for the *mémoire*.

21 Hampson, *Robespierre*, p. 37.

22 *Ibid.*, p. 67. See also G. Walter, *Robespierre*, édition définitive, 2 vols. (Paris, 1961), vol. I, pp. 68–76.

23 Dumont, *Souvenirs sur Mirabeau*, p. 63, though he suggested the cleric was the Archbishop of Aix.

24 M. J. Mavidal *et al.* (eds.), *Archives Parlementaires de 1781 à 1860*, première série, 96 vols. (Paris, 1879–1990), vol. XVI, p. 237.

remarks. Moreover, if he detested the upper clergy, Robespierre was better disposed towards the lower clergy. There was no criticism of them in his *mémoires* of 1783 and 1789, for example. He attempted, unsuccessfully, to persuade the Assembly to increase the state pension paid to former *curés*. 'Look to the mass of poor clerics who have grown old in an active ministry and have nothing to show for it but infirmities and misery,' he urged. 'You must choose between them and the bishops.'[25] Yet as his contributions to the debates on the civil constitution of the clergy reveal, he had little understanding of, or sympathy for, the priest's rôle in the sacerdotal mysteries of the Catholic church. He viewed the parish clergy as 'public officials', paid for by the nation and charged with responsibilities over 'public welfare and happiness'.[26] Accordingly, he argued that all clerics should be elected. To do otherwise would have meant that the clergy remained a discrete body, as they had been under the old régime, capable of setting themselves up against the general will.[27] By the same token, he wished priests to wear clerical dress only when they were performing their religious functions. 'No public official should be distinguished from other citizens by a distinctive dress, except during the exercise of his public functions,' he declared.[28] On similar grounds he favoured ending clerical celibacy, a proposal he unsuccessfully attempted to put forward at the end of May 1790.[29]

For Robespierre, then, a cleric was above all a citizen. At first, this point of view led him, quite logically, to oppose the legislation directed against those clerics who opposed the civil constitution and who refused the ecclesiastical oath imposed in 1791. It was wrong in principle, he argued, to have specific legislation against a class of people: priests were citizens with the same rights of expression as everyone else. To single them out merely gave them a discrete status within society. Troublemakers should be prosecuted under legislation that had a universal application.[30] Time was to modify this approach, however. By the end of 1791 Robespierre had become convinced of the existence of an ecclesiastical counter-revolution. Defence of the Revolution justified the imposition of savage penal laws against nonjurors. They thus fell victim to his Manichaean vision that placed opponents and supporters of the Revolution in two hostile camps.

What of his attitude towards the church? Like most reflective people

25 *Ibid.*, vol. XVI, pp. 408–9, 535.
26 *Ibid.*, vol. XVI, pp. 408, 3.
27 *Ibid.*, vol. XVI, p. 156.
28 *Ibid.*, vol. XVIII, p. 756.
29 Thompson, *Robespierre*, pp. 85–6. He thus appears to have changed his mind on this issue, having expressed a contrary view in 1786 in *Les droits et l'état des bâtards*: N. Hampson, *Will and Circumstance: Montesquieu, Rousseau and the French Revolution* (London, 1983), pp. 134–5.
30 *Archives Parlementaires*, vol. XXIV, p. 214.

in late eighteenth-century France, the Robespierre who arrived in Versailles in 1789 was critical of the Catholic church and in favour of its reform, though not in favour of its abolition. His attitude towards reform, much like his attitude towards the clergy, derived from the dominating principle of popular sovereignty. That the Assembly had the right to reform the church, he had no doubt. The church was a 'social institution', he declared, and, as such, it was as much subject to the will of the nation as any other public body.[31] He therefore supported the thrust of the ecclesiastical legislation passed by the Assembly in 1789 and 1790, which aimed effectively to nationalise the church. It was right to appropriate ecclesiastical property, he argued, since this belonged to the nation.[32] It was right to restructure the church along lines proposed under the civil constitution of the clergy since this brought it into line with what the nation needed and wanted. He thus favoured a state church in 1789–90, but he did not yet advocate a state religion.

Overall, it is probable that Robespierre's religious opinions only began to crystallise as the revolutionary crisis broke. In the 1780s he had been a critic of the clergy and the established church, but his approach towards their reform was conditioned by the revolutionary principle of popular sovereignty. It is surely significant that the fullest, indeed the only known, articulation of his deism before his election to the Estates General was in the *mémoire* for the Dupond case, in the context of a discussion of the principles of the Revolution. His belief in a creator-God who maintained a tutelary oversight over human affairs and in the immortality of the soul would have been familiar to others of his social class in the late eighteenth century. The original features of his otherwise eclectic deism – his grounding of the social contract upon divine intention, his association of the divinity with the ideals of the Revolution and his acknowledgement that Providence had intervened in history to give the French nation a once-for-all opportunity to restructure society in line with divinely sanctioned moral principles – were only comprehensible in the context of the unfolding crisis of 1789. Robespierre's ideology, at least in respect of his religious views, was thus essentially complete when he went as a deputy to the Estates General. Events between 1789 and spring 1792 strengthened the beliefs he already held.

Robespierre's discourses concerning the cult of the Supreme Being constitute the third textual landmark on which to base an assessment of his religious opinions. The cult was instituted by the decree of 18 Floréal Year II (7 May 1794) and inaugurated by the great festival at Paris on 20 Prairial Year II (8 June 1794) staged by David and presided

[31] *Ibid.*, vol. XVI, p. 3.   [32] *Ibid.*, vol. XI, p. 231.

over by Robespierre. It had been prefaced by Robespierre's attack in the Jacobin club on atheism and the dechristianising campaign on 1 Frimaire Year II (21 November 1793) and his report to the Convention on the 'Principles of Political Morality' on 17 Pluviôse Year II (5 February 1794). Robespierre's speech on 18 Floréal represents the frankest and fullest exposition of his religious views since the Dupond *mémoire* of 1789. There can be little doubt that the cult of the Supreme Being reflected his deepest personal religious convictions. 'If one searches Robespierre's writings for the piece that most intimately and profoundly reflects his thought, it is without doubt the report of 18 Floréal,' wrote Gérard Walter.[33] Not only is the tenor of the speech and the passion with which it was delivered testimony to this,[34] but it is surely significant that this was one of only three occasions (the others being the speeches on education and the self-denying ordinance) when Robespierre put forward his own explicit proposals for action. Generally, he was content to analyse and hint at the action that he felt was necessary.

The speech shows clearly that Robespierre had abandoned none of the religious beliefs that he had earlier held. God remained totally identified with the Revolution. Article I of the decree of 18 Floréal made the connection: 'The French people recognise the existence of the Supreme Being.'[35] It did not say it, because it did not need to be made explicit in the embattled Republic, but no other people on earth recognised His existence. Rather like Yahweh and the Jews, the Supreme Being had a unique relationship with the French people. The characteristics of the divinity, as enunciated by Robespierre, were precisely those of the Revolution: liberty, justice and, above all, *vertu*. (These qualities, not coincidentally, were precisely those that Robespierre claimed to manifest in his own person.) God thus provided the grounding for the moral order that was at the very heart of the Revolution. 'Immorality is the basis of despotism, just as *vertu* is the essence of the Republic,' Robespierre declared. 'Let us attach morality to its eternal and sacred foundations; let us inspire in men that religious respect for their fellows, that profound sense of duty, which are the only guarantee of social order.'[36] In 1789 the revolutionaries had wanted to nationalise the

33 Walter, *Robespierre*, vol. II, p. 399 and see also pp. 133–40.
34 Dumont, *Souvenirs sur Mirabeau*, p. 144, recalled Robespierre's confession that generally he was as timid as a child and trembled as he approached the podium. But not on this occasion: Mathiez, *Fall of Robespierre*, p. 95.
35 Robespierre's speech and the text of the decree are in Robespierre, *Œuvres*, vol. X, pp. 442–62.
36 *Ibid.*, vol. X, pp. 447, 458.

church; in 1794, with the cult of the Supreme Being, Robespierre nationalised God.

How was the Supreme Being to be discovered? Here, Robespierre elaborated upon what he had said in the Jacobin club on 26 March 1792. He again confirmed that God was accessible through intuition (he had previously talked about feeling the divine presence in his heart). Now he added that God might be found through the contemplation of Nature. He therefore called upon his hearers on 18 Floréal to look inside themselves, suppress all passion and listen to the inner voice of conscience. Contradicting the conventional wisdom of the Enlightenment which urged that the truth that was in men's hearts might be discovered by the use of reason, he declared that reason handicapped man in his search for truth. 'Man's reason', he said, 'resembles the earth on which he lives: half is sunlit, while the other half is plunged into darkness.'[37] This allowed Robespierre to contrast the intuitive knowledge of God and his laws evidenced by the people with the flawed conceptions of the divine manifested by the rational *philosophes*. This was a theme first broached in the *mémoire* of 1789. He had returned to it in his attack on the dechristianisers on 1 Frimaire, declaring that 'The idea of a superior being who watches over oppressed innocence and who punishes triumphant crime is wholly popular.'[38] And it had been most recently touched upon in the speech of 17 Pluviôse when he had noted, 'Happily, *vertu* is natural to the people.'[39]

Similarly, the apocalyptic vision of a God who worked through history with France as His chosen instrument, first signalled in the *mémoire*, had in no wise been altered by the passage of time. 'Those two opposing spirits [vice and *vertu*] in conflict with one another for the empire of nature, are struggling in this great epoch of human history to establish irrevocably the destinies of the world, and France is the theatre of this mighty battle,' he declared on 17 Pluviôse.[40]

The cult of the Supreme Being was not a lifeline to the Catholics as Aulard suggested.[41] But nor, though Robespierre denounced the clergy, was it a frontal attack on Catholicism, such as he had condemned in November 1791. Here too there was consistency in his approach. He argued that, if left free of persecution, Catholicism and all other faiths would be won over by the self-evident truth of the cult and subsumed into this 'universal religion of Nature'.[42] Consistent but unrealistic. For although the language that Robespierre adopted when talking of his God was drawn eclectically from the stock of vocabulary used by

[37] *Ibid.*, vol. X, p. 444. [38] *Ibid.*, vol. X, p. 196. [39] *Ibid.*, vol. X, p. 355.
[40] *Ibid.*, vol. X, p. 356. [41] Aulard, *Culte de la raison*, p. 457.
[42] Robespierre, *Œuvres*, vol. X, p. 457.

Christians since the early seventeenth century,[43] there was nothing that was Christian left in his narrow vision of an implacable and unforgiving deity, who presided over a Manichaean universe divided between upholders and opponents of the Revolution.[44]

Academic debate about the motives for the introduction of the cult of the Supreme Being has tended to polarise. On the one hand, it is argued that it was an expression of Robespierre's genuine religious convictions; on the other, that it was politically inspired.[45] In fact, the two points of view are not mutually exclusive and ought not be seen as alternatives. As we have seen, the cult did indeed represent Robespierre's innermost convictions; other considerations influenced the timing of its introduction. To understand this, we need to take a long view rather than concentrating on the events of the autumn and spring of 1793–4, crucial though these were.

Robespierre's view of the Revolution had always been a moral one, as the Dupond *mémoire* initially made clear. This was why he adopted the rôle of an inquisitor after his election to the Estates General, constantly questioning people's motives. It also explains why, following his appointment to the Committee of Public Safety in July 1793, which put him into a position of executive authority, he undertook no specific responsibilities but instead articulated the theoretical and moral basis of the new government. Saint-Just complemented him in this rôle. By 1792, both men were coming to perceive a problem. The institutions of the Republic had effectively been established, and in this sense the Revolution was complete. Yet in another sense, everything remained to be done, for the citizens of this Republic were not yet morally worthy of the institutions created for their benefit. 'It is not an empty word that makes a republic,' Robespierre wrote late in that year, 'it is the character of its citizens.'[46] He came back to this dilemma in his speech of 18 Floréal, contrasting the astounding advances made in the arts and the sciences with the continuing ignorance of people with respect to public morality. What was to be done about this? The answer was to change men, and initially education was perceived as the means of transforming them.

In February 1792, Robespierre had urged the adoption of a national system of education, not based on routine pedagogy, but designed to

43 J. Deprun, 'A la fête suprême: les "noms divins" dans deux discours de Robespierre', *AHRF* 44 (1972), 161–80.

44 As Jordan, *Robespierre*, p. 197, notes: 'He is a God who easily would have survived a purification scrutiny at the Jacobins, who would have sat on the Mountain.'

45 For a résumé of the arguments see M. Ozouf, *Festivals and the French Revolution* (Cambridge, Mass., 1988), pp. 107–10.

46 P. Gueniffey, 'Robespierre', in F. Furet and M. Ozouf (eds.), *Dictionnaire critique de la Révolution française* (Paris, 1988), p. 328.

inculcate the principles of the Revolution through propaganda techniques, of which the most important were public festivals.[47] He returned to the theme twelve months later when he took up the educational proposals of his assassinated friend, Lepeletier de Saint-Fargeau, and argued vigorously for them in a report presented to the Convention on 13 July 1793. Had they been fully implemented, these would have provided France with a national system of boarding schools designed to remove children from the malign influence of the family and to rear them on the 'divine principles of morality and equality'.[48] To be sure, the process of moral regeneration through education would not take place overnight. But this did not matter too much. *Vertu* was natural to the people. It currently lay dormant, but it was only a matter of time before it would be fully awakened. Meanwhile, the Revolution would be kept on course by the people's leaders, the Mountain, whose own moral rectitude had apparently been assured by the expulsion of the Girondins from the Convention on 2 June.

Against this background, one can imagine the horror that Robespierre experienced as evidence began to accumulate that even among the vanguard of the Revolution there was moral turpitude and counter-revolutionary plotting. Matters began to come to a head with revelations of a 'Foreign Plot', a widespread set of conspiracies against the Republic, first signalled by Fabre d'Eglantine in October 1793. There is no need here to engage with the plot's bizarre details. But it should be stressed that, for Robespierre, the concurrent campaign to dechristianise France, the leaders of which were to be found among the Mountain, lay at the very heart of the web of conspiracy.[49] His attitude was made clear in his speeches of 1 Frimaire and 18 Floréal, and we should take at face value the words of a man who had spent his whole political life sniffing out and exposing treachery. Dechristianisation, he proclaimed, carried with it several dangers: it allowed the corrupt to hide their misdeeds; it was a means to discredit the Revolution and provoke further foreign intervention; it stoked the fires of internal counter-revolution by attacking the peasants' religious prejudices. But dechristianisation was above all threatening because it was the culmination of a series of conspiracies, stretching back decades. These conspiracies included the efforts of the Enlightenment writers, and they all aimed to undermine

47 Robespierre, *Œuvres*, vol. VIII, pp. 178–9.

48 *Ibid.*, vol. V, p. 209.

49 Easily the clearest exposition of the plot is N. Hampson, 'François Chabot and his plot', *Transactions of the Royal Historical Society*, 5th ser., 26 (1976), 1–14. For an outline of the origins and course of the dechristianising campaign, see P. de la Gorce, *Histoire religieuse de la Révolution française*, 5 vols. (Paris, 1923–5), vol. III.

the very essence of the Revolution – its moral basis – through the preaching of atheism.

Thus, by the spring of 1794 Robespierre was faced by moral turpitude among the vanguard of the Revolution and an underdeveloped moral sense among the people. He responded to the former by inaugurating a series of purges at the Paris Jacobin club and its affiliates, and then struck down his opponents on both left and right with the executions of the Hébertists and the indulgents in March and April.[50] He responded to the latter by seeking to speed up the moral regeneration of France. He reaffirmed his faith in education on 18 Floréal, but additionally a more affirmative course of action was to be undertaken in the shape of the new cult of the Supreme Being. 'Hitherto', he declared, 'the art of government has been the art of cheating and corrupting the governed; henceforth, it is to be changed into the art of enlightening them, and making them better.'[51] A system of national festivals, beginning with the festival of the Supreme Being, would be 'both the most persuasive bond of fellowship, and the most powerful means of regeneration', he proclaimed. 'Assemble men together and you will make them better.'[52] The cult would teach people the elements of morality which was the 'one and only foundation of civil society'.[53] Robespierre seems to have felt that if people came to know God they would also become aware of the eternal verities that God had inscribed on the heart of every individual. In this way, the cult would produce citizens who were worthy of the institutions created for their benefit. Simultaneously, the knowledge that the laws had a divine sanction would endow them with a moral force that they would not otherwise possess.

A substantial section of the speech on 18 Floréal was devoted to a condemnation of atheism. This, Robespierre argued, dissolved the bonds of society. It led people to believe that the fate of all, good as well as wicked, was decided by blind chance. Society was left at the mercy of the strongest and the cleverest. By contrast, religion reinforced the social bonds by differentiating between the regenerate and the unregenerate. It is not altogether clear how Robespierre saw this working. He did not explicitly suggest that in the after-life God would punish the wicked and reward the good, although he hinted at this. Thus, for the first time, there was an unequivocal assertion of the immortality of the soul, which

50 Significantly, Danton was not executed for corruption, though there was plenty of evidence for this, but for failure to match up to a moral standard. Robespierre noted, 'The word virtue made Danton laugh. How could a man, to whom all idea of morality was foreign, be the defender of liberty?': W. Doyle, *The Oxford History of the French Revolution* (Oxford, 1989), pp. 274–5.

51 Robespierre, *Œuvres*, vol. X, p. 445.

52 *Ibid.*, vol. X, pp. 458–9.

53 *Ibid.*, vol. X, p. 444.

was a 'constant call to justice'.[54] But he was absolutely certain that punishment ought to come in the here-and-now rather than, or perhaps as well as, in the hereafter. Accordingly, he coupled the teaching of *vertu*, through a state religion, with the punishment of vice, through the Terror.

It is often thought incongruous that just two days after the first festival of the Supreme Being, celebrated with displays of flowers, fruit and vegetables and for which the grisly scaffolding of the guillotine had been dismantled, the Prairial law was enacted. This inaugurated the bloodiest period of the Terror. Yet there was nothing coincidental about the timing. An intensification of the Terror and the establishment of the cult of the Supreme Being were related means by which Robespierre sought to achieve the moral regeneration of France. The connection between the two was signalled for all those who could discern the meaning of Robespierre's words. On 17 Pluviôse, he stated, 'The resource of popular government in time of revolution is simultaneously *vertu* and terror: *vertu*, without which terror is harmful; terror, without which *vertu* is powerless.'[55] On 18 Floréal, again counterpoising two apparent antitheses in that fashion that was characteristic of his discourses, he exhorted the deputies: 'Establish your actions on the immutable foundations of justice and revive public morality [i.e. create a state religion]. Hurl thunderbolts at the heads of the guilty and rain lightning on your enemies.'[56] He concluded his address to the crowd on 20 Prairial by urging: 'Be generous towards the good, sympathetic towards the unfortunate, pitiless towards the wicked.'[57] In reality, then, the cult and the Terror were two sides of the same coin. The former gave an ideological justification for the use of violence that might otherwise have seemed capricious and uncontrolled. Jean Jaurès recorded that Jacques-Alexis Thuriot, a former member of the Committee of Public Safety and President of the Convention on 9 Thermidor, remarked in a stage whisper as Robespierre gave his speech to the assembled crowd at the festival of the Supreme Being, 'It's not enough for him to be in charge, he has to be God.'[58] There was more than a grain of truth in the charge. Robespierre had made God in his own image; and, certain of his own moral convictions, he now proposed 'to usurp divine justice by using the guillotine as an instrument of moral regeneration'.[59]

[54] *Ibid.*, vol. X, pp. 451–2. The immortality of the soul was also recognised in Article I of the decree, after the existence of the Supreme Being.

[55] Robespierre, *Œuvres*, vol. X, p. 357.

[56] *Ibid.*, vol. X, p. 462. [57] *Ibid.*, vol. X, p. 483.

[58] J. Jaurès, *Histoire socialiste de la Révolution française*, revised edition, 8 vols. (Paris, 1922–4), vol. VIII, p. 400.

[59] J. McManners, *The French Revolution and the Church* (London, 1969), p. 103.

Robespierre went to the guillotine seven weeks and one day after the first festival of the Supreme Being. The cult was so bound up with its creator's personality and political fortunes that its demise seems inevitable. But was it doomed to failure? Did it leave no echoes behind? There is little evidence to substantiate claims that it was widely welcomed by Catholics. Indeed, such acceptance would have been surprising. It failed to fulfil any of those remedial functions that were an essential element of old-régime popular Catholicism. It provided no Marian girdles to ease the pain of childbirth; no exorcisms of insects to protect the crops; no blessings to ensure the fertility of the soil and the marriage bed. Cold and abstract, it brought no magic to living and little consolation to dying. Even the cult's adherents regretted that no provision had been made to obtain *protection* from the Supreme Being.[60] In any event, the cult was always going to be rejected by those with counter-revolutionary sentiments precisely because it was so closely linked with the Revolution. And there was an additional factor in its rejection. The mayor of one village in the Auxerre was later to refer to the peasants' 'spirit of perversity' which led them always to act in ways which flouted authority.[61] Thus under the old régime, they played cards and ostentatiously frequented the *cabaret* during the hours of mass; during the Revolution, they worked on the *décadi* and boycotted the revolutionary festivals.

Yet there was a constituency for the cult. We should not ignore the well-founded reports of substantial crowds who turned out to celebrate the first festival of the cult of the Supreme Being. At Paris, their numbers ran into thousands, on what was admittedly a beautiful day in a carnival atmosphere. Robespierre was greatly moved by their obvious manifestation of support, which stood in sharp contrast to the scarcely concealed cynicism of some of his colleagues.[62] The research of Michel Vovelle also suggests some popular support for the cult from among those committed to the Revolution. His analysis of almost one thousand petitions to the Convention on the subject of dechristianisation shows that the Supreme Being was already the predominant figure in those festivals which are often placed under the heading of the cult of Reason

60 M. Ozouf, 'Religion révolutionnaire', in Furet and Ozouf, *Dictionnaire critique*, p. 610. On 29 Floréal, the mayor of Paris, Lescot-Fleuriot, sought to reassure the inhabitants about the food supply by announcing: 'The Supreme Being . . . has commanded nature to prepare you abundant harvests.' Such evocations of the Supreme Being by the authorities were unusual: A. Aulard, *The French Revolution: a Political History*, trans. of 3rd edition, 4 vols. (London, 1910), vol. III, p. 188.

61 H. Forestier, 'Le culte laïcal: un aspect spécifiquement auxerrois de la résistance des paroisses rurales à la déchristianisation', *Annales de Bourgogne* 24 (1952), 106–7.

62 Charles Nodier, *Souvenirs de la Révolution et de l'Empire*, 2 vols. (Paris, 1865), vol. I, pp. 288–90, for a good description of the event; Jordan, *Robespierre*, pp. 199–200.

and which began to be organised spontaneously in the autumn of 1793.[63]

If we focus a little higher up the social scale, there is further evidence that Robespierre was not whistling in the wind when he inaugurated the cult of the Supreme Being. So much of it was to be reborn in the cult of theophilanthropy, inaugurated in Nivôse Year IV, and in the deism of the educated classes in the nineteenth century: a concern with Nature, a tutelary Providence, the immortality of the soul.[64] Yet, even if some elements of his religious thought were present in others, Robespierre's beliefs ultimately comprised an original synthesis by their holder himself. That unique distillation of religious opinions, which had been his consistent concern and driving passion since 1789, died with him on 10 Thermidor.

[63] M. Vovelle, 'The adventures of reason, or from reason to the Supreme Being', in C. Lucas (ed.), *Rewriting the French Revolution* (Oxford, 1991), pp. 134–5.

[64] A. Mathiez, *La Théophilanthropie et le culte décadaire 1796–1801* (Paris, 1904).

Part III

Robespierre's politics

7 Robespierre and the press

Hugh Gough

Robespierre was a journalist for less than a year of his political career. Unlike Brissot or Carra, who moved effortlessly from the world of pre-revolutionary letters into the maelstrom of journalism and national politics, he only published his first newspaper when his political reputation was already well known. Unlike fellow deputies in the Constituent Assembly such as Mirabeau and Barère, who launched newspapers in the summer of 1789 to maintain contact with their constituents and create a national profile, he only followed them when he was no longer a deputy and his profile was already well established. As in so many other ways, Robespierre was different. Journalism for him was a means rather than an end, something which he used to support his political career when under attack in the spring of 1792 and abandoned shortly before joining the Committee of Public Safety in the summer of 1793. Yet although only a transitory journalist he owed some of his reputation to the press and had a healthy respect for its rôle in the new political world that the Revolution created. As both politician and journalist he held strong views on press freedom and the journalist's political function which were formed while he was out of power, then modified and enforced while he was in.

When elected to the Estates General in the spring of 1789, Robespierre already had some contact with journalism, for he and his sister Charlotte were on friendly terms with Madame Marchand, the owner and editor of the *Affiches d'Artois* in their home town of Arras. Madame Marchand may have helped him in his election campaign in Arras and some sources suggest that she lent him money and a clothes chest for his journey to Versailles.[1] Whatever the truth of this, the relationship rapidly deteriorated as she became a critic of the Revolution by late 1789, causing a violent quarrel with Charlotte in the following spring, which ended both the friendship and the Robespierre household's free

1 Norman Hampson, *The Life and Opinions of Maximilien Robespierre* (London, 1974), p. 41; Louis Jacob, *Robespierre vu par ses contemporains* (Paris, 1938), p. 91.

copy of her paper.[2] Madame Marchand was soon to encounter more serious political problems as her printer, de la Sablonnière, refused to print a number in May 1790 because of its critical attitude towards the Revolution, forcing her to print it in Douai instead.[3] She promptly bought her own presses to avoid future printing problems, but her attitude continued to offend local revolutionaries and in February 1791 the Jacobin club in Arras denounced her to the municipality, which passed on the complaint to the Constituent Assembly and expressed its regret that it had no legal power to close the paper down.[4] In the following October, when she published a satirical account of Robespierre's triumphal return from Paris at the end of the Constituent Assembly, she was visited by a group of army officers garrisoned in nearby Bapaume who, unaware of the fact that they were talking to her, threatened to cut off the editor's ears as a punishment:

> These gentlemen ordered me to radically change the tone of my newspaper. They wanted me to be more serious in my treatment of Robespierre and disliked the mocking tone of my article. But I asked their permission to use a little humour from time to time: so many people are sad these days![5]

Shortly afterwards Madame Marchand moved to Tournai where the paper finally ceased publication after the fall of the monarchy in August 1792.[6]

If Robespierre quickly crossed swords with Madame Marchand, his political career nevertheless rapidly caught the attention of the Parisian press because of his dogged support for radical democracy as a deputy. The right-wing press was understandably hostile to him, the counter-revolutionary *Défenseur des opprimés* comparing his oratory to a warm water tap and the satirical *Sabbats jacobites* ridiculing him as a descendant of the would-be regicide Damiens idolised only by criminals.[7] The *Babillard* attacked his reputation for incorruptibility, the *Gazette de Paris* called him an 'inflexible' person motivated only by a 'spirit of hatred', and while the *Actes des apôtres* initially adopted a typically light-hearted tone of waspish cynicism, airing doubts over his intellectual reputation, it had adopted a more corrosive and hostile approach by the summer

[2] *Correspondance de Maximilien et Augustin Robespierre*, ed. Georges Michon (Paris, 1926), pp. 70–1.

[3] *Affiches d'Artois, du Boulonnais et du Calaisis* 52 (28 May 1790), p. 468 (Archives Départementales du Pas-de-Calais B1659).

[4] AN, DXXIXbis doss. 296, pièce 5.

[5] Jacob, *Robespierre*, p. 91.

[6] Pierre Bougard and Ghislaine Bellart, 'La presse arrageoise des origines à 1870', *Mémoires de l'Académie des Sciences, Lettres et Arts d'Arras* 5e série, 4 (1960–5), 67–71.

[7] Jean-Paul Bertaud, *Les amis du roi. Journaux et journalistes royalistes en France de 1789 à 1792* (Paris, 1984), pp. 103–5; Marc Bouloiseau, 'Aux origines des légendes contre-révolutionnaires. Robespierre vu par les journaux satiriques', *AHRF* 30 (1958), 28–49.

and autumn of 1790.[8] Not all the right-wing press was hostile, for on one occasion the abbé Royou's *Ami du roi* expressed a grudging admiration for his courage and sincerity even if it rarely had sympathy with his viewpoint.[9] Yet it was from the left of the political spectrum, from the Parisian radical press, that Robespierre was to receive his most sympathetic treatment. Marat praised his courage in his *Ami du peuple*, François Robert admired his principled approach to politics in the *Mercure national*, Fréron enthused over his 'pure and celestial mind' in the *Orateur du peuple* and Elysée Loustallot in the *Révolutions de Paris* noted that:

We have few of these kind of men who, in the search to fulfil their duty rather than seek applause, hold to principles like Monsieur Robespierre, and take the risk of appearing too enthusiastic in their support for the rights of the people, knowing full well that they will suffer in the process.[10]

Camille Desmoulins, in the *Révolutions de France et de Brabant*, was particularly enthusiastic, for he had been a pupil at the Collège Louis-le-Grand with Robespierre, who acted as a witness at his wedding with Lucille in the winter of 1790. For Desmoulins, Robespierre was 'this excellent citizen, the ornament of the northern deputies':

Quand il parle c'est moins un orateur dont les discours varient qui se lève, que le livre de la loi qui s'ouvre, non pas toujours de la loi écrite, mais de la loi insérée et gravée dans tous les cœurs. (When he speaks it is less an orator whose speeches can vary from one occasion to another who rises to his feet, than the book of the law which opens – not always the book of the written law but of the law engraved in all our hearts.)[11]

Although frequently mentioned by other journalists, Robespierre differed from several of his colleagues in the Constituent Assembly by seeing no need to launch his own newspaper until the spring of 1792. He may well have found political life as a deputy and active member of the Paris Jacobin club demanding enough without the added regular grind that a newspaper required, and most of his speeches were well covered in the national press anyway. When they were not, or when he wanted to gain access to a wider audience, he sent copies of them to selected provincial Jacobin clubs, or published letters in sympathetic papers such as the *Révolutions de Paris*.[12] There have been suggestions that he was the anonymous editor of an Anglo-French paper, *L'Union*, in the winter of 1789–90 and secretly contributed to Marat's *Ami du*

8 *Actes des apôtres* 5, pp. 12–13.
9 *Ami du roi*, 21 May 1791, p. 2.
10 *Révolutions de Paris* 43 (1–8 May 1790), p. 258.
11 *Révolutions de France et de Brabant*, 21 February 1791, pp. 576–7; Bertaud, *Amis du roi*, pp. 101–2, 128.
12 Michael L. Kennedy, *The Jacobin Clubs in the French Revolution. The First Years* (Princeton, 1982), pp. 248–9.

peuple in the spring of 1792.[13] Yet there is no evidence to support either claim, and there seems little doubt that the launch of the *Défenseur de la constitution* in the spring of 1792 marked his first step into active journalism. His reasons for doing so were political rather than financial, for, now that he was no longer a deputy, his conflict with the Girondins over the war issue left him with the need for a national platform to defend his reputation against a political group which had largely built its reputation on the popularity of its newspapers, which included the *Patriote français* and the *Chronique de Paris*. December 1791 and January 1792 had seen his dramatic confrontation with Brissot over war, February had seen him clash with Brissot's colleagues on the Jacobin club's correspondence committee over the content of its circulars to provincial clubs and, during March, he had taken issue with Guadet over the question of religion.[14] In mid-April several Girondin journalists had accused him of political desertion for resigning as public prosecutor of the Parisian criminal court, and on 25 April Brissot had attacked him in the Jacobin club for causing unnecessary political division among supporters of the Revolution. Before the end of the month both Girey-Dupré, in the *Patriote français*, and Sylvain Maréchal, in the *Révolutions de Paris*, had raised the possibility that his behaviour was the result of a secret pact with the court to promote the cause of counter-revolution:

> There are three opinions on Robespierre: some think him mad, others put his conduct down to wounded pride, and a third view believes him to be in the pay of the civil list. We never believe in corruption unless there is ample proof, but we do believe that, whether through madness or vanity, Robespierre is obviously at the root of the divisions which are tearing the Jacobin club apart and that the only way for him to regain his reputation is to renew his links with the true friends of liberty and the constitution.[15]

There were no secret deals with the court. Instead it was the veiled accusation of treason and crypto-royalism from his former political allies that prompted Robespierre to launch the *Défenseur de la constitution* in late April 1792. As is so often the case with the revolutionary press, we know little or nothing about the business side of the venture. The cost of launching a journal during the Revolution was not prohibitive, but it was probably beyond the reach of Robespierre's personal resources and it seems reasonable to assume that he had outside financial backing. He appears to have been offered help by Dumouriez, from the Ministry of

[13] *Actes des apôtres* 5, p. 10; Gustave Rouanet, 'Robespierre et le journal "L'Union"', *Annales révolutionnaires* 9 (1917), 145–65; Olivier Coquard, *Marat* (Paris, 1993), pp. 322–3.

[14] G. Walter, *Robespierre*, 2 vols. (Paris, 1961), vol. I, pp. 285–319.

[15] *Patriote français*, 28 April 1792, p. 473; *Révolutions de Paris* 147 (28 April–5 May 1792), p. 209; *Chronique de Paris*, 30 April 1792, pp. 460–1.

Foreign Affairs, in the form of cheap printing rates; but that was an offer with strings because of Dumouriez's close links with the Girondins, and he emphatically turned it down.[16] Instead the help probably came from his landlord, the wealthy cabinet-maker and property owner Maurice Duplay, with whom he had been lodging since the previous autumn. Gérard Walter also suggested that Robespierre may have been given a subscription list by a young admirer, Sébastien Lacroix, who had published the prospectus for a newspaper, *L'Accusateur public*, in early April but never taken it into print. Lacroix came from a fervently Robespierrist family and was to make a political career for himself on the radical wing of Jacobinism over the next two years, publishing a newspaper in Marseille after the collapse of the federalist revolt in the winter of 1793.[17] The *Défenseur*'s printer, Léopold Nicolas, also lived in the Duplay household. Desmoulins later claimed that Nicolas acted as Robespierre's personal bodyguard during the early years of the Revolution, accompanying him around Paris with a large stick, 'worth a whole company of young fancy thugs by himself'.[18] Certainly Nicolas was to do well out of Robespierre's patronage, for he went on to become a major printer for the Ministry of War during the Terror, printer of the Jacobin club's journal, the *Journal de la montagne*, and of the Committee of Public Safety's *Feuille du salut public*, and a member of several of the club's committees. His critics resented him as a bully who threw his political weight around in the search for influence and profit, but he remained loyal to Robespierre until the end and was guillotined four days after him on 14 Thermidor Year II.[19] As for the distribution of the paper, this was looked after by Pierre-Jacques Duplain, a printer and bookseller on the cour du Commerce, who was a member of the Cordelier club, a friend of Danton and Marat and distributor for Camille Desmoulins's newly launched – and short-lived – *Tribune des patriotes* as well.[20]

In his prospectus, published on 25 April, Robespierre described his purpose in publishing the *Défenseur de la constitution* as being to combat the division and ignorance which had enabled the constitution's enemies – the Girondins – to seize the political initiative. Like almost every other

16 Walter, *Robespierre*, vol. I, p. 304.

17 *Ibid.*, vol. I, p. 305; *Journal républicain de Marseille et des départements méridionaux*, 1 October 1793 to 20 Pluviôse Year II, *passim*.

18 *Vieux Cordelier* 5 (5 Nivôse Year II), pp. 61–5.

19 E. Hamel, *Histoire de Robespierre*, 3 vols. (Paris, 1865–7), vol. III, p. 316; *Vieux Cordelier* 5 (5 Nivôse Year II), pp. 78–80; E. Courtois, *Papiers inédits trouvés chez Robespierre, Saint-Just, Payan etc.*, 3 vols. (Paris, 1828), vol. III, pp. 90–3; F.-A. Aulard (ed.), *Recueil des actes du comité de salut public*, 27 vols. (Paris, 1889–1933), vol. VI, p. 88; AN, AFII 66 reg. 484, pièce 51; $F^7 4774^{57}$.

20 AN, $F^7 4744^{57}$, doss. 3.

journalist during the 1790s, he also modestly proclaimed his intention of saving 'la chose publique' by encouraging patriotism and unity. The journalistic form which he chose for that was a weekly periodical, published in octavo size with forty-eight to sixty-four pages in each edition, none of which carried any advertisements or illustrations to lighten the impact of the printed word. Twelve numbers of the *Défenseur* were published at weekly intervals, between 17 May and 20 August 1792. There was then a gap of a little over five weeks before he resumed under a new title, *Lettres à ses commettans*, reflecting the resumption of his career as a deputy in the newly elected National Convention. Some twenty-two numbers of this appeared between 30 September 1792 and mid-April 1793, before he abandoned it without warning. A pamphlet-size weekly was a common enough format for a newspaper in the Revolution, used on the left by titles such as the *Révolutions de France et de Brabant* or the *Révolutions de Paris*, and on the right by the *Actes des apôtres* or the *Journal de M. Suleau*. The weekly rhythm allowed editors time to reflect on events and – at least in theory – to provide a balanced commentary for their readers instead of the breathless narrative of the daily press. Yet Robespierre's format was more commentary-based than most, for he published few articles of hard news in either paper and made no attempt to cover current events in provincial France or abroad. Instead his aim was clearly to attract support for his own political views by reprinting speeches that he or his political allies made in the Jacobin club or the Convention, and by publishing editorial comment on current events. He was a journalist catering for a clientele in search of views rather than news.

Historians of the Revolution and biographers of Robespierre have already drawn extensively on both newspapers in their analyses of his political career, and there is little point in reworking their analysis in any great detail here. Initially the *Défenseur* concentrated on the political and military crisis of the summer of 1792, blaming it as much on the Girondins as on the king. Robespierre accused Brissot of having divided patriot opinion since the previous summer through his support for a republic in the aftermath of Varennes, and of compounding this by linking his political fortunes to Narbonne and Lafayette during the winter of 1791–2.[21] This, he claimed, was proof of a long-term plot to undermine political liberty, and, although he stopped short of accusing Brissot of treason, he did accuse him and his fellow Girondins of using patriotism to mask their political ambition. Initially his remedy for the crisis was to rally support for the 1791 constitution – hence the title of

[21] *Défenseur de la constitution* 3.

the *Défenseur* – but by mid-June he had begun to express pessimism over the ability of the Legislative Assembly to tackle counter-revolution and by mid-July was clearly moving towards support for a republic. 'The main cause of all our woes is in both the executive and the legislature; in an executive which wants to ruin the state and in a legislature which either cannot or will not save it.'[22] This led him into support for the *fédérés* in their demand for the king's removal and into endorsing the insurrection of 10 August. By the time the *Défenseur* had given way to the *Lettres* in late September, Robespierre's activity on the Paris Commune and the shadow of the September massacres had opened up a gulf between himself and the Girondins which largely defined the three major issues that dominated the paper in the months that followed: the struggle for control of the Convention, the king's trial and the spring crisis of 1793. The early numbers of the *Lettres* focused on the Girondin attacks on himself and Marat, which began in the Convention on 25 September and peaked with Louvet's attack in early November. From the fifth issue onwards the king's fate began to dominate, as Robespierre published his own views on the issues at stake in the trial, while the final numbers in the spring of 1793 dealt with the catastrophe in Holland and Belgium, blaming it on Dumouriez, the high command and their Girondins allies.

The lack of business records for both titles makes their circulation and influence difficult to estimate. Robespierre had a national reputation and enjoyed a loyal following in certain provincial Jacobin clubs, yet the majority of clubs supported the Girondins during the winter of 1792–3 and it was the Girondin press that dominated the national market until it was forcibly removed from the political scene after the *journée* of 2 June. Given the limited appeal of Robespierre's views and the austere format of both papers, it seems probable that both the *Défenseur* and the *Lettres* reached only a small, if committed, audience.[23] That may be one reason why he abandoned journalism in mid-April 1793, although the overriding factor was probably political, for the conflict with the Girondins was coming to a head. Within four months of abandoning the *Lettres*, Robespierre was to become a member of the Committee of Public Safety and wield political power on the national stage for the first time. Once there his views on the rôle and function of the press were to play a crucial rôle in the Committee's dealings with the press.

Robespierre stated his views on the rôle of the press on several occasions during the Revolution and until the spring of 1793 was an

22 *Ibid.*, 11, p. 319.

23 Michael L. Kennedy, *The Jacobin Clubs in the French Revolution. The Middle Years* (Princeton, 1988), p. 179.

unequivocal supporter of press freedom. As early as August 1789 he intervened in the debate on Article XI of the Declaration of the Rights of Man, opposing the wording that was finally adopted. The provision that the abuse of press freedom would be punishable by law under conditions to be specified in later legislation seemed to him an unnecessary restriction of the statement of principle. Instead he favoured a straight assertion of principle, leaving subsequent modifications to the constitution, and cited the American precedent in support of his case. 'There is no tyrant on earth who would hesitate to sign an article as restricted as the one that you are proposing. Press freedom is an inseparable element of the freedom of communicating one's thought to others.'[24] His objections were ignored and he made no significant contribution to discussions on press legislation again until March 1791 when, in the context of disturbances in Douai caused by religious opposition to the civil constitution of the clergy, the *comité des recherches*, *comité militaire* and *comité des rapports* recommended legislation against priests who encouraged violence, in speech or in print. Robespierre opposed the proposal on the grounds that the link between word and action was impossible to prove and that no distinction should be drawn between the actions of priests and ordinary civilians.[25] He later expanded these views in a long speech to the Jacobin club in May 1791, in which he defended press freedom on the grounds of individual freedom and social utility. Freedom of expression was an innate human right, there could be no objective way of judging the impact of the printed word on events, and good ideas would always eliminate the bad if an intellectual free market were allowed to flourish. He referred once more to the American precedent, went on to cite the persecution of Galileo and Descartes and also rolled out the ghost of Rousseau in support of his case:

> Quel sera donc le sort de ceux qui, inspirés par le génie de la liberté, viendront parler des droits et de la dignité de l'homme à des peuples qui les ignorent? Ils alarment presqu'également et les tyrans qu'ils démasquent, et les esclaves qu'ils veulent éclairer. (So what would be the fate of those who, inspired by the spirit of liberty, go to talk of the rights and dignity of man to people who have never heard of them? They will alarm, in almost equal proportion, both the tyrants that they are exposing and the slaves that they want to enlighten.)

He then went on to make a passionate defence of public opinion as the sole judge of private opinion and, in words that contradicted his later

24 *Moniteur universel*, 23–6 August 1789, p. 380; M. J. Mavidal *et al.* (eds.), *Archives Parlementaires de 1781 à 1860*, première série, 96 vols. (Paris, 1879–1990), vol. VIII, p. 83.

25 *Moniteur universel*, 21 March 1791, p. 668; Robespierre, *Œuvres*, vol. VII, pp. 135–48.

actions on the Committee of Public Safety, denied the validity of any form of censorship law:

Public opinion is the sole competent judge of private opinions and the sole legitimate censor of publications. If it approves of them, what right have those in power to condemn them? If it condemns them, why do you need to repress them? How would you dare to stop the free trade in thought ... The control of public opinion over private opinion is gentle, salutary, natural and irresistible; the hold of authority and force is, by its very nature, tyrannical, odious, absurd and monstrous.

Robespierre's conclusion at this time was that neither the state nor politicians should have the power to prosecute journalists, as that would give them the power to stifle criticism at source. Instead it was a citizen's public duty to denounce those in power without fear of retaliation and the only people free to use the courts against the press should be private citizens, defending their reputation through the ordinary law of libel.[26]

Robespierre later reiterated these arguments in the *Défenseur* and the *Lettres à ses commettans*. In the very first edition of the *Défenseur*, he pointed out that he had himself been the victim of sustained press criticism, but that he had never complained and would rely solely on public opinion to defend his reputation. In a later edition he went on to argue that journalism played a crucial rôle in democratic politics, by creating a free circulation of ideas which informed public opinion, thus exerting a control over the activity of politicians who would otherwise follow policies of their own. He then adapted this to Rousseau's vocabulary, arguing that the press mobilised the general will against the particular will, and enabled the Revolution to avoid Rousseau's reservations on the imperfections of representative democracy.

Si vous l'enchaînez, les représentants, déjà supérieurs à toute autorité, délivrés encore de la voix importune des censeurs, éternellement caressés par l'intérêt et par l'adulation, deviennent les propriétaires ou les usufruitiers paisibles de la fortune et des droits de la nation; l'ombre même de la souveraineté disparaît, il ne reste que la plus cruelle, la plus indestructible de toutes les tyrannies; c'est alors qu'il est au moins difficile de contester la vérité de l'anathème foudroyant de Jean-Jacques Rousseau contre le gouvernement représentatif absolu. (If you restrict press freedom, deputies who are already above all other authority, once free of the unwanted attention of their censors, and perpetually flattered by self-interest and adulation, will become the owners and sole users of the wealth and the rights of the nation; even the shadow of sovereignty will disappear and all that will remain will be the most cruel and indestructible of all tyrannies; that is why it is, to say the least, difficult to contest the truth of the crushing

[26] *Discours sur la liberté de la presse, prononcé à la société des amis de la constitution, le 11 mai 1791, par Maximilien Robespierre, député à l'Assemblée Nationale, et membre de cette société* (Paris, 1791).

condemnation of completely representative government by Jean-Jacques Rousseau.)[27]

Robespierre's position remained largely unchanged well into the spring of 1793 and the very last edition of the *Lettres* contains his proposed text for a Declaration of the Rights of Man for the constitution that the Convention was debating, in which Article IV asserts: 'The right to meet peacefully and the right to express one's opinions in print or in any other manner are such necessary consequences of human liberty that the need to state them supposes the presence or the recent memory of despotism.'[28] Yet, behind the words, his position had already begun to change for, since the collapse of the monarchy on 10 August 1792, press censorship had become a fact of political life. Many royalist newspapers had been closed down and although several survived by camouflaging their royalism behind a cover of moderate republicanism, legislation on 4 December 1792 laid down the death penalty for those who advocated the return of the monarchy. On 29 March 1793, anyone who advocated land redistribution or who attacked national sovereignty was also made liable for execution, and the climate of opinion was clearly running in favour of censorship.[29] Robespierre made no objection to this, and in the Convention on 19 April opposed Buzot's call for total press freedom, on the grounds that revolutions were exceptional events which required the state to use exceptional powers to crush conspiracies: 'The interests of the Revolution can require certain measures against a conspiracy based on press freedom.'[30] His growing reservations were prompted by regular attacks being made on him in the Girondin press and by the impact of Roland's work at the Ministry of the Interior in setting up the *bureau d'esprit public* to dispense subsidies to Girondin pamphleteers and journalists.[31] In late November 1792, he accused Roland of spending enough money to feed 100,000 poor families and queried whether press freedom had not developed into a mechanism for enabling governments to mislead public opinion and crush individual freedom.[32] Initially he clung to his original belief that truth would naturally triumph over error and in the Jacobin club in mid-December 1792, during a venomous debate on the activity of the *bureau d'esprit public*, he recommended that the club should meet earlier every

27 *Défenseur* V. 28 *Lettres à ses commettans* 2e série, 10, p. 361.

29 A. Soderjhelm, *Le régime de la presse dans la Révolution française*, 2 vols. (Helsingfors and Paris, 1900–1), vol. II, pp. 221–53.

30 *Archives Parlementaires*, vol. LXII, p. 707; Robespierre, *Œuvres*, vol. IX, p. 452.

31 Marc Bouloiseau, 'Robespierre d'après les journaux girondins', in *Actes du colloque Robespierre. XIIe congrès international des sciences historiques (Vienne, 3 septembre 1965). Avant-propos par Albert Soboul* (Paris, 1967), pp. 3–17.

32 *Lettres à ses commettans* 1er série, 6, p. 77.

day, so that the *Patriote français* and the *Chronique de Paris* could be publicly read out to members to provide instruction in error. As late as May 1793, he opposed coercive measures and warned deputies against the temptation of trying to mould public opinion.[33]

Over the summer of 1793, once the Girondins had been expelled from the Convention, those beliefs collapsed. Robespierre then attacked journalists as 'the most dangerous enemies of liberty', and, on 16 June, when the Minister of the Interior complained of attacks being made on him in the *Tableau politique*, claimed that these attacks were part of a conspiracy to systematically denigrate the institutions of state; until that conspiracy was crushed, no man of virtue could be safe. He urged deputies to give the Committee of Public Safety power to take severe measures against journalists who undermined popular freedom and, according to one report, concluded with the assertion that press freedom was only applicable in peacetime and periods of calm.[34] At least one journalist wisely read the writing on the wall, for two days later the political editor of the *Moniteur*, Grandville, wrote an obsequious letter to him assuring him that the *Moniteur* had been giving tacit support to the Mountain since the previous autumn, by deliberately reducing its coverage of Girondin speeches: 'All you need is to cast a glance over our copies for the last month, to see that no newspaper has contributed more to blighting public regard for the faction that will soon be brought to account.' According to Grandville, this had cost him a thousand subscribers in the federalist areas of the Midi.[35]

Once he joined the Committee of Public Safety in late July, Robespierre was in a position to enforce his attitudes on the press, and he wasted little time in doing so. On 2 August, Couthon presented a report for the Committee of Public Safety which alleged that the editor of the *Annales patriotiques*, Carra, had advocated supporting the Duke of Brunswick in the previous summer. The Convention promptly ordered Carra's arrest and, when he tried to defend himself, Robespierre intervened with the allegation that Carra had wanted to put Brunswick on the throne. When Carra tried to reply, he retorted, 'Ce n'est point aux conspirateurs à interrompre le défenseur de la liberté.' ('Conspirators have no right to interrupt the defender of liberty.') Carra was sent to the Revolutionary Tribunal and executed two months later.[36] At the

[33] Robespierre, *Œuvres*, vol. IX, pp. 159–60; Albert Laponneraye, *Œuvres de Maximilien Robespierre*, 3 vols. (Paris, 1842), vol. III, pp. 372–3.
[34] *Archives Parlementaires*, vol. LXXVI, p. 582; Robespierre, *Œuvres*, vol. IX, p. 452.
[35] Courtois, *Papiers inédits*, vol. II, p. 129.
[36] Robespierre, *Œuvres*, vol. X, pp. 47–9.

Jacobin club in early September, Robespierre turned on Prudhomme, owner of the *Révolutions de Paris*, and in late December reprimanded the *Moniteur* for its omissions and inaccuracies. He was particularly irked by the fact that his own speech on the principles of revolutionary government had included a reference to 'la république une et universelle' instead of 'la république une et indivisible', an error which played into the hands of the cosmopolitan radicals whom by now he suspected of working for France's enemies to undermine the Revolution.[37]

None the less, the most prominent example of Robespierre's hostility to journalism came during the political conflict between *Exagérés* and indulgents during the winter of 1793–4. This was a conflict spearheaded by two journalists, Hébert and Desmoulins, in which Robespierre appears to have initially encouraged Desmoulins's campaign in the *Vieux Cordelier* for a scaling-down of the Terror and the restoration of press freedom.[38] Yet after Collot's return from Lyon and Fabre d'Eglantine's arrest in the East India Company investigations, he changed direction, closed ranks with colleagues on the Committee of Public Safety and denounced both extremists and moderates as equally intent on destroying the Revolution. On 18 Nivôse Year II (7 January 1794), he criticised Desmoulins in the Jacobin club, concluding with the light-hearted suggestion that copies of his *Vieux Cordelier* should be burnt in the middle of the room. Desmoulins's retort that burning was no reply made him adopt a more menacing tone with the accusation that Camille was the unwitting dupe of a 'wretched faction' intent on ruining the Revolution.[39] His attitude towards such 'dupes' was clarified in the speech on political morality that he delivered to the Convention on 17 Pluviôse Year II (5 February 1794), in which he denounced the 'mercenary scribblers who are bribed to dishonour the cause of the people, to extinguish public virtue, fan the fire of civil discord, and prepare the way for political counter-revolution by encouraging a moral counter-revolution first'.[40] Within a month these were the charges levelled by Fouquier-Tinville against Hébert in the Revolutionary Tribunal, as he cited articles from the *Père Duchesne* from as far back as the previous June that were critical of the Convention and the Committee of Public Safety. Desmoulins too, who followed Hébert to the guillotine a matter of days later, was condemned

[37] AN, AFII 66 reg. 484, pièces 18, 27; *Correspondance de Maximilien et Augustin Robespierre*, p. 237.

[38] Jean-Paul Bertaud, *Camille et Lucille Desmoulins* (Paris, 1986), pp. 239ff.

[39] Robespierre, *Œuvres*, vol. X, pp. 307–8.

[40] *Rapport sur les principes de morale politique qui doivent guider la Convention Nationale dans l'administration intérieure de la République* (Paris, n.d.).

for 'crimes' that included his attack on the Terror in the third number of the *Vieux Cordelier*.[41]

Robespierre's hostility to the press continued into the summer of 1794 with biting criticism of the Jacobin club's newspaper, the *Journal de la montagne*, and an attack on the *Moniteur*. Both reflected his belief that journalists worked for their private interest rather than for the general good, on behalf of a counter-revolutionary conspiracy that was undermining the Revolution.

> Anyone who knows anything about the Revolution and its enemies must realise their tactic: they have several, but the simplest and most powerful is to mislead public opinion over principles and men: that is why newspapers always have a rôle to play in revolutions. Enemies have always paid writers; as a result journalists habitually provide moral support for internal and external enemies . . .[42]

A free press was now, by definition, an enemy press, the only reliable press was one that lay under government control and Robespierre played a central part in encouraging this control through the Committee of Public Safety's policy of subsidising compliant journalists. For the most part this was done by taking out block subscriptions to the *Moniteur*, the *Antifédéraliste*, the *Journal universel* and the *Journal des hommes libres* for distribution to Jacobin clubs and administrations.[43] Yet Robespierre's signature was also on the decision taken in early August 1793 to create an unofficial government newspaper, the *Feuille du salut public*, which was used to defend the Committee's policies and control the flow of news.[44] The Committee of Public Safety was not alone in doing this, for individual ministries, and particularly the Ministry of War, played a major rôle too.[45]

Robespierre's attitude towards the press by the time of his arrest and death in the summer of 1794 was diametrically opposed to the one that he had defended so tenaciously just two years previously. The defender of press freedom had become the champion of censorship, just as the political democrat had developed into the apologist for revolutionary

[41] A. Tuetey, *Répertoire général des sources manuscrits de l'histoire de Paris pendant la Révolution française*, 11 vols. (Paris, 1890–1914), vol. X, p. 116; Bertaud, *Camille et Lucille Desmoulins*, pp. 283–4.

[42] Robespierre, *Œuvres*, vol. X, pp. 387, 503.

[43] M. Bouloiseau, 'Les débats parlementaires pendant la terreur et leur diffusion', *AHRF* 35 (1963), 337–45; AN, AFII 66 reg. 484, pièces 6, 12, 31; F.-A. Aulard, 'La presse officieuse sous la terreur', in *Etudes et leçons sur la Révolution française*, 1er série (Paris, 1890), pp. 227–40.

[44] AN, AFII 66 reg. 484, pièces 2, 3, 4, 5; Aulard (ed.), *Recueil des actes du comité de salut public*, vol. V, pp. 459, 506.

[45] A. Mathiez, 'La presse subventionnée en l'an II', *Annales révolutionnaires* 10 (1918), 112–13.

dictatorship. The reasons for that change, and the degree to which the events of 1789 ever offered the chance of establishing a genuinely liberal political régime, have been bitterly debated since François Furet published his *Penser la Révolution française* in 1978.[46] This short study of one aspect of Robespierre's activities, his journalism, can offer only a very tangential contribution to the debate. Yet his attitude to the press and to journalists does point the way towards two potential weaknesses in the revisionist argument. The first relates to his early defence of press freedom, for despite the revisionist argument that Rousseauist ideas of regeneration combined with the early development of plot theory to build political intolerance into revolutionary discourse from the outset, Robespierre's views on the press until the spring of 1792 were clear and consistent. He was a follower of Rousseau, a passionate believer in the need to inject virtue into personal and political behaviour, and convinced that plots and conspiracies lay behind almost every setback that the Revolution suffered. His political world was polarised between the virtuous and the wicked, the friends of the people and its enemies, and this polarity was stated frequently in both his newspapers. Yet this was an outlook that he shared with his Girondin rivals, many of whom also admired Rousseau, believed passionately in the need for social regeneration and were intolerant of political pluralism.[47] Moreover, Robespierre remained adamant until the spring of 1793 that political conflict could only be resolved by free argument, based on the Enlightenment belief in the ability of reason to discover truth and discount error. Because of this he was both consistent and tenacious in his defence of press freedom: intolerant of his opponents' views, but tolerant of their right to express them until the tide of political events from the autumn of 1792 onwards convinced him, and many of his Jacobin colleagues, that treason threatened the achievements of the Revolution. It was not ideology that drove Robespierre towards intolerance but the impact on that ideology of events and fears. This makes it difficult to accept that his actions of 1794 were already embedded in his ideology of 1789.

The second contribution of Robespierre's press activity to the revisionist debate centres on the nature of the repression which he shaped and supported during the Terror. Many journalists and printers were guillotined in Year II, either for their journalism or for their political activity, and Robespierre clearly regarded a free press as a potential ally of

[46] F. Furet, *Penser la Révolution française* (Paris, 1978).

[47] Marcel Dorigny, 'François-Xavier Lanthenas et la formation du citoyen: les paradoxes du libéralisme girondin?', in Claude Mazauric (ed.), *La Révolution française et l'homme moderne* (Paris, 1988), pp. 409–17; Norman Hampson, *Will and Circumstance. Montesquieu, Rousseau and the French Revolution* (London, 1983), pp. 149–266.

counter-revolution.[48] Yet by concentrating too closely on the guillotine's blade and Robespierre's words, we run the risk of overstating the scale of the repression that took place. For journalists arrested and executed during the Terror were charged under the provisions of the law of 4 December 1792 which banned support for the monarchy, the law of 29 March 1793 which banned attacks on the Convention and on property, and the law of suspects of 17 September 1793 which provided a blanket definition of political crime. There was no specific press law to match the legislation that the Directory enforced in 1796 and 1797, and, despite the Committee of Public Safety's decision on 14 Frimaire (4 December 1793) to take out a block subscription to all Parisian newspapers, it never had a press bureau to exercise regular surveillance on journalists in the way that the Directory later did. There was no return to the prior censorship of the ancien régime under Robespierre and no anticipation of the executive censorship of Napoleon. Instead it was the bourgeois republic of the Directory that first introduced a restrictive press law, closed down newspapers by executive decree and exiled journalists for their political views, setting a precedent that Bonaparte was to follow. The number of political journals published in Paris certainly dipped during the Terror from around fifty-eight to just over forty, and some of this decline may have been due to the repressive political atmosphere. Yet economic factors also played a major rôle, and the number of provincial papers may even have risen. The Terror was certainly arbitrary towards journalists but it could be tolerant too and several royalist newspapers were able to continue in existence, making token gestures towards Jacobin orthodoxy while expressing their latent hostility to the régime through nuances of phrase or selective reporting.[49] Even within the Jacobin press, the newspapers which the régime subsidised and promoted, there was a wide divergence of approach and opinion and no attempt to create a unified 'party line'. The press of the Terror, which Robespierre denounced, was by no means as monolithic, and the scale of censorship by no means as severe, as has often been suggested. The most eloquent testimony to this came in the weeks after Robespierre's execution as journalists throughout the country queued up to condemn him as a dictator and tyrant but then rapidly scattered to all parts of the political spectrum as the Terror collapsed and parliamentary politics returned.[50] The impact that Robespierre had on the press

[48] Hugh Gough, *The Newspaper Press in the French Revolution* (London, 1988), pp. 100–3.

[49] Jeremy Popkin, 'The royalist press in the reign of Terror', *Journal of Modern History* 51 (1979), 685–700; Jean-Paul Bertaud, 'An open file: the press under the Terror', in Keith Michael Baker *et al.* (eds.), *The French Revolution and the Creation of Modern Political Culture*, 4 vols. (Oxford, 1987–94), vol. IV, pp. 297–308.

[50] For a short selection, see Walter, *Robespierre*, vol. II, pp. 360–5.

during the Terror was to prove transitory and his earlier endorsement of it as an essential part of the liberal parliamentary process, viewed from the perspective of the nineteenth and twentieth centuries, was to prove more long lasting.

8 Robespierre, the war and its organisation

Alan Forrest

Most of Robespierre's biographers have given scant attention to his rôle as an organiser of war or as a military strategist.[1] He talked relatively little of these matters, preferring to leave them to others, to men more versed in the culture of the military and the science of war. In this he showed a wholly appropriate discretion. After all, the Convention was not short of men with military skills and battle experience: like other able men of their generation, they were drawn into politics in the 1790s as the forum where the most vital decisions were taken and where French society could most effectively be reformed. Carnot and Prieur de la Côte-d'Or were just two of the revolutionary leaders whose previous experience of the army gave them precious insights into military organisation and troop motivation,[2] while others, and most notably Saint-Just, learned much from practical missions to the armies in the field.[3] Robespierre, in contrast, stayed in Paris, maintaining his power base in the political arena of the Convention and the Jacobin club. He never left Paris on mission, either to the provinces or to the frontiers; he made no attempt to visit the troops once the war was declared. In political terms this was undoubtedly a valid choice to make, but it was not one that gave him any special prestige in military circles, nor did it acquaint him with the practical problems faced by the troops on the ground. This may help explain why so many of his pronouncements on the war retained a high degree of theoretical aloofness which reflected his intellectual preference but which also betrayed serious areas of inexperience. He knew that he could never hope to master the military brief as he could the political stage, and he confessed to Fréron that his greatest regret was his failure to learn the art of war.[4] He was

[1] See, for instance, J. M. Thompson, *Robespierre*, 2 vols. (Oxford, 1935); Norman Hampson, *The Life and Opinions of Maximilien Robespierre* (London, 1974); and David P. Jordan, *The Revolutionary Career of Maximilien Robespierre* (New York, 1985).
[2] A. Kuscinski, *Dictionnaire des Conventionnels* (Paris, 1916), pp. 110–14, 509–11.
[3] Jean-Pierre Gross, *Saint-Just, sa politique et ses missions* (Paris, 1976).
[4] Jordan, *Robespierre*, p. 83.

surely right to conclude that others were better equipped than he to advise on the day-to-day issues of the military campaigns.

Indeed, Robespierre often comes across in his speeches and his writings as a man consumed by the ideological context of the war and bored, even alienated, by the detail of military tactics. His dislike of army officers and their closed, exclusive culture was barely concealed, and he was always ready to believe that it was their plots and machinations that were responsible for checks and defeats on the battlefield. Once at the height of his power, he had little to say about the conduct of hostilities: his months on the great Committee of Public Safety (from July 1793 until his fall from grace at Thermidor) were punctuated by only occasional references to military matters, and then almost exclusively to their political implications. Thus, on 12 August 1793, he spoke in support of Thirion's plea for a *levée en masse* to drive back the enemy.[5] On 8 September, he opposed the Mâcon Jacobin club when they heaped praise on General Kellermann, arguing that it was Kellermann's errors that had delayed the surrender of Lyon during the summer months.[6] And he responded to the threat along the northern frontier by urging a sustained effort against all France's enemies and insisting that no distinction should be made between them. For, he argued, 'since the start of the Revolution, one has had to observe that there are in France two quite distinct factions – the Anglo-Prussian faction and the Austrian – both united against the Republic'.[7]

Robespierre's principal contribution to the military debate, indeed, was his courageous stand in 1792 against any French declaration of war and his reasoned case that involvement in a European conflict must necessarily play into the hands of those who had shown themselves the most ruthless enemies of the revolutionary cause. Even after hostilities had been declared he would remain suspicious of politicians who sought to distract opinion on to foreign targets when there were, in his eyes at least, far more pressing battles to be won at home. Robespierre refused to share in the national tendency to glory in military victories or in the massive human sacrifice which they involved. He remained, even at the height of the war, a political animal for whom the primacy of politics was a matter of faith. The Revolution could only be made secure by political initiatives, by the creation in France of a stable political culture, and in that process unnecessary foreign adventures were a damaging irrelevance. He believed devoutly that civic virtue remained the most important ingredient in victory, just as he suspected treachery behind every setback in the field. On the eve of Wattignies, for instance, he told

[5] Robespierre, *Œuvres*, vol. X, p. 69. [6] *Ibid.*, vol. X, p. 102.
[7] *Ibid.*, vol. X, p. 155.

the Convention that victory could only come through public vigilance and patriotism. He feared the work of enemy agents in the armies, and warned that 'if a setback occurs, if the army retreats, the whole of the French nation must rise up and act as its rearguard'.[8] It was an outlook that did little to endear him to the generals, and one which, in more conventional circumstances, might seem to make him curiously ill-prepared for the rôle of war leader which he was destined to assume.

Indeed, his attitude towards the declaration of war suggests that Robespierre inherited this mantle very much against his will. His opposition was founded not just on a deep distrust of the motives of his political opponents, but also, as David Jordan has noted, on his own reading of history.[9] This reading had little time for wars of liberation, since he was persuaded that the interests of war and of revolution were irrevocably opposed. Foreign peoples, whatever the Girondins might think, were most unlikely to welcome armed missionaries from France, bringing the message of revolution in their knapsacks. And the cost to France, and particularly to her volunteers, could become too terrible to contemplate. So while he was in no doubt that the ambitions of the Austrian emperor must be contained – in his own words, 'it is necessary to contain him in the manner that Popilius [*sic*: Pompey?] contained Mithridates'[10] – that did not mean that France must rush to declare an impossible and unwinnable war across a whole continent. In January 1792, in a chamber stirred to heights of bellicose patriotism by Brissot and his supporters, this was not an easy message to get across, and Robespierre seemed a rather isolated figure. Yet he persisted in his opposition to what he saw as a war party forming within the majority. On 18 December 1791, he raised his first public objections to war; and in two of his most memorable speeches, on 2 and 11 January 1792, he hammered his message home. Certainly, he admitted, 'I favour, just as much as M. Brissot, a war to further the reign of liberty, and would also give myself over to the pleasure of regaling you with all the successes in advance.' But the best-laid plans could be rendered hollow by events, as by treason. 'In the circumstances in which I find my country, I look around uneasily and wonder whether the war we shall wage will be the one which enthusiasm promises us.'[11] And he went further, questioning the motives of those advocating conflict, and warning that war would simply play into the hands of France's enemies.

This stance was a difficult one to maintain once war was declared and French soldiers were fighting and dying in the North and along the Rhine. In wartime all politicians must to some degree close rank and

[8] *Ibid.*, vol. X, p. 146.
[9] Jordan, *Robespierre*, p. 85.
[10] Robespierre, *Œuvres*, vol. VIII, p. 25.
[11] *Ibid.*, vol. VIII, pp. 75–6.

support the men who are fighting in their name. And Robespierre was acutely conscious that his public image and his reputation as a patriot were at risk. He answered his opponents' charges with typical rhetorical skill, drawing a fine distinction between what he termed the patriotism of the true republican and that which pertained in non-revolutionary times. A revolutionary war must be waged, he claimed, to free subjects and slaves from unjust tyranny, not for the traditional reasons of defending dynasties and expanding frontiers. In 1792, the war that stretched out before the French had little about it that was truly revolutionary. Indeed, argued Robespierre, such a war could only favour the forces of counter-revolution, since it would play into the hands of those who opposed the sovereignty of the people. The risks of Caesarism were clear, for in wartime the powers of the generals would grow at the expense of ordinary soldiers, and the power of the king and the court at the expense of the Assembly. These dangers should not be overlooked, he reminded his listeners; in troubled periods of history, generals often became the arbiters of the fate of their countries.

> If they are Caesars or Cromwells, they seize power for themselves. If they are spineless courtiers, uninterested in doing good yet dangerous when they seek to do harm, they go back to lay their power at their master's feet, and help him to resume arbitrary power on condition they become his chief servants.[12]

The future of the Revolution itself was at risk.

But if Robespierre opposed the declaration of war, he could do nothing to prevent it, and, when the Jacobins came to power, he, as much as any other leader, had to live with its consequences. He might not see the necessity for war or appreciate the wisdom of dissipating France's energies across her frontiers. He might equate the enthusiasms of the Brissotins with the intrigues of the court and the siren voices of counter-revolution; there was, after all, a paranoic streak in Robespierre's psychology which found it easier to believe that others were seeking to undermine the Revolution than to accept that virtue might not always have its immediate reward. But within the constraints which this ideological vision imposed, he was not deaf to the needs of the military, nor was he unmoved by the calls for reform. He was a war leader in spite of himself, and of the problems which the Revolution faced in the summer of 1793 the most urgent by far was to reverse a series of defeats and restore morale in the armies. Whatever his personal inclinations, Robespierre had no choice but to give priority to the military, even at the cost of sacrificing parts of his domestic programme. He could not do otherwise; it was a responsibility he could not shirk.

[12] *Ibid.*, vol. VIII, p. 49.

In particular, Robespierre had to seek ways to improve the capability of the French armies in the field. He did this in characteristic fashion, taking up the cause of root-and-branch reform that would destroy many of the old mentalities in the army and promote a new vision, one compatible with the ideals of the Revolution itself. Most significant, perhaps, was his rôle in the political battle for the *amalgame*, the debate over the method to be adopted to integrate the two very different armies which the Revolution had brought into existence. There was increasing agreement in political circles that the *status quo* was no longer sustainable: an army which contained different kinds of soldiers, different kinds of regiments, different kinds of ambition and honour, even different levels of pay. But how could the new volunteers and the old line troops – including, of course, those who had been recruited into the line since 1789 – be blended into a single and effective fighting force? Robespierre rejected the simplest administrative answer, that of incorporation, on the grounds that the identity of the volunteers, with all their enthusiasm and patriotic commitment, would be lost. Their units would be dissolved as the men who composed them were incorporated into the old regiments of the line, and that for Robespierre was politically unthinkable. But the more radical solution of amalgamation – the creation of a new army in which it would be the line units that would be submerged into large new volunteer battalions – would take too long, given the gravity of the emergency which the country was facing. Hence Robespierre argued for Dubois-Crancé's compromise solution, that of *embrigadement*, the creation of new fighting units, or *demi-brigades*, by bringing together two battalions of volunteers and one of the line to fight alongside one another under a common command. In Dubois-Crancé's proposal he saw a pragmatic answer to the needs of the military that was compatible with his own democratic ideology.[13]

This instance is instructive as it shows how far Robespierre gave priority to political considerations, even in the face of an immediate military threat. He would not have understood this dichotomy in such terms: for him – unlike several other prominent republicans of his day – there could be no possible conflict between political reliability and executive efficiency, no reason why Jacobin militants like Lavalette should not be entrusted with key military commands.[14] Indeed, when Lavalette was suspended from his command in July 1793, Robespierre rushed to his defence, pointing to his record in stifling moderate and anti-revolutionary plots in the Armée du Nord. It was, he told the

[13] Jean-Paul Bertaud, *La Révolution armée: les soldats-citoyens et la Révolution française* (Paris, 1979), pp. 158–60.

[14] Alan Forrest, *The Soldiers of the French Revolution* (Durham, N.C., 1990), pp. 97–9.

Convention, astonishing that 'he who has made so many efforts to advance the cause of the people should have succumbed at the tribunal of your agents'.[15] For Robespierre believed devoutly that an effective army must be dependent on sound political ideology, since it was axiomatic that free men would fight with greater bravery and determination than those whose commitment was bought by kings and tyrants. This meant, in turn, that a revolutionary army had to be one whose principles were compatible with the message of the Revolution itself. Its soldiers had to be able to see the value of the work they did and of the sacrifice that was expected of them. Propaganda was therefore almost as crucial as field training in Year II, and lessons in republican principle as necessary a preparation for battle as the science of war.

This was an issue that would continue to divide revolutionary leaders throughout the 1790s, though, by the time of the Directory, it was generally accepted that professionalism was the most vital attribute and that ideological militancy was no substitute for good training in tactics and the manipulation of arms. In the restructuring of the army Robespierre would always number himself among those who urged greater democracy and a wider range of responsibility for the common soldier. This was all the more important in view of the authoritarian traditions of the old royal regiments, traditions which made the line army seem a highly inappropriate vehicle for revolutionary change. Punishments were savage, officers remote and uninterested in the welfare of their men. Soldiers obeyed through fear rather than by consent.[16] In the Jacobin debates on restructuring the army, Robespierre favoured much freer movement between the ranks and spoke out strongly for the principle of election, at least for junior officers and NCOs. It was a startlingly novel notion – that soldiers knew the qualities which they most admired in others and were therefore the best judges of those who should lead them into battle. In the event, the Convention opted for a compromise solution, whereby the troops would put forward three names and the relevant officers would make the final decision. Robespierre saw this as a contradiction and as a betrayal of a fundamental democratic principle. He wanted direct elections by those of the rank below that in which the appointment was being made, and he castigated the Convention's war committee for its lack of courage in violating what he saw as one of the central principles of the Revolution. What they were proposing, he regarded as a fudge that could satisfy no one. 'It is a kind of incomplete election which mixes two contradictory

[15] Robespierre, *Œuvres*, vol. IX, p. 628.

[16] E. Léonard, *L'armée et ses problèmes au dix-huitième siècle* (Paris, 1958), pp. 43ff.

systems – selection by the officers and selection by lower ranks.'[17] They should have followed the logic of their convictions, argued Robespierre, and opted for one system or the other.

Behind this principled assault lay another motive, however, in which ideology played a less obvious part – Robespierre's almost pathological distrust of the officer class. This had its roots in the nature of the royal army which, as Isser Woloch has noted, was suffering a serious crisis of confidence even before the disorders of 1789 'corroded its discipline and coherence'.[18] The officers of the ancien régime were aristocrats whose oath of loyalty had bound them to the king, and they did, of course, contain among their number many who had no love for the new order, no allegiance to the sovereign people or the ideals of the Revolution. Just how dubious was their loyalty had been demonstrated by the colossal rates of resignation and defection during the months of the constitutional monarchy, when more than one-third of all officers had abandoned their posts, and by the refusal of many to serve the state once Louis XVI had taken the road to Varennes.[19] Robespierre shared the widespread revolutionary fear of an aristocratic plot, and, if that plot were to end in military insurrection, it was clear where its leaders would be found. Besides, he had an almost pathological dislike of Lafayette, mirrored shortly afterwards by his dislike of Dumouriez.[20] Their defections merely convinced him that the armies must contain others, even other former revolutionary heroes, whose loyalty to the people was suspect and who might at any time turn their firepower against Paris. So great was his fear of the officer class that he could contemplate only one solution, its immediate dissolution. In January 1792, he even argued that winning battles was not everything, since victories which further enhanced the powers and prestige of the officers could be deeply damaging to the cause of the nation. 'The violation of the principles on which liberty rests,' he declared, 'the corrosion of public spirit, are more terrible disasters than a battle lost.' Indeed, he went on, in present circumstances 'the very victories of our generals might be more lethal than our defeats'.[21]

This anti-noble, anti-officer prejudice led Robespierre in a number of different directions. It prejudiced him against the line and in favour of the new volunteer battalions whose officers might be assumed to share his revolutionary ideology. It encouraged him to seek new ways of

17 Robespierre, *Œuvres*, vol. V, p. 295.
18 Isser Woloch, *The New Regime* (New York, 1994), p. 381.
19 Samuel F. Scott, *The Response of the Royal Army to the French Revolution* (Oxford, 1978), p. 109.
20 Jordan, *Robespierre*, p. 94.
21 Robespierre, *Œuvres*, vol. VIII, p. 101.

finding individuals to promote to the officer grades: after all, the Ecole Militaire had long been an exclusively aristocratic preserve, and there was no established tradition whereby commoners could aspire to the higher ranks of the military. It led him to argue that the political loyalties of army officers were at least as important under a revolutionary régime as their technical competence – an approach which opened up a larger debate between those who argued for a revolutionary army, loyal to republican ideals, and those who felt that only a mastery of tactics and strategy could bring the successes in the field which France so desperately sought. And it persuaded him of the need to extend police surveillance to the armies in the same way as to the departments – with deputies on mission, committees of surveillance and revolutionary committees all operating in the larger armies on the frontiers, and with revolutionary justice handed down and carried out inside the military camps themselves. By 1793, Robespierre and his highly ideological Minister of War, Bouchotte, were arguing that soldiers should not only be encouraged to join Jacobin clubs in their regiments or in the towns where they were garrisoned, but that their opinions should be actively sought on the conduct of the war by the officers who were placed in command of them. They were, after all, the principal victims of incompetent and treasonable commanders, and they should not be expected to suffer in silence.

Robespierre believed passionately that the simple rank of general should not suffice to protect an individual from the consequences of his crimes. He demanded, for instance, that General Dillon should be investigated after his unauthorised communication with the landgrave of Hesse in 1792;[22] and gave credence to every rumour coming out of Lille. Everyone, he assured the Convention (without producing a single shred of evidence to support his claim), believed that Custine and Lamarlière had been plotting to hand over the city of Lille to the Austrians. Immediate retribution was called for.[23] And defeats in the Vendée could be explained only by treason on a massive scale. When Saumur fell, for instance, he demanded that all those responsible be called to account, proposing the arrest of two republican commanders, Westermann and Ligonier, the dismissal of General Menou, and the instant recall of two deputies on mission to the army in the West.[24] In short, he listened keenly to the stream of denunciations that came from soldiers and political societies within the armies, and was among the first to insist that they be acted upon. Given that such denunciations were frequent, especially in the Armée du Nord, a number of generals,

[22] *Ibid.*, vol. V, p. 39. [23] *Ibid.*, vol. IX, p. 629. [24] *Ibid.*, vol. IX, pp. 576–7.

among them Custine, Luckner and Houchard, would pay for their indiscretions on the guillotine.[25]

If he showed his distrust of the officer class, Robespierre never tired of protesting his interest in the welfare of the ordinary soldiers under its command.[26] They had sprung from the people; many of them had volunteered for service; it followed that they shared the outlook of the mass of the population, and the people, as Robespierre persistently told his audiences, were trustworthy, moral, good. There was, of course, a strong element of populism in this. The eighteenth-century soldier was not used to hearing his praises sung by his political masters; liberated by 1789 and driven to mutiny by the brutality of his superiors, the revolutionary soldier was now ready for his new rôle as a soldier-citizen, a rôle which Robespierre preached with fervent passion. The troops were national guardsmen, answerable to the people, and nothing should be done that would jeopardise that special relationship. In particular, he urged that they should remain in touch with the people, that it was not the duty of revolutionaries to drill them into alien thinking, removed from the population they represented. 'Carefully avoid', he urged the deputies, 'everything that could ignite in the souls of the *citoyens-soldats* such military spirit as cuts off soldiers from citizens and which yokes glory and self-interest to things that make for the ruin of citizens.'[27] Civilians and soldiers must think of themselves as one.

An army of volunteers was composed of ordinary Frenchmen, including those who had attacked the Bastille and stormed local *châteaux* in the outburst of fraternal triumphalism that was 1789. For Robespierre, their enthusiasm and revolutionary commitment were themselves a source of military strength. France should have an army in its own image, an army which shared the essential aspirations of the people. That army, he was convinced, must be committed to a revolutionary ideal. For this reason he approved the voluntary principle which underpinned the first levies, in 1791 and 1792, but distrusted the reluctant and resentful armies produced by the *levée des 300,000* in the spring of 1793, and was driven by pragmatism to accept the more democratic *levée en masse* in August. The troops raised by levies, he argued, were not true volunteers, but men condemned to fight by the drawing of lots or

25 John A. Lynn, *The Bayonets of the Republic: Motivation and Tactics in the Army of Revolutionary France 1791–94* (Urbana, 1984), pp. 13–14.

26 An earlier version of this discussion of Robespierre's concern for the ordinary soldier was given to the bicentennial conference on Robespierre at Arras in 1993. This has since appeared as 'Robespierre: la guerre et les soldats', in Jean-Pierre Jessenne, Gilles Deregnaucourt, Jean-Pierre Hirsch and Hervé Leuwers (eds.), *Robespierre: De la Nation artésienne à la République et aux Nations* (Lille, 1994), pp. 359–68.

27 Robespierre, *Œuvres*, vol. VII, p. 263.

by some system of designation. They did not necessarily share a commitment to the common cause of the nation. In contrast, Robespierre persisted in his faith in the volunteers, in men who had risen from the ranks of the people burning with a fierce love of liberty. Such men, he insisted, could never endanger the freedom enjoyed by their fellow citizens, since it was illogical that the people should wish to oppress themselves.[28] Besides, equality demanded that the sacrifice should be shared. 'In a republic', he said,

> every citizen is born a soldier. The arduous profession of arms is not the lot of one class or a part of the citizen body, destined to go alone to face the dangers of combat, whilst the rest perpetually enjoy the honours and the benefits of administration, legislation or teaching and enjoy all the pleasures of domestic life, reading peacefully by the fireside about the joyous outcomes or the disasters of the campaigns.[29]

Such inequality could only be an affront to citizenship.

If the national guardsmen were naturally good and devoted to the interests of France, it followed that blame for defeats and humiliations could not reasonably rest with them. Soldiers were the victims of the misconduct of others. Yet under the ancien régime it had been the ordinary infantryman who had been shot, hanged or broken on the wheel for his crimes, while aristocratic officers had been judged by a different, and altogether more lenient, disciplinary code. To Robespierre, as to others on the radical wing of politics, this represented intolerable injustice, rendered even more flagrant by the sentences handed down to the mutineers at Nancy in 1790. He repeatedly demanded that the law be made equal for all, since all were citizens and all must enjoy equal access to justice. This was a principle which could not be overlooked merely because the men in question were soldiers; that fact alone did not imply that they had forfeited their rights as citizens, even if army life did mean that they owed total obedience to the state. The whole question of military discipline in a society of free men worried Robespierre. For while he recognised that an army had to obey orders, he refused to accept that that excluded all possibility of independent thought. Discipline should be by consent, not blindly imposed. In September 1790, in the course of one of his many speeches on this theme, he urged that in the matter of punishment the soldier should be treated in exactly the same way as his superiors, since 'sentiments of honour are the same in both ranks'. But the level of instruction, of political understanding and acumen, was not the same; and whereas the existing law tended to punish the ranks more harshly than their officers, Robespierre argued that it was often the officers who had misled them in

[28] *Ibid.*, vol. VII, p. 266. [29] *Ibid.*, vol. V, p. 282.

the first place. At Nancy, Bouillé wanted to impose summary sentences on those who had joined the mutiny as a deterrent to others. But Robespierre took the side of the men. 'Do you not see', he harangued the Assembly, 'that the officers have sought to mislead the men? And it is against these deceived soldiers, against these soldiers whose patriotism has blundered, that you wish to send other soldiers!'[30] The injustice of a system geared to the interests of the officers was, he implied, quite unashamed.

In this the army was, of course, a symbol, a metaphor for society as a whole. It was also an invaluable training ground for the next generation of citizens, whose attitudes would be shaped by their experience in the battalions. Robespierre's public pronouncements reflected this very faithfully. On the one hand, he argued the material case of the troops, deploring the shortage of supplies and arms, denouncing crooked or exploitative suppliers, insisting that the common soldiers had as much right to decent pensions as their superiors. They also had some claims on land. Robespierre shared the concern of some of his radical colleagues that serving soldiers should not be arbitrarily denied the benefits of *partage* simply because they chanced to be absent from their villages. On the other hand, he idealised the young soldiers for their sacrifice and their heroism, emphasising the unity that must exist between them and the civilian population of France. In the many festivals of 1793 and the Year II, the theme of military–civilian unity was reiterated again and again, with the armies represented symbolically on the parade ground or in front of the town hall, alongside the departmental and municipal officials, their representatives always young soldiers, fresh-faced and enthusiastic, breathing the spirit of a youthful and militant France.[31] In the armies themselves, the symbolism was just as strong. It was drilled home in the newspapers soldiers read, in the uniforms they wore, and in the songs they sang round the camp fires after the evening meal. In Year II, Robespierre was particularly insistent that the cult of the Supreme Being should be preached to the soldiers, recognising its moral value to men who were repeatedly asked to risk their lives in the cause of the *patrie*. It did not merely bestow temporal approval; it gave the young soldiers reassurance and appeared to offer the promise of eternity. In the words of Jean-Paul Bertaud, 'the cult of the Supreme Being incorporated the cult of the martyrs of liberty. The cult soothed the anguish felt by soldiers facing death.' Bertaud adds that in a number of units the worship of the Supreme Being seems to have arisen spontaneously from

[30] *Ibid.*, vol. VI, p. 530.
[31] Robert Legrand, 'Les fêtes civiques à Abbéville', *Bulletin de la Société d'émulation historique et littéraire d'Abbéville* 24 (1978), 373–426.

the ranks themselves; unlike in so much of civilian France, it did not have to be imposed artificially as an instrument of policy.[32]

There is no doubt that Robespierre's policies were impelled by a determination to combat what he perceived as the threat of Caesarism. But did they also contain a clear strategic vision? That is less certain. What does seem clear is that, before the arrival of Carnot as a member of the Committee of Public Safety, military policy had tended to drift, with political judgements given more weight than strategic considerations. It was, as Marcel Reinhard made clear, Carnot, and not Robespierre, who had sufficient military vision to put the new armies to a telling military use. Reinhard was not rash enough to give Carnot all the credit for this, or to discuss him in the heroic terms in which he has often been discussed by military commentators. But his contribution was considerable. He and Prieur de la Côte-d'Or were deliberately placed on the Committee to bring an element of military experience and technical competence at a moment when French military policy lacked focus and the political leadership had little idea which generals to trust. They recognised that the classic tactics adopted by French armies in the past could no longer work effectively with the new volunteer force at their disposal – sieges, cordons of troops protecting the frontiers and slow, methodical build-ups of strength aimed at forcing the enemy to retreat. These tactics could only succeed with well-trained and seasoned troops, and these France no longer had. If Carnot can lay claim to the title of 'organiser of victory', it is because he gave due thought to these problems, and to the technical difficulties which his generals were encountering in the field. He recognised that a new strategy was called for, one that exploited their superior numbers of young and inexperienced soldiers. This was the doctrine of the *masse*, a commitment to rapid attacks and manoeuvres, the emphasis on revolutionary *élan*. It was here, as Reinhard recognised, that questions of strategy blended neatly with political imperatives.[33] To achieve these goals on the ground, Carnot needed to have a country organised for war, a country that would remain 'révolutionnaire jusqu'à la paix'. Providing that, largely through the twin mechanisms of political surveillance and terror, was Robespierre's greatest contribution to victory. He had the foresight to understand that France's military effort could succeed only if supply routes were assured, if political opposition were quelled, if, in a word, the home front were tightly secured.

But what of Robespierre's more democratic vision of the army itself, with its elected officers and citizen-soldiers? Did that play any construc-

32 Bertaud, *La Révolution armée*, p. 210.
33 Marcel Reinhard, *Le Grand Carnot*, 2 vols. (Paris, 1950–2), vol. II, pp. 102–3.

tive part in the defence of the Republic, or should it be consigned to the realm of ideology, of eighteenth-century political correctness? The question needs to be approached with some caution. It was, after all, from the reforms of 1793 and the Year II that the victorious armies of the Directory sprang, even though by then professionalism had largely replaced ideology as the mainstay of the military machine. And, during the Jacobin months, Robespierre and Carnot in their different ways succeeded in renewing military morale and turning round a war which France had been in danger of losing. The young, poorly trained, often poorly equipped recruits performed very well in what were often highly unpropitious circumstances. But did they do so because their self-belief was sustained by ideology? Eighteenth-century military history has tended to be written in terms of carefully planned strategies and brilliant generals – who, like Hoche or Bonaparte, plucked victory out of the jaws of defeat – but this is an approach which underplays the motivation of the individual soldier and presents republican symbols and army reforms as part of a system of propaganda imposed from the top. Yet we know from the journals, personal letters and *carnets de route* of many of these soldiers that they were persuaded by that propaganda, that they read republican newspapers and joined Jacobin clubs, that they rapidly came to see themselves as the defenders of the new political order. In some armies, notably the Nord, cells of radicalised soldiers manipulated civilian clubs to put pressure on their officers and on the political leadership in Paris. In such instances the soldiers were not at the mercy of radical politicians but were themselves the agents of radicalisation and political reform.[34]

John Lynn, in his study of the Nord, raises some important questions about troop motivation, arguing that, in any war, group cohesion makes a vital contribution to performance in battle. In the Year II, morale remained surprisingly high in the ranks because, he suggests, the soldiers were aware that their own self-interest merged with the defence of the *patrie* and the survival of the Revolution.[35] Equality played a real part in this. Men who did well in the field were promoted, and such advancement demonstrated the reality of claims that military careers were open to talent. This verdict sits easily with the results of recent research on twentieth-century warfare, whether on the morale of American soldiers in Vietnam or of French troops in the trenches of the First World War. Military historians increasingly recognise that armies are motivated at a number of different levels and that the history of battles cannot be satisfactorily subsumed into that of great war leaders or of far-sighted

[34] Forrest, *Soldiers*, pp. 94–9.

[35] Lynn, *Bayonets*, pp. 21–3.

generals. Leonard V. Smith, for instance, in his recent monograph on the French Fifth Infantry Division in 1914–18, argues that, once they were in the field, the soldiers increasingly took decisions of their own, independently of the formal command structure. NCOs played a pivotal rôle in the decision-making process, as battlefield soldiers determined how they would and would not fight their sector of the war.[36] Perhaps this is an argument more appropriate to a twentieth-century army than to one at the end of the eighteenth century, but the self-belief inculcated by revolutionary doctrine did contribute to sharing responsibility among the troops to a degree not seen previously. Ideology here reinforced strategy, and Robespierre should be given credit for his part in creating an army that could perform effectively in a new kind of warfare.

[36] Leonard V. Smith, *Between Mutiny and Obedience: the Case of the French Fifth Infantry Division during World War I* (Princeton, 1994), especially pp. 79–89.

9 Robespierre and the insurrection of 31 May–2 June 1793

Morris Slavin

By the spring of 1793 the French Revolution seemed at an impasse. It had not elevated the status or raised the living standards of the great mass of the common people. The *menu peuple* had become disillusioned and disheartened. Hébert paraphrased their disappointment in a bitter diatribe. 'We no longer believe anyone ... They steal from us, plunder us as in the past ... There is no bread, *foutre*, at any price ... We are without work ... For four years now we have suffered. What have we gained from the Revolution?'[1]

An *assignat* note of 100 *livres* had fallen in May 1793 to 52 per cent of its face value and plunged to 36 per cent the following month. Prices, as could be expected, had risen correspondingly. A rough estimate is that the cost of necessities, including rent, had risen about 100 per cent. Wages, too, had gone up but not in the same proportion as prices.[2]

The military defeats suffered by the French in the spring of 1793 were aggravated by the defection of Dumouriez in April. This undermined still further the confidence of common soldiers and civilians alike in their commanders. As a result the armies of the first coalition successfully invaded France from all directions. Meanwhile, the Vendée was in revolt, and by June the insurgents were threatening Nantes. These military defeats, in turn, sharpened the party struggles that led to the confrontation between the Girondins and the Jacobins. The latter became convinced not only that the Girondin policies had to be defeated, but also that their advocates had to be ejected from the Convention. The question was how to do it.

Robespierre faced this problem on the eve of 31 May 1793 – how to expel the leading Girondins from the Convention without undermining that institution itself. If the whole Girondin party were to be ejected, the Convention would become a mere rump. Robespierre knew enough of English history to recall how ineffective England's Parliament had

1 *Le Père Duchesne* 233 (5 May 1793).

2 Pierre Caron, *Tableau de dépréciation du papier-monnaie* (Paris, 1909), p. iii. AN, F 11 218; George Rudé, *The Crowd in the French Revolution* (Oxford, 1959), p. 252, n. 2.

become after Pride's Purge in December 1648, and how that action had paved the way to the dictatorship of Oliver Cromwell. An accusation of being a 'Cromwelliste' was a serious charge hurled by revolutionaries against each other.[3] Robespierre had no intention of installing himself as a dictator. He was still committed to the parliamentary system. Moreover, he knew that old saying: 'smite the shepherd and the sheep will scatter'.

On 3 April, he exculpated these sheep, that is the deputies who allegedly had been misled by their leaders, and he opposed the expulsion of those who had voted for 'the appeal to the people' after the king's trial. Only 'les grands coupables' (the truly guilty ones), the leading Girondins, deserved to be expelled, he insisted.[4]

A week later Robespierre attacked them together with 'the aristocratic bourgeoisie' whose members 'hold equality in horror' and 'who fear for their property', an unusual appeal to class hatred for one who championed the ideal of republican unity. Accusing the Girondins of wanting to re-establish a monarchy, he charged his opponents with hiding under the mask of moderation and the love of order. Still asserting that the majority of deputies were pure, he repeated that many had been fooled by 'deceptive newspapers of the faction'.

The same day, in the Jacobins, Robespierre endorsed the radical petition of the Halle au Blé section which had indicted the majority of the Convention as corrupt and threatened direct action to save the Republic if the Montagnards were too weak to do so. At the same time, Robespierre declared that certain expressions in the petition should be changed. He could hardly have agreed that the majority of the deputies were corrupt or that the Montagnards were too weak to save the Republic.[5]

Equally important, there was a real danger that, if the Convention were to be subverted, advocates of the *mandat impératif* would be strengthened in their campaign to substitute direct democracy for representative government. The *mandat impératif* had strong historic roots. Under the old régime a deputy was expected to defend the interests of his own order, not to represent all France. Since each estate, theoretically, knew its own interests, it could direct the mission of its delegate. This obligation, imposed by the electors upon their emissaries,

[3] See Roger Barny, 'L'image de Cromwell dans la Révolution française', *Dix-huitième siècle* 25 (1993), 387–97. Between 13 and 25 Thermidor Year II, Robespierre was denounced as a Cromwell thirteen times by his enemies: *ibid.*, 395.

[4] Robespierre, *Œuvres*, vol. IX, pp. 370–1.

[5] *Ibid.*, vol. IX, pp. 376–412, 413–16. Robespierre warned that certain 'indiscreet expressions' should be avoided because, although they may have appeared as trifles, these trifles played into the hands of their enemies in the provinces.

to vote in a predetermined manner upon questions considered in advance was what was meant by the term *mandat impératif*.[6]

It is obvious, of course, that lifting the immunity of the leading Girondins by evicting them endangered the parliamentary system. After the insurrection of 2 June 1793, Danton was to complain that 'the majesty of the National Convention had been outraged'. Yet there was no way out of this dilemma faced by Robespierre. If it were true, as he argued, that the Revolution was endangered by the mistaken or criminal policies of the Girondins, then it was essential to eliminate Brissot, Vergniaud, Gensonné and the others from the Convention. This meant that the Jacobins had to maintain a tight control of the uprising that would oust their opponents on the right, and yet not allow their antagonists on the left to take advantage of this action.

Did Robespierre and the Jacobins have something to fear from the left, or were they striking at mere shadows? Consider this revealing confession of the *Chronique de Paris* during the insurrection: 'Many misguided men, distinguishing between neither Plain nor Mountain, accused the whole Convention of stupendous increases [in the price] of foodstuffs, and believed they would find an end to their ills in its dissolution.'[7] That this sentiment was shared by those who wanted to substitute a form of direct democracy for the parliamentary system will be seen later. Among them were leaders of the uprising.

Five days before the insurrection, Robespierre, speaking in the Jacobin club, declared that since the law had been violated and since 'despotism' had reached a new height 'the people must rise'. It is interesting to note that he used the word 'mandatories', not deputies, in referring to representatives of the people. He declared:

> We republican deputies want to establish a government of the people, by its mandatories ... I believe that the sovereignty of the people is violated, when its mandatories surrender [donnent] ... the posts that belong to the people ... I urge the people to go to the Convention [and place themselves] in insurrection against the corrupt deputies.[8]

Was his use of the term 'mandatories' mere demagogy? It is difficult to say. Obviously, Robespierre was embracing a doctrine foreign to his

[6] Camille Koch, *Les origines françaises de la prohibition du mandat impératif* (Nancy, 1905); M. Genty, 'Mandataires ou représentants: un problème de la démocratie municipale. Paris, 1789–1790', *AHRF* 44 (1972), 1–27.

For the arguments of Sieyès against the *mandat impératif* and those of Talleyrand and Barère, see M. J. Mavidal *et al.* (eds.), *Archives Parlementaires de 1781 à 1860*, première série, 96 vols. (Paris, 1879–1990), vol. VIII, pp. 200–3, 107.

[7] P. J. B. Buchez and P.-C. Roux (eds.), *Histoire Parlementaire de la Révolution française*, 40 vols. (Paris, 1834–8), vol. XVII, p. 49.

[8] Robespierre, *Œuvres*, vol. IX, pp. 526–7.

thinking during this crisis. If the deputies of the Convention had been misled by the 'eloquence' of the Girondin orators, as Robespierre believed, then they were not representing the will of the people and not acting as its mandatories. Assuming this were true, as many sections, the Paris Commune and the Jacobins thought, the removal of the Girondins would restore a will which, as Rousseau had taught, could not be represented.[9] In short, Robespierre was willing to use extra-legal means to resolve the political crisis. But in order to succeed he had to embrace the slogans of those section radicals who looked upon the deputies of the Convention, not as their representatives, but as their proxies. Of course, Robespierre may have been resorting to mere rhetoric. The term 'mandatories' had a familiar sound in the ears of his *sans-culotte* supporters.

The question still remains: how was it possible to accomplish this goal without surrendering to the *Enragés*, the Hébertists and those left-wing Jacobins who sympathised with the radical sections? The Paris Commune and its sections had long championed such measures as the maximum, a price ceiling on the necessities of life, and a guarantee of provisions through forced requisitioning of foodstuffs in the countryside. Needless to say, these measures were at variance with laissez-faire economics favoured by Girondins and Jacobins alike. To carry out a purge of the Convention, the Commune and its sympathetic sections launched an extra-legal assembly sitting in the archbishop's palace, the Evêché. It was modelled on the sectional assembly that had organised the uprising against the king on 10 August 1792. Out of this assembly in the Evêché would rise the *Comité des Neuf*, which, in turn, would give way to the *Comité central révolutionnaire* destined to complete the insurrection of 2 June.[10]

The Evêché Assembly was open to the public, not a secret conclave. Originally it had been convoked by the Commune to discuss measures against suspects, to levy a contribution on the wealthy and to make requisitions – all authorised by the Convention. Nevertheless, the Commune could not associate itself overtly with a revolutionary assembly sitting in the Evêché, legal though it may have been. The general council of the Commune, its directing body, served, however, as an intermediary among the sections and between them and itself. On 14

[9] 'Sovereignty cannot be represented for the same reason that it cannot be alienated. It consists essentially in the general will, and the will cannot be represented ... The deputies of the people are not, nor can they be its representatives. They are only its commissioners.' Jean-Jacques Rousseau, *Du contrat social*, in *The Political Writings of Jean-Jacques Rousseau*, ed. C. E. Vaughan, 2 vols. (Cambridge, 1915), vol. II, p. 96.

[10] See Morris Slavin, *The Making of an Insurrection. Parisian Sections and the Gironde* (Cambridge, Mass., 1986), chapter 4.

May, the municipal police suggested that a list of suspects be drafted, which everyone knew was to contain the leaders of the Gironde.[11]

In order to defend themselves, the Girondins, still dominant in the Convention, established a Committee or Commission of Twelve that issued warrants of arrest against their enemies. In addition to interrogating the municipal authorities, it demanded and received the minutes of the general council. Shortly afterwards it imprisoned Hébert.

If the struggle in the sections between the supporters of the Montagnards and those of the Girondins is examined, it will be found that few had a consistent majority during the weeks before 31 May. It is true, of course, that the sections of the West End tended to be moderate or conservative, while those of the centre inclined to the radical. This was largely, but not exclusively, a result of their social composition. The bourgeois sections tended to support the Girondins, while the more *sans-culotte* divisions favoured the Montagnards. Nevertheless, majorities shifted from week to week, and the invasion by militants from neighbouring regions could overthrow a moderate majority by expelling its members from the assembly.[12]

The conflict in the section du Mail, one of the more conservative sections, illustrates this action. Robespierre had encouraged his supporters by declaring bluntly: 'Don't be frightened by the success of intriguers in a few corrupt sections. The faubourg Saint-Antoine will crush the section du Mail.'[13] And, indeed, this is what ultimately happened. On the evening of 21 May, when most of the section du Mail's members had left the general assembly, a delegation of fifty or sixty militants from four neighbouring districts stormed into the hall and took over the meeting. Armed with sabres and clubs, they must have terrified the remnant of the section's membership.

A spokesman of the militants announced that he had no intention of addressing 'the aristocrats' in the section, but, rather, its '*sans-culottes*'. A leading defender of section Mail tried to appease the invaders by asserting, 'We are all brothers ... We want to fraternise with all sections of Paris and have declared war on tyranny and anarchy.' A delegate of the militants immediately replied: 'The aristocrats call the *sans-culottes* anarchists. They are mistaken.' Another shouted: 'There are other aristocrats ... All the rich, all the big merchants.' Others took up the cry: 'None are more cowardly than the rich ... We will *foutre* them out of here.' Finally, a leading militant warned that they would not allow a closed ballot on a resolution about to be presented. About midnight the assembly broke up with everyone, ironically enough, singing 'a hymn to

[11] *Ibid.*, p. 69. [12] *Ibid.*, pp. 43–63.
[13] Robespierre, *Œuvres*, vol. IX, pp. 525–6.

liberty'. The following day, predictably, the resolution forced upon the section the previous evening was repudiated.[14] This struggle between the two sides continued even after the insurrection.

How different were the political biographies of those who supported the Girondins in the sections from those who favoured the Montagnards? An investigation of the people whose records exist demonstrates conclusively that there were no significant differences. Both sides had members who were present at the storming of the Bastille. Both had repudiated Lafayette and the Feuillants. Both became republican after Louis's flight to Varennes. Both suffered casualties in the attack on the Tuileries on 10 August, and both were active in the affairs of their neighbourhoods. Yet the policies pursued by their respective leaders were different – from support of General Dumouriez to the tactics for crushing the insurgents in the Vendée.

Some weeks before the uprising an assembly of delegates from the more radical sections recognised these differences. Commissioners of thirty-three sections had been elected to take extraordinary measures to bring the political crisis to an end. Sitting in the archbishop's palace, located in the heart of section la Cité, they declared Paris to be in insurrection against 'the aristocratic and liberty-oppressive faction' – that is the Girondins. And just as during the uprising against the king a similar assembly had elected leaders to launch the attack on the Tuileries, so, on the eve of 31 May, the Evêché gathering elected a *Comité des Neuf* to begin the assault.

The temporary president of this committee was the well-known *Enragé* Jean-François Varlet. It was he who gave the order in the early hours of 31 May to sound the alarm and call the sections to arms. Within a few hours, however, Varlet was replaced by the president of section la Cité, Claude-Emmanuel Dobsen, whose rôle was to direct the insurrection into safer channels. While there is no documentary proof, indirect evidence makes clear the plan of the Montagnards to which Dobsen must have been an important party.

Writing in the autumn of 1794 from prison, Varlet charged that among those elected to organise the insurrection were true republicans but also a number of emissaries from what he called 'the most destructive of factions', that is the Jacobins. This 'league of Caligula', he continued, saw nothing in the overthrow of the Girondins but the possibility of a vast scope for their ambition. 'The insurrectionary committee [the *Comité des Neuf*] contained the germ of a revolutionary government . . . The false insurgents substituted Robespierre for Brissot

[14] *Ibid.*, vol. IX, pp. 44–5.

... As for me, I was too sincere to be initiated into it, I was set aside.'[15] Who had the power to set Varlet aside? Those who took control of the insurrection, that is the Montagnards and their supporters in the sections and the Paris Commune.

Robespierre knew Varlet well. In addition to the many brochures published by Varlet that could hardly have escaped Robespierre's notice, both belonged to section Piques. In September 1793, Varlet made an ill-conceived proposal to reject the payment due to those who had taken up arms during the uprising. Robespierre denounced this petition by recalling that before the insurrection only the rich could afford to attend sectional assemblies and confessed that he himself could not afford to serve the people without pay.[16]

Another member of section Piques who had been proposed for the *Comité des Neuf* but was 'set aside' was a naturalised French citizen born in Granada by the name of André-Marie Gusman (or Andres Maria Guzman). He was given the sobriquet Don Tocsinos because it was he who had sounded the tocsin on 31 May. Gusman accused the Jacobins of wanting to pull back from the insurrection. 'Never have they played more indecently with the majesty of the people', he complained, and he declared 'that the insurrection was betrayed by those who had prepared it'.[17]

From Gusman's point of view it could indeed be argued that the insurrection had been betrayed by the Jacobins – but only if we concede that the latter intended to go beyond the goal of removing the Girondins from the Convention. There is no evidence for such a belief. It is true, of course, that the demonstration on 4 and 5 September 1793 which forced the Convention to adopt a maximum, organise the 'revolutionary army' in order to requisition foodstuffs from the peasants, encourage the spread of popular societies, and take other such measures demanded by the *sans-culottes* could be seen as fulfilling the goal of the sections during the revolt against the Girondins. But there is no evidence that Robespierre and his fellow Jacobins intended to adopt such a programme on 31 May.

Nevertheless, this *journée* of September demonstrates that the *sans-culottes* had interests of their own that went beyond the limited action proposed by Robespierre and the Montagnards. Assuming this was

[15] BN, Lb 41 4090, *L'explosion* (Paris, 1 October 1794) and another brochure written shortly thereafter with no noticeable changes, *ibid.*, Lb 41 1330, *Gare l'explosion!* (Paris, 5 October 1794). The quotation is from the first brochure.

[16] *Journal de la montagne*, 19 September 1793; Madival *et al.*, *Archives Parlementaires*, vol. LXXIV, pp. 311–13; Buchez and Roux, *Histoire Parlementaire*, vol. XXIX, pp. 114–15.

[17] Cited by Jules Michelet, *Histoire de la Révolution française*, ed. Gérard Walter, 2 vols. (Paris, 1961), vol. II, pp. 381, 387.

realised by the latter, how could they control the uprising in addition to removing Jean Varlet as president of the insurrectionary committee? As we have seen, the original *Comité des Neuf* became a body of ten members by the addition of Claude-Emmanuel Dobsen. Let us suppose for the moment that, under pressure from the radical sections, nine of the ten members wanted to go beyond the goal of expelling the Girondins. One obvious way to frustrate their desires was to dissolve this body into a larger committee made up principally of Jacobins or their supporters so that the original *Comité des Neuf* became a minority. This is precisely what happened.

On 29 May, the general council of the department of Paris had convoked an assembly of commissioners to meet two days later in the halls of the Jacobin club. These commissioners represented, in addition to the authorities of the Paris department, the general councils of two neighbouring districts (those of Saint-Denis and Bourg-de-l'Egalité), the general council of the Paris Commune and the Evêché assembly of the Paris sections. This assembly of the department appointed eleven members to the Evêché's *Comité des Neuf*. About the same time, the general council of the Paris Commune added another four members.[18] Thus the original insurrectionary *Comité des Neuf* had become enlarged to one of twenty-five members: ten from the Evêché assembly of the sections (including Claude-Emmanuel Dobsen), four from the Paris Commune and eleven from the department of Paris. The new name of this enlarged insurrectionary committee, as it took control of the uprising in the early hours of 31 May, was the revolutionary central committee, *Comité central révolutionnaire*.[19] The president was Jean-Baptiste Loys who had been appointed to Evêché's *Comité des Neuf* and was the Jacobins' chief spokesman on it.[20]

This enlarged committee organised itself into ten different departments – from correspondence with the Convention's Committees of Public Safety and General Security to interior police, public works and *émigrés*. Exercising the powers embodied in these departments made the committee, for a few days, the real government of France.

The committee made clear, however, that it was subject to recall by

18 Maurice Tourneux, *Procès-verbaux de la Commune de Paris (10 août 1792–1er juin 1793)* (Paris, 1894); BN, MSS., Nouv. acq. fr. 2716, fol. 57, 31 May 1793; Alexandre Tuetey, *Répertoire général des sources manuscrits de l'histoire de Paris pendant la Révolution française*, 11 vols. (Paris, 1890–1914), vol. VIII, no. 2658; Paul Saint-Claire Deville, *La Commune de l'an II: vie et mort d'une assemblée révolutionnaire* (Paris, 1946), p. 87.

19 AN, BB^3 80, dos. 1, pc. 141, 31 May 1793. The document, mistakenly dated 'du 1er mai 1793', reads as follows: 'Le Conseil général arrête que la Comité Révolutionnaire existant actuellement à la Maison Commune sera appelé le *Comité Révolutionnaire crée par le peuple du département de Paris*.'

20 Slavin, *Making of an Insurrection*, pp. 78–80.

the sections, despite the fact that it had usurped the powers of the legally constituted authorities.[21] This admission that the sections were the ultimate source of its power did not prevent the *Comité des Neuf* from taking the initiative so necessary during the confusing first moments of the insurrection. Theoretically even its members could be recalled by their individual sections, but in practice, once the uprising was launched, the enlarged body of twenty-five members assumed authority over the revolt. Its personnel included a variety of militants ranging from *sans-culottes* to ex-noblemen. Despite their different social origins, all were united in the practical and immediate task before them. Only after the forced removal of the leading Girondins would the differences between the original *Comité des Neuf* and the enlarged *Comité central révolutionnaire* manifest themselves.

Having established control over the *Comité central*, the Jacobins still had to compel the Convention to surrender its Girondins. This was to be done by surrounding the assembly with a large armed force. The commander of this force, François Hanriot, was appointed by the *Comité des Neuf*. He was a strong supporter of Robespierre and was destined to perish with him on 10 Thermidor. Hanriot was ordered to seize the arsenal and the artillery park in the early morning of 31 May.[22]

Among the measures taken in the early hours of 2 June was that to authorise Hanriot to surround the Convention with a substantial armed force. This was intended to intimidate the majority of the Convention should that body refuse to surrender the accused deputies. At the same time, as noted above, the *Comité* was aware of the demands from people like Varlet to purge the Convention not only of the Girondins but also of the so-called moderates. This would have made the uprising the 'brutal insurrection' that the *Comité* wished to avoid.

The *Comité* was also aware that an armed clash might occur with the forces of moderate sections which still supported the besieged deputies. Furthermore, no one wanted a repetition of the September massacres, with the Girondins as the new victims. To avoid this possibility it was decided to surround the Convention with 80,000–100,000 Parisian guardsmen, with cannon pointed at the assembly hall. But in order to avoid an unauthorised, 'brutal' act, Hanriot stationed a force of 6,000 men in an inner ring immediately around the hall. This armed force was directly under his command. Thus the insurgents had to protect the

[21] AN, BB[3] 80, dos. 16, pc. 15, 31 May 1793; *ibid.*, pc. 51, n.d.

[22] *Ibid.*, BB[3] 80, dos. 16, 31 May 1793. 'Hanriot is appointed provisional commanding general of the Parisian army by the *Comité des Neuf*.' See also Tuetey, *Répertoire*, vol. VIII, nos. 2646, 2670.

Convention with Hanriot's 'reliable troops',[23] yet bring sufficient pressure upon the body for it to give up the Girondin deputies.

Even with this precaution several deputies suffered indignities. A number had their clothes torn and were turned back when they tried to leave the hall. Even Jean-François Lacroix, a member of the Committee of Public Safety, was not permitted to leave. And when, on his motion, the Convention demanded that the armed force surrounding it be immediately withdrawn, Hanriot shouted his defiance: 'Tell your *foutre* president that I *foutre* him and his assembly, and that if within one hour he doesn't deliver to me the twenty-two [Girondins], I'm going to blast it.'[24] Now even the Montagnards were embarrassed, and, according to Barère, Robespierre whispered to him: 'What are you doing? You're making a mess of it.' In reply, Barère allegedly called Robespierre a hypocrite for not speaking out.[25]

Why would Robespierre have accused Barère of making a mess of it unless he knew that Hanriot was carrying out the orders of those who had decided on the tactics to follow? Did the Committee of Public Safety and/or the leading Jacobins give the orders to Hanriot to bring pressure on the Convention to expel the Girondins? Or was Hanriot acting on his own? Obviously they would hardly have agreed to something which threatened the Convention and themselves. Still, it might be assumed that the plan of surrounding the Convention with an armed force had been adopted by the leading Jacobins. If so, Robespierre would have agreed to it, or, at least, been aware of it. This unexpected turn of events was indeed 'a mess', and Robespierre was holding Barère responsible for it.

Let us assume for the moment that what Barère wrote in his memoirs really happened, and that he recalled accurately the exchange between Robespierre and himself. Why would he call Robespierre a 'hypocrite' for not speaking out? Against whom and against what did Barère expect Robespierre to speak out? It could only have been against Hanriot and his threat to the Convention. Whoever was responsible for the 'mess' it seems certain that neither Barère nor Robespierre favoured this 'outrage' to the Convention.

To demonstrate that the Convention was still free, about a hundred deputies of the right, joined by several Montagnards, followed their

[23] Jean Jaurès, *Histoire socialiste de la Révolution française*, ed. A. Mathiez, 8 vols. (repr. New York, 1973), vol. VII, p. 506. See the references to additional sources in Slavin, *Making of an Insurrection*, p. 206.

[24] Louis Mortimer-Ternaux, *Histoire de la Terreur 1792–1794*, 7 vols. (Paris, 1868–81), vol. VII, pp. 404, 406.

[25] Bertrand Barère, *Mémoires de B. Barère*, 4 vols. (Paris, 1842–4), vol. II, p. 92.

president, Hérault de Séchelles, down the great stairs of the Tuileries into the garden. Robespierre, meanwhile, remained in his seat together with the other deputies. When Hérault de Séchelles walked out he found Hanriot on horseback confronting him. Upon his refusal to surrender the proscribed Girondins, Hanriot shouted theatrically: 'Cannoneers to your guns!' The helpless deputies then turned back and meekly re-entered the hall.[26] Shortly thereafter the Convention voted to exclude those Girondins on the proscribed list who had failed to resign.

It is interesting to note just what happened in the garden of the Tuileries on 2 June. Anaxagoras Chaumette, the popular *procureur* of the Paris Commune, wrote: 'All armed Parisians bend their steps toward the hall of the Convention. Their numerous phalanxes inundate the avenues, fill the approaches, surround from all sides the premises of the Convention. *Indignation and respect are painted on all faces.*'[27] This is quite revealing. The *sans-culottes* are described by Chaumette as being indignant that the Convention still had not surrendered the Girondins. Nevertheless, representatives of the people deserved their respect. Chaumette wrote, moreover, that, when deputies went out to mingle with the armed force, the latter opened a wide path to permit them to walk about freely. No one touched or menaced a single deputy, Chaumette insisted. This is not quite true, but there can be no doubt that the *sans-culottes* were still somewhat in awe of the nation's representatives.[28]

Months later, Hébert related the following incident to the Cordeliers club. As the Convention was being surrounded, Lacroix of the Committee of Public Safety complained that he had been insulted. A gunner standing nearby replied: 'You would like to be insulted very much, scoundrel, but we will not give you that pleasure.'[29] Although this remark bespeaks more indignation than respect, respect is not totally lacking in it.

It should be emphasised that the departmental authorities who had created the *Comité central* did so on the initiative of the Jacobins. The delegates chosen by the sections, the department and the Paris Commune met in the hall of the Jacobins. This new centre of the insurrection was created, in the words of Louis Blanc, in order 'to destroy the prestige of the Evêché committee'. Once the *Comité central*

[26] Buchez and Roux, *Histoire Parlementaire*, vol. XXVIII, pp. 45–6, n. 1; François-Nicolas Buzot, *Mémoires sur la Révolution française* (Paris, 1828), pp. 332–52.
[27] *Papiers de Chaumette*, ed. F. Braesch (Paris, 1908), p. 183 (my italics).
[28] *Ibid.*, pp. 183–4.
[29] Pierre Caron, *Paris pendant la Terreur. Rapports des agents secrets du ministre de l'intérieur*, 6 vols. (Paris, 1910–64), vol. V, p. 247.

took control of the insurrection, it ended 'the influence of the violent on the Hôtel de Ville', Blanc concluded.[30]

Was Robespierre aware of what was happening? It is inconceivable that, as the most prestigious of the Jacobins, he would not have been informed of the manoeuvre to tame the *Comité des Neuf*. Almost a year after the insurrection, on 15 April 1794, Robespierre attacked Louis-Pierre Dufourny, president of the directory of the Paris department, in the following words: 'On 31 May, Dufourny was introduced into the committee of insurrection [i.e. the *Comité central*]; when he saw that the popular movement would succeed, he left the committee and sought means to make it impotent.'[31] Robespierre was not accusing Dufourny of destroying the power of the *Comité des Neuf*, but, rather, that of the *Comité central révolutionnaire*, under the control of the Jacobins. Dufourny criticised the trial of Danton, which may have been the real reason for Robespierre's attack on him. Still, it appears that Robespierre was resorting to demagogy when he posed as a defender of the *Comité central*.

After Robespierre's fall, Dufourny justified his rôle on 31 May by admitting that he helped to remove those he called 'conspirators and their agents'. Furthermore, he stated the following:

> Fearing, with reason, that the powers delegated temporarily by the people might be debased or treacherously used by a dictatorship ... I took steps for a new convocation of the people which, suppressing the *Comité central révolutionnaire*, replaced it by a committee of public safety for the department [of Paris] ... Robespierre reproached me at the Jacobins ... for having *shackled the popular movement at that time*.[32]

Yet, as late as October 1794, Dufourny proposed that the insurrection of 31 May be celebrated because, he insisted, it was the greatest event of the Revolution, 'after [that] of 10 August'.[33] Thus, there seems to have been a conflict between Robespierre's conception of the rôle still to be played by the *Comité central* and Dufourny's fear of it.[34] In any case,

[30] Louis Blanc, *Histoire de la Révolution française*, 2nd edition, 12 vols. (Paris, 1866), vol. VIII, p. 411.

[31] After being interrupted by Dufourny, Robespierre warned him: 'Remember that Chabot, that Ronsin were impudent like you ...'. *Œuvres de Maximilien Robespierre*, ed. Albert Laponnaraye, 3 vols. (repr. New York, 1970), vol. III, p. 604. For the quotation, *ibid.*, vol. III, pp. 606–7; also in Buchez and Roux, *Histoire Parlementaire*, vol. XXXII, p. 409. Gérard Walter pointed out that Dufourny was one of the organisers of the insurrection but we know little of his rôle as president of the Paris department. See Michelet, *Histoire de la Révolution française*, vol. II, p. 1372.

[32] BN, Lb 41 4136, L.-P. Dufourny, *Justice Sévérité Vélocité Sentinelle, prends garde à toi* (Paris, 31 October 1794), pp. 6–7, italics in the original.

[33] *Ibid.*, p. 15.

[34] But Henri Calvet thought the statement by Dufourny was 'impudent' (the same word used by Robespierre) because, on 3 June, Dufourny and a colleague called the arrest of

both agreed that the original objectives of the Evêché assembly and its *Comité des Neuf* had to be curbed and the goals of the insurrection envisaged by it had to be changed.

Considering these events what can we conclude regarding Robespierre's rôle? It seems obvious that, in keeping with his mistrust of the more radical demands of the *Enragés* and their supporters, Robespierre refused to embrace their programme of direct democracy. He never ceased defending the republican institutions established after the overthrow of the king. At the same time, he appealed to the *sans-culottes* to expel the Girondins. He had proclaimed publicly that he was in 'insurrection' against the ruling group in the Convention and, thereby, strengthened the revolutionary forces in the more radical sections. Could the more conservative deputies trust him once the Revolution swerved to the right?

Still, enough deputies of the Plain recognised Robespierre's popularity among the *sans-culottes* and his rôle as spokesman for the Convention. Less than two months after the insurrection they joined with the Mountain to elect Robespierre to the Committee of Public Safety. The date was 27 July 1793 – exactly one year to the day before 9 Thermidor Year II.

Could the Montagnards have replaced the Girondin leadership of the Convention without an armed coup? It is possible but unlikely. In time, enough deputies of the Plain might have become convinced that without mobilising the sections, the Paris Commune and the popular societies, victory against the coalition and the internal counter-revolution was unlikely. The Girondins seemed incapable of arousing the energies of the *menu peuple*, something the Jacobins and their allies in the Commune could do. It is possible also that they were unwilling to impose the harsh measures demanded of them. But, in addition, revolutionaries, as is well known, are highly impatient. The one element that was lacking, especially in the critical spring of 1793, was time. Moreover, in revolutionary situations, majorities are often not added up, but, rather, won over. Robespierre, despite his call for insurrection against those he termed 'corrupt deputies', needed a majority in the Convention. He was no Cromwell – a factor which proved his undoing on 9 Thermidor.

We can only speculate as to Robespierre's true feelings when the uprising occurred. He surely must have been troubled when the Con-

the Girondins a 'mere dilatory measure that will muffle the revolutionary movement'. This was the same opinion as expressed by Varlet, Gusman and Loys, as seen above. See Calvet's *Un instrument de la Terreur à Paris: le comité de salut public ou de surveillance du département de Paris (8 juin 1793–21 Messidor an II)* (Paris, 1941), p. 46, n. 38.

vention was surrounded by armed men. A false step could have brought disaster. No one could have guaranteed that Hanriot would keep his men in line. The majesty of the Convention had, indeed, been outraged. It should also be noted that Robespierre kept silent throughout the eventful three days of the uprising and some days after. Nor did he say a word during the heated discussion in the Convention on who and how many of the Girondins were to be purged. This is hardly the mark of a true revolutionary. Still, he had accomplished his end. The Girondins were broken. Terror and virtue were about to stride on to the stage of history, giving a new direction to the French Revolution.

10 Robespierre and the Terror

Norman Hampson

I

Robespierre's association with the Terror was the product of the interaction between his temperament, his principles and his reaction to the political events in which he was totally absorbed from 1789 onwards. The first of these is the most elusive, since the evidence is scanty and often distorted by political bias. The little that has survived from the first thirty years of his life suggests that he grew up as a typical eighteenth-century provincial intellectual with some literary aspirations. His membership of the Arras Academy and of the light-hearted literary society, the Rosati, for which he produced occasional poems, together with one or two rather formal letters to young ladies, all conform to this pattern. He also enjoyed a reputation for disinterestedness.[1] There are hints of a somewhat acerbic attitude towards his legal adversaries: in 1786, he was reprimanded by the Arras bar for 'outrageous remarks respecting the authority of the law and jurisprudence and insulting to the judges'.[2]

The essays that he wrote for academy prizes drew heavily on Montesquieu, stressed the leading rôle of men of letters in the formation of public opinion and emphasised the social importance of religion, on the ground that 'philosophy is unknown to the people'. In one of his cases, in 1786, he made three references to 'the scum of society'. When treating the legal status of bastards, he asserted that 'politics itself is nothing save public morality'. In an *éloge* of the minor poet Gresset, he praised both Frederick II and the bishop of Amiens who had helped to send the chevalier de la Barre to his death, and he refused to opt between Voltaire and Rousseau on the merits of the theatre. This suggests caution rather than conviction.

During the last years of the ancien régime both Robespierre's legal

[1] Louis Jacob, *Robespierre vu par ses contemporains* (Paris, 1938), p. 195; V. Daline, 'Robespierre et Danton vus par Babeuf', *AHRF* 32 (1960), 389.

[2] *Œuvres complètes de Robespierre*, ed. V. Barbier and R.-C. Vellay (Paris, 1910), p. 275.

arguments and the language in which he expressed them suggest a growing attachment to Rousseau. Somewhat ironically, in view of what was to come, he argued that:

A feeble, timid creature ... could blanch, stammer, contradict himself ... and yet be innocent ... At the sight of so many scaffolds steaming with innocent blood ... I hear inside myself a powerful voice telling me to shun for ever that savage tendency to convict merely on the basis of presumption.[3]

This Rousseauist tendency became sharply accentuated towards the end of 1788, as Robespierre responded to the prospect of major political changes, to which he hoped to make a personal contribution. He was perhaps influenced by the publication of the second part of Rousseau's *Confessions* during the autumn. He referred specifically to the *Confessions* in his *Dédicace aux mânes de Jean-Jacques Rousseau*, which was one of the most significant things that he ever wrote.[4] Describing himself as 'called to play a rôle in the midst of the greatest events which have ever convulsed the world', he invoked Rousseau, not as a source of ideas, but as a 'prodige de vertu', and dedicated himself to emulate Rousseau's life rather than to implement his thoughts. He accepted Rousseau's claim that he was the victim of man's injustice. 'I wish to follow in your revered footsteps.'

The reward of the virtuous man is the conviction of having wanted the good of mankind; next there is the recognition of the peoples, which envelops his memory, and the honours which are bestowed on him by his contemporaries. Like you, I should wish to purchase these blessings at the cost of a laborious life, at the cost even of a premature death.[5]

Much of the future Robespierre is already here: the self-dedication to the general good, the expectation of public recognition and the prospect of eventual martyrdom. It did not escape contemporaries. Dubois-Crancé wrote in 1792 that 'this man, sustained by the morality of Rousseau, felt within himself the courage to emulate his hero, with regard to his austerity of principles and manners, morality, unsociable character, uncompromising spirit, proud simplicity and even his morose nature'.[6]

Further evidence of a Rousseauist cast of mind emerged during the Dupond case at the end of 1788. In an extraordinary digression into current politics, Robespierre offered a foretaste of what were to become his regular themes. There had been an 'affreuse conspiration' from

[3] *Le véritable portrait de nos législateurs* (Paris, 1792), pp. 107–11.
[4] *Œuvres complètes*, pp. 317–18.
[5] Quoted in Hector Fleischmann, *Charlotte Robespierre et ses mémoires* (Paris, n.d.), pp. 290–2.
[6] Jacob, *Robespierre*, p. 83.

which the king had sought refuge in the bosom of his people. France was a uniquely generous nation which, thanks to its magnanimity and the virtuous character of its king, had recovered those ancient and imprescriptible rights that had been violated through the ages. The mission of Louis XVI was to 'lead men to happiness and virtue through legislation grounded on the unchanging principles of universal morality'. Providence had offered France the challenge of 'this great and difficult task which the most illustrious sovereigns of the earth were unable to implement'. 'This is perhaps the unique moment provided for us by the benevolence of the Almighty, who orders the destiny of empires; and, if we allow it to escape us, it is perhaps decreed that He will in future only light the way towards times of trouble, desolation and calamities.' 'O my *patrie*, save yourself from this deadly spirit of discord.' If everything ended disastrously, there was the consoling vision of an afterlife in which the virtuous would meet with their reward.[7] Henceforth the script was not to change, despite the succession of actors who were rejected for the leading parts. The Paris *parlement* disappeared almost at once. Louis XVI and Necker went soon afterwards, to be followed by Mirabeau and the constitutional monarchists, Pétion and the Girondins, Danton and Desmoulins, eventually by almost all of his former friends and colleagues.

Like a good many of his contemporaries, Robespierre was determined to get himself elected to the Estates General. He wrote two pamphlets in support of his candidature. The first of these, *A la nation artésienne*, was mainly concerned with the attempt of the Arras municipality to manage the elections. At one of the numerous local meetings, Robespierre defeated a proposal to convey the thanks of the Third Estate to the other two orders for their offer to renounce their fiscal privileges, on the ground that the belated rectification of an injustice was no occasion for expressions of gratitude.[8]

Later in the campaign, Robespierre produced a second pamphlet with the more aggressive title of *Les ennemis de la patrie démasqués*, in which he worked himself up into a state of hysterical alarm. 'Citizens, the *patrie* is in danger; enemies within, more formidable than the foreign armies, plot its ruin in secret ... What does it matter to me that ... they already think of martyring all the defenders of the people?' Once on this tack, there was no holding him back and he concluded with an extraordinary evocation of what he clearly envisaged as a pilgrimage to his own shrine. 'Ah, then may the tears of friendship mingle on his tomb with those of the hapless people whom he aided ... whilst his soul rises to enjoy, in

[7] *Œuvres complètes*, pp. 579, 618, 661, 670, 673, 680.
[8] Robespierre, *Œuvres*, vol. VI, p. 19.

the everlasting abode of order and justice, the happiness which the tyranny and injustice of men have banished from the earth.' In that dawn when most people thought it bliss to be alive, Robespierre was already consoling himself with thoughts of what would happen after sunset.

The Bibliothèque Nationale's copy of *A la nation artésienne* contains as a postscript a handwritten *Supplément au journal d'Artois*, dated 1 May 1789, which describes the qualities of the newly elected deputies as though they were racehorses. The lampoon is dismissive of the clergy, deferential towards the nobility and critical of the men from the Third Estate, but only really hostile in the case of Robespierre, who is described as '*L'Enragé*': 'quick-tempered, responding to neither the bit nor the stick, vicious as a mule, daring to bite only from behind, afraid of the whip.'[9] This entry is astonishing. That was, of course, a caricature, but a caricature only exaggerates what is perceived to be there.

II

During the first two years of the Constituent Assembly, Robespierre probably saw himself as part of the mainstream of the revolutionary movement. He was certainly on its radical wing, one of the 'thirty voices' whom Mirabeau ordered to be quiet – but he supported the proposal to put Mirabeau's remains in the Pantheon.[10] As the conscience of the *patriotes*, he was continually reminding them of the democratic implications that ought to have followed from the Declaration of the Rights of Man. He attacked the limitation of the franchise, defended the political rights of coloured men in the colonies and insisted on the election of all administrative officials. This included the clergy, 'who are only magistrates'.[11]

Like most of his colleagues, Robespierre adapted his views on the location of sovereignty to the political situation. Sovereignty derived, of course, from the general will, which was not the will of all (as expressed in the primary assemblies) but something that emerged from the debates in the National Assembly. Where Robespierre was concerned, this was not a cynical conjuring trick to transfer power from people to parliament. In a speech that he had printed when there was no time for him to deliver it in the Assembly, in September 1789, he advocated frequent elections, with no re-eligibility for retiring deputies. Belief in the existence of a general will implied that a majority vote – at least when it went the right way, as it usually did – expressed the real will of

[9] BN, 8^{0} Lb^{39} 6607. [10] Robespierre, *Œuvres*, vol. VII, p. 179.
[11] *Ibid.*, vol. VI, p. 398.

the nation as a whole. The minority was therefore obliged, not merely to comply with it, but to adopt it as its own opinion. Any future attempt at revision was illegitimate. This was not quite the end of the question. 'The first of all laws is the well-being of the people'[12] and 'the march of revolutions is not subject to the ordinances which govern the peaceful state of an established constitution'.[13] That left the way open for direct action by the sovereign people, as in July 1789. It is reassuring to be told that public opinion was the sole judge of what was in conformity with the law,[14] but Robespierre claimed in the case of Avignon that, since all peoples aspired to be free, any Avignonnais who had not voted for incorporation into France 'must be deemed oppressed'.[15] Avignon was a local example of a more general problem. The goodness, patience and generosity of the mass of ordinary people meant that they were an easy prey to self-serving hypocrites. It was therefore the duty of the Assembly to 'raise our fellow citizens' souls ... to the level of ideas and feelings required by this great and superb revolution',[16] Robespierre maintained in an undelivered speech of September 1789. It was to take some years for the practical consequences of all this to become apparent, but Robespierre's future policies were already implicit in his early attempts to reconcile Rousseauist principle with the practice of parliamentary government.

During the first two years of the Revolution, he was still inclined to stand up for the freedom of the individual, even when it seemed to conflict with the security of the revolutionary government. He defended the principle of parliamentary immunity in the case of the comte de Toulouse-Lautrec, even though he had been arrested on a charge of plotting counter-revolution. He insisted on the secrecy of the mails,[17] and, if he had taken a different view on 27 July 1789, he could reasonably argue that the circumstances had been exceptional. He opposed putting any legal restrictions on the right to leave the country.[18] On occasion he put humanity before rigorous adherence to principle, defending anyone who gave asylum to a friend who was fleeing from a criminal charge,[19] and opposing Mirabeau's motion to have Condé declared a traitor.[20] Unlike his revered Rousseau, he opposed capital punishment.[21]

Like many of his colleagues on the left, Robespierre saw himself as defending 'the Revolution' against the hostility of those whose pretences of moderation concealed their determination to restore the ancien

[12] *Ibid.*, vol. VI, p. 46.
[13] *Ibid.*, vol. VI, p. 514.
[14] *Ibid.*, vol. VII, p. 19.
[15] *Ibid.*, vol. VII, p. 257.
[16] *Ibid.*, vol. VI, p. 95.
[17] *Ibid.*, vol. VII, pp. 85–7.
[18] *Ibid.*, vol. VII, pp. 87–9.
[19] *Ibid.*, vol. VI, p. 514.
[20] *Ibid.*, vol. VI, pp. 489–93.
[21] *Ibid.*, vol. VII, pp. 432–46.

régime: the court, the ministers and the great majority of the nobility and upper clergy. Where he was somewhat exceptional was in his credulity, which led him to take alarm at every vague rumour of a counter-revolutionary plot. By the spring of 1791, he had convinced himself that France was caught between 'conspirators and treacherous people who profess themselves her friends'.[22]

It was at this time that he parted company with most of the left, whom he accused of continuing to pose as friends of the Revolution when they had actually sold out to the court and the aristocracy. Men like Duport and the Lameths, possibly alarmed by the growing social unrest in Paris, seem to have decided to try to effect a reconciliation with the royal government, in the hope of securing the king's positive support for the new constitution, when the Assembly was visibly approaching the end of its labours. Robespierre, who regarded every compromise as a *compromission*, had begun to denounce this 'betrayal' before the king's flight. He saw the Feuillant secession from the Jacobins and the fiction that Louis had been 'abducted' not as a mistaken political choice but as proof that his opponents had gone over to the court and to counter-revolution. On 16 July 1791, he told the Jacobins that most of the deputies were corrupt. 'It is here that the standard of liberty is planted.' If the general will could only emerge within the Assembly and most of the deputies were corrupt, it was not clear what should happen next. Robespierre was certainly not thinking in terms of an insurrection. He piloted the remnant of the Jacobins on a course of constitutional propriety at the time of the Champ de Mars petition. Although this preserved him from any personal danger when Danton and Marat thought it prudent to go into hiding, it did not deter him from presenting himself as the martyr of the Revolution.

> I dedicate myself to all the hatreds; I know the fate which awaits me ... I have sacrificed my life to truth, liberty and the *patrie* ... I shall receive almost as a boon a death which will prevent me from being an observer of the evils which I regard as inevitable.[23]

He did not die; he was not even arrested, but in September he found himself without a parliamentary mandate because of the self-denying ordinance that he himself had proposed.

III

Robespierre greeted the Legislative Assembly with relief and a brief period of optimism. He wrote to his friend Buissart, in Arras, 'I find

[22] *Ibid.*, vol. VII, p. 90. [23] *Ibid.*, vol. VII, pp. 522–3.

great resources in the present Assembly, which I regard . . . as very much superior to its predecessor.'[24] He believed that if 'mon cher Pétion' could defeat Lafayette, the perpetrator of the Champ de Mars massacre, in the election for mayor of Paris, this would constitute a 'triumph of patriotism and frank integrity over intrigue and tyranny'.[25]

Things reverted to normal a few months later when Robespierre found himself once more in a minority, even within the Jacobins, over the question of going to war. This was Brissot's policy, in the expectation that war would either force the king to resign himself to a subordinate rôle within the constitution or reveal him as a man in league with the enemy in order to restore the ancien régime. Robespierre, taking the second alternative for granted, had no difficulty in exposing the vacuous optimism with which Brissot dismissed any talk of danger. His arguments were cogent and prescient, but their precise nature has not been generally understood. What he most feared was that the royal government would be able to conceal its hostility to the Revolution behind a pretence of patriotic unity: 'By declaring war, you deprive yourself . . . of the means whereby you can defy the executive power.'[26] He repeatedly insisted that he was not opposed to war itself, but that, as things stood, either victory or defeat could be made to serve the hidden agenda of the counter-revolution. 'A law which is received by two parties unanimously is never good.'[27] The king's ministers had always to be regarded as enemies. 'What matters to us is to frighten them by great examples, not to change them.'[28] If Louis were to choose ministers from the Jacobins, Robespierre would conclude that the men involved had sold themselves. What was needed was a resolute defence of the constitution, which meant that the Assembly should have disregarded the two royal vetoes of the autumn! 'We should have grasped that opportunity to overthrow despotism.'[29] At first he thought that Brissot, 'un législateur patriote', was merely naïve. He was particularly shocked by Brissot's suggestion that a patriotic war might put an end to the 'état affreux' of mistrust between the Assembly and the ministers, which he himself regarded as an essential safeguard of the Revolution. When Brissot persisted in disregarding Robespierre's increasingly impatient correction, it eventually became clear that he had followed Lafayette in selling himself to the court.

The trouble with Robespierre's view of the situation was that it failed to attract much support. Amongst the public at large, in the Assembly,

[24] *Correspondance de Maximilien et d'Augustin Robespierre*, ed. Georges Michon (Paris, 1926), pp. 130–1.

[25] *Ibid.*, p. 130.

[26] Robespierre, *Œuvres*, vol. VIII, p. 37.

[27] *Ibid.*

[28] *Ibid.* vol. VIII, p. 171.

[29] *Ibid.*, vol. VIII, p. 140.

even in the Jacobin club, the majority favoured war. Robespierre disposed of public opinion with a convenient quotation from Rousseau: 'The people always wants the good but it does not always recognise it.' The Assembly had gone the way of its predecessor and the Jacobins had become the instrument of a cabal.[30] Perhaps to convince himself as much as his audience, both of his *vertu* and his judgement, Robespierre treated the club to repeated recapitulations of all that he had achieved in the Constituent Assembly. *He* was not dividing the *patriotes*; there could be no collusion between probity and perfidy, virtue and vice, and his past record was the proof of his entitlement to distribute the rôles in this morality play. When the Girondin ministers were dismissed in June, he offered them rehabilitation 'if they want to join with the *patriotes*, and particularly with me'.[31] This was rather surprising if he really believed that they had sold themselves to the court.

With the Prussian army approaching the frontier and the Assembly the prisoner of its constitutional scruples, the salvation of the Revolution was coming to depend on another act of direct intervention by the sovereign people. On 8 June, Robespierre told the Jacobins that the Assembly was subject to the general will (which he had previously believed to be the product of its discussions) 'and when it plainly opposes it, the body can no longer exist'. If this looked like making constitutional principles dance to his tune, he remained some kind of a democrat: 'I know of nothing so appalling as the concept of an unlimited power, amalgamated to a large assembly which is above the law.'[32] He therefore suggested deposing the king and replacing the Legislative Assembly with a convention, elected by universal suffrage, from which all members of the two previous assemblies would be excluded, with the right of recall in the hands of the primary assemblies.

When the essential elements of this programme had been achieved as a result of the insurrection of 10 August – which the Girondin leaders had tried to prevent by negotiation with the king – Robespierre behaved as though popular sovereignty was for the time being in the hands of the Paris Commune. As its spokesman, he threatened the deputies: 'The people rests, but it does not sleep.'[33] He handled the Parisian elections to the Convention like a veteran party manager. It was he who secured the elimination of any of the electors chosen by the sovereign people who had previously belonged to a club or signed a petition that the Jacobins held to be counter-revolutionary. When the remaining electors hesitated to vote for Desmoulins, Robespierre persuaded them to agree to the preliminary discussion of the merits of the candidates. This

[30] *Ibid.*, vol. VIII, p. 326.
[31] *Ibid.*, vol. VIII, p. 374.
[32] *Ibid.*, vol. VIII, p. 411.
[33] *Ibid.*, vol. VIII, p. 437.

allowed him to get Desmoulins preferred to Kersaint, Marat to Priestley and to keep out Tallien. It is difficult to believe that Augustin Robespierre, who was unknown in Paris, could have been elected without the pulling of political strings. On 2 September, when the prison massacres were already starting, Robespierre and Billaud-Varenne denounced Brissot and other Girondin leaders as agents of Brunswick. It was some months since he had begun to argue that death was the only penalty for traitors.

IV

In the Convention, it was open war from the start. Understandably, if unwisely, the Girondins opened hostilities by trying to exclude Robespierre, Danton and Marat, and by denouncing Paris as the home of anarchy and murder. Robespierre naturally presented this as a personal attempt on his life and proof that the Girondins were the latest embodiment of a plot that went back as far as 1789. 'This accusation is a crime ... to destroy the common weal.'[34] No one had been persecuted so much as he. 'I covet the honour of being the first to be murdered by the Brissotins.'[35] 'I alone offer to defy them. They will be able to kill me but I single-handedly, as long as I live, will be terrible to all the plotters.'[36] Where martyrdom was concerned, whether in the metaphorical or the literal sense, a fellow Montagnard had a more obvious claim. When the Convention was making up its mind whether to send Marat before the Revolutionary Tribunal, Robespierre seemed to feel left out. 'I deserve a *décret d'accusation* ... all you who ally together against me ...' If Marat's prosecution was due to hatred, 'perhaps I myself will be encompassed in this loathing'.[37] His reaction to Marat's murder was too much even for the Jacobin club, where Bentabole accused him of being envious. Robespierre said that his only reason for joining in the debate was that 'the honours of the dagger are also destined for me'. The Jacobins were indulging in too many 'hyperboles outrées' about Marat instead of discussing how to avenge him. Robespierre therefore opposed putting his remains in the Pantheon and suggested postponing any state funeral until the end of the war.

After the overthrow of the monarchy and the execution of Louis XVI in January 1793, Robespierre could no longer think of his enemies as the paid agents of the court. The declaration of war against Britain almost immediately afterwards allowed Pitt (occasionally seconded by

[34] *Ibid.*, vol. IX, pp. 18–19.
[35] *Ibid.*, vol. IX, p. 157.
[36] *Ibid.*, vol. IX, p. 327.
[37] *Ibid.*, vol. IX, p. 430.

the Austrian commander-in-chief, Coburg) to step into the breach as bogeyman and paymaster. His scheming went back as far as the beginning of the Revolution and his latest agents, the Girondins, were 'more criminal in their means than all the factions that have gone before them'.[38] 'All our misfortunes must be attributed to the same cause – a perpetual indulgence towards all those who have betrayed the *patrie*.'[39] It therefore followed that 'mercy which compounds with tyranny is barbarous'.[40] On 5 November, he had been evasive on the subject of the September massacres: almost all those who had perished had been guilty, but even they deserved some sympathy. By 10 April, the whole grisly business had become 'Paris rising to crush the enemies of France'. He told the readers of his newspaper that revolutionary measures were acts of cruelty and oppression when taken by despots and aristocrats but became 'salutaires et actes de bienfaisance' if carried out by the people.[41]

Robespierre's problems were the product of what he believed to be his unique grasp of the political situation. The mass of the population meant well but, 'aussi léger que généreux', it was continually misled by 'cowardly libellers'.[42] On 3 March, he suggested sending the latter before the Revolutionary Tribunal, but that was merely striking at the symptoms. 'Public feeling has lagged behind the Revolution ... the people still lacks political sense.'[43] 'Our enemies have public opinion in their hands.'[44] There had been sound political reasons for not submitting the fate of the king to a referendum, which would have made the division within the country explosively obvious, but that was not why Robespierre had opposed it. He asserted that 'simple folk' would be misled by 'intriguers' and that working people would not spare the time to attend the meetings of the primary assemblies. This was an argument, of course, that applied to all forms of democratic election. When, on 13 April, Gensonné proposed referring the Girondin–Montagnard quarrel to the electorate, Robespierre denounced such proposals as 'blasphemies against liberty'.

One could always argue that, since the general will emerged from the discussions in the Assembly, it was for the Convention to educate public opinion. 'Is it not for you to direct it?'[45] The trouble with that was that Robespierre's opponents tended to be in the majority, at least until the king's trial. As he told his readers:

> this is the time of factions. Now, the time of factions is not conducive to the launching of a system of public instruction ... I might regale you with polished

[38] *Ibid.*, vol. IX, p. 58.
[39] *Ibid.*, vol. IX, p. 309.
[40] *Ibid.*, vol. IX, p. 184.
[41] *Ibid.*, vol. V, p. 322.
[42] *Ibid.*, vol. IX, pp. 51, 54.
[43] *Ibid.*, vol. IX, p. 297.
[44] *Ibid.*, vol. IX, p. 512.
[45] *Ibid.*, vol. IX, p. 127.

descriptions of national festivals and perhaps produce a moment of illusion by conjuring up the image of some Spartan institutions.[46]

Robespierre's attitude towards the Convention fluctuated with the changing political balance. At the beginning of 1793, he seems to have believed that the outcome of the king's trial had put the Montagnards in control, or, as he defined it, restored concord between the Assembly and the nation. It was perhaps the despatch of a good many Montagnards into the provinces to supervise the implementation of the conscription act of 20 February that swung the political balance the other way and Robespierre resumed his customary pessimism.

He was not averse to another act of direct intervention by the sovereign people, provided that its success could be guaranteed. He suspected his opponents of trying to provoke a 'mouvement partiel' that would give them a pretext for a new Champ de Mars massacre. As he told the Jacobins on 7 December, an insurrection was 'the most sacred of duties' but too dangerous to contemplate in the immediate future. In March, he was evasive and ambiguous. On 8 March, he was 'the supporter of all necessary insurrections'. A fortnight later, 'The people must rise all over France to crush the enemy within . . . The people must save the Convention and the Convention will, in its turn, save the people.' The Paris sections should arrest all 'mauvais citoyens', 'without infringing the deputies' inviolability'. By 8 May, he was advocating the creation within Paris of an *armée populaire*, to be paid by the rich, the arrest of suspects and the purging of 'aristocrats' from the sections, but he claimed that this could be done 'la loi à la main' and discounted any talk of armed revolt. The creation of the Committee of Twelve, which took the offensive against leading Parisian radicals, may have convinced him of the imminence of the Girondin coup that he had been predicting for months. Changing tack, on 26 May he called for an 'insurrection against all the corrupt deputies'. When it came, on 2 June, he was one of the few who professed to regard the forcible purge of the Girondin leaders as an affirmation of popular sovereignty rather than a capitulation to Hanriot's National Guards.

One of the more striking features of Robespierre's evolution at this time, if what he said corresponded to what he actually thought, was his growing inability to distinguish between fantasy and the awkward complexities of real life. On 13 March, he claimed that Brissot had been acting as Lafayette's agent when he provoked the Champ de Mars massacre which had killed 500 people. The actual figure was probably about a dozen. If Dumouriez had been allowed to invade the Nether-

[46] *Ibid.*, vol. V, pp. 210–11.

lands towards the end of 1792, 'revolution would have broken out in England. The despots would have been unable to recoup and liberty would have been established within France itself.' It was because of the treachery of the foreign ministers that all the governments of Europe in turn had declared war on France. The only one that had actually done so was Prussia. A year earlier, Robespierre's level-headed view of the situation had been in striking contrast to Brissot's windy bombast. The rôles were now reversed and it was Robespierre who claimed that 'no one dares doubt that a French army, properly led against the tyrants, would be invincible'.[47] On 4 December 1792, he proposed that the Convention vote the principle that 'no nation is entitled to give itself a king'.

V

After the *coup d'état* of 2 June, the Convention consisted entirely of *patriotes* and for the next six months Robespierre concentrated half of his attention on discouraging them from quarrelling with each other. His fluctuations of mood were becoming increasingly extreme. On 28 June, he was improbably euphoric in the Jacobin club. 'Who could have believed that this Assembly, comprising all the blackguards sold to the counter-revolutionaries, would become in a fortnight the most popular and democratic of all the assemblies?' On 8 July, he defended the Committee of Public Safety, even though its members were not equally *éclairés* and *vertueux*. His own election to the Committee on 27 July reinforced his belief that it was the main bastion of the Revolution. He therefore opposed the proposal to bring the new constitution into force, on the ground that national elections would return 'the emissaries of Pitt and Coburg',[48] supported the limitation of the meetings of the Paris sections,[49] and expressed his suspicions of the popular societies that were created to evade this restriction.[50] On 25 September, he helped the Committee to survive what amounted to a vote of no confidence. Between August and November, he used his authority in the Jacobin club to guarantee the *patriotisme* of Barère, Bourdon de l'Oise, Julien de Toulouse and Duquesnoy, even when he disagreed with their policies, and he protected the seventy-three deputies arrested for protesting against the purge of the Girondin leaders.

At the same time he was becoming increasingly violent in his demands for the exemplary punishment of foreign agents, which meant anyone whom he believed to pose a threat to the revolutionary govern-

[47] *Ibid.*, vol. IX, p. 308.
[48] *Ibid.*, vol. X, p. 65.
[49] *Ibid.*, vol. X, pp. 110–13.
[50] *Ibid.*, vol. X, p. 166.

ment, like Jacques Roux, whom he described as an Austrian agent. The activity of the Revolutionary Tribunal had to be accelerated.[51] It should be given the power to end trials after three days.[52] He wanted an intensification of repression after the recapture of Lyon and Bordeaux.[53] From its beginning, the Revolution had been dominated by 'la faction anglaise' which had now penetrated 'the purest of the popular societies'.[54] Every surrender of a French fortress had been due to treason.[55] The men responsible for everything that was going wrong were generals, administrative officials and 'those atrocious journalists', not Montagnard deputies.

A couple of the latter encouraged Robespierre to link the two sides of the picture by suggesting that one of the aims of the counter-revolutionaries was to manipulate the more gullible deputies and induce them to attack each other. In mid-October, Fabre d'Eglantine denounced the intrigues of Proli and his quartet of Jacobin busybodies who were hoping to use Hérault-Séchelles and Chabot as their dupes.[56] When Chabot in his turn went to Robespierre to tell him about the Batz plot to set leading Montagnards at each others' throats, Robespierre advised him to 'ménager les patriotes', which may have induced Chabot to suppress his intended insinuations against his chief tormentor, Hébert.[57]

During the autumn, Robespierre had been able to accommodate within his scenario the attempt of Hébert and Vincent to commit the Revolution to more violent policies, designed to intimidate their rivals and to enhance their own importance. Their endorsement of the dechristianisation campaign of mid-November put an end to that. Robespierre's first reaction was to dismiss this as a plot by Proli designed to set him against Hébert,[58] but his suspicions grew when Hébert persisted in what seemed to be a policy and began to close in on Danton. Robespierre may have been influenced by what looks like one of Fabre's more imaginative productions.[59] The *Précis et relevé des matériaux sur la conspiration dénoncée par Chabot et Basire* drew attention from time to time to Fabre's perspicacity and rearranged Chabot's testimony so that the Batz plot became primarily an attempt to mislead the *sans-culottes* by 'the exaggeration of liberty and equality; to preach atheism and formally suppress the tenet of the immortality of the soul'. This was being conducted by the *Armée révolutionnaire*, the War Office

51 *Ibid.*, vol. X, pp. 79–81.
52 *Ibid.*, vol. X, p. 159.
53 *Ibid.*, vol. X, p. 86.
54 *Ibid.*, vol. X, pp. 62, 71.
55 *Ibid.*, vol. X, p. 61.
56 See Albert Mathiez, *La conspiration de l'étranger* (Paris, 1918), pp. 1–38.
57 AN, F[7] 4637, *François Chabot à ses concitoyens*, fo. 50. Chabot amended the phrase to read 'm'a recommandé la prudence'.
58 Robespierre, *Œuvres*, vol. X, p. 200.
59 AN, AFII 49.

(alias Vincent) and a section of the Jacobin club. Hébert, in other words, was one of Batz's chief agents and dechristianisation – to which Chabot had not paid any attention – was designed to stir up opposition to the Revolution. This was preaching to the credulous, if not yet the converted. Robespierre very sensibly believed that the attack on Catholicism *was* bound to provoke unnecessary opposition. Since he chose to see it as militant atheism and he was convinced that the success of the Revolution so far could only be attributed to the special intercession of Providence, it was rather more than a matter of politics and it had to be stopped at almost any price.

Robespierre became, in the first half of December, the accessory, if not the tool, of the 'indulgents' whose offensive broadened into an attack on revolutionary government. Danton joined him in opposition to dechristianisation but then retired into the background. On 5 December, Robespierre accused those who criticised the 'half-heartedness' of the government of being in British and Prussian pay. Four days later, he claimed that the aristocracy had launched a new attack 'under the cloak of patriotism'. He read in proof the first two numbers of the *Vieux Cordelier* in which Desmoulins implied that the extremists were British agents. In the Jacobin club, he guaranteed the revolutionary credentials of Danton and Desmoulins on 3 and 14 December. He was, however, becoming suspicious. The vote on 12 December (rescinded on the following day), to renew the membership of the Committee of Public Safety, probably confirmed his fears. That night he told the Jacobins that there were traitors, not merely in the administration but within the committees of the Convention. 'The foreign party holds sway in the midst of the Jacobins. The destruction of the *patrie* is at hand.'

Various factors contributed to Robespierre's growing conviction that the 'indulgents' were yet another faction in foreign pay. On the day after Robespierre had defended him in the Jacobins, Desmoulins published the third issue of the *Vieux Cordelier* which attacked revolutionary government. Early in January, the revelation of Fabre's complicity in the East India Company scandal that formed the hard core of the so-called Batz plot must have been particularly humiliating to a man who boasted of his perspicacity. As recently as 26 December he had told the Jacobins, 'I am in a better position than anyone to judge and pronounce on individuals' and he was now exposed as Fabre's dupe. Perhaps in desperation, he urged the club, on 7 January, to turn its back on the pernicious pleasures of recrimination and unite in an examination of the crimes of the British government. He still tried to protect Desmoulins but when Camille invoked Rousseau – 'to burn is not to answer' – in reply to his proposal to destroy the third number of the *Vieux Cordelier* unread, Robespierre lost his temper and suggested that Desmoulins was 'possibly more than misled'. Recovering himself, he continued, 'I should not have uttered these truths, had not Desmoulins been so stubborn' – which was a rare admission that he sometimes preferred to leave some 'truths' unsaid.

Faced with this discouraging situation, Robespierre looked with a new urgency for ways of defining and consolidating revolutionary government. In his speeches of 25 December and 5 February, the repressive edge was keener than ever: the Revolution 'owes only death to the enemies of the people'. Those who wanted to confine it within constitutional bounds were 'cowardly assassins'. Appeals for 'parricidal gentleness ... seem to me only escaped sighs for England and Austria'. 'To punish the oppressors of humanity – that is clemency.' To compensate for all this necessary blood-letting, there was a new tendency to elaborate on the moral Utopia that lay at the end of the road. This amounted to an anticipation of Marx's dream of a communist society in which the repressive state would have withered away, conceived in ethical rather than in economic terms. 'We want a system in which all base and cruel passions would be fettered, and all beneficent, generous passions promoted by the laws.' To attain this unprecedented goal, the country and the Convention had to unite behind the Committee of Public Safety.

Robespierre may have been convinced by now that moderates and extremists were part of the same foreign plot but he was not primarily responsible for their destruction. The Hébertists signed their own death warrants when they began toying with the idea of another forcible purge of the Convention. Robespierre, who had been out of action for a month, perhaps because of nervous prostration at the prospect of the coming battles, only returned to duty on the day that the government struck. The case of Danton and Desmoulins is rather more complicated. The trial of Fabre and the other East India Company racketeers had been set for 2 April and seemed unlikely to provide Fouquier-Tinville with any problems. On 30 March, to Fouquier's consternation, the arrest of Fabre's 'accomplices', Danton, Desmoulins, Philippeaux and Delacroix, against whom he had neither charges nor evidence, transformed a corruption trial into a political crisis. The most likely explanation for this sudden decision is that the governing committees panicked at the prospect of Danton coming to Fabre's rescue and turning the Convention against the government. Billaud-Varenne claimed, after Robespierre's fall, that when he first proposed the proscription of Danton, Robespierre accused him of wanting to destroy the best *patriotes*. If that were so, he soon changed his mind – so completely that he provided Saint-Just with much of the material for his denunciation of the four deputies and silenced such opposition as the Convention dared to offer to the raising of their parliamentary immunity. The deputies were probably less reassured by his assurance that few of them were guilty than they were intimidated by 'whoever trembles at this moment is guilty'.[60] Those who did, began to seek each other out for their mutual protection.

Without consulting his colleagues on the Committee, Robespierre now persuaded the docile Assembly to adopt the cult of the Supreme Being, which marked a new stage in his identification of republicanism with morality. Since 'the sole foundation of civil society is morality', the prime objective of the enemy was 'to corrupt public morals'. Crime was now equated with sin and vice versa, which meant that the scope for repression was virtually unlimited. Robespierre's attempt to implement the penultimate chapter of the *Social Contract* was accompanied by a tribute to Rousseau whose 'profound loathing of vice' had earned him 'hatred and persecution by his rivals and his false friends'. The parallel was too obvious to need elaborating. Robespierre ended his speech with a programme for those 'fêtes nationales' that he had rejected when they would have been under Girondin control.[61]

The attempt by Admiral (or 'Admirat') to shoot Collot d'Herbois and Cécile Renault's even more ineffectual attempt to get at Robespierre reinforced the Incorruptible's conviction that he was the predestined martyr of the Revolution. Collot's competition was as unwelcome as Marat's. At the Jacobins on 25 May, Robespierre denounced the 'cunning trap' offered by someone who proposed civic honours for the man who challenged Admiral, together with a thanksgiving service to the Supreme Being for preserving the lives of the two deputies. Almost any initiative was now suspect. Two days later, Robespierre returned to a favourite theme: 'When we have fallen beneath their blows ... there will not be a Frenchman who will not wish to come before our bloody corpses to swear to kill the last of the people's enemies.'

One did not have to wait until that dreadful day. The bill for the reorganisation of revolutionary justice that Couthon sprang on the Convention on 10 June, apparently without previous discussion in the Committee of Public Safety, transformed the Revolutionary Tribunal into a 'people's court' in which conviction depended on the sentiment of the jury and defendants were denied the right to employ counsel and to call witnesses. Intervening in support of Couthon, Robespierre implied that anyone who opposed the immediate passage of the bill – which could be construed as depriving deputies of their parliamentary immu-

[60] Robespierre, *Œuvres*, vol. X, p. 414.
[61] *Ibid.*, vol. X, pp. 458–61.

nity – was part of an aristocratic plot. But for 'a fortunate chance of the Revolution', he himself would have been the first victim of calumny and proscription. He seemed to have forgotten about Lepeletier and Marat. On 1 July, it was Providence rather than chance that was responsible for his preservation.

His tendency to retreat into fantasy was growing all the time. On 17 November, the British had helped to start the Revolution. Together with Austria, Russia, Prussia and 'Italy' they had set up a secret government in France that was responsible for food shortages and religious disturbances.[62] By the end of March, the casualties in the Champ de Mars massacre had risen to 2,000.[63] Danton had been 'cold and mute when liberty faced its gravest dangers'.[64]

By now, Robespierre had some reason to refer to himself as a 'patriote isolé', though he alone was responsible for his isolation. He had alienated his colleagues on the Committee by proposing his own policies without consulting them. After a violent quarrel, he began to boycott their sessions.[65] He gave hints of his frustrations to the Jacobins, where Couthon implied that the Committee of Public Safety was obstructing another 'final' purge of half a dozen deputies. Montagnards who thought it safer not to sleep at home were not being alarmist. Robespierre made a note that Bourdon 'constantly walks about with the air of an assassin contemplating a crime'.[66] What he saw as their plotting was no more than self-defence. On 23 July, the Committee of Public Safety held a meeting that Robespierre consented to attend, in the hope of resolving its divisions. He appears to have said nothing but Couthon and Saint-Just accepted the compromise and Saint-Just was commissioned to draft a united report to the Convention.

Three days later Robespierre, presumably believing himself to be the victim of another plot, broke the truce with a speech to the Assembly that summed up his whole political life. He was the innocent victim in a fight to the finish between absolutes of good and evil. The proof that he was right was to be found in his unique career. 'Who has defended the National Convention at the peril of his life?' He was 'a slave of liberty, a living martyr of the Republic'. Once again, it was the government's refusal to engage in effective repression that was allowing its enemies to endanger the Revolution. 'It is terror of crime that provides the security of innocence' and the 'cowardly weakness' of the revolutionary govern-

62 *Ibid.*, vol. X, pp. 278–9.
63 Albert Mathiez, *Etudes sur Robespierre* (Paris, 1958), p. 140.
64 Robespierre, *Œuvres*, vol. X, p. 456.
65 Mathiez, *Etudes sur Robespierre*, pp. 148–76.
66 B. Courtois, *Rapport fait au nom de la commission chargée de l'examen des papiers de Robespierre* (Paris, An III), p. 192.

ment meant that Paris was threatened with an insurrection. The only culprits he named were three members of the Finance Committee but he insinuated that the Revolution was at risk because of the activities of the Committee of General Security and its agents and compromised by his colleagues, Carnot, Barère, Lindet and Billaud-Varenne. He therefore demanded the replacement of the Committee of General Security and its subordination to a purged Committee of Public Safety. His intention, he assured the deputies, was merely to 'end the specific quarrels' and he asked for the last time, 'What can be held against a man who is in the right and who knows how to die for his country?' He had said it every time that he had exposed and destroyed a batch of false friends who had turned out to be in foreign pay and there was no reason to suppose that he would not go on saying it indefinitely. This time, the Convention had had enough.

VI

Robespierre's contribution to the Terror raises two main questions, neither of them allowing of an easy answer: how far did he actually believe what he said and how much difference had he made? The first of these was epitomised by his attitude towards Danton. When he supplied Saint-Just with a list of Danton's counter-revolutionary activities from 1789 onwards, this contained only two pieces of information that he had not known when he had dismissed all the charges against Danton in the previous December. In a recent conversation, Danton had accused Desmoulins of a 'vice privé et honteux' and he had supported Delacroix's bill for the abolition of slavery, in the hope of destroying the French colonies.[67] Saint-Just thought it prudent to omit the second of these from his own speech. If Robespierre believed what he wrote, how could he have defended a man whom he knew to be a villain and a foreign agent? To argue that the evolving situation had opened his eyes and led him to perceive the perfidy behind what he had previously taken to be errors of judgement, does not say much for his self-advertised political acumen. More seriously, if one examines the actual charges, it means conceding that the truth was whatever corresponded to anything that Robespierre wanted to believe at any particular time. That was why no one was safe. As he brooded over the situation in the summer of 1794, he noted that Bourdon had once proposed draining marshes at a time of fish shortages![68] To suggest that he was innocently mistaken is also to overlook the contrast between his public speeches and his more

[67] Mathiez, *Etudes sur Robespierre*, chapter 6.
[68] Courtois, *Rapport*, p. 191.

confidential activities. Smiting the unrighteous looked rather less heroic when it came to writing *Approuvé* against Herman's proposal to 'purge the prisons at a stroke and clear the soil of the Republic of this refuse, these rejects of humanity'.[69]

Robespierre's political influence may well have been exaggerated. After his death he was everyone's scapegoat and he was subsequently canonised by a school of twentieth-century historians. His rôle had been to provide the justification for movements that others had set in motion: the overthrow of the Girondins, the extremist offensive in the summer of 1793 and the 'indulgent' counter-attack a few months later, the proscription of Danton that he had abetted when he had been unable to prevent it. He never exercised any departmental responsibility and his influence on policy-making was confined to a few initiatives, such as the self-denying ordinance of 1791, the cult of the Supreme Being and (presumably) Couthon's Prairial law that transformed the Revolutionary Tribunal. All this is true enough but it tends to overlook the fragility of revolutionary government in the Convention, where the powers of the Committee of Public Safety expired every month. Robespierre's justified reputation for incorruptibility and his self-advertised *vertu* gave him a unique, if not always an unquestioned, authority in the Jacobin club and the Convention. He helped to win the vote of confidence for the Committee of Public Safety in September 1793 and he silenced Danton's would-be defenders on 31 March 1794. By the summer of that year, he was the man who was feared by all the Montagnard deputies whose past activities had associated them with discredited policies or people. His colleagues on the Committee, who were not afraid to challenge him in secret session, were apprehensive about provoking a political crisis by public dissent. To the extent that the revolutionary dictatorship was an instrument for winning the war, it had lost its justification after the battle of Fleurus on 26 June and the main problem was how to negotiate an orderly return to constitutional government. By now Robespierre had committed himself to the creation of an ideal society which, in his mind, was indistinguishable from the extermination of the corrupt and the self-seeking. That meant the indefinite prolongation of the Terror. Since he was incapable of distinguishing between dissent and treason, it also implied his personal rule. However one assesses his contribution to the complex of events, policies and attitudes that made up the Terror, the Thermidor crisis, which was his sole responsibility, left those who overthrew him with an unmanageable legacy.

[69] AN, F^7 4436.

Part IV

Robespierre in retrospect

11 Carlyle's seagreen Robespierre and the perilous delights of picturesque history

Mark Cumming

When Thomas Carlyle's history of the French Revolution first appeared in 1837, reviewers applauded Carlyle's ability to bring history to life before his readers' eyes. John Stuart Mill, for instance, effusively praised his friend's graphic powers in the *London and Westminster Review*:

> Mr Carlyle ... brings us *acquainted* with persons, things, and events, before he suggests to us what to think of them: nay, we see that this is the very process by which he arrives at his own thoughts; he paints the thing to himself – he constructs a picture of it in his own mind, and does not, till afterwards, make any logical propositions about it at all. This done, his logical propositions concerning the thing may be true, or may be false; the thing is there, and any reader may find a totally different set of propositions in it if he can; as he might in the reality, if *that* had been before him.[1]

While Mill's generous remarks suggest why the images of *The French Revolution* were so appealing to Carlyle's contemporary audience, they gloss over some of the problems arising from his visual techniques. Some of Carlyle's most compelling pictures are simply unfactual, as the historian Oscar Browning showed late in the nineteenth century. As he tricycled from Paris to Varennes, Browning came to the conclusion that many of the details in Carlyle's celebrated account of the flight to Varennes are 'inexact' and 'some of them quite wrong and misleading'. 'This is the danger of the picturesque school of historians,' he complained. 'They will be picturesque at any price.'[2] And Carlyle's images, far from offering a neutral account of historical events, embody many of his fundamental prejudices, most notably his belief that the French were not equipped spiritually or intellectually to understand their own Revolution. While it might be comforting to assume that the historian moves in an orderly fashion from facts to 'logical propositions', it seems as

1 From an unsigned review reprinted in Jules Paul Seigel (ed.), *Thomas Carlyle: the Critical Heritage* (New York, 1971), p. 61. Compare Albert J. LaValley's similar observation that Carlyle's habitual first response to a historical subject was 'to look and see rather than to theorize and judge' (*Carlyle and the Idea of the Modern* (New Haven, 1968), p. 155).

2 Oscar Browning, *The Flight to Varennes and Other Historical Essays* (London, 1892), pp. 52, 76.

likely, especially with an author of such concentrated visionary power as Carlyle, that his personal and aesthetic predispositions invariably shape his facts.

More credible to a late twentieth-century reader are Carlyle's own remarks on historians of the French Revolution published a few months before Mill's review and in the same journal:

> Each individual takes up the Phenomenon according to his own point of vision, to the structure of his optic organs; – gives, consciously, some poor crotchety picture of several things; unconsciously some picture of himself at least. And the Phenomenon, for its part, subsists there, all the while, unaltered; waiting to be pictured as often as you like, its entire meaning not to be compressed into any picture drawn by man.[3]

Carlyle anticipated recent critical theory in his recognition that the historical image is two-faced, pointing outwards to the historical subject and inwards to the author's psyche. It is the self-expressive content of the historical image that makes the practice of picturesque or visionary history both appealing and treacherous. As Lionel Gossman, a staunch detractor of visionary history, has argued in his distinguished work on Michelet, the visionary historian's narrative can 'prompt a vicarious participation in Revolution as . . . a kind of political pornography'. It can 'excite a potentially dangerous inclination to play out personal, probably erotic fantasies on the stage of politics, using other people as props'. The visionary narrative can make history the raw material for a personal mythology which the reader is encouraged to accept by faith rather than criticise by reason.[4]

Carlyle's narrative replays the Revolution as a heroic, deeply personal battle between truth and falsehood, between the realities of hunger and injustice and the human formulae (a corrupt monarchy and an inadequate political radicalism) that failed so miserably to address them. It transforms historical events generated by chance, coincidence and complex personalities into the morally inevitable events of myth.[5] When

[3] Thomas Carlyle, 'Parliamentary history of the French Revolution', in *The Works of Thomas Carlyle*, Centenary Edition, ed. H. D. Traill, 30 vols. (London, 1896–9) (hereafter cited as *Works*), vol. XXIX, p. 2. The three volumes of *The French Revolution* (cited below as *French Revolution*, vol. I, *French Revolution*, vol. II and *French Revolution*, vol. III) occupy vols. II, III and IV of this edition.

[4] Lionel Gossman, 'Michelet and the French Revolution', in James Heffernan (ed.), *Representing the French Revolution: Literature, Historiography and Art* (Hanover, N.H., 1992), pp. 100–1, 104. See also Gossman's *Towards a Rational Historiography*, Transactions of the American Philosophical Society 79:3 (Philadelphia, 1989) and *Between History and Literature* (Cambridge, Mass., 1990). While I continue to enjoy the kind of narrative history written by Carlyle and Michelet, I have found Gossman's scepticism helpful and enlightening.

[5] Carlyle himself depicted his book as the product of an intensely personal battle for self-expression, and his friend Ralph Waldo Emerson greeted it in similar terms: 'You have

Carlyle depicts the Montgolfier brothers' balloon as an emblem of pre-revolutionary ardour and warns of an explosion to come, he evokes the fate of Icarus and represents the Revolution as an inevitable progression to the Reign of Terror.[6] When he portrays the abbé Siéyès building 'Constitutions (as many as wanted) skyhigh, – which shall all unfortunately fall before he get the scaffolding away',[7] he recalls the tower of Babel and its attendant biblical notions of pretension and divine punishment. Carlyle's visionary conception of history encourages metaphorical identification of the visual fact with mythic meaning.

Of crucial importance in this transformation of fact into myth is Maximilien Robespierre, for Carlyle the living embodiment of the revolutionaries' spiritual and intellectual limitations and the fatal product of their predisposition to narrow rhetoric and constitutional panaceas. The figure of 'seagreen Robespierre', so vividly conceived that it assumes an imaginative existence distinct from its historical original, reveals both the aesthetic delights and the attendant dangers of Carlyle's visual techniques. Carlyle's image of the 'resolute-tremulous incorruptible sea-green man'[8] is, in its way, quite brilliant, yet the factual basis for this portrait is tenuous – Carlyle made his greenish veins the distinguishing feature of his whole physical being – and what Carlyle did with the fact, when he had established it to his own satisfaction, is extreme. He used the physical greenness to characterise the whole man as an unnatural figure distinguished by cowardice, effeminacy and 'cheap magnanimity'[9] and to characterise the Revolution itself in its final anarchic phase. Carlyle's memorable portrait, rather than reflecting the ever-shifting conditions under which the revolutionary leader worked, is entirely suffused with mythic inevitability. In Robespierre's green face, Carlyle suggested, we can discern with moral certainty the Reign of Terror, the confusion of Babel, the explosion of the balloon.

I

If Carlyle's portrait of Robespierre is the product of his own preconceptions, it is hardly alone in this respect, for the whole corpus of Robespierre studies is a hall of mirrors, where startlingly different images confront us, and the possibility of establishing an actual, original Robespierre imperfectly reflected in them seems remote.[10] The sequence of

broken away from all books, & written a mind' (letter of 13 September 1837, in *The Correspondence of Emerson and Carlyle*, ed. Joseph Slater (New York, 1964), p. 167).

6 *French Revolution*, vol. I, p. 51.

7 *Ibid.*, vol. I, p. 144. 8 *Ibid.*, vol. II, p. 202. 9 *Ibid.*, vol. II, p. 199.

10 Among the useful surveys of Robespierre's changing image are *Actes du colloque Robespierre. XIIe congrès international des sciences historiques (Vienne, 3 septembre 1965).*

images and counter-images started with Robespierre himself. As David P. Jordan has usefully established in his study of *The Revolutionary Career of Maximilien Robespierre*, Robespierre's success stemmed largely from his fashioning of himself, through his humble lodgings, his self-effacing oratory and the propriety of his dress, as a prototype of the ardent revolutionary; this fashioning, Jordan argues, effected the 'total politicization of the inner and outer man'.[11] For the Thermidorians who overthrew Robespierre, it was necessary to recast the self-denying revolutionary as the self-absorbed tyrant and to transform his lodgings in the rue Saint-Honoré, formerly 'the ideal setting for a champion of the people', into 'the sinister refuge of a would-be dictator'.[12] The *Mémoires de Barbaroux*, for instance, depict Robespierre's chamber as a shrine in which 'his own likeness was repeated in every form, and by every art – in paintings on the right-hand wall, in engravings on the left; his bust at one end of the room, and his bas-relief at the other – not to mention half a dozen small engravings of his portrait on the tables'.[13]

The process of redefining Robespierre's image returned to prominence during times of revolutionary tension throughout the nineteenth century. Ann Rigney has demonstrated how French historians of the 1840s used images of Robespierre as vehicles for authorial ideology. While the 'prototypical' characteristics of Robespierre's appearance (his paleness, his thinness and his meticulous dress) remain constant from history to history, those characteristics are invested with quite different significance. In describing Robespierre's slender physique, Rigney writes, 'the different historians choose a different property from within the semantic field of "noncorpulence," along an evaluative scale running from meager to slim'. The pallor that in Louis Blanc's writings signifies 'the strength of [Robespierre's] conviction as defender of the people's rights' in Michelet's work signifies his 'lack of color', 'the rigidity of his posture' and 'the lack of creativity in his thinking and writing'. And as Rigney documents, the debate over Robespierre's

Avant-propos par Albert Soboul (Paris, 1967); François Crouzet, *Historians and the French Revolution: the Case of Maximilien Robespierre* (Swansea, 1989); George Rudé (ed.), *Robespierre*, Great Lives Observed (Englewood Cliffs, N.J., 1967); George Rudé, *Robespierre: Portrait of a Revolutionary Democrat* (New York, 1975), pp. 55–92; and J. M. Thompson, *Robespierre* (Oxford, 1935; 3rd edition, 1988), pp. 593–633, with an updated 'Bibilographical note' by Colin Lucas, pp. 635–40.

11 David P. Jordan, *The Revolutionary Career of Maximilien Robespierre* (New York, 1985), p. 4.

12 Thompson, *Robespierre*, p. 526.

13 *Mémoires de Barbaroux*, ed. A. Chabaud (Paris, 1936), p. 144, translated in Thompson, *Robespierre*, p. 526.

appearance has continued well into the twentieth century.[14] As recently as 1985 Jordan provides an appendix on the 'Portraits of Robespierre' and offers an alternative description of the furnishings in his room: 'His own room at the Duplays' was simply furnished, with a bed, a writing table, a small bookcase. Only a terra-cotta bust in a niche, his portrait on the wall, declared the place his.'[15]

Carlyle's image of Robespierre was formed early in his preparation for writing *The French Revolution* and remained essentially unchanged. Early in 1833, he wrote to Mill concerning a 'series of Revolution Portraits' he had recently obtained (the *Collection complète des tableaux historiques de la Révolution française*), which confirmed his conception of Robespierre as 'a narrow, exasperated, exacerbated Methodist Precentor'.[16] Although Mill subsequently wrote to Carlyle to warn him of the possible inaccuracy of the 'Revolution Portraits',[17] the image of Robespierre was so fixed in his mind that, in a letter of February 1835, he felt free to compare an English radical whom he had just met to Robespierre:

> Roebuck the Radical [is] our main man; a smallest and neatest of men, miniature classical head, with miniature aquiline nose, screeching argumentative voice; radical-logic, limitation, vehemence, self-conceit – all in the superlative. The little face, when you look close to it, is all minutely wrinkled; anger, dissatisfaction, vinaigrous ... unrest looks painfully out from it: a hidebound barren man, with only audacity considerable; likest Robespierre of anything I have seen.[18]

The readiness with which Carlyle identified Roebuck and Robespierre suggests the degree to which his conception of Robespierre depended on a preconceived notion of the political radical rather than a consideration of the man himself. Carlyle's image of Robespierre remained unchanged in the 1837 essay on 'Mirabeau', despite John Wilson Croker's sympathetic reassessment in his important study for the *Quarterly Review* in

14 Ann Rigney, 'Icon and symbol: the historical figure called Maximilien Robespierre', in Heffernan, *Representing the French Revolution*, pp. 113, 114–15, 121 n. 14.

15 Jordan, *Robespierre*, p. 58.

16 From a letter of 22 February 1833, in *The Collected Letters of Thomas and Jane Welsh Carlyle*, Duke-Edinburgh edition, ed. Charles Richard Sanders, Kenneth J. Fielding, Clyde de L. Ryals *et al.* (Durham, N.C., 1970–) (hereafter cited as *Letters*), vol. VI, pp. 331–2.

17 See his letter of 9 March 1833, in *The Earlier Letters of John Stuart Mill 1812–1848*, ed. Francis E. Mineka, vols. XII and XIII of the *Collected Works of John Stuart Mill* (Toronto, 1963), vol. XII, p. 146.

18 *Letters*, vol. VIII, p. 51. Later in the same year, Carlyle noted that 'Roebuck seems to be becoming a kind of English Marat. He has not the stuff of Marat; is more like some poor acidulent cold-implacable Robespierre.' (*Ibid.*, vol. VIII, p. 175.)

1835.[19] The 'Mirabeau' essay cites Robespierre as an instance of the Revolution's 'rabid triviality' and offers him as a painful contrast to its 'original men', Napoleon, Danton and Mirabeau:

Consider Maximilien Robespierre; for the greater part of two years, what one may call Autocrat of France. A poor sea-green (*verdâtre*) atrabiliar Formula of a man; without head, without heart, or any grace, gift, or even vice beyond common, if it were not vanity, astucity, diseased rigour (which some count strength), as of a cramp: really a most poor sea-green individual in spectacles; meant by Nature for a Methodist parson of the stricter sort, to doom men who departed from the written confession; to chop fruitless shrill logic; to contend, and suspect, and ineffectually wrestle and wriggle; and, on the whole, to love, or to know, or to be (properly speaking) Nothing: – this was he who, the sport of wracking winds, saw himself whirled aloft to command *la première nation de l'univers*, and all men shouting long life to him: one of the most lamentable, tragic, sea-green objects whirled aloft in that manner, in any country, to his own swift destruction, and the world's long wonder![20]

At the end of Carlyle's researches Robespierre is still the 'Methodist parson' fervently devoted to an insufficient cause. The single feature that distinguishes this final image of Robespierre from the earlier one is the seagreen hue.

In March 1835, Carlyle wrote to Mill saying that he wanted to consult Madame de Staël's *Considérations sur les principaux événements de la Révolution française*, and it is from her portrait that he took the fact of Robespierre's greenish complexion: 'Ses traits étaient ignobles, son teint pâle, ses veines d'une couleur verte' or, in the English translation Carlyle cites, 'His features were mean, his complexion pale, his veins of a greenish hue.'[21] When Carlyle first introduces Robespierre in *The French Revolution*, he is apparently hesitant to insist on his subject's greenness. The Robespierre who joins the procession of the Estates General in May 1789 is an 'anxious, slight, ineffectual-looking man, under thirty, in spectacles; his eyes (were the glasses off) troubled, careful; with upturned face, snuffing dimly the uncertain future time; complexion of a multiplex atrabiliar colour, the final shade of which may

19 Reprinted in John Wilson Croker, *Essays on the Early Period of the French Revolution* (London, 1857, repr. New York, 1970), pp. 299–430.

20 *Works*, vol. XXVIII, p. 409. For the source of the phrase 'without head, without heart', see *French Revolution*, vol. III, p. 130, which quotes Condorcet's description of '"a Robespierre without an idea in his head . . . or a feeling in his heart"'.

21 *Œuvres posthumes de Madame la Baronne de Staël-Holstein* (Paris, 1861, repr. Geneva, 1967), p. 183. The English version is given in Rudé, *Robespierre*, Great Lives Observed, p. 123. Carlyle's repeated substitution of 'verdâtre' for Madame de Staël's 'verte' may derive (as David Sorensen has generously informed me) from Helen Maria Williams's description of his greenish spectacles ('lunettes verdâtres') as noted in the third edition of Barbaroux's *Mémoires* (Paris, 1827), p. 64n.

be the pale sea-green'.[22] The 'may be' appears tentative enough, yet it masks the substantial leap Carlyle has already made by transposing the greenish colour of the veins to the entire complexion. And in the very next sentence, the qualifying 'pale' is dropped and the greenness is solidly established as the distinguishing feature of the subject's entire physical being: 'That greenish-coloured (*verdâtre*) individual is an Advocate of Arras; his name is *Maximilien Robespierre*.' Very quickly, the possibility of Robespierre's greenish complexion has become an ineradicable fact of his essential nature and, by extension, of the Revolution's. Carlyle's phrase 'seagreen Robespierre' – sometimes coupled with the historically derived term 'Incorruptible' – becomes one of his most celebrated epic epithets, and the *leitmotiv* of Robespierre's greenness recurs throughout the three long volumes.[23] Robespierre's appearance and nature become frozen. His career becomes not a series of responses to particular challenges but a working-out of what has been in the self from the beginning; and his miserable fate is not the product of alterable circumstances but the inevitable result of his own meanness and greenness. The face becomes the story of the man.

While Carlyle's use of physiognomy may seem to be an obviously literary technique for drawing a character, there is an important context for it in earlier memoirs and histories of the French Revolution. Carlyle's adjective 'atrabiliar', which draws on the time-worn theory that specific humours determine individual personalities, recalls the suggestion, made in the *Mémoires de Barras* (and elsewhere), that Robespierre was always 'atrabilaire' and 'triste'. These same memoirs read the relative fates of Robespierre and Danton in physiognomic terms: they quote 'a physiognomist of the Revolution' as arguing that Robespierre 'was bilious, that is to say full of hatred and distrustful', while Danton 'was sanguine, that is to say generous and confident. The confident temperament had to yield to the envious one.'[24] Merlin de Thionville went so far as to assert that Robespierre's appearance actually changed as the Revolution progressed and as he became more consumed by violence

[22] *French Revolution*, vol. I, p. 141.

[23] Among the many available discussions of *The French Revolution* and epic tradition, readers may wish to consult LaValley, *Carlyle and the Idea of the Modern*; John D. Rosenberg, *Carlyle and the Burden of History* (Oxford, 1985); and my *A Disimprisoned Epic: Form and Vision in Carlyle's 'French Revolution'* (Philadelphia, 1988).

[24] George Duruy (ed.), *Mémoires de Barras*, 4 vols. (Paris, 1895–6), vol. III, p. 278: 'Un physiologiste de la Révolution a dit, avec raison peut-être, que toute l'histoire de Robespierre et de Danton pouvait se résumer en deux traits décisifs des causes et des conséquences de leur destinée différente. Le premier, Robespierre, était bilieux, c'est-à-dire haineux et défiant; le second, Danton, était sanguin, c'est-à-dire généreux et confiant. Le tempérament de la confiance devait succomber devant celui de l'envie.' For 'atrabilaire' and 'triste', see *ibid.*, vol. I, p. 145.

and envy: 'In the Constituent Assembly his complexion was pale and wan; in the Convention it became livid and yellow.'[25] Whether Robespierre's enemies profoundly believed in the theory of the humours or merely used it for the purposes of self-serving rhetoric, the art of physiognomy allowed them to transfer their disagreements with Robespierre from history to nature.

Carlyle's use of physiognomy also placed the problem with Robespierre in nature rather than particular circumstances, but his understanding of Robespierre's career differed from those of his predecessors. Robespierre's early detractors, if they did not portray him as positively tyrannical, tended to argue that his vices overcame his virtues as the Revolution progressed. Carlyle, however, was less interested in his alleged vices than in his inadequate virtues, his unyielding devotion to the insufficient creed of the French Revolution, 'the Gospel according to Jean-Jacques'.[26] Consequently, Robespierre's appearances in *The French Revolution* delineate not a development from ardour to despotism but a manifestation of his essential nature in time. From the beginning of the history until the end, Robespierre is the 'thin lean Puritan and Precisian' who 'would make away with formulas; yet lives, moves, and has his whole being wholly in formulas, of another sort'.[27] From beginning to end, he is the self-deceived and impercipient man unable to fathom the reality of the event in which he plays such a major rôle.[28]

II

The first crucial instance of Robespierre's impercipience appears in Carlyle's account of the crisis following the flight to Varennes, which offers an unflattering recreation of an unflattering anecdote from Madame Roland's memoirs. To some historians this anecdote has displayed Robespierre's admirable caution in a difficult situation,[29] but to Carlyle it is a moment of fateful ignorance. He writes that Robespierre's patriot friends

> would fain have comforted the seagreen man; spake of Achille de Châtelet's Placard; of a Journal to be called *The Republican*; of preparing men's minds for a

[25] Quoted in Rudé, *Robespierre*, Great Lives Observed, pp. 106–7.

[26] *French Revolution*, vol. III, p. 211.

[27] *Ibid.*, vol. I, p. 221.

[28] One of the rare instances in which Carlyle praised Robespierre's insight is the debate on the execution of Louis XVI. While many attempted to use pre-revolutionary law to justify a revolutionary execution, Robespierre had the vision to see that 'it was needless to speak of Law; that here, if never elsewhere, our Right was Might' (*French Revolution*, vol. III, p. 91). Croker advanced a very similar argument in his essay on Robespierre (*Essays*, p. 363).

[29] See, for instance, Thompson, *Robespierre*, pp. 158–9 and Ralph Korngold, *Robespierre: First Modern Dictator* (London, 1937), pp. 110–11.

> Republic. 'A Republic?' said the Seagreen, with one of his dry husky *un*sportful laughs, 'What is that?' O seagreen Incorruptible, thou shalt see![30]

Carlyle's apostrophe, with its prophetic biblical language, evokes the eternal truth which Robespierre and his shallow revolutionary gospel cannot fathom. The entire anecdote, dramatically isolated at the end of a chapter of the second volume, recalls a strikingly similar anecdote from the first volume, also located at a chapter's end, which recreates the evening of 14 July 1789, when Louis XVI is informed of what has transpired in Paris:

> In the Court, all is mystery, not without whisperings of terror; though ye dream of lemonade and epaulettes, ye foolish women! His Majesty, kept in happy ignorance, perhaps dreams of double-barrels and the Woods of Meudon. Late at night, the Duke de Liancourt, having official right of entrance, gains access to the Royal Apartments; unfolds, with earnest clearness, in his constitutional way, the Job's-news. '*Mais*,' said poor Louis, '*c'est une révolte*, Why, that is a revolt!' – 'Sire,' answered Liancourt, 'it is not a revolt, – it is a revolution.'[31]

Through the structural parallel of the two anecdotes Carlyle suggests that Robespierre is as ignorant as Louis XVI of the Revolution's essential nature – its colossal assertion of the need to re-establish true and just relations among men – which dwarfs an effete monarchy and an ineffectual political radicalism alike.

A second moment of impercipience appears in Carlyle's account of the September massacres of 1792, his most devastating portrait of Robespierre as self-deceived Methodist. Carlyle suggests, as J. M. Thompson does in his chilling account of this episode,[32] that Robespierre was so caught up in revolutionary dogma that he could ignore massive human suffering:

> A Thousand and eighty-nine lie dead, 'two-hundred and sixty heaped carcasses on the Pont au Change' itself; – among which, Robespierre pleading afterwards will 'nearly weep' to reflect that there was said to be one slain innocent. One; not two, O thou seagreen Incorruptible? If so, Themis Sansculotte must be lucky; for she was brief![33]

Once again, the apostrophe underscores how inadequate a response Robespierre's cheap sentimentality is to the appalling reality of the situation, presented in the Goyaesque vision which follows:

> Carts go along the streets; full of stript human corpses, thrown pell-mell; limbs sticking up: – seest thou that cold Hand sticking up, through the heaped embrace of brother corpses, in its yellow paleness, in its cold rigour; the palm opened towards Heaven, as if in dumb prayer, in expostulation *de profundis*, Take pity on the Sons of Men![34]

[30] *French Revolution*, vol. II, p. 168.
[31] *Ibid.*, vol. I, p. 200.
[32] Thompson, *Robespierre*, p. 290.
[33] *French Revolution*, vol. III, p. 41.
[34] *Ibid.*, vol. III, p. 42.

A third and definitive moment of impercipience is the feast of the Supreme Being, the apotheosis of Robespierre's career as a formula and windbag. This apotheosis is positioned in history where we might expect it to occur in a novel or drama, immediately before Robespierre's downfall. Carlyle's chapter on the festival, provocatively entitled 'Mumbo-Jumbo', explores hollow and insufficient images: Robespierre's image of himself and the contrived religious images created by his ally 'Painter David'. 'All the world is there, in holiday clothes: foul linen went out with Hébertists; nay Robespierre, for one, would never once countenance that; but went always elegant and frizzled, not without vanity even, – and had his room hung round with seagreen Portraits and Busts.'[35] The detail of Robespierre's room full of self-icons is used here with deft satiric effect (the image being rendered doubly comic if we take the adjective 'seagreen' to govern 'Busts' as well as 'Portraits'). The physical detail, which for Barbaroux signified a dangerous dictatorial ambition, for Carlyle signifies a grotesque superficiality.[36] In Carlyle's vision, 'Mahomet Robespierre, in sky-blue coat and black breeches, frizzled and powdered to perfection' is a figure of ridicule, engaged in a pathetic feeble charade:

> The seagreen Pontiff takes a torch, Painter David handing it; mouths some other froth-rant of vocables, which happily one cannot hear; strides resolutely forward, in sight of expectant France; sets his torch to Atheism and Company, which are but made of pasteboard steeped in turpentine. They burn up rapidly; and, from within, there rises 'by machinery,' an incombustible Statue of Wisdom, which, by ill hap, gets besmoked a little; but does stand there visible in as serene attitude as it can.[37]

This jauntily satiric presentation of Robespierre as the ungainly 'Mahomet' and Pope of his own religion (and here again Carlyle appears to take his imagery from Robespierre's contemporaries)[38] quickly gives way to biblical denunciation:

> Mumbo-Jumbo of the African woods to me seems venerable beside this new Deity of Robespierre; for this is a *conscious* Mumbo-Jumbo, and *knows* that he is machinery. O seagreen Prophet, unhappiest of windbags blown nigh to bursting,

[35] *Ibid.*, vol. III, p. 266.

[36] Carlyle appears to suggest that Robespierre himself was responsible for the self-icons in his room, but others ascribe their presence to the Duplay family. See, for instance, Max Gallo, who comments on a description of Robespierre's study in the memoirs of La Révellière-Lépeaux very similar to Barbaroux's: 'They [the busts and portraits] were certainly signs of affection that Robespierre had not asked for; yet they could only influence the psychology of a man who felt himself to be predestined.' *Robespierre the Incorruptible: a Psycho-Biography*, trans. Raymond Rudorff (New York, 1971), p. 124.

[37] *French Revolution*, vol. III, p. 267.

[38] See for instance the *Memoirs of Bertrand Barère*, trans. De V. Payen-Payne, 4 vols. (London, 1896), vol. II, p. 165, where the ideas of Robespierre as 'revolutionary Pope' and 'Mahomet' are coupled.

what distracted Chimera among realities art thou growing to! This then, this common pitch-link for artifical fireworks of turpentine and pasteboard; *this* is the miraculous Aaron's Rod thou wilt stretch over a hag-ridden hell-ridden France, and bid her plagues cease? Vanish, thou and it! – '*Avec ton Etre Suprême*,' said Billaud, '*tu commences [à] m'embêter*: With thy *Etre Suprême* thou beginnest to be a bore to me.'[39]

The phrase '*Etre Suprême*', which Carlyle here doggedly repeats rather than translates, is reiterated insistently in the following pages as the emblem of Robespierre's inflated triumph and as the supreme indictment of his revolutionary faith.

The physical complement to Robespierre's impercipience is his physical impotence, cowardice and effeminacy, which are exposed most starkly in his encounters with Danton. The Robespierre–Danton pairing, which has been treated so often in books and films, exemplifies for Carlyle the ultimate confrontation of the superficial with the elemental:

One conceives easily the deep mutual incompatibility that divided these two: with what terror of feminine hatred the poor seagreen Formula looked at the monstrous colossal Reality, and grew greener to behold him; – the Reality, again, struggling to think no ill of a chief-product of the Revolution; yet feeling at bottom that such chief-product was little other than a chief windbag, blown large by Popular air; not a man, with the heart of a man, but a poor spasmodic incorruptible pedant, with a logic-formula instead of heart; of Jesuit or Methodist-Parson nature; full of sincere-cant, incorruptibility, of virulence, poltroonery; barren as the eastwind! Two such chief-products are too much for one Revolution.[40]

Carlyle's reading of the Robespierre–Danton conflict in gender terms (which, as Ann Rigney notes, is repeated by Michelet)[41] once again exemplifies the dual reference of the image to the historical subject and the author's psyche. It reveals Carlyle's longstanding preference for those who act to those who talk and perhaps betrays something about his own psychic uncertainty concerning his rôle as a writer rather than as a warrior or activist. It might even be read as Carlyle's repudiation of a perceived femininity in his own nature. Certainly the antithesis between the feminine Robespierre and the masculine Danton underscores his sense of Danton as one of the 'original men' of the Revolution.

Carlyle's Danton always impresses us with his size and force, his 'careless, large, hoping nature'.[42] As an unsympathetic John Wilson noted in *Blackwood's Edinburgh Magazine* in 1837, 'Danton is one of his

[39] *French Revolution*, vol. III, pp. 267–8. [40] *Ibid.*, vol. III, p. 254.

[41] Ann Rigney, *The Rhetoric of Historical Representation: Three Narrative Histories of the French Revolution* (Cambridge, 1990), pp. 159, 163.

[42] *French Revolution*, vol. III, p. 255.

darlings, chiefly on account of his huge bulk, vast voice, hideous aspect, and prodigious *tout ensemble*.'[43] At his trial, Danton exudes fierce energy in the face of imminent death. He scorches his accusers with 'passionate words, piercing with their wild sincerity, winged with wrath'. 'Your best Witnesses he shivers into ruin at one stroke ... He raises his huge stature, he shakes his huge black head, fire flashes from the eyes of him, – piercing to all Republican hearts ...'[44] Carlyle's Robespierre, by contrast, is always physically insubstantial: a 'slight, ineffectual-looking man',[45] a 'thin lean Puritan and Precisian',[46] the 'most consistent, incorruptible of thin acrid men',[47] a 'mean meagre mortal',[48] 'the glass of incorruptible thin Patriotism'.[49] He lacks even the rabid vitality of other short revolutionaries like Marat and Louvet,[50] mustering at best a 'resolute timidity'.[51] And unlike Danton, he repeatedly shrinks and cringes before a physical threat. (Indeed, to a Freudian reader, this image of the shrinking Robespierre might suggest a figure of detumescence.) Following the flight to Varennes, Carlyle's Robespierre fears for his life, and here, as elsewhere in the narrative, his greenish complexion reflects his physical cowardice: 'Perhaps, we may say, the most terrified man in Paris or France is – who thinks the reader? – seagreen Robespierre. Double paleness, with the shadow of gibbets and halters, overcasts the seagreen features ...'[52] When Robespierre is unsuccessfully challenged in the Convention by Barbaroux in September 1792, he offers only a passive (feminine?) resistance to his accuser, which recalls, though only by contrast, Christ's behaviour towards his tormentors: 'With such sanctified meekness does the Incorruptible lift his seagreen cheek to the smiter; lift his thin voice, and with jesuitic dexterity plead, and prosper ...'[53] When Robespierre is later challenged by Louvet, there is an unmistakable contrast between the energy of the accuser and the cowardice of the accused:

For, one day, among the last of October, Robespierre, being summoned to the tribune by some new hint of that old calumny of the Dictatorship, was speaking and pleading there, with more and more comfort to himself; till rising high in heart, he cried out valiantly: Is there any man here that dare specifically accuse

43 'Poetry by our new contributor', *Blackwood's Edinburgh Magazine* 42 (1837), 592.
44 *French Revolution*, vol. III, pp. 257–8.
45 *Ibid.*, vol. I, p. 141.
46 *Ibid.*, vol. I, p. 221.
47 *Ibid.*, vol. II, p. 114.
48 *Ibid.*, vol. II, p. 136.
49 *Ibid.*, vol. II, p. 202.
50 *Ibid.*, vol. III, pp. 74, 86.
51 *Ibid.*, vol. II, p. 202.
52 *Ibid.*, vol. II, p. 167. J. M. Thompson pointed out that others besides Robespierre – Madame Roland included – shared similar fears (*Robespierre*, pp. 155–6). But the impression of a terror unique to Robespierre conveniently fits Carlyle's impression of his subject's physical cowardice.
53 *French Revolution*, vol. III, p. 75.

me? '*Moi!*' exclaimed one. Pause of deep silence: a lean angry little Figure, with broad bald brow, strode swiftly towards the tribune, taking papers from its pocket: 'I accuse thee, Robespierre,' – I, Jean Baptiste Louvet! The Seagreen became tallowgreen; shrinking to a corner of the tribune: Danton cried, 'Speak, Robespierre; there are many good citizens that listen'; but the tongue refused its office.[54]

Robespierre's silence on this occasion foreshadows his inability to act effectively when challenged by the men of Thermidor.

Robespierre's futile attempt to address the Convention on 27 July 1794 is a final instance of his inability to triumph in a physical confrontation. Last words, in life and in novels, are often held to have definitive significance, not just because they come at the end, but because they offer some kind of ultimate comment on the character of the speaker. But whereas Danton departs Carlyle's stage with 'passionate words, ... winged with wrath', Robespierre leaves with desperate shrieks and impotent muteness:

Robespierre is struggling to speak, but President Thuriot is jingling the bell against him, but the Hall is sounding against him like an Aeolus-Hall: and Robespierre is mounting the Tribune-steps and descending again; going and coming, like to choke with rage, terror, desperation: – and mutiny is the order of the day!

O President Thuriot, ... sawest thou ever the like of this? Jingle of bell, which thou jinglest against Robespierre, is hardly audible amid the Bedlam storm; and men rage for life. 'President of Assassins,' shrieks Robespierre, 'I demand speech of thee for the last time!' It cannot be had. 'To you, O virtuous men of the Plain,' cries he, finding audience one moment, 'I appeal to you!' The virtuous men of the Plain sit silent as stones. And Thuriot's bell jingles, and the Hall sounds like Aeolus's Hall. Robespierre's frothing lips are grown 'blue'; his tongue dry, cleaving to the roof of his mouth. 'The blood of Danton chokes him,' cry they. 'Accusation! Decree of Accusation!' Thuriot swiftly puts that question. Accusation passes; the incorruptible Maximilien is decreed Accused.[55]

While this scene has undoubted dramatic eloquence, its historical authority is called into question by an alternative version of the same scene, contained in Croker's essay, which shows a much more defiant and heroic Robespierre:

In the height of the terrible conflict, and at a moment when Robespierre seemed deprived by rage and agitation of the power of articulation, a voice cried, '*It is Danton's blood that is choking you!*' Robespierre, indignant, recovered his voice and his courage to exclaim, – 'Danton! Is it, then, Danton you regret? *Cowards! – lâches – Why did you not defend him?*'[56]

[54] *Ibid.*, vol. III, pp. 86–7. [55] *Ibid.*, vol. III, pp. 279–80.

[56] Croker, *Essays*, pp. 420–1. Croker was quoting here, though he did not indicate his source.

Both scenes are undoubtedly compelling. Both scenes have the kind of literary reality that marks the last words of Hamlet or Othello or Macbeth. And – to use Gossman's metaphor of visionary history as political pornography – both scenes might be welcome additions to our private collection of images. The first scene evokes the *topoi* of the wheel of Fortune and the fall of tyrants, while the second recalls the motif of the epic hero speaking valiantly in the face of death (the very motif Carlyle applies to Danton). But the historical events reconstituted in the two scenes are fundamentally different and it is possible that neither is historically accurate. J. M. Thompson, who ascribed to Lacretelle the version of the episode Croker presents, argued that it 'misses the point' and offered his own, more prosaic, account: '"It's Danton's blood that's choking him," taunted Garnier. "Is it Danton, then," said Robespierre, "that you are avenging?" and it was a fair retort, considering that he had just been charged with trying to save Danton's life.'[57]

III

Carlyle's handling of 'seagreen Robespierre' offers a telling if extreme instance of his historical practice. It certainly offers good measure of the literary delights that have always attracted readers to *The French Revolution*: a fine sense of history as pageant, an intensely vivid recreation of fact and an overwhelming verbal energy. Yet its inveterately exterior perspective betrays one of Carlyle's fundamental paradoxes, that, while he asserted the importance of people in history, he remained reluctant to explore the complexities of the inner self. In Carlyle's treatment of Robespierre, we do not get what we get in J. M. Thompson's biography, for instance – the author reaching across the gulfs of time (and the English Channel) to recreate a mind differently constituted and differently situated from his own; we have an external caricature in the Hogarth–Dickens vein which always tends to oversimplify this complex man.

The process of oversimplification is encouraged by the almost total suppression of Robespierre's voice in Carlyle's narrative. While critics often praise the multivocality of *The French Revolution* (Andrew Sanders, for instance, describes the text as 'a mosaic of many voices'),[58] Carlyle's Robespierre is notable for how little he says. Robespierre is seldom

57 Thompson, *Robespierre*, pp. 571, 571n.

58 Andrew Sanders, '"The French are always at it" – the impact of the French Revolution on nineteenth-century English literature, 1815–1870', in H. T. Mason and W. Doyle (eds.), *The Impact of the French Revolution on European Consciousness* (Gloucester, 1989), p. 111.

allowed to speak directly in Carlyle's narrative and his words, when rendered indirectly, are presented briefly and dismissively. Note, for instance, this comically abbreviated account of Robespierre's ill-fated last speech to the Convention on 26 July 1794, in which he argued that one more purge was needed to cleanse the Revolution:

The biliary face seems clouded with new gloom: judge whether your Talliens, Bourdons, listened with interest. It is a voice bodeful of death or of life. Longwinded, unmelodious as the screech-owl's, sounds that prophetic voice: Degenerate condition of Republican spirit; corrupt Moderatism; *Sûreté*, *Salut* Committees themselves infected; backsliding on this hand and on that; I, Maximilien, alone left uncorruptible, ready to die at a moment's warning. For all which what remedy is there? The Guillotine; new vigour to the all-healing Guillotine; death to traitors of every hue![59]

Carlyle does energise his text by directing divergent voices towards Robespierre, but these are not evidence of conflicting views, as in Norman Hampson's explicitly multivocal study of him,[60] but merely different modes of negativity. As Carlyle plays cat-and-mouse with his subject, Robespierre is repeatedly bandied back and forth between the left paw of satire and the right paw of moral indignation. Carlyle silences Robespierre much as Thuriot does, as if he suspects that the revolutionary leader's voice might disrupt his personal replaying of the Revolution.

There are, of course, moments of sympathy towards the end of *The French Revolution* which appear to temper Carlyle's dismissive approach to Robespierre. Immediately after the feast of the Supreme Being, Robespierre is shown walking alone, as if in some way prescient of his downfall. In this vignette – reminiscent, as John D. Rosenberg argues, of Christ in the Garden of Gethsemane[61] – Carlyle comes close to making him a person rather than a walking caricature:

The Incorruptible himself sits apart; or is seen stalking in solitary places in the fields, with an intensely meditative air; some say, 'with eyes red-spotted,' fruit of extreme bile: the lamentablest seagreen Chimera that walks the earth that July! O hapless Chimera, – for thou too hadst a life, and heart of flesh, – what is this that the stern gods, seeming to smile all the way, have led and let thee to! Art not thou he, who, few years ago, was a young Advocate of promise; and gave up the Arras Judgeship rather than sentence one man to die?[62]

And Carlyle presents Robespierre just before his death with a warm and generous pathos:

[59] *French Revolution*, vol. III, p. 276.

[60] Norman Hampson, *The Life and Opinions of Maximilien Robespierre* (London, 1974).

[61] Rosenberg explores the Christ-like features of the fallen Robespierre in *Carlyle and the Burden of History*, pp. 104–9.

[62] *French Revolution*, vol. III, p. 275.

Robespierre lay in an anteroom of the Convention Hall, while his Prison-escort was getting ready; the mangled jaw bound up rudely with bloody linen: a spectacle to men. He lies stretched on a table, a deal-box his pillow; the sheath of the pistol is still clenched convulsively in his hand. Men bully him, insult him: his eyes still indicate intelligence; he speaks no word. 'He had on the sky-blue coat he had got made for the Feast of the *Etre Suprême*' – O Reader, can thy hard heart hold out against that? His trousers were nankeen; the stockings had fallen down over the ankles. He spake no word more in this world.[63]

Carlyle's eulogy for Robespierre rather touchingly accepts him as a fellow human being and reintegrates him with humanity:

Stricter man, according to his Formula, to his Credo and Cant, of probities, benevolences, pleasures-of-virtue, and suchlike, lived not in that age. A man fitted, in some luckier settled age, to have become one of those incorruptible barren Pattern-Figures and have had marble-tablets and funeral-sermons. His poor landlord, the Cabinet-maker in the Rue Saint-Honoré, loved him; his Brother died for him. May God be merciful to him and to us![64]

Yet Carlyle could empathise with Robespierre only when he considered him as a private individual separated from his political self. His sympathy for the man becomes one more way of dismissing the revolutionary. And the final effect of Carlyle's portrait of this most famous orator, even to the very moment of his death, is to suggest an ultimate, impotent muteness: 'Samson wrenched the coat off him; wrenched the dirty linen from his jaw: the jaw fell powerless, there burst forth from him a cry; – hideous to hear and see.'[65]

Carlyle's Robespierre says so little partly because Carlyle felt compelled to say so much through him. For Carlyle the Revolution was not a completed event that lent itself to disengaged study. While the part of the Revolution that belonged to France and the years 1789 to 1794 had passed, the larger story of the Revolution had not yet been closed. In his 1839 essay on 'Chartism', Carlyle proclaimed that the Revolution was

not a French revolt only; no, a European one; full of stern monition to all countries of Europe. These Chartisms, Radicalisms, Reform Bill, Tithe Bill, and infinite other discrepancy, and acrid argument and jargon that there is yet to be, are *our* French Revolution: God grant that we, with our better methods, may be able to transact it by argument alone![66]

In his rejection of Robespierre, Carlyle rejected all 'Radicalisms', all strictly political and legislative remedies to the grievous maladies of Europe, which could be cured, in Carlyle's view, only by a return to love, reverence, work and worship. Witness the following remarkable excerpt from *Past and Present* (1843), where a memorable quotation from *The French Revolution* reappears unexpectedly in an English

[63] *Ibid.*, vol. III, pp. 284–5.
[64] *Ibid.*, vol. III, p. 286.
[65] *Ibid.*, vol. III, p. 285.
[66] *Works*, vol. XXIX, pp. 149–50.

context. Pondering the massive social unrest of England, Carlyle launches an attack on the anti-slavery agitations of the Exeter Hall philanthropists. At the conclusion of his tirade, he tells the reformers: 'thy eyes are of the sodden sort; and with thy emancipations, and thy twenty-millionings and long-eared clamourings, thou, like Robespierre with his pasteboard *Etre Suprême*, threatenest to become a bore to us: *Avec ton Etre Suprême tu commences à m'embêter!*'[67] If history is the medium through which Carlyle addressed his own age, it is the exasperated Billaud rather than the zealous Robespierre who speaks for him.

Carlyle's pictures of Robespierre and his age are limited by their sometimes tenuous relation to fact, their exterior perspective and their subservience to the author's personal mythology. Yet the gripping pictures of *The French Revolution* still have the power to make us feel that history matters, that something cosmic and elemental was going on in the last years of the eighteenth century, even if not quite as Carlyle depicted it. The very audacity of Carlyle's images encourages us to question the validity of other historical images which are less obviously (and more insidiously) products of the imagination. Moreover, Carlyle's emphasis on the visual reinforces our sense (undoubtedly heightened by studies of the past few decades) of the degree to which the French Revolution itself depended on the creation and refashioning of images. Carlyle still commands a great deal of respect for his astute insight into the private (if sometimes guilty) aesthetic pleasures we take from historical images and for his recognition of their potency in affecting historical understanding. Whether we enjoy such images serially, as Gossman fears we are likely to do, or work beyond them to propositions that can be tested by rational debate, we will remain gripped by the historical pictures that touch our imaginations: the shrine of the tyrant in Barbaroux's account, the chaste lodgings of the ardent revolutionary in Jordan's study, or Carlyle's cartoon-like chamber filled with the seagreen portraits and seagreen busts of 'seagreen Robespierre'.

[67] *Ibid.*, vol. X, p. 279.

12 Robespierre through the Chartist looking-glass

Gwynne Lewis

A chief whose name will live for evermore,
The man of men, whom myriads will deplore;
For Maximilien's dead! great Robespierre,
(Cropt in his flower – his five-and-thirtieth year),
And nowhere, on this earth, hath left his peer.

(Bronterre O'Brien, *Elegy on the Death of Robespierre* (1857))

If he had been a contemporary historian, Lewis Carroll would have opted for the post-modernist school. Some readers may recall the lines in *Alice Through the Looking-Glass*: 'how nice it would be if we could only get through into Looking-glass House! I'm sure it's got ... such beautiful things in it! ... Let's pretend the glass has got soft like gauze, so that we can get through.'[1] In our revisionist, deconstructionist, neo-idealist world, such flights of fancy have become commonplace for the historian. In *Citizens*, Simon Schama returns to the Victorian narrative form of history-writing, adopting a *cinéma-vérité* technique: 'In Holland his encyclopedic mind raced ...' 'As he peered into the thinning Vendéan morning mist ...'[2] Another fanciful flight into the invented past has been undertaken by Amitav Ghosh in his brilliantly inventive, anecdotal history of Egypt covering eight centuries. Referring to a letter written in AD 1148, the author suggests that 'Within this tornado of grand designs and historical certainties, Kalaf Ishaq's letter seems to open a trapdoor into a vast network of foxholes where real life continues uninterrupted.'[3] With Alice and her rabbitholes, Schama and his historical video-time-machine, Kalaf and his foxholes, history is being reconstructed in some strange places these days. But then, as Marx might have said to Hegel, 'Any shift from the ethical to the aesthetic, my

[1] L. Carroll, *Alice Through the Looking-Glass and What She Found There*, Everyman edition (London, 1965), p. 113.
[2] S. Schama, *Citizens: a Chronicle of the French Revolution* (London and New York, 1989), pp. 98, 691.
[3] A. Ghosh, *In an Antique Land* (London, 1992), pp. 15–16.

friend, from the material to the idealist, will leave us lost in the mists of time.'

However, let us use Alice's looking-glass to see why, during the 1830s and 40s, the French Restoration image of Maximilien Robespierre as the devil incarnate began to assume a more human form for the radical wing of British Chartism; how this focus on Robespierre and continental 'democratic socialism' produced one of the principal divisions within the Chartist camp; and how the debate in Britain affected the Marxist interpretation of Robespierre and the Revolution of 1789. François Furet remarked that 'Toutes les interprétations marxistes de la Révolution française sont postérieures à Marx',[4] which is clever and hence only partly true. The fact is that, during the 1830s and 40s, Marx and Engels haltingly developed their own interpretation of Robespierre and the French Revolution, one that was influenced more by the internationalist, democratic-socialist wing of the Chartist movement in Britain, spearheaded by the British 'Triumvirate' of Bronterre O'Brien, Julian Harney and Ernest Jones, than by Hegel and Feuerbach.

I

According to the 'classic historiography' of the Revolution, the association of Jacobinism with modern communism – personalised as the link between neo-Robespierrism and neo-Babouvism – began to take shape with the publication in 1828 of Filippo Buonarroti's *Conspiration pour l'égalité*. Its features were then sharpened by a succession of socialist politicians and writers, like Louis Blanc, before being twisted into its modern Marxist and Marxist-Leninist forms through the writings of historians like Jean Jaurès, Albert Mathiez, Georges Lefebvre and Albert Soboul.[5] There clearly was a laying-on of historical, socialist hands from Blanc to Albert 'Marius' Soboul, but what this very French historiographical assembly-line misses is the contribution, *at a crucial phase in the creation of Robespierre's image*, of foreign admirers of the Revolution such as Bronterre O'Brien.

O'Brien, educated as a lawyer, has not always been sympathetically treated by British historians, perhaps because he was an Irishman who became an adopted son of England *and France*. The majority of English radical historians have been as keen to protect the virginity of their own revolutionary tradition as their French colleagues have of the Revolution of 1789. Dorothy Thompson in her authoritative work on the Chartists prefers the nationalist O'Connor to the internationalist O'Brien, con-

[4] F. Furet, *Marx et la Révolution française* (Paris, 1986), p. 13.

[5] See E. Hobsbawm, *Echoes of the Marseillaise* (London, 1990), chapter 3.

cluding that the latter's influence was most positive during the early years of Chartism, the 1830s and early 40s: thereafter, the 'enigmatic' and 'unstable' aspects of his personality contributed to the personal quarrels which plagued the Chartist movement.[6] From the standpoint of international democratic socialism, it could – and will – be argued that O'Brien's influence was most positive *after 1845*, the date which marks the launch – by Julian Harney, who had been a printer's apprentice under O'Brien's editorship of the *Poor Man's Guardian* – of the Society of Fraternal Democrats. As one might expect, one of his biographers, Alfred Plummer, has a high opinion of O'Brien, not just as a brilliant journalist – the editor of the *Poor Man's Guardian* in the early 1830s – but as someone who linked the radicalism and 'socialism' of Tom Paine and Thomas Spence with post-1830 French 'Jacobin' democratic socialism.[7] Like Plummer, Margot Finn, in her recent, penetrating study of British radicalism after Chartism, lays particular emphasis on the way in which O'Brien strove to weave the internationalist and socialist aspects of his personal ideology into the fabric of British radical socialism. Even Finn, however, underestimates the importance of O'Brien's debt, not so much to the French Revolutionary tradition as to its neo-Robespierrist and neo-Babouvist legacy. For example, although she notes that O'Brien had been '[s]chooled in the tradition of the first French Revolution', she states that his work on Robespierre was published in 1859.[8] In fact, Bronterre had published the first volume of his projected two-volume biography of Robespierre in 1838, the culmination of a prolonged and formative study of the Revolution, of Robespierre and of Gracchus Babeuf. Few, if any, British Chartists were more profoundly influenced by the example of French revolutions, or learned more from the history of the defeats of the French working class than Bronterre O'Brien. It is one of the main contentions of this essay that this detailed and continual study of revolutionary movements in France represents the determining influence upon his actions as a leading figure in British radical and socialist movements, distinguishing him from both the British Owenite socialists and the sometime admirers of Marx and Engels like Harney and Jones. It will also be argued that, as a result of his influence and, in particular, his championship of Robespierre, O'Brien made a major, not a minor,

[6] D. Thompson, *The Chartists* (London, 1984), pp. 101–4.

[7] A. Plummer, *Bronterre: a Political Biography of Bronterre O'Brien 1804–1864* (London, 1971).

[8] M. Finn, *After Chartism: Class and Nation in English Radical Politics 1848–1874* (Cambridge, 1993), p. 83. Finn is probably referring to the *Dissertation and Elegy on Maximilian* [*sic*] *Robespierre*, a re-issue of the poem first published two years earlier.

contribution to the left-wing 'classic historiography' of the French Revolution.

II

In the summer of 1835, O'Brien crossed the Channel to undertake research in Paris for a biography of Robespierre: he would make two further trips during the summers of 1836 and 1837. *The Life and Character of Maximilien Robespierre*, volume one of a projected two-volume work which was published in 1838, is an extraordinary work for its time which merits close examination. Over 500 pages long, it represents an important stage in the development of O'Brien's analysis of the relationship between the French Revolutionary experience and radical movements in Britain. Like his other French Revolutionary 'hero' (such individual figures are now recognisable again in our post-modernist mirror), Gracchus Babeuf, O'Brien had first cast Robespierre in the rôle of a villain, having denounced 'l'Incorruptible' in 1831 along with 'the Marats, the Dantons and other such demons of the day'.[9] His first undertaking in *The Life*, therefore, was to rescue Robespierre from the error of his own ways and the historiographical embrace of aristocratic and bourgeois historians, the most exaggerated of whom had described Robespierre as 'a filthy beast that finished his daily orgies of lust and the guillotine by a nocturnal debauch amongst common prostitutes' – a description better fitted to Danton than to the prim Maximilien![10] Contributing to a general historiographical tradition that has seen Robespierre reflected in history's looking-glass as both angel and devil, O'Brien decided to line up firmly, and deliberately, on the side of the angels, clearly conscious of the magnitude of his task: 'The more virtuous therefore – the more magnanimous – the more godlike I prove Robespierre to have been, the greater will be the terror in which his memory is held by the upper and middle classes.'[11]

There can be little doubt that the man who led O'Brien – and many others – to reassess his opinion of Robespierre was Filippo Buonarroti. In 1828, Buonarroti had published his famous account of the Babouvist conspiracy – *Conspiration de l'égalité dite de Babeuf* – which not only contained an account of the conspiratorial and ill-fated revolt against the French Directory in 1795–6, in which Buonarroti had been a

[9] *Carpenter's Political Letter*, 21 February 1831.

[10] R. G. Gammage, *History of the Chartist Movement 1837–1854*, ed. F. Cass (London, 1969), p. 74.

[11] B. O'Brien, *The Life and Character of Maximilian* [*sic*] *Robespierre*, vol. I (London, 1838), pp. 6–7.

principal actor, but which also laid the foundations for the rehabilitation of Robespierre as the harbinger of modern democratic socialism.[12] We know that O'Brien had been working on a translation of Buonarroti's work as early as 1832, although it was to be four years before O'Brien's English version appeared.[13] It would not be an exaggeration to argue that the political and social ideology, which the young Bronterre O'Brien – he was only twenty-six when the French Revolution of 1830 occurred – had begun to construct before and during his days on the *Poor Man's Guardian* between 1831 and 1835, was given its mature form by his assimilation of Buonarroti's 'Robespierrist-Babouvist' thesis. O'Brien stated: 'I was so forcibly struck by the coincidence of Buonarroti's ideas with my own, that I immediately resolved to translate the book, and thereby present to the English reader the doctrines of the *Poor Man's Guardian* under a new form and dress . . .' O'Brien knew his semiotics and that it was necessary to describe French revolutionaries as John Bull! He actually went to see the 75-year-old Buonarroti in Paris in 1836. The memory of this meeting with one of the 'grand old men' of European conspiratorial politics must have remained with O'Brien throughout his life.[14]

Clearly, O'Brien's publications on Babeuf and Robespierre were not to be found on the shelves of every Yorkshire handloom weaver or Dorset farm labourer: they presumed some knowledge of French history; each book was around 500 pages long; and they cost a poor man's fortune at six shillings each. However, it should be noted that Henry Hetherington published O'Brien's translation of Buonarroti's work on Babeuf in twenty parts, each at twopence. As for the more learned and literary radical, the Chartist activist and historian R. G. Gammage considered O'Brien's biography of Robespierre to be 'one of the most masterly productions of the kind that had ever been given to the world';[15] whilst, in more measured tones, Alfred Plummer concludes that 'the few devoted enthusiasts who did read O'Brien's writings no doubt talked to others, and in so doing contributed more than they knew to that slow seepage of democratic thought and feeling which later became a swelling flood'.[16] As for O'Brien himself, his obsession – the word is possibly not too strong – with 'l'Incorruptible' continued throughout his life. Although the second volume of his biography never

[12] F. M. Buonarroti, *Conspiration de l'égalité dite de Babeuf, suivie du procès auquel elle donna lieu, et des pièces justificatives*, ed. Robert Brécy and Albert Soboul (Paris, 1957).

[13] *Buonarroti's History of the Babeuf Conspiracy for Equality*, trans. B. O'Brien (London, 1836). O'Brien had notified the readers of the *Poor Man's Guardian* of his intention to publish the translation as early as 1832. Plummer, *Bronterre*, p. 59.

[14] Plummer, *Bronterre*, pp. 59–66.

[15] Gammage, *Chartist Movement*, p. 74.

[16] Plummer, *Bronterre*, pp. 71–2.

appeared (was the Terror too controversial a subject to tackle after the British government's own 'Reign of Terror' in 1839?), O'Brien published an essay on Robespierre in 1848 and, in 1857, the twenty-stanza *Elegy on the Death of Robespierre* which sold at just twopence a copy.

The link with the French Revolutionary tradition which, during the 1830s, assumed an increasingly moderate, but more republican and socialist emphasis – a point to which we shall return – was strengthened by the activities of the two other members of the Chartist radical and internationalist 'Triumvirate', Julian Harney and Ernest Jones. Harney, who hailed from humble stock, apparently liked to be known as 'the English Marat'; Jones, on the other hand, had been raised in Germany, the son of an English officer with aristocratic pretensions. Again, apparently – the source is Gammage who had his own axe to grind against both Harney and Jones – Jones also liked to compare himself, in his more romantic moments, to a Frenchman – no less a figure than Charlemagne![17] On a more serious note, both Harney and Jones extended the network of contacts between British Chartists and continental radicals, strengthening the internationalist nature of the movement but also introducing even more contradictions to the tangled ideological web of British Chartism. In 1845, as we have noted, Harney created his Chartist Society of Fraternal Democrats, primarily to introduce Polish, Italian, German and French political *émigrés* to their English sympathisers. As Margot Finn states: 'What had begun in the Jacobin era as an abstract alliance between English and continental democracy was transformed by the Chartist leadership into an active collaboration between English and continental agitators.'[18] By 1848, the contradictions between Fergus O'Connor's 'home, sweet home' version of Chartism and the internationalist perspective of the Chartist 'Triumvirate' had unquestionably provoked not only bitter personal feuds, but also profound policy splits within the already debilitated body of Chartism.[19]

III

We have argued that, long before the 'hydra of European revolution' had emerged once again in 1848, Bronterre O'Brien had developed an ideology whose constituent parts had been taken from his Irish background, the English radical-socialist tradition and the French neo-

[17] Gammage, *Chartist Movement*, p. 281.

[18] Finn, *After Chartism*, p. 58.

[19] In January 1848, O'Connor attacked Harney for devoting too much time and space in the *Northern Star* to foreign affairs, 'matters in which the Star readers and the English people take not the slightest interest'. *Ibid.*, p. 108.

Robespierrist and neo-Babouvist legacy of '1789', as interpreted by Filippo Buonarroti; and that he was ably – if erratically – supported in his task by fellow internationalists like Harney and Jones. But what were the main planks of this truly internationalist and democratic-socialist programme which not only widened the ever-present fissures within Chartism but also provided the element of consistency to O'Brien's otherwise quarrelsome and sometimes contradictory career? For brevity's sake, we shall confine our answer to 'the political' and 'the social'. So far as the metaphysical was concerned, the Irish Catholic O'Brien seemed happy with a modified version of Robespierre's anti-clericalism and cloudy deism, modified in Harney's direction – Christ as the 'sansculotte Jesus'.[20]

Top of the political agenda was the demand for universal male suffrage. Throughout his long political life, O'Brien never really wavered in his conviction that extending the franchise to the respectable, male working class was the *prerequisite* for the ultimate attainment of social justice and equality. This, for O'Brien, represented the essential bridge linking continental democratic socialism and the English radical tradition, one on which Maximilien Robespierre and Tom Paine could both stand. In his biography, O'Brien had written that Robespierre had 'lived and died in defence of *political equality* for all'.[21] So did O'Brien. In 1842, he was even prepared to join with the rich Quaker Joseph Sturge in launching the latter's short-lived Complete Suffrage Movement, an act of apostasy in the eyes of Fergus O'Connor, which led to the first really vicious dispute between the two prickly Irishmen. The fact that, at this time, O'Connor was playing the 'working-class card' against O'Brien appears to be paradoxical, given O'Brien's dedication to his 'fellow labourers' since the early 1830s. It can only be resolved by emphasising O'Brien's espousal of the Jacobin belief that political action and universal male suffrage were the keys which unlocked the doors to social equality. It was this fundamental article of faith which made it impossible for O'Brien to join forces, permanently, with the Owenite socialists – he sympathised with their social analysis of the evils of unfettered capitalist competition and private property but could not accept their rejection of political action. O'Brienites and Owenites disagreed over means, not ends, but it was a crucial difference.

The term 'Jacobin', as employed in the 1830s and '40s, of course, did not necessarily imply a slavish adherence to the ideas of Robespierre; neither, despite its much later identification with French nationalism,

[20] Plummer, *Bronterre*, pp. 210–16. [21] O'Brien, *Robespierre*, p. 310.

should it be used in opposition to 'international democratic socialism'. In the first place, the Parisian Jacobin club of the early 1790s had been the most international of venues for late eighteenth-century radicals; in the second, though Buonarrotti had successfully bathed Robespierre and Babeuf in the same healing waters of time to produce what some French activists in the 1830s and '40s termed 'neo-Robespierrism' and 'neo-Babouvism', an increasing number combined both under the capacious umbrella of 'Jacobinism'. After all, what was good for Karl Marx, who told the Poles in 1848 that the 'Jacobin of 1793 has become the Communist of today', was good enough for French republican socialists.[22] To throw more light on the *apparent* inconsistencies of the internationalist Chartists, more work should be done to compare political and ideological developments in France and Germany with those in Britain in the 1830s and '40s. For example, Raspail, one of the founders of the *Société des droits de l'homme* in the early 1830s, agonised over whether or not he should 'opt for the path of legality, setting, as an overriding priority, the goal of a political, republican revolution'. His contemporary, Lebon, argued for violent insurrection and the suspension of democracy, a policy more closely identified with Buonarotti's account of Babeuf's conspiracy.[23] The debate over the evolutionary or revolutionary path to the promised land was, of course, both prolonged and heated amongst British Chartists. Can there be much serious doubt that O'Brien eventually opted for the more pacifist and 'élitist' strategy, having studied, in depth, the lessons learned by Babeuf and Buonarroti – that mass, 'popular movements' can easily be smashed by the mightier forces of the state? If he had harboured any doubts, they seem to have been dissipated by his eighteenth-month prison experience in 1840–1. Henceforward, he would be extremely suspicious of mass demonstrations and rallies.

Recent accounts of Chartism, influenced by the emphasis which certain socio-cultural historians have placed on 'the language of labour', have emphasised the point that Chartism was fundamentally propelled by political forces. Gareth Stedman-Jones has intelligently argued that Chartism was, essentially, a political movement. He has also suggested that the essential thrust of Chartism was against 'capitalists' accused of exploiting a corrupt political and legal system, not their economic power over the working class. Hence his conclusion that Chartism represents the dusk of the traditional English radical movement, not the dawn of a

22 Hobsbawm, *Echoes of the Marseillaise*, p. 42.

23 *Présence de Babeuf: Lumières, Révolution, Communisme. Actes du colloque international Babeuf, Amiens, 7–9 Dec. 1989* (Paris, 1994), pp. 315–19.

modern, socialist era.[24] Patrick Joyce has given very qualified approval to this analysis, arguing that there is something to the argument that class identities were 'rooted in the economic categories of labour and capital and gave rise to conflictual conceptions of society which, unlike in previous times, were anchored firmly in the area of industrial production, rather than economic exchange or distribution'. However, eager to place labour history within broader cultural boundaries, he concludes that 'it is the strength of the moral categories of custom rather than of the economic categories of the market that is most evident'.[25] Our argument would be, first, that this concentration on 'an oppressive political system' was not due to any lack of understanding of the exploitative nature of industrial modes of production, but was, in part, an espousal of neo-Jacobin and, more precisely, neo-Babouvist methods of tackling these problems; secondly, that Marx and Engels themselves learned from the debate amongst radical Chartist leaders concerning the fundamental difference between what would be termed 'Utopian' and 'scientific' socialism, with all that this entailed for the socio-economic analysis of capitalism and the political struggle; and, thirdly, that, following the failure of the 'Parisian Spring of 1848', even greater emphasis would be placed on 'the social question', though never to the exclusion of political strategies.

One of the distinguishing features of neo-Robespierrist thought, in France as in England, was the belief that social equality and justice could only be achieved by the working class *acting in conjunction with the radical elements of the bourgeoisie*. This 'popular front' strategy informed the historical writings – and, to a certain degree, the political actions – of *marxisant* historians from Jean Jaurès, through Lefebvre, to Albert Soboul in France, and, it could be argued, from Tawney, through to George Rudé and Edward Thompson in Britain. Following the failure of the 1839 insurrectionary movement, and his related imprisonment, Bronterre O'Brien leaned increasingly towards the neo-Robespierrist notion of 'class collaboration'. Replying to O'Connor's denunciation of his 'unholy alliance' with Sturge in 1842, O'Brien declared that

> there is a considerable and growing minority of the middle classes with whom I deem a union not only possible but probable ... This portion is composed partly of good and wise men, whose probity and love of justice raise them above

[24] G. Stedman-Jones, *Languages of Class: Studies in English Working-Class History 1832–1982* (Cambridge, 1983). See the criticisms of N. Kirk, 'In defence of class: a critique of recent revisionist writing upon the nineteenth-century English working class', *International Review of Social History* 32 (1987), 2–47.

[25] P. Joyce, *Visions of the People: Industrial England and the Question of Class 1848–1914* (Cambridge, 1994), pp. 87–90.

class-prejudices; and partly of tradespeople and others in embarrassed circumstances who see no hope.[26]

However, it does not follow that, *because of his emphasis on political action and cross-class alliances*, O'Brien did not develop an intelligent critique of the social consequences of modern forms of capitalism. R. G. Gammage, a disciple of O'Brien, noted in 1854 that, although universal male suffrage and political action represented for O'Brien the means to achieve social justice, 'he also comprehended ... that the highest amount of political influence would never be of the slightest utility in enabling them to burst the bonds of social misery, unless they understood the true basis of society'.[27] As early as 1838, O'Brien had taken on the editorship of a new radical publication entitled *The Operative*, which he described as a journal 'established *by* the working classes *for* the working classes, to defend the rights of labour from the aggressions of Capital'.[28] In many of his articles – for example in 'The Rise, Progress and Phases of Human Slavery' (1849) in which he argued that a social revolution would be necessary to emancipate the working class from 'wage-slavery' – O'Brien developed theories on surplus value which were evidently read by Marx.[29] No less an authority than Harold Perkin believes that O'Brien was 'a critic of capitalist society who anticipated and rivalled Marx'.[30]

If O'Brien's attachment to universal male suffrage and the importance of political action was neo-Robespierrist, his ideas on 'the social question' were certainly influenced more by Gracchus Babeuf. Much ink has been spilt on what kind of communism Babeuf and his followers advocated, but there is now general acceptance that it was based upon eighteenth-century notions of 'distributive agrarian communism'. In the words of François Furet,

During the revolutionary years Babeuf abandoned the idea of an 'agrarian law' providing for equal distribution of land to individuals and adopted instead that of communal land ownership and elimination of private property: the fruits of the earth were to be distributed equally among citizens, all of whom were to be called upon to play an equal rôle in their production.[31]

Here again, however, O'Brien adapted, rather than adopted, French ideas. His Irish background, and the profound individualism and attachment to private property which remains one of the cultural imperatives of British history, led him to focus his critique on the monopoly of

26 Plummer, *Bronterre*, p. 173.
27 Gammage, *Chartist Movement*, p. 75.
28 Plummer, *Bronterre*, pp. 87–8.
29 *Ibid.*, pp. 249–50.
30 H. Perkin, *The Origins of Modern English Society 1780–1880* (London, 1969), p. 392.
31 F. Furet, 'Babeuf', in Furet and M. Ozouf (eds.), *A Critical Dictionary of the French Revolution*, trans. A. Goldhammer (London, 1989), pp. 179–85.

landownership enjoyed by aristocrats and the richer middle class, a song sung by most Chartists. However, as opposed to Fergus O'Connor's ill-fated, and ill-conceived, 'Land Plan', which retained the concept of petty peasant production, O'Brien went much further in the direction of Babouvism, explaining that

> By means of fraud and brigandage the people's rights to the national territory had been usurped by sinister private interests, by 'usurpers and tyrants of the soil' ... Over the years, landlordism had driven masses of men into the towns, there to become the 'hired slaves of middle-class demons', and no mere tinkering could effectively alter 'a system based on so hideous a foundation'.

O'Brien's remedy was land nationalisation. However, conscious of the deep-rooted British belief in the 'sanctity of property', he agreed that no owner of land should be deprived of his or her rights during their lifetime; only after a landlord's death would the property pass to the state. Following Babeuf – but not to the letter – land would be redistributed fairly and national warehouses created to redistribute surplus produce. Local banks would receive the rents charged for the redistributed national lands and from this fund would provide loans to deserving cases: 'the stock and labour of every such man would be mortgaged, as it were, to the public, for the repayment of the loan out of the future proceeds of his industry'. O'Brien also argued for the nationalisation of public utilities and what would become known in the twentieth century as 'the commanding heights of the economy'.[32] To justify these policies, which form a bridge between seventeenth- and eighteenth-century 'communism' and mid-twentieth-century socialism, O'Brien claimed – incorrectly – that his mentor, Maximilien Robespierre, had also sought to do away with 'all property qualifications, with all exclusive privileges, with all class distinctions'.[33] In O'Brien's looking-glass, the images of Robespierre and Babeuf merged into one another and, as we noted above, were more often than not dressed in the apparel of John Bull. In this historical reconstruction, Maximilien Robespierre emerged with more democratic and socialist features than would ever have been recognisable to his colleagues on the Committee of Public Safety!

IV

Whether because of the identification of Robespierre with Babeuf, or because of the English dress, Marx and Engels had some difficulty in

[32] Plummer, *Bronterre*, pp. 181–4. Some of O'Brien's best journalistic writing and political ideas can be found in his *National Reformer* which he published from Douglas, Isle of Man, to avoid newspaper taxes and postage costs, from 1844 to 1847.

[33] O'Brien, *Robespierre*, p. 313.

recognising Robespierre as a socialist, certainly as a 'scientific' one. François Furet recorded the ambivalence about Robespierre and the French Revolution which can be found in the early works of Marx and Engels, particularly before 1848.[34] It is an essential part of our argument that the confused, rather cubist, picture of 'l'Incorruptible' which had emerged by 1848 was the joint work of British internationalist Chartists, French *dém.-socs.* and German communists – the 'Jacobin of 1793' had become 'the Communist' of 1848. Julian Harney knew Engels well: their friendship was, in fact, to last to Engels's death. It was Harney who had contracted Engels to write for the *Northern Star*, having met him for the first time in 1843. From 1843 to 1845, during which time Engels was writing *The Condition of the Working Class in England*, Harney was instrumental in weaning him away from his sympathy for Owenite communitarian socialism: the collapse of Owen's plans by 1845 and Marx's first clearly articulated statements on his materialist theory of history sealed Harney's efforts.[35] Harney also met Marx, probably for the first time, in November 1847 when the latter came to England to address a meeting of the Fraternal Democrats. Ernest Jones, who had been raised in Germany and spoke several European languages, became, for Marx and Engels, 'their man in Britain', after his two-year spell in prison from 1848 to 1850. Jones had met Marx and Engels through Harney's Fraternal Democrats, and, according to John Saville, their influence 'in the development of his understanding was to be decisive'.[36]

The importance of *The German Ideology* in the evolution of Marx's thought has been stressed by many commentators.[37] As we have seen, it was precisely during the middle years of the 1840s, when Marx was writing this seminal work and Engels his *Condition of the Working Class*, that contacts between them and the British 'Triumvirate' had begun in earnest. In his earlier works, Marx had been keen to stress the divide which separated bourgeois civil society from the Jacobin Terror – the alienated revolutionary state, the 'modern State' which distinguished itself from socio-economic reality during the revolutionary experience.[38] According to this reading of history, Napoleon's empire became the revolutionary state, operating through military conquest rather than through the bureaucratic Terror of 1793–4. Robespierre and the Jacobins, unable to discern their true bourgeois, capitalist reflections in

[34] Furet, *Marx et la Révolution française*, particularly pp. 33–43.

[35] G. Claeys, 'The political ideas of the young Engels, 1842–45', *History of Political Thought* 6 (1985), 456.

[36] J. Saville, *Ernest Jones: Chartist* (London, 1952), pp. 22–7.

[37] See, for example, the preface and pp. 37–47 of Norire Ter-Akopyan, *Marx–Engels: Pre-Capitalist Socio-Economic Foundations* (London, 1979).

[38] S. Avineri, *The Social and Political Thought of Karl Marx* (Cambridge, 1968), p. 190.

history's looking-glass, had chosen to peer into the mists of classical times to find a legitimation for their actions – revolutionaries dressed up in Roman togas.

In *The German Ideology*, Marx – prompted perhaps by Engels – developed a more sympathetic approach to Robespierre who now became the radical bourgeois spokesman of the future working class. The really exploitative wing of the (mainly commercial) capitalist bourgeoisie was the Girondins and their spiritual heirs, the Thermidorians, the representatives of the *possédants*; the Robespierrist dictatorship had its roots in 'la seule classe réellement révolutionnaire, la masse innombrable'.[39] It could be argued, however, that the contrast with earlier pronouncements is more apparent than real, and is to be explained by the involvement of Marx and Engels in the political struggles and strategies leading up to 1848; and in deciding these strategies the 'Triumvirate' of O'Brien, Harney and Jones were far from being of peripheral importance. Again, too little attention has been paid to the common strategy involved in the public celebrations, the dinners and fraternal speeches in Britain, the 'banquet movement' in France, which evoked stirring memories of '1789' and '1830'. Living their double lives as historical sociologists and political activists, Marx and Engels frequently deviated from the path of academic righteousness, attracted by the sound of gunfire. The ambivalence between 'thought' and 'action' is present in *The Class Struggle in France* as it is in *The Civil War in France*, subjective sympathy for the exploited and slaughtered masses clashing with more objective and cerebral thoughts. Marx's formative ideas concerning the rôle of the bourgeoisie and the proletariat in history were formed from a combination of Hegelian idealism and the tragic history of the French left from 1789 to 1848.[40]

V

The year 1848 started promisingly for the 'Triumvirate'. Dorothy Thompson conveys the excitement felt by one young Chartist attending a meeting of the Fraternal Democrats in London when news of the February revolution in Paris arrived: 'The effect was electrical. Frenchmen, Germans, Poles, Magyars sprang to their feet, embraced, shouted and gesticulated in the wildest enthusiasm.'[41] However, despite wild talk of 'bloody revolution' and enthusiastic demonstrations in the North, the Midlands and the capital, there was to be no mass uprising.

[39] *Ibid.*, pp. 48–57.
[40] F. Furet, *Le passé d'une illusion: essai sur l'idée communiste au XXe siècle* (Paris, 1995).
[41] Thompson, *Chartists*, pp. 317–8.

The petitioning of Parliament on 10 April only served to prove the strength of the authorities and the relative weakness of popular opinion, and, although meetings and disturbances continued for many months, there can be no disguising the fact that, for a variety of reasons, London in that bloody summer of 1848 was not Paris, nor even Vienna. Throughout the first half of 1848, however, Bronterre O'Brien was mainly conspicuous by his absence from public affairs. It may have been that he was privy to inside information concerning insurrectionary activity which he felt was doomed to fail – events in his home country of Ireland suggested the exhaustion of a people and a cause, not a prelude to revolution – but this does not altogether explain why he temporarily withdrew his support from the national executive of the Chartist movement, much to the disgust of Harney and Jones.[42] They should not have been surprised at his refusal to heed romantic calls to the barricades. Had he not learned the futility of 'popular movements' from his reading of Babouvism in the 1790s? Had they not learned anything from the failure of popular insurrectionary movements in Britain during the late 1830s?

If they had not, Marx and Engels had: for them 'Utopian' ideologies had failed and 'scientific socialism' had been vindicated. Just as for O'Brien, the massacre of working-class demonstrators in the Parisian streets in June 1848 would evoke memories of the Thermidorian repression of 1795 – once again, the 'innocent' working class had been enticed on to the streets only to be crushed by the forces of reaction, and historical necessity. Following the counter-revolutions of 1848–9, the Marxist analysis of Robespierre would veer more towards the depiction of 'l'Incorruptible' as the unwitting tool of the bourgeoisie. The contradiction of the Marxist concept of Robespierre as a bourgeois 'dictator', but one who still represented the best interests of the people, would pose a problem for left-wing historians of the Revolution from Jean Jaurès to Albert Soboul.[43]

In Britain, after the damp squib of the April demonstrations in London and the bloody explosion of the June Days in Paris, the 'Triumvirate' would also shift the focus of their attention to the social, as opposed to the political, analysis of history. Jones would look to Germany and Marx; Harney to continental revolutionaries and radicals of various hues. O'Brien, however, continued to seek inspiration, and legitimation for his own ideas, from France. Margot Finn puts it like this: 'Without abandoning the national identities that linked them to middle-class radicals, they [the radical Chartists] embraced French

42 Plummer, *Bronterre*, pp. 191–2.
43 Hobsbawm, *Echoes of the Marseillaise*, pp. 89–90.

Revolutionary theories that propelled the radical tradition beyond its Puritan and Jacobin roots to the politics of class.'[44] By the spring of 1849, Harney had mended his ideological and strategic fences with O'Brien, inviting him to join him and his fellow Fraternal Democrats in a commemoration of the 1848 French revolution. On 1 May, Harney dined with the French *dém.-soc.* leader, Louis Blanc. Through his several newspapers – the *Democratic Review*, June 1849–May 1850, and the *Red Republican*, June–December 1850 – Harney would now preach the message of 'The Charter and Something More', that 'something more' being a pretty strong brew of French, German and British socialism and class struggle. In June 1850, Harney, citing Saint-Just's saying that 'those who make half revolutions, dig a grave for themselves', wrote in his *Red Republican*:

> With the experience of other nations to guide them, it would be culpable in the highest degree for the Democrats of this country to neglect the duty of enlightening the masses as to their social rights, while agitating for the enactment of the political franchise embodied in the People's Charter.[45]

For Marx, this meant that the (scientific) horse had finally been put before the (Utopian) Chartist cart. In November, Harney published the first English translation of *The Communist Manifesto* in the *Red Republican*. For a relatively brief period, in the late 1840s and early '50s, the influence of Marx and Engels on British radicalism was quite pronounced. When the German-speaking Ernest Jones came out of prison in July 1850 – 'a socialist' not a Chartist – the association would grow stronger. It was Jones who helped to engineer the defeat of the O'Connorites and the election of a very radical national executive in 1850, marking 'the high peak of socialist influence within the Chartist programme'.[46]

During this period when Harney and Jones were moving closer to a Marxist class analysis, Bronterre O'Brien was listening, but continuing to plough his own particular Franco-British furrow. His activities from the autumn of 1848 confirm the impression that no leading reform figure in Britain did more to lay the intellectual foundations for the bridge which links Chartism and twentieth-century English democratic socialism.[47] Once again, there can be little doubt that he was influenced by events in France where, since the failures of 1848 and the election of Louis Napoleon as President of the Second Republic, moderate socialists like Louis Blanc had been working hard to effect a coalition of

44 Finn, *After Chartism*, p. 59.

45 *Red Republican and Friend of the People*, vol. I, no. 1.

46 P. Cadogan, 'Harney and Engels', *International Review of Social History* 10 (1965), 72–4.

47 This is one of the main conclusions reached by Plummer in his final 'Appraisal' of O'Brien: *Bronterre*, pp. 247–60.

reformers to unite the left and radical centre, precisely O'Brien's strategy for the past decade. The themes which recur in his speeches and writings from 1848 to his death in 1864 are those with which any follower of O'Brien would have been familiar – the need for co-operation between the working class and the radical bourgeoisie; universal male suffrage as the essential route to social justice; nationalisation and reform of the banking and taxation systems to secure that justice. They are in line with early nineteenth-century neo-Robespierrist and neo-Babouvist ideas, but, crucially for O'Brien, they were also in the tradition of Tom Paine and Thomas Spence.

Possibly it was O'Brien's age and deteriorating health, aggravated by drinking, which determined that the last phase of his career during the 1850s and early '60s would be as 'the schoolmaster of Chartism', a journalist, teacher, even a prophet. However, we should remember that the education of the masses before the advent of mature democratic socialism had always been an important aspect of neo-Robespierrist and neo-Babouvist ideology. As early as the winter of 1848–9, O'Brien had begun to organise his lecture series at the John Street Literary and Scientific Institution. The following winter, O'Brien would play a rôle in the creation of the National Reform League for the Peaceful Regeneration of Society. His Eclectic Institute in Denmark Street, Soho, was founded in the winter of 1850–1. Throughout these years, indeed until his death, O'Brien would be chairing discussions and giving lectures at his John Street and Denmark Street meeting places. There is more than the occasional overtone of the Workers' Educational Association in O'Brien's support in later life for educational evening classes in mathematics, English and French for working people. As if all this were not enough, O'Brien was still writing and editing newspapers, beginning with *The Power of the Pence* in late 1848, and acting as 'foreign correspondent' for the *Glasgow Sentinel* for several months. Finally, it was during the last decade of his life that he published a series of influential works. In 'The Rise, Progress and Phases of Human Slavery', O'Brien defined the nineteenth-century working class as the slaves of modern capitalism; in *State Socialism*, he laid down a programme of political and economic reform that has discernible links with the nationalisation policies of the Labour party after World War II; whilst in *European Letters and Tracts* (produced for the National Reform League), he attempted to untangle the threads of British and continental reform movements.[48]

[48] The first part of 'The Rise' appeared in *Reynold's Political Instructor* on 17 November 1849; *State Socialism* was published in May 1850; *European Letters* began on 6 October 1851.

VI

When Bronterre O'Brien died, on 23 December 1864, Victor Hugo was invited to speak at the funeral. Explaining from his exile in the Channel Islands that circumstances made it impossible for him to attend, he wrote that, had he spoken at the graveside, he would have 'seized with earnestness this occasion of proving that national differences do not exist for democrats, and of blending a French voice with English voices at the tomb of a man of courage and virtue. Progress, democracy and liberty have lost much in losing [this] ... valiant and generous man.'[49] It was an appropriate tribute. It is a pity that contemporary historians have not followed suit. When Alfred Plummer wrote his biography of Bronterre, over a generation ago, he was told 'that too little was known of James Bronterre O'Brien's life and writings'.[50] Despite the unquestioned value of Plummer's work, it remains true that 'the English Robespierre' is still a curiously incomplete and enigmatic figure. To solve the enigma, more research and analysis need to be undertaken of O'Brien's relationships and appraisal of French democratic socialism and, indeed, Irish radicalism, which itself owed a particular debt to the French Revolutionary tradition.

It may be that the times are now propitious for such an undertaking. 'Post-modernism' and 'the linguistic turn' have certainly caused new mists to cloud history's looking-glass, but, of late, they seem to be clearing. Of course, as we wrote at the beginning of this chapter, Lewis Carroll knew a thing or two about what is now termed 'post-modernism', to say nothing of 'deconstructionism':

> 'When I use a word,' Humpty Dumpty said in a rather scornful tone, 'it means just what I choose it to mean – neither more nor less.'
>
> 'The question is,' said Alice, 'whether you *can* make words mean different things.'
>
> 'The question is,' said Humpty Dumpty, 'which is to be master – that's all.'[51]

The focus on word-play, the importance conferred upon 'the language of labour', has recently made it very difficult to discern almost any radical or revolutionary group in history's looking-glass: Diggers, Levellers, *sans-culottes* have all been temporarily lost in the mists of time. Words like 'democracy' and 'socialism' have been – and are being – twisted to fit any ideology. But there is an honesty, a remarkable consistency in Bronterre O'Brien's approach to democratic socialism which is reassuring. Margot Finn is right to point to the essential continuity of O'Brien's influence on the radical democratic tradition in

49 Plummer, *Bronterre*, p. 244. 50 *Ibid.*, preface.
51 Carroll, *Alice Through the Looking-Glass*, p. 159.

Britain, reminding us that 'the Eclectic Hall that housed the Eclectic Institute provided a meeting place in London first for the O'Brienite National Reform League, later for the British section of the First International, and ultimately for a republican club established during the radical revival that followed the outbreak of the Paris Commune'.[52] On the socialist front, Royden Harrison is also right to stress that men like O'Brien *were* early socialists, even if his brief is not to enquire into the provenance of his socialism, one strand of which was the French Revolutionary tradition.[53] Of course, O'Brien's words were often coined to sell to the British working class of the mid-nineteenth century, not terribly well versed in the theses of Hegel or Feuerbach. As an Irishman, he was peculiarly well placed to appreciate the weight of British capitalist and cultural power, the power of an unreformed Parliament, monarchy, church and educational system. Yet he remained optimistic to his rather sad, poverty-stricken end, believing, as he wrote in his *Elegy on the Death of Robespierre*, that:

> As time and progress shall make facts more clear
> And truths divine illumine our hemisphere;
> These will reveal that helmsman without peer,
> Who taught what course republics ought to steer;
> Whose virtues only Vice thought too austere;
> Whose life was grand – whose death was sad and drear.

A final thought. It is interesting, given his determination to present 'Marianne' as 'John Bull', that his *Elegy* to Robespierre was modelled on Milton's *Lycidas*!

52 Finn, *After Chartism*, p. 135.
53 R. Harrison, *Before the Socialists: Studies in Labour and Politics 1861–1881* (London, 1965), p. 12, n. 1.

13 Rehabilitating Robespierre: Albert Mathiez and Georges Lefebvre as defenders of the Incorruptible

James Friguglietti

On 28 July 1794 (10 Thermidor Year II), Maximilien Marie Isidore Robespierre was taken from the Conciergerie prison and carted through Paris streets lined with shouting crowds. Deposited in the place de la Révolution, he watched as two of his colleagues from the Committee of Public Safety and his younger brother Augustin mounted the scaffold and were beheaded. When he himself finally climbed the steps and was tied to the plank, the executioner ripped away the bandage that bound his jaw, shattered by a bullet at the time of his capture. The celebrated orator died shrieking an animal cry of pain. Within a few hours his corpse along with those of his companions disappeared into a common grave at a Parisian cemetery.

Two hundred years have passed since Robespierre's mortal life ended and his posthumous one began. His career has been closely scrutinised by historians, repeatedly narrated by biographers, vividly described by novelists, and melodramatically depicted by film-makers. But if the outline of his political career is familiar, his complex personality remains rather cryptic and the controversy over his behaviour continues to be lively.

To his many admirers, Robespierre was the leading figure of the Revolution; to his detractors, he was its great villain. The sharp and prolonged debate between defenders and opponents greatly exasperated the historian Marc Bloch, who, in his *Historian's Craft*, written in 1941, exclaimed: 'Robespierrists, anti-Robespierrists, we've had enough. We say, for pity's sake, simply tell us what Robespierre was really like.'[1]

Two prominent Robespierrists, whose work Bloch may surely have had in mind, were Albert Mathiez and Georges Lefebvre. For a half century, these historians employed their prodigious scholarship to rehabilitate the memory of the Incorruptible. But Mathiez and Lefebvre

[1] Marc Bloch, *Apologie pour l'histoire ou métier d'historien* (Paris, 1964), p. 70.

sought not only to refute the calumnies levelled against him by his numerous detractors; they also sought to enshrine him in the pantheon of republican heroes. At times their efforts resembled an effort at canonisation.

Such intense partisanship can be ascribed to their patriotic desire to strengthen the Third and Fourth Republics by linking them to the achievements of the First. In this sense, Robespierre might serve as a heroic model for their own age. At the same time, deep personal and psychological reasons existed that led Mathiez and Lefebvre to engage in what must often have seemed a quixotic enterprise. Only an examination of their own lives can explain their efforts on behalf of Robespierre.

Mathiez and Lefebvre both came of age when Robespierre's reputation had reached a low point. As his historiographers J. M. Thompson, Jacques Godechot and François Crouzet have demonstrated, two rival traditions developed after 9 Thermidor. Republican and socialist historians such as Etienne Cabet, Louis Blanc and Ernest Hamel had extolled his revolutionary leadership. But far more frequently Robespierre was denounced by a succession of writers who ranged from the monarchist Adolphe Thiers, the conservative Hippolyte Taine and the moderate republican Jules Michelet to the Radical-Socialist Alphonse Aulard. The moderates who had gained control over the Third Republic by 1879 exalted Robespierre's rival, Georges-Jacques Danton. In his memory a statue was erected in the place de l'Odéon in Paris where it stands today.[2]

The historian who long dominated the 'official' Dantonist school of revolutionary history was Alphonse Aulard, appointed by the Paris city council to teach the subject at the Sorbonne in 1886. Aulard used his numerous publications and the historical journal that he edited to praise Danton's memory and execrate that of Robespierre. First as secretary, then as president of the Société de l'histoire de la Révolution, he assembled an impressive array of scholars whose aim was to defend the work of the Revolution and political figures whose careers were spent establishing and preserving the Third Republic. All equated the régime with the progressive achievements of the Revolution: republicanism, parliamentarism, democracy and the rights of man and the citizen proclaimed in 1789. Aulard's scholarship, combined with his university

[2] For summaries of how Robespierre has been treated by historians, see J. M. Thompson, *Robespierre*, 2 vols. (Oxford, 1935), vol. I, pp. xv–lv; Jacques Godechot, 'L'historiographie française de Robespierre', in *Actes du colloque Robespierre. XIIe congrès international des sciences historiques (Vienne, 3 septembre 1965). Avant-propos par Albert Soboul* (Paris, 1967), pp. 167–89; and François Crouzet, *Historians and the French Revolution: the Case of Maximilien Robespierre* (Swansea, 1989).

instruction, journalism and political activity on behalf of the Radical-Socialist party, made him a formidable intellectual figure.[3]

Ironically, it was Aulard's prize pupil and associate, Albert Mathiez, who did most to topple Danton from his pedestal as the hero of the Third Republic and install Robespierre in his place. Initially, Mathiez appeared to accept Aulard's Dantonist orthodoxy. He later claimed that as a young man he 'was nurtured on the legend and believed in the generous Danton, treacherously murdered by the ambitious Robespierre, [and] had no defence against the official history'.[4] Mathiez became the most vocal advocate of Robespierre as well as the harshest critic of his mentor and friend Aulard.

Why did Mathiez develop into such an outspoken Robespierrist? What accounts for his fierce partisanship? There are three likely explanations: first, his social origins; second, his remarkable intellect; and third, his fiery temperament.

Mathiez sprang from a modest background. Born in 1874, the son of a small peasant landowner turned innkeeper living in rural Franche-Comté, he never knew wealth or luxury. His peasant origins, then his excellent education in the state school system, led him to convert to socialism. By the time he left the Ecole Normale Supérieure in 1897, Mathiez believed that the existing economic and social order was unjust and that the ruling political parties had proved incapable of instituting necessary reforms. When, as a young historian, he turned his attention to the French Revolution, he discovered in the Incorruptible one of the few leaders truly committed to improving the lot of the French masses. Robespierre he considered a genuine democrat, sincere republican and ardent defender of social equality, in effect an ancestor of modern French socialism. Mathiez deemed him no mere historical figure but rather the perfect model for politicians of the twentieth century and hero for the ordinary citizen.

Equally important in converting Mathiez to Robespierrism was his considerable intelligence. Throughout his school years, Mathiez's first-rate mind won him one academic success after another. By the early age of thirty, he had earned his doctorate at the Sorbonne for an impressive dissertation concerning republican cults. Consequently, Mathiez became an authority on the Revolution.

It was Aulard who directed Mathiez's thesis and who, for several years afterwards, remained his mentor and friend. When the two men first

[3] For a survey of his career, see Georges Belloni, *Aulard historien de la Révolution française* (Paris, 1949).

[4] James Friguglietti, *Albert Mathiez, historien révolutionnaire (1874–1932)* (Paris, 1974), p. 74.

met in 1900, they appeared quite compatible: both were provincials who had attended the Ecole Normale Supérieure and both were loyal republicans who admired the ideals of the Revolution. Aulard did much to assist his pupil, advising him on his dissertation and arranging the publication of his scholarly articles. But differences in age, temperament and political outlook soon caused Mathiez to distance himself from the Sorbonne professor. His own extensive research in the archives convinced him that Aulard's work was shallow and his intellectual integrity questionable. Mathiez concluded that Aulard remained essentially a journalist promoting the Radical-Socialist party, an opportunist profiting from historical publications subsidised by the state. The more he doubted Aulard's reliability as a historian, the more Mathiez identified the older man with Danton. In contrast, the younger scholar increasingly equated himself with Danton's rival, Robespierre.

Mathiez eventually broke openly with his mentor and in 1907 founded the Société des Etudes robespierristes. In a statement of purpose almost certainly drafted by Mathiez, the new organisation declared its aim to 'research, organise and publish all historical documents that can throw fresh light on [the] biography of Robespierre . . . It considers Robespierre as the one who, from the convocation of the Estates General until 9 Thermidor, most perfectly incarnated the Revolution . . .'[5]

From the outset, Mathiez presided over the society, transforming it into a virtual Jacobin club, and extolled Robespierre and the Revolution at every opportunity. In addition, he edited the organisation's journal, *Annales révolutionnaires*, becoming its most frequent contributor. In its pages Mathiez published any article or document that could enhance Robespierre's reputation and denigrate Danton's. Repeatedly, he condemned Danton as venal, dishonest and immoral, the exact opposite of the Incorruptible. Mathiez kept his society alive during the First World War and during the 1920s developed its journal, known from 1924 as the *Annales historiques de la Révolution française*, into the foremost periodical in its field. He thus came to outshine his longtime rival Aulard.

During the First World War, which saw the mobilisation of France's army, German invasion, censorship, economic controls, inflation, war profiteering and defeatism, Mathiez greatly broadened his understanding of the revolutionary era. Henceforth, he perceived Robespierre not only as the leader of the democratic movement and social reformers, but also as the courageous defender of the Revolution against foreign invasion and domestic insurrection, the heroic figure who led France to

[5] *Ibid.*, p. 81.

victory in the Year II. In his *Robespierre terroriste* (1921), Mathiez described him as the 'most noble, most generous and most sincere face of the French Revolution'.[6] In succeeding works, notably his three-volume survey *La Révolution française* (1922–7), his study of economic and social unrest during the Year II entitled *La vie chère et le mouvement social sous la Terreur* (1927) and his collection of articles on political affairs, *Girondins et Montagnards* (1931), Mathiez focused his attention on Robespierre, continually praising the revolutionary's courageous leadership and personal integrity.

But Mathiez did not confine himself to publishing books and articles. In October 1923, he proudly delivered an address to the citizens of Arras when they placed a commemorative plaque on the house where Maximilien lived from 1787 to 1789. 'For the first time', he declared,

> the birth-place of Robespierre has associated itself . . . with the rehabilitation of this great citizen, so odiously slandered for more than a century . . . Truth is on the march. The efforts we have been making for sixteen years have not been in vain. If our task has not finished, we can draw the strength to continue from these first successes, with the certainty of approaching victory.[7]

Mathiez travelled tirelessly across France and even abroad to present lectures, including one entitled 'Robespierre, history and legend'. In it, he passionately refuted every charge ever levelled at his hero since 9 Thermidor. The portrait Mathiez drew was that of an upright man and infallible leader persistently besmirched by his many enemies. Mathiez did mention one flaw he had discovered: 'If I had to reproach Robespierre for anything, it would be that he perhaps waited too long to abandon Danton, with whom he had been linked since the outbreak of the Revolution by an old political comradeship.'[8]

Tragically, Mathiez never completed the biography of Robespierre that he had long planned. He died suddenly on 25 February 1932, after suffering a cerebral haemorrhage in his lecture room at the Sorbonne. His death at the age of fifty-eight was certainly hastened by his volcanic personality. As early as his student days at the Ecole Normale Supérieure, Mathiez had displayed a violent temper and capacity for quick anger. Throughout his career, he often allowed his emotions to dominate his intellect. He treated anyone who disagreed with his own historical interpretations with both anger and contempt. His writings, clear and vigorous in their style, were rarely free of personal invective hurled against his numerous enemies. In one of the first issues of the *Annales révolutionnaires*, he published a twelve-page review of Aulard's

[6] Albert Mathiez, *Robespierre terroriste* (Paris, 1921), p. 34.
[7] 'L'hommage d'Arras à Robespierre', *Annales révolutionnaires* 15 (1923), 441.
[8] Albert Mathiez, 'Robespierre, l'histoire et la legende', *AHRF* 49 (1977), 21.

book *Taine historien*. By turns scholarly and personal, it chastised the elderly scholar for lapses in understanding, superficial judgements and inadequate use of sources. 'He treats Taine as he would a candidate for the doctorate on the day of his thesis defence,' Mathiez contended. 'Monsieur Aulard does not wish to admit that his book is in a sense a work of polemic. He believes that he is truly impartial. But he says this a little too often.'[9]

Aulard, whose personality was far more placid than Mathiez's, never deigned to reply in kind to his critic. His very refusal to trade insult for insult only further angered Mathiez. Over a period of twenty years, until Aulard's death in 1928, Mathiez continued to assail the individual who, in his eyes, incarnated the enemy of Robespierre. His repeated emotional outbursts, combined with daily physical and mental exertion, no doubt cut short his life.

Mathiez left behind a substantial legacy of scholarship, much of it devoted to rehabilitating Robespierre. The organisation that he founded and dominated for almost a quarter century, the Société des Etudes robespierristes, proved one of his most enduring creations. By stimulating original research into the revolutionary period and publishing a journal of high scholarly standards, he contributed significantly to historical studies.

When Mathiez died in 1932, Georges Lefebvre succeeded him as president of the society and editor of its journal. But if he continued his predecessor's crusade on behalf of Robespierre, Lefebvre differed from him both in personality and public behaviour.

It is far more difficult to determine when and how Lefebvre became a Robespierrist. Most of his writings from his first scholarly articles to the works he published in the early 1930s make few or no allusions to the revolutionary leader. Lefebvre's primary interest lay in studying agrarian history and rural sociology, as his monumental doctoral dissertation, 'Les paysans du Nord pendant la Révolution française' (1924), and his study of rural panic in 1789, *La Grande Peur* (1932), attest.

By his late fifties, however, Lefebvre had developed into a vocal partisan of the Incorruptible. In *La Révolution française*, published in 1930, he made his opinions quite clear. Though Lefebvre's discussion of Robespierre occupied scarcely one page, it encapsulated the arguments that he expounded for the rest of his scholarly career. For him, Robespierre appeared the staunch defender of democracy, determined opponent of foreign war, saviour of the Republic and man of integrity and vision. As Lefebvre commented:

[9] Albert Mathiez, review of A. Aulard, *Taine historien de la Révolution française*, *Annales révolutionnaires* 1 (1908), 349.

Before the Constituent Assembly and then at the Jacobin club and in the press, [he] tirelessly defended democratic principles [and] won the esteem of the revolutionary people ... By a tragic turn of events, it was he who was charged with saving the Revolution during the [war] he had vainly sought to prevent. The confidence of republicans was well placed ... He respected the principles that he professed, but he was not the abstract theoretician he has been made out to be. In the long crisis that followed, he proved ... singularly attentive to circumstances and was able to confront them with the flexibility of a statesman.[10]

Unlike Mathiez, however, Lefebvre did not remain blind to Robespierre's shortcomings. He conceded, for example, that the law of 22 Prairial, passed with his support in June 1794, accelerated the Terror, while Robespierre's denunciation of atheism as a political crime helped turn many of the deputies in the Convention against him. As a person Robespierre was neither corrupt nor vicious, for, as Lefebvre observed, he 'remained without wealth despite his talent and lived a modest domestic life in the home of the furniture-maker Duplay'. What eventually brought Robespierre down in 1794 was a combination of extremists and moderates who coalesced against the 'supposed dictator'.[11]

After Lefebvre became president of the Société des Etudes robespierristes, he presented his longest and most eloquent defence of his hero. The occasion was the dedication of a bust of Robespierre held in Arras on 15 October 1933. Attended by a host of local notables, the ceremony fulfilled the dream that Mathiez had cherished when, ten years earlier, he had inaugurated the plaque on the house in that same town where Robespierre had lived before the Revolution. Lefebvre delivered two separate speeches before his distinguished audience. The first recounted the history of Robespierre's reputation since 9 Thermidor. He summarised all the charges that had been levelled against the revolutionary leader by his detractors from royalists to conservative republicans. Lefebvre also recalled those historians, notably Jaurès and Mathiez, who had laboured to rehabilitate him. Concluding his speech with a rare burst of emotion and enthusiasm, he declared:

Citizen Maximilien Robespierre! The descendants of the Jacobins and sans-culottes ... remain faithful to your memory. They have erected this bust in remembrance of you as a sign of their esteem and friendship. In all their names I hail you as their fathers would have done in the Year II of the Republic. Citizen Robespierre, 'Salut et fraternité!' Long live the Republic, one and indivisible![12]

In the second and longer oration delivered in the municipal theatre of

[10] Georges Lefebvre, Raymond Guyot and Philippe Sagnac, *La Révolution française*, Peuples et Civilisations, vol. XIII (Paris, 1930), p. 212.

[11] *Ibid.*, p. 258.

[12] 'Le buste de Robespierre à Arras (15 octobre 1933)', *AHRF* 10 (1933), 488.

Arras, Lefebvre extolled the noble qualities that Robespierre displayed. He praised his personal honesty and virtue, noting that Robespierre was 'chaste and sober, taciturn and often melancholy, with his chief source of relaxation being the modest pleasures of the family and a close circle of friends'. Lefebvre lauded his 'honesty, industry, dignified morals, outward decency and distrust of excessive wealth and disorderly luxury'. Reviewing Robespierre's political career from 1789 to 1792, before he became an active republican, the historian hailed his staunch defence of social equality and political democracy. Robespierre, he declared, showed great foresight in denouncing the Girondins for provoking war and even greater courage in leading France during the most dangerous months of the military conflict in 1793–4.

Lefebvre strenuously denied that Robespierre had ever been a dictator, claiming that he had always acted in collaboration with the Committee of Public Safety and the Convention. Realism, touched by a certain cynicism, allowed him to grasp the political consequences of a prolonged conflict: the eventual appearance of a military tyrant who would seize political power. The historian hailed the Incorruptible for his statesman-like qualities, popularity with the people and parliamentary eloquence. The Great Terror, Lefebvre concluded, was not the work of Robespierre, who sought to curb its excesses as well as to protect the innocent from its rigours. Had he lived during the Revolution, Lefebvre declared, he would have remained loyal to Robespierre and not have 'turned against the leader who seemed most worthy of esteem'. He added that, 'as Jaurès expressed it, we would take our place beside him in the Jacobin club'.[13] Throughout the rest of his long life, Lefebvre held to his exalted opinion of the revolutionary leader.

Lefebvre regularly used his editorship of the *Annales historiques de la Révolution française* to defend the Incorruptible. In 1936, for example, he devoted six pages of the journal to a review of J. M. Thompson's two-volume life of Robespierre. Although he called the English historian 'conscientious and well informed', Lefebvre sharply criticised him for describing the Incorruptible as a 'fanatic', a 'dictator' and an 'Inquisitor'. He repudiated Thompson's accusations and referred to his idol as a 'realist', 'one who sought to assure the triumph of the Revolution and equally an idealist who saw in it the progressive realisation of his desires . . . though it, none the less, moved with a force that overwhelmed him'. Lefebvre justified Robespierre's behaviour during the Terror by declaring it to be a manifestation of the same 'collective mentality'

[13] Georges Lefebvre, 'Discours sur Robespierre', *ibid.*, 510.

responsible for the Great Fear and the September massacres, 'a new reaction against the aristocratic plot'. In short, the Terror was not the direct personal responsibility of the man he revered and defended so passionately.[14]

Under Lefebvre's strong leadership the Société des Etudes robespierristes continued its work of rehabilitation until 1940, when the German occupation forced the organisation to suspend its activities. After the Liberation, it resumed one of its most important projects, the publication of Robespierre's complete works, an undertaking that Mathiez had initiated in 1908. This well-edited collection, which includes his *Lettres à ses commettans* and five volumes of speeches, was not finally completed until 1967. It represents a monument in print, the scholarly equivalent of the statue in bronze or stone that was never raised to his memory within the capital.

As a French patriot, Lefebvre rejoiced at the liberation of his country from German domination. His joy was mixed, however, for his younger brother Théodore, a geographer who had taught at the University of Poitiers, had been arrested for resistance activity, deported to Germany, tried and beheaded in 1943.[15] This tragedy helps explain why Lefebvre trembled with emotion when he quoted from a speech that Robespierre delivered in September 1793:

> It is weakness for traitors that is destroying us. There are those who sympathise with the most criminal men, with those who deliver our country to the enemy's arms. I can sympathise only with unhappy virtue ... oppressed innocence [and] the fate of an unhappy people being murdered so villainously.[16]

Years later, one of his young students, Madeleine Rebérioux, recalled how, after Lefebvre learned of his brother's execution, he 'came to the school [the Ecole Normale Supérieure de Sèvres] and perhaps spoke more ardently to us about the Incorruptible'.[17]

The apogee of Lefebvre's adoration of Robespierre came in June 1958, when the Société des Etudes robespierristes celebrated the bicentennial of his birth. A day-long colloquium was convened in the Amphithéâtre Michelet, the same lecture hall where Mathiez had suffered his fatal stroke in 1932, to honour the Incorruptible. Lefebvre greeted the assembly with an eloquent speech that concluded with the same peroration he had delivered twenty-five years earlier at Arras:

14 Georges Lefebvre, review of J. M. Thompson, *Robespierre*, *AHRF* 13 (1936), 468–73.
15 Georges Six, 'In Memoriam', *AHRF* 19 (1947), 68–70.
16 Georges Lefebvre, 'Pro domo', *ibid.*, 190.
17 Madeleine Rebérioux-Amoundruz, 'Georges Lefebvre, professeur à l'Ecole Normale Supérieure de Sèvres', *AHRF* 32 (1960), 78.

'Citizen Robespierre, "Salut et fraternité!" Long live the Republic one and indivisible.'[18]

An impressive array of scholars, French and foreign, examined various aspects of Robespierre's life and achievements, throwing fresh light on his behaviour and policies. One speaker, Maurice Dommanget, summed up the reasons for devoting so much attention to a single man: 'The cause of Robespierre', he maintained, 'is identified with democracy, the people and the highest egalitarian aspirations, and, finally, the cause of the French Revolution in particular and revolutions in general . . .'[19]

Concurrently, Lefebvre arranged for the publication of a collection of studies written by Mathiez and reissued under the title *Etudes sur Robespierre (1758–1794)*. This attractive volume allowed the former president of the society to pay tribute to his idol from the grave.

That same spring, the elderly Lefebvre presented an address entitled 'Robespierre and the popular societies' to the Société d'histoire moderne. The text, partially translated and published in the first issue of *French Historical Studies*, represents his final word on Robespierre. Its conclusion is worth quoting:

> Robespierre appears to me as the resolute and faithful representative of [the] revolutionary mentality; he was the intrepid defender of the Revolution of 1789 which destroyed in France the domination of the aristocracy; the immovable and incorruptible head of revolutionary Resistance. This place in history can never be taken from Robespierre.[20]

That Lefebvre revered Maximilien Robespierre is all too obvious. But the reasons *why* he devoted much of his long life to rehabilitating the revolutionary leader are not so readily apparent. Certainly they differed from those of Mathiez, who completely identified himself with the Jacobin statesman. Although born in the same year as Mathiez, Lefebvre sprang from a dissimilar background and had an entirely different temperament. While far less tempestuous and aggressive, he nevertheless found strong reasons for sympathising with Robespierre.

First, there was the fortuitous circumstance that, like his hero, Lefebvre was born in northern France. Only thirty miles separate their respective birth-places, Arras and Lille. Both men spent the decisive years of their childhood and youth living in the same region of cool, damp climate and grey skies, populated by industrious peasants and

[18] Georges Lefebvre, 'Assemblée générale du 15 juin 1958', *AHRF* 30 (1958, special issue), 3.

[19] Maurice Dommanget, 'La Société et les Annales. Cinquante ans d'histoire (1908–1958)', *ibid.*, 26.

[20] Georges Lefebvre, 'Remarks on Robespierre', *French Historical Studies* 1 (1958), 10.

urban labourers. The dual influences of geography and climate cannot be underestimated in appreciating Lefebvre's empathy with Robespierre.

Second, in addition to geographical propinquity, the two northerners shared rather similar social origins. Both arose from modest circumstances, Robespierre being the son of a failed lawyer, Lefebvre the grandson of a woolcarder and son of a book-keeper. Both were worthy scholarship students who made their way in society thanks to their intelligence and industry. When he eulogised Robespierre at Arras in 1933, Lefebvre described him as 'the son of an unsuccessful lawyer, an orphan from his childhood, the brilliant pupil at the Collège Louis-le-Grand, a poor scholarship boy [who] lived by his labours ... beginning in 1781'.[21] Lefebvre himself received financial aid so that he could attend the *lycée* at Lille, then the university there. Because he learned classical languages too late, he never sought admission to the prestigious Ecole Normale Supérieure. A teacher in various provincial schools, he earned his doctorate in history only when he reached the age of fifty.[22]

Living modestly, even austerely, his entire adult life, Lefebvre could readily sympathise with the revolutionary deputy who spent his last years inhabiting a small room of the Duplay household in Paris. As his student and long-time friend Richard Cobb observed of Lefebvre, 'In Robespierre ... he saw the personification of the French *petit bourgeois*, [the qualities] of probity, economy and hard work.' Cobb further noted of his mentor that he lived a life of austerity, was constantly short of money until he was over fifty and never travelled first class on trains until he was over eighty. In the elderly scholar's home there were no carpets and the furniture was sparse, with a broken armchair for reading; but there was a bust of Robespierre.[23] As François Crouzet has noted, 'It was impossible not to think of the Duplay household ... when visiting G. Lefebvre in his small house at Boulogne-Billancourt.'[24] Nor could a visitor there fail to notice the four portraits that hung in his modest living room, those of Robespierre, Jaurès, his brother Théodore and the historian Marc Bloch, all of them 'martyrs' who fell in the cause of liberty.[25]

Third, and perhaps most important, were Lefebvre's strong republican and socialist convictions, which almost certainly stemmed from his social origins. He turned to socialism early in his career in large measure because of the influence of Jean Jaurès, the ardent socialist politician

[21] Lefebvre, 'Discours sur Robespierre', 492.

[22] Richard Cobb, *A Second Identity: Essays on France and French History* (New York and Toronto, 1969), pp. 84–100.

[23] *Ibid.*, pp. 85–6.

[24] Crouzet, *Historians*, p. 32.

[25] René Garmy, 'Georges Lefebvre et l'homme (Souvenirs)', *AHRF* 32 (1960), 82.

and orator. In a rare personal statement published in 1947, Lefebvre acknowledged his debt to Jaurès: 'I saw and heard [him] only twice, lost in the crowd ... but if anyone can be called my master, I would recognise no one except him.'[26] Jaurès's republican spirit, belief in democracy and optimism about transforming society through parliamentary action were all absorbed into Lefebvre's thinking by 1914. He esteemed the four volumes dealing with the French Revolution that Jaurès contributed to the *Histoire socialiste*. From this work Lefebvre borrowed the phrase he used to dedicate the bust set up in Arras: 'Here, beneath this sun of June 1793, that warms your fierce struggle, I am with Robespierre, and beside him I take my seat at the Jacobin club.'[27] And not insignificantly, when Lefebvre died in 1959 at the age of eighty-five, it was in the home where he had lived for twenty years, located on the boulevard Jean Jaurès.

The death of Lefebvre ended a half century of Robespierrist activism. He had loyally carried on Mathiez's work as president of the Société des Etudes robespierristes and as editor of its journal. Lefebvre lived long enough to commemorate the bicentennial of Robespierre's birth, the high point of his determined effort to rehabilitate the Incorruptible. Had Mathiez lived until 1958, he would surely have done the same. It is a tribute to their efforts that both their society and its publication still exist today, while those directed by Aulard have disappeared.

Whatever their personal and professional reasons for doing so, Mathiez and Lefebvre served as Robespierre's posthumous defenders in a trial that the Incorruptible never had before he was dispatched to the guillotine on 10 Thermidor and passed forever into history. Surely he never had finer ones.

[26] Lefebvre, 'Pro domo', 190.
[27] Quoted in Madeleine Rebérioux, 'Jaurès et Robespierre', in *Actes du colloque Robespierre*, pp. 194–5.

14 Robespierre in French fiction

Malcolm Cook

I

It hardly needs to be said that the demands of historical writing and those of fiction are quite different. In his *Eléments de littérature*, Marmontel wrote:

> Of all characteristics, the most vital to history is, then, truth – and absorbing truth. But truth implies learning, discernment, sincerity, impartiality. Now learning is unsure, discernment difficult and sincerity rare; and complete detachment, that freedom of the spirit and the soul, that utter impartiality which is the hallmark of a faithful witness, is scarcely ever to be found.[1]

It might be supposed that writers of fiction would work according to different criteria. Certainly, truth could hardly be a requirement and yet, in the eighteenth century at least, theorists (and Marmontel was just one of many in this respect) claimed that fiction requires a solid foundation, one that is based on truth. Quoting Marmontel again, we read:

> Fiction, then, must be the representation of truth, but truth established by the choice and mix of colours and the characteristics which it draws from nature. There is no picture so perfect in the natural ordering of things that the imagination might still not add to it . . . History has few subjects which poetry is not obliged to correct and embellish, to adapt it to its medium.[2]

Clearly, history and fiction have common interests and may share similar working practices. But the subjects treated, the emphasis and the aims of each will differ. The French Revolution, to speak generally for a moment, is likely to inspire writers: Dickens, of course, and, more recently, Hilary Mantel, whose *A Place of Greater Safety* was published in 1992. In the author's note to the latter, we read: 'I have tried to write a novel that gives the reader scope to change opinions, change sympathies: a book that one can think and live inside. The reader may ask how to tell

[1] Jean-François Marmontel, *Eléments de littérature*, in *Œuvres complètes*, 19 vols. (Paris, 1818), vol. XIV, p. 46.
[2] *Ibid.*, vol. XIII, p. 464.

fact from fiction. A rough guide: anything that seems particularly unlikely is probably true.'[3] Such a guide is not likely to be of much use. We will return to this text to find a description of Robespierre, which will illustrate how his portrait has evolved over two centuries. The text itself does not lend itself to serious study. What it does show is that, even two hundred years after the event, the reading public is willing to buy fictional accounts of the Revolution. Perhaps the explanation for this is to be found nearly two hundred years earlier, in Sénac de Meilhan's fascinating account of the life and exile of an *émigré*. In the preface to the novel, the author wrote:

> A tragic poet, when asked at the start of the Revolution's bloody scenes whether he occupied himself with such work, replied: 'tragedy currently roams the streets.' Anything is possible and romantic in the French Revolution ... the most extraordinary encounters, the most astonishing circumstances, the most deplorable occurrences become commonplace events and surpass those which novelists can envisage.[4]

The debate about the relationship between fiction and history was a real one in the eighteenth century. Perhaps, indeed, it has never been satisfactorily resolved. It must, of course, be the starting point for any discussion concerning the appearance of historical figures in fiction. The subject, for the purpose of this essay, is necessarily restricted and concentrates almost entirely on French fiction. It begins by looking at the way in which Robespierre figures in fiction that is contemporary with the events, including texts of the period 1792–1800. Then, it examines ways in which Robespierre is used as a point of reference in texts in which he plays no real part. Finally, and this is the most substantial part of the essay, there is a detailed examination of three novels and an assessment of the way in which Robespierre plays a particular part.

II

Readers of fiction of the period 1789–1800 showed a clear preference for sentimental fiction of the kind made popular in France by Richardson and imitated by, amongst many others, Rousseau. Robespierre is unlikely to be a fictional hero of such novels. Fictional heroes are, on the whole, young romantic figures with a taste for adventure, who discover the meaning of life through a series of devised events; fictional texts, in the eighteenth century at least, often conveyed a moral message. No

[3] Hilary Mantel, *A Place of Greater Safety* (Harmondsworth, 1992), p. x.

[4] Sénac de Meilhan, *L'Emigré*, in *Romanciers du dix-huitième siècle*, 2 vols. (Paris, 1965), vol. II, p. 1549.

doubt Robespierre was familiar with Rousseau's great novel *La nouvelle Héloïse* of 1762. But it is equally certain that he did not see himself as Saint-Preux. Indeed, and this is not surprising, Robespierre hardly appears in the fiction of the last decade of the eighteenth century. It could be suggested that his presence is felt in a number of texts, especially the pastoral tales of writers like Pierre Blanchard. But he does not appear as a living character. In an interesting recent book entitled *Sentimental Narrative and the Social Order in France 1760–1820*, David Denby, analysing Robespierre's speech against dechristianisation at the Jacobin club on 21 November 1793, claims that 'Robespierre is affirming that History can be a sentimental narrative, or rather that the social subject should be allowed to imagine History in those terms'.[5] While the present author is not convinced that Robespierre was making that affirmation, one can accept the view that sentimental narrative can inform history and, more precisely, that the lack of certain figures in popular narrative is itself meaningful.

Robespierre is a name which is found, with great regularity, in the many fictional pamphlets produced by the Revolution. These pamphlets had a short life and, of course, were published and printed anonymously. A few titles will indicate the nature of this fiction, starting with *Robespierre chez les orphelins ou Histoire secrette des derniers jours de Robespierre* (London, 1794). In this account we learn why Robespierre was absent from the Convention for the last three weeks of his life: he got drunk, lost his way home and fell asleep in the countryside. He is woken up by a child who is chasing a swarm of bees, who regrets that the bees have lost their queen. This remark puzzles Robespierre. He catches the queen in his snuff box and is surprised that the other bees discover the queen's whereabouts and become organised and orderly. There is clearly a message here. Robespierre gets badly stung, he is taken to an orphanage and the account finishes with a dialogue between Robespierre and two orphan boys, during which he admits the errors of his ways.

It is the period immediately following Robespierre's death which saw the publication of a number of fictional pamphlets in which he is a figure of ridicule: for example, *Robespierre en cage*, *Robespierre aux enfers* and so on. By 1795 biographical accounts were appearing. For example, we find *La vie et les crimes de Robespierre, surnommé le tyran, depuis sa naissance jusqu'à sa mort* (Augsburg, 1795), attributed to Proyart under the pseudonym Le Blond de Neuvéglise. This is a full-length study (of 370 pages) which includes a warning to the readers. History cannot, as Voltaire suggests, be disguised as a pleasant novel whose aim is to charm

[5] D. Denby, *Sentimental Narrative and the Social Order in France 1760–1820* (Cambridge, 1994), p. 160.

the reader: 'le vrai but, le but sublime de l'histoire est de rendre les hommes et plus sages et meilleurs' ('The true aim, the most sublime aim of history, is to make men wiser and better').[6] This biography includes a full descriptive account of Robespierre, the kind of portrait which we will find of him in the fiction of a later age. It is too long to quote in full but a brief extract will at least allow us to appreciate the tone:

He bore on his broad shoulders a rather small head. He had light brown hair, a round face, an indifferent, pock-marked complexion, a livid hue, a small, round nose and pale blue, slightly sunken eyes. He never laughed. He hardly ever smiled; moreover, it was generally only a mocking smile which revealed all the peevishness of a bilious nature.[7]

We find a similar portrait of Robespierre in Duperron's *Vie secrette, politique et curieuse de M. J. Maximilien Robespierre* (Paris, An II). This is a much shorter text, written and published soon after Robespierre's death (there is an engraving in the Bibliothèque Nationale edition which depicts Robespierre's head being held by the executioner, dripping with blood).[8] This pamphlet, full of printing errors and poorly produced, includes another long descriptive portrait of Robespierre, of which this is a brief extract:

He often clenched his fists, as if through a kind of nervous convulsion; the same movement affected his shoulders and neck, which he moved convulsively from right to left; his clothes were elegant, his hair always neat; his somewhat frowning features were quite unremarkable; his hue was livid, bilious; his eyes gloomy and dull; a frequent flickering of the eyelids seemed to follow the spasm.[9]

Obviously, portraits are used to define character and there is little distinction to be drawn between the selection of detail in a pamphlet which claims authenticity and a novel which seeks to convince the reader. Certain features will, of course, be expected. It may be that the caricatural elements which would dominate later portraits were not yet clearly established in this early period. In this period following Robespierre's death, there is, clearly, a sudden explosion of critical propaganda whose rôle is to destroy the image of Robespierre as founder of the Republic.

III

Naturally, Robespierre will figure as a character who defines an age, in fiction describing the reality of the Revolution. Two examples come to

6 M. Le Blond de Neuvéglise, *La vie et les crimes de Robespierre, surnommé le tyran, depuis sa naissance jusqu'à sa mort* (Augsburg, 1795), pp. 14–15.

7 *Ibid.*, p. 67. 8 BN, Lb41 1161. 9 *Ibid.*, p. 24.

mind: Lebastier's *Dorbeuil et Céliane de Valran, leurs amours et leurs malheurs pendant la tyrannie de Robespierre* of An III and the *Voyageur sentimental en France sous Robespierre* of An VII. In the latter, the narrator is present in the Convention and hears Robespierre speaking. To put it simply, Robespierre appears in the fiction, saying things he is known to have said and he is heard by a narrator who has no historical reality. The narrative is enhanced, of course, by such a method and the process of making the unreal seem real (which is the aim of much fiction) is advanced. What is lacking, in the presentation of Robespierre in these texts, is a philosphical discussion about the nature of his political status. He gives weight to fictional characters but is, himself, devalued.

Let us now move forward into the nineteenth century. Michelet, of course, dominated the scene and his descriptions and accounts flavoured many others. There are times when Michelet's history reads like fiction. For example, his poetic account of Marat's death and his remarkable description of the festival of the Supreme Being, in which Robespierre stands out from the crowd: 'Robespierre, as usual, walked quickly, with an agitated air. The Convention did not move nearly so fast. The leaders, perhaps maliciously and out of a perfidious deference, remained well behind him, thereby isolating him. From time to time, he turned round and saw he was alone.'[10] There can be no doubt that Michelet's history was to set the the tone for the writers of fiction who followed his methods, writing historical accounts in which characters come to life whilst the reader is constantly seduced by the most captivating style. As we shall see later, Hugo and Anatole France owed him a large debt. If history reads like fiction, it must also be said that, on occasions, fiction reads like history.

Major French texts of the nineteenth century paid homage to the Revolution and their fictional characters seek inspiration in the ideals of the First Republic. For example, in Flaubert's *Education sentimentale*, published in 1869, we see the events of 1848 and different characters look back to the earlier period; Robespierre is barely mentioned in this nostalgic view of the past, in which the novelist's primary concern is the gradual devaluation of the hero, Frédéric. Novels which, today, are rather less well known also have a revolutionary setting. Two examples provide useful points of reference. The prolific Paul Féval (1817–87) chose the Vendée in 1793 for his setting of *Le Docteur Bousseau* and the two co-authors Erckmann/Chatrian chose a revolutionary setting for their novel, *Histoire d'un paysan*, of 1868–74. This novel begins: 'Many people have told the story of the great revolution of the people and the

10 Jules Michelet, *Histoire de la Révolution française* (Paris: Club français du livre, 1971), p. 581.

bourgeoisie against the nobility in 1789. They were learned men, *hommes d'esprit*, who observed events from above. But I am an old peasant and I shall speak only of our concerns.'[11] The chronological progression of the novel eventually leads to the appearance of Robespierre. The portrait is not sympathetic:

> I saw this man. He crossed the large room and went up the little staircase opposite, a scroll of paper in his hand and green-tinted spectacles on his nose. Beside the other deputies, nearly all dressed in black, you would have said a fop: his hair was dressed and combed; he had a white cravat, a white waistcoat, frills, cuffs; it was clear that this was a man who looked after himself and gazed at his reflection in the looking-glass like a young girl. I was astonished. But when he turned round, seated himself and unrolled his papers, giving the impression of hearing everything, and I saw him watch from behind his spectacles those in every part of the room, it struck me that he resembled a fox, the sprucest and cleanest of animals, which grooms, washes and preens itself all over. I said to myself: 'I still wouldn't trust you, even if you were a thousand times more virtuous.'[12]

It will become increasingly evident, as we look at different novels and compare different portraits of Robespierre, that attitudes towards him and, in particular, detailed portraits of him give the text a political definition and situate the author. Robespierre does not play a major part in these texts – but his presence is felt and the attitude towards him is crucial.

IV

We must now look, in more detail, at novels where there is a real presence. We will take them in order of publication, starting with Vigny's *Stello*. Published in 1832, *Stello* is, essentially, a first-person narrative in which the main character, the Docteur Noir, recounts his experiences and his consultations. One of these takes him to visit Robespierre and this introduces a lengthy section in which, for example, the Doctor finds himself with Robespierre and Saint-Just. They have summoned Marie-Joseph Chénier, the playwright, to come to see them and the four characters find themselves in the same room, discussing, amongst other things, the nature of poetry. The scene allows Vigny to make a direct satirical attack on both Robespierre and Saint-Just; it also allows him to introduce his admiration of Chénier's brother, André the poet, one of the victims of the Terror. Robespierre has also invited the father of the two Chéniers. This domestic scene against the backcloth of cynical disrespect for human life is a striking example of political

[11] Emile Erckmann/Alexandre Chatrian, *Histoire d'un paysan* (Paris, 1868), p. 1.
[12] *Ibid.* (repr. Colmar: Bentzinger, 1988), p. 366.

propaganda in which the two republicans manage to condemn themselves through their words. Dialogue, clearly, is important, as too is the presence of the Doctor, whose impartial comments provide the reader with a sense of objectivity. As far as we know, the scene did not take place in reality – but it is so vividly described that the reader is drawn into the net, enticed by the very realism of the presentation. This, to think back for a moment, is the kind of fiction imagined by Marmontel.

The section on Robespierre makes fascinating reading: it allows Vigny to express his hate for the Reign of Terror, his scorn for the two leaders, Robespierre and Saint-Just, and also his admiration for the dead poet, since we witness the execution and the response of the brother, accused, by his enemies, of having done nothing to save André. Eventually, we see the arrival of 9 Thermidor and the death of Robespierre and his allies. Vigny provides the reader with a portrait of Robespierre which is based very much on the accepted view of him:

> He was thirty-five years old, his face squashed between his brow and his chin, as if both his hands had wanted to force them together above the nose. His face was as colourless as paper, dull and as though cast in plaster. It was deeply pock-marked. Neither blood nor bile circulated there. His small eyes, dejected and dull, never looked at one directly, and a constant, unpleasant flickering made them seem smaller still, when, by chance, his green spectacles did not completely hide them. His mouth was contracted convulsively by a kind of smiling grimace, prim and wrinkled, which led Mirabeau to compare him to 'a cat that has drunk vinegar'. His hair was tidy, over-dressed and pretentious. His fingers, shoulders and neck were constantly and involuntarily clenched, convulsed and twisted when little nervous spasms seized him. He was dressed first thing in the morning, and I never caught him not attired. That day, a yellow silk coat with white stripes, a jacket with flowers, a jabot, white silk stockings and buckled shoes gave him a very elegant appearance.[13]

This long, detailed portrait picks up a number of common factors: the pock-marked face, the green glasses, the elegant mode of dress. There are similarities here with the portrait found in the later novel by Erckmann/Chatrian – but this should not surprise us. What Vigny manages to incorporate into his physical description is a precise attack on the character of his subject. Ill at ease, twitching nervously, unable to look one straight in the face, Robespierre was clearly not a man to be trusted.

Two other features of this novel are of interest in the context of this essay. Unusually, we find Robespierre engaged in conversation and making a number of precise political points. He lavishes praise on Saint-Just in words which follow a discussion on poetry:

[13] Alfred de Vigny, *Stello* (Paris: Garnier, 1979), p. 139.

'There's the man I'd call a poet', said Robespierre, pointing to him. 'He sees things on a grand scale. He doesn't amuse himself with stylistic forms that are more or less conventional: he deploys words like lightning flashing across the darkness of the future, and he feels the destiny of petty men who bury themselves in the detail of ideas lies in serving our vision.'[14]

The Doctor and Chénier are stunned into silence by these remarks. In this fiction, Robespierre is endowed with a language which is so literary, so contrived, that the reader's willingness to accept the illusion is stretched to the limit. Finally, in a speech which will be familiar to those who know Robespierre's political writings, we see Robespierre in discussion with Marie-Joseph Chénier, extolling republican virtues and threatening all those who fail to support the Republic: 'Il faut une volonté *une*. Nous en sommes là. Il la faut républicaine, et pour cela il ne faut que des écrits républicains; le reste corrompt le peuple.' ('We need a single will. That is where we are. It must be republican, and for that we need republican writing; the rest corrupts the people.')[15]

Vigny's novel is complex and stylised and the author's own opinions are never far away. Here, though, is the first appearance of Robespierre in a text by a major writer; it is deliberately and carefully interwoven with an account of the death of Chénier the poet – and the reader is given little freedom in his response to the tragic events.

Hugo's novel *Quatrevingt-treize*, which was published in 1873, is set in 1793 and recounts a series of royalist uprisings against the Republic. It involves three main characters: the marquis de Lantenac, the leader of the *blancs* who will stop at nothing to defend the cause he supports; his nephew, Gauvain, who leads the republican troops; and Gauvain's former tutor, Cimourdain, a former priest and now a fanatical revolutionary. The setting is the woods and villages of Brittany and the Vendée and the tone is sombre yet poetic. Hugo's ability to create atmosphere and his constant use of symbolic structures provide the reader with what, surely, is the most complex novel to depict the French Revolution. For Hugo there are no easy answers in the struggle which is taking place. The war in the Vendée is a civil war which leads to confusion and massacres of the innocent. The novel defies a simple explanation. Within it, almost as an interlude to the fighting taking place in the Vendée, we are taken to Paris to see the Republic at work. We see the Convention seething with people and bubbling with ideas. It is a Convention in which individuals play themselves, real people who lived through the Revolution and who participated in the debates there.

Also in Paris is a small bar and in its back room an important meeting

[14] *Ibid.*, p. 160. [15] *Ibid.*, p. 157.

is taking place: 'On 28 June 1793, three men met around a table.' They are described in the following terms:

> The first of these men was pale, young, serious, with thin lips and a cold expression. He had a nervous tick in his cheek which pinched it when he smiled. He was powdered, brushed, wearing gloves and buttoned up; his pale blue coat had no creases. He wore nankeen breeches, white stockings, a high cravat, a pleated jabot and shoes with silver buckles. The other two men were respectively a giant and a dwarf . . .[16]

In an early undated heavily illustrated edition of this novel, we are given a portrait of the three characters. They are immediately recognisable in a setting which is quite false. Danton is drinking wine, Marat has a cup of coffee in front of him and in front of Robespierre is a pile of papers. The illustrator has provided perfect caricatures of these three figures, in a way which somehow eludes the writer.

The three are discussing the progress of the Revolution and they fail to agree. Suddenly, unannounced, a fourth man enters: Cimourdain ('this powerful, unknown man whom the people saluted').[17] He warns: '"If the Revolution perishes, it will perish at the Vendée's hands. One Vendée is more dangerous than ten Germanies. For France to live, the Vendée must be slain." These few words gained him Robespierre.'[18] Cimourdain is made a delegate of the Committee of Public Safety and sent to the Vendée with orders to seek out and kill Lantenac.

The next chapter takes us from the intimacy of the small group to the cauldron which is the Convention. Hugo emphasises the status and power of this body, saying 'the Convention is possibly the zenith of history'.[19] He offers a precise description of the building and its architecture and then proceeds to describe the people who work within it. No novel of the Revolution can equal this, in terms of historical detail. Hugo's goes through enormous numbers of people and defines their various rôles. We glimpse the Convention at work (we see the darker side of its activities too). There are two sides – the Girondins and the Montagnards; one man stands out: 'Outside these two parties, and holding them both at a distance, is one man – Robespierre.'[20]

Hugo focuses on the principal actors: 'Condorcet was a man of dreams and clarity; Robespierre was a man of implementation; and sometimes, in the final crises of old societies, implementation means extermination.'[21] Robespierre, of course, plays a leading rôle in the Convention and Hugo gives him a voice:

[16] Victor Hugo, *Quatrevingt-treize* (Paris, n.d.), p. 136. [17] *Ibid.*, p. 154.
[18] *Ibid.*, p. 155. [19] *Ibid.*, p. 165. [20] *Ibid.*, p. 177.
[21] *Ibid.*, p. 180.

Robespierre takes the floor and speaks for two hours, looking at Danton, sometimes fixedly, which is grave, sometimes indirectly, which is worse. His denunciation is uncompromising. He ends with an indignant explosion, full of dismal expressions: 'we know the plotters, we know the traitors, we know the corrupters and the corrupted, we know the traitors; they are in this assembly. They hear us, we see them and do not let them out of our sight. When they look up, they will see the sword of the law; when they look into their hearts, they will see their infamy.'[22]

Hugo emphasises Robespierre's use of rhetorical devices and successfully conveys to the reader the sense of menace which this speech produces. Before long the reader's attention is taken back to the Vendée. Again we become involved in the tragic struggle so evocatively described by Hugo. But Robespierre has left his mark. His presence in the novel is not great but its effects are striking: Cimourdain's departure from Paris and his arrival in the Vendée move the story along towards its conclusion. One gets a very definite sense of the isolated province, cut off from Paris. But one senses too that the political centre of France is Paris and that the confusion of the Convention is an omen for the future.

On the face of it, Hugo tries to give Robespierre the characteristics which are generally attributed to him: detached, intellectual, eloquent and passionate in his beliefs. His presence in the novel endows a sense of historical reality to a text where the imagination of the author is in need of restraint. In our final example, *Les dieux ont soif* by Anatole France, the context is very different.

Les dieux ont soif was published in 1912. It is set entirely in Paris and recounts the adventures of Evariste Gamelin, an unsuccessful painter who is a convinced republican and admirer of Robespierre. The view of Paris is an intimate one, gleaned, no doubt, from the author's perusal of the revolutionary documents that passed through his father's hands in his capacity of antiquarian bookseller. The novel has a particular significance for us – it is, in this reading of the text, the first (perhaps the only) attempt in French fiction to rehabilitate Robespierre: the author's republican views are gently conveyed in this novel which, unlike *Stello* or *Quatrevingt-treize*, has a strong sentimental strand in the love affair between Gamelin and Elodie. Obviously Anatole France does not come out in favour of the Terror – but he shows the respectability of republican thought against a backcloth of over-zealous interpretation.

In the closed world of eighteenth-century Paris, the reader follows the progress of Gamelin with interest and curiosity. The view of revolutionary events differs starkly from that offered by Hugo. France chooses the period 1793–4 and includes the death of Robespierre. He shows us

[22] *Ibid.*, p. 191.

the trials before the Revolutionary Tribunal and the petty concerns of insignificant officials. Only two major historical figures have any stature: Marat and Robespierre. Danton and Saint-Just do not make an appearance. Robespierre is present throughout in the thoughts of the hero. But he also appears as himself. Gamelin admits that it was Robespierre, whom he refers to as Maximilien, who had educated him about the nature of deism:

> Through his virtuous eloquence, this great man revealed to him the true character of atheism, and its nature, designs and effects. He showed that that doctrine, created in the salons and boudoirs of the aristocracy, was the most treacherous invention which the enemies of the people had devised to corrupt and enslave it.[23]

Gamelin is impressed by the calm intellectual authority which Robespierre exerts; he is persuaded by his manner and by the force of his ideas. He recognises the need of the Revolution to defend itself from its enemies and he understands that, in such circumstances, certain actions are inevitable. But Evariste is much closer to the bloody action – on the same page on which his belief in the Supreme Being is explained, we read that, the following week, he sent forty-five men and eighteen women to their deaths. We find no simple caricature in this novel, rather a genuine attempt to explain Robespierre's actions in the context of the threat to the Revolution. Robespierre's intellectual authority dominates the text. Nowhere is this better felt than in chapter twenty-six in which Evariste recognises Robespierre walking in the jardins Marbeuf. It is Thermidor and the sun is setting, giving off a bloody purple colour. Robespierre appears pale and thin, his face showing the wrinkles of anxiety. Gamelin's comment – 'it is a thankless task working for the happiness of mankind' – is said without the slightest trace of irony.[24] It is surely no exaggeration that in this text alone we sense tragedy – a great life destroyed, a task unfinished. Gamelin's eulogy is sincere:

> I have seen your sadness, Maximilien; I have understood your thought. Your melancholy, your weariness, that expression of fear stamped on your glances all say: 'The Terror is over and the reign of fraternity begins! Frenchmen, unite, be virtuous, be righteous. Love one another . . .' Well, I will serve your plans; in order that you may be able, in your wisdom and goodness, to put an end to civil discord . . .[25]

The following chapter charts the last days of Robespierre. He is still talking, as Gamelin says, with purity, eloquently. But there is no salvation. Gamelin witnesses the moment when Robespierre's jaw is shattered and the young man attempts to end his own life before, eventually,

[23] Anatole France, *Les dieux ont soif* (Paris: Gallimard Folio, 1989), p. 167.
[24] *Ibid.*, p. 251. [25] *Ibid.*, p. 252.

going to the guillotine. The novel comes to an end with a description of Paris on 10 Thermidor. There is a sense of liberation in the air but one recognises that the values now extolled are false ones. A new order is being established in which the solid virtues of the Republic are swept away: the Revolution has failed and the death of Gamelin and his hero signify the end of an era.

V

What general conclusions can we draw from this analysis of Robespierre in fiction? First of all, of course, it must be said that Robespierre fits uneasily into a fictional setting. He plays himself, on the whole, and, perhaps inevitably, he is true to his character. Robespierre is not the conventional novel hero – he is aloof, detached, intellectual, shunning the trivial and full of political ambition. He is shrewd and cunning with a vision of the future that is felt in the majority of these novels. In physical terms, of course, novelists are constrained by external evidence – elegant and neat, he is always immaculate. There is no doubt that the novelists sought details which were commonplace so that the reader always recognised the very real person about whom they were reading. Various points of interest emerge. All the texts recognise that Robespierre is a shrewd politician and that he is a dangerous enemy; we find him in a number of different locations and it is this variety which, perhaps, deserves our final attention. In the early satirical pamphlets he is put, quite deliberately, in a number of comic situations – this is a simple means of devaluing the character. In Vigny's text we find him at home; there is a fascination for the writer and the reader here, which may remind us of Michelet's description of Marat's home. The cosy intimacy is out of keeping with high political office and the reader recognises this embarrassment. Hugo places him first of all in a neutral venue, the café where the three characters meet. It is barely described and the artist has had little help from the author in his representation of it. We also find Robespierre at the Convention. He is, in a sense, more at home here, dominating the audience with his power and eloquence and speaking for the Revolution. But the picture is a threatening one and the reader is uneasy. Finally, and in many ways this is the most interesting example of all, we see Robespierre in revolutionary Paris, forming part of the population which he dominates. This portrait is carefully drawn: Robespierre comes across as a sincere republican, one who deserves our sympathy and one whose death is, in the end, tragic. It is practically impossible to trace sources and routes through the various portraits of Robespierre. There is little doubt that Michelet was read and known by the two later writers, but one suspects that they read much else as well.

Two hundred years on, what remains? The corpus of texts in which Robespierre appears is not large. He is not the stuff of fiction, perhaps. However, when he does appear Danton, Saint-Just, even Marat disappear into the background. This alone must make us think that Robespierre did have a rôle in French fiction, even if that rôle is a complex one which authors will use for their own purposes.

It is now useful to return to a portrait of Robespierre given in *A Place of Greater Safety.* Certain features appear regularly but there is an intimacy in this most recent portrait that no writer of French fiction has ever dared to adopt. A brief example will suffice, and will serve as a conclusion:

> Max is quiet, calm and easy to live with; he has a neat build and wide, light eyes of a changeable blue-green. His mouth is not without humour, his complexion is pale; he takes care of his clothes and they fit him very well. His brown hair is always dressed and powdered; once he could not afford to keep up appearances, so now appearances are his only luxury.[26]

[26] Mantel, *Place of Greater Safety*, p. 99.

15 The representation of Robespierre in European drama

William D. Howarth

In many plays concerned with the French Revolution, the clash between the two great leaders, Danton and Robespierre, constitutes a major theme.[1] This is inevitable, given the obvious dramatic potential of the opposition of these figures who imposed their personalities on the events of the time, and have fascinated the imagination of historians and creative writers over the two centuries since those events took place. And it cannot be denied that of the two, it is Danton who has appealed more often to the creative imagination, as a larger-than-life, almost mythic example of the tragic hero; Büchner's *Dantons Tod* is no doubt the best-known, but is by no means the only, example of such an interpretation, in which the hero is destroyed by a fatal flaw within himself as much as by the historical forces of the times in which he lived. Such an interpretation almost inevitably requires the identification of Robespierre with these historical forces, as a functional agent, or catalyst, for the destruction of the tragic protagonist, the irony of his own death forming at best a sort of epilogue. Saint-Georges de Bouhélier, whose play *Le sang de Danton* was performed at the Comédie-Française in 1931, wrote, 'It is not a historical drama in the conventional meaning of the term. It is a tragedy in the mould of the *Oresteia* or *Oedipus Rex*.' He saw Robespierre's death as the end-term of a fatalistic process: '9 Thermidor echoes 9 Germinal'; and his Robespierre, as he is led to the guillotine, cries out: 'Germinal! Germinal! It is because of you that I am dying! O Danton, Danton! You have haunted me, hunted me, pursued me! The vengeance of the dead – therein lies the whole drama!'[2]

But let us return to the period of the Revolution itself; for the first examples of the portrayal of Robespierre on the stage date from a time when the rôle of the theatre was becoming more than a detached

[1] W. D. Howarth, 'The Danton/Robespierre theme in European drama', in H. T. Mason and W. Doyle (eds.), *The Impact of the French Revolution on European Consciousness* (Gloucester, 1989), pp. 21–34.

[2] Saint-Georges de Bouhélier, *Le sang de Danton* (Paris, 1931).

commentary on events that were already past history, and some dramatists were ready to intervene actively in the making of history. Having said that, one must regretfully dismiss the claim that the outstanding dramatist of the day was doing just that by a savage lampoon on Robespierre in 1792. It is well known that in the third of his Figaro plays, *La mère coupable*, Beaumarchais based the portrait of Bégearss, one of the blackest villains to appear in the melodramas of this period, on his personal enemy, the lawyer Bergasse; and it has been alleged that 'it does not take much imagination now to understand that Beaumarchais, who had suffered through Robespierre, had him also in his mind'. There is no evidence at all for this, and the suggestion is all too clearly a product of wishful thinking on the part of the person who put it forward: Eleanor Jourdain, one of the two academic ladies who in the 1920s achieved a certain notoriety by seeing the ghosts at Versailles – and whose imagination seems to have led her astray here as well.[3]

It is possible, however, to be more positive about the contribution of the Paris theatres, and of the topical plays put on there, to the events of the revolutionary years. In particular, there was a running battle between the Commune de Paris and the Théâtre de la Nation (that is, the more moderate half of the Comédie-Française company, which remained behind at the Salle du Luxembourg when the 'rouges' under Talma broke away in 1791). The principal cause of this conflict was Laya's *L'ami des lois*, first performed in January 1793. Though quite undistinguished from a literary point of view, this play showed great courage in presenting a reversal of the situation portrayed in many so-called revolutionary dramas of this period: here, it is the former aristocrats who are shown in a sympathetic light, while the Jacobin characters are seen to be self-seeking hypocrites. It is universally accepted that the Jacobin Nomophage ('devourer of laws') is a representation of Robespierre, while the journalist Duricrâne is generally supposed to be based on Marat. In Act II, Nomophage addresses his confidant:

> Soyons justes d'ailleurs, mon cher: sous l'ordre ancien
> Qu'étions-nous vous et moi? parlons franc; moins que rien.
> Qu'avions-nous? j'en rougis! pas même un sol de dettes,
> Car il faut du crédit pour en avoir de faites.
> Or, d'un vaste pays maintenant gouverneurs,
> Nous aurons des sujets, des trésors, des honneurs,
> Nous qui, riches de honte et surtout de misère,
> N'avions en propre, hélas, pas un arpent de terre.

[3] See E. F. Jourdain, *Dramatic Theory and Practice in France 1690–1808* (London, 1921), p. 24. See also Appendixes B and C.

(Let us be honest, my friend: under the old régime, what exactly did the two of us amount to? Nothing at all. I am ashamed to remember the extent of our possessions: not even a handful of debts, for to run into debt you need some sort of credit. Now we find ourselves rulers of a large country; we shall be obeyed by our subjects, and loaded with wealth and honours: we who a short time ago hadn't an acre of land to our name, and were rich only in disgrace and destitution.)[4]

In his edition of the play, Jacques Truchet calls it 'a very searching indictment of the Mountain';[5] and although the Commune did not succeed in banning *L'ami des lois*, it was a source of friction between the patriots and the moderates until September, when the Théâtre de la Nation was closed and the members of its company arrested – at which point the author went into hiding until after the fall of Robespierre. Although his dramatic method is that of conventional comedy rather than a more realistic portrayal of contemporary events, and although both his picture of Robespierre and his anti-Jacobin satire are totally lacking in subtlety, Laya's play provides a clear contrast with the politically 'correct' offerings of the day (pro-Jacobin before the *coup* of 9 Thermidor, rabidly anti-Jacobin afterwards); and throughout the first half of 1793, performances of *L'ami des lois* served as a rallying-point for the waning Girondin cause.

When we move on a generation or more, to a period during which the events of the Revolution provide subject-matter for historical drama as we generally understand the term, there is an obvious critical distinction to be made between the melodramas which Alexandre Dumas *père* and others contributed to the Paris theatres for more than twenty years from 1830 (and of which *Le chevalier de Maison-Rouge, ou les Girondins* (1847) is a late example) and the more academic treatment of a historical subject in dramatic form, to appeal to the discerning reader rather than the spectator in the theatre. The latter was the genre known as the *scène historique*; and Duchatellier, the author of *Le théâtre historique de la Révolution*, published in 1828–9, described his approach to the history play as follows: 'in our work, there is not a word, an interjection or an action which could not be found in the newspapers and broadsheets of the period'. Duchatellier's *La mort de Louis XVI* was followed in 1829 by *La mort des Girondins*: a good example of the *scène historique* in its lack of focus (there are fifty-eight named characters, plus crowds of supernumeraries) deriving from the author's attempt to reproduce the genuine complexity of the historical event. Though a third instalment, *Le 9 thermidor*, was announced, it does not appear that it was ever published. A trilogy that was completed, however, and published in

4 *Théâtre du xviiie siècle*, ed. J. Truchet (Paris, 1972–4), vol. II, p. 1250.

5 *Ibid.*, vol. II, p. 1545.

1830, by one Ducancel, begins with *L'intérieur des comités révolutionnaires* which is actually a contribution to the *local* history of the revolutionary period, for it is set in Dijon in 1795. It is typical of the *scène historique* in that there is no focus on a central protagonist or protagonists; the notes to the play make it clear that the author saw little to choose between Marat, Danton and Robespierre. The subject he adopted is historically authentic, in that the Dijon committee did support Robespierre after 9 Thermidor, and denounced the Convention as counter-revolutionary conspirators; but the presentation of Robespierre, as dictated by the genre of the *scène historique*, is deliberately non-committal. The same is true of *Les septembriseurs* (1829) whose author, Regnier-Destourbet, wrote that he had set out to prove that 'history is more dreadful than the most dreadful fiction; that to be more monstrous, more appalling, more awful than the material our young writers produce in those stories called "printed nightmares", it would be enough to record human history realistically, without disguising anything'.

In *Robespierre, ou le 9 thermidor* by Anicet-Bourgeois and Francis (1830), however, the dispassionate stance of the *scène historique* is not maintained. The play takes a thermidorian, anti-Robespierre line; and in addition the dramatic writing is popular, anecdotal and romanesque, both as regards the private lives of the ordinary people who are foregrounded by the plot, and the more public relationships of Robespierre and the Cordeliers. A scene in the Conciergerie prison, for instance, shows us André Chénier in a corner, writing verses on his knee: inevitably, he is writing 'Comme un dernier rayon . . .', while Robespierre is made to express to a confidant, like the villain of a contemporary melodrama, his intention to become an out-and-out dictator. The balance is redressed, however, in what is the most interesting of the plays of the period, *Le 9 thermidor, ou la mort de Robespierre, drame historique* (1831) by one Bonnias. This play presents a not unfamiliar mixture of the public and the private; but what distinguishes it from other offerings considered so far is its lengthy pro-Robespierre preface:

> This is a work inspired by a profound conviction; it is a response, which if not complete is at least conscientious, to the slanders and attacks which, over a period of forty years, have unceasingly been made on the reputations of the illustrious leaders of the popular cause, those great men who fell under the blows of intrigue during the crisis of 9 Thermidor.

Though another indifferent play – it was never performed – this is the first of the Robespierre plays deliberately to espouse the revisionist cause which was to be central to Robespierre historiography later in the century. Ernest Hamel's controversial rehabilitation of Robespierre in his biography of 1865–7 finds an equally partisan echo, for instance, in *Robespierre, ou les drames de la Révolution*, published at Lyon in 1888 and played in the Paris *banlieue* in the same year, after being refused for nearly a decade, according to its author, Combet, by the leading theatres of the capital. Combet wrote that his play, which was dedicated to Hamel, was finally being published 'with the aim of telling the non-reading public the truth about Maximilien Robespierre, and openly doing justice to one of the noblest victims of the hatred, slander and cowardice of men, through the medium of the theatre (which must act so as to complement the schools)'. The philosophical intention behind Combet's play could not be clearer: 'The play is not a party manifesto, rather it is an essay concerned to make amends and do justice. It is a call for impartial history, for the revising of an ill-considered judgement passed on the most upright man of the French Revolution.'[6] Nevertheless, the author's creative inspiration owes more to the colourful spectacle of the historical melodrama than to the sober documentation of the *scènes historiques*. The penultimate tableau, for instance, has the significant title 'Le Golgotha', and we are clearly invited to interpret Robespierre's death as a kind of martyrdom:

> The cloud which has become very dense and dark is pierced from time to time by flashes of lightning whilst thunder rumbles. An opening gradually emerges and there is seen, as in a frame, Robespierre at the Hôtel de Ville [*sic*], wounded and lying on a table, in the midst of a howling crowd. Then the clouds close in again whilst the rumbling of thunder continues. Flashes of lightning rend the sky and everything is bathed in a bloody glow. The cloud half opens and part of the place de la Révolution, with the scaffold and the tumbrils, comes into view. Among those about to die is Robespierre, his head swathed in blood-stained bandages. There is a thunder-clap, then a black cloud envelops the dreadful scene, and everything is plunged into darkness.

This scene is followed by an apotheosis in the Elysian Fields, in which the martyr is admitted to the company of Justice, Truth and History; the stage-direction is too long to quote more than its conclusion:

> Then Robespierre appears, borne on clouds. At his entry, the heavenly choir bursts into song. Truth and History lead him to the foot of the throne of Justice, who offers him the golden palm of the immortals. Thereupon, Dante, Jesus, Socrates, Joan of Arc, Voltaire, Rousseau, Saint-Just, Lebas and the rest come up to Robespierre, surrounding him, whilst the crowd redoubles its singing, triumphantly accompanied by the orchestra. The back of the stage is lit up, as though by an aurora borealis, and there, in letters of fire, are the words:
>
> *République universelle. – Etats-Unis d'Europe. –*
> *Alliance des peuples.*
>
> There is majestic singing, whilst the clouds are illuminated.

[6] Louis Combet, *Robespierre, ou les drames de la Révolution* (Lyon, 1888), preface.

Combet's play was followed a few years later by another pro-Robespierre play, *Le neuf thermidor* by a trio of authors, La Rode, Rolle and Crémieux, performed at the Théâtre des Bouffes-du-Nord in 1892. This play is much more moderate in its dramaturgical conception; a distinguishing feature is the fact that it presents Madame Tallien as the villain of the piece, motivated by a desire for vengeance on a mild, peace-loving Robespierre for spurning her advances. The critic of *Figaro* commented that this went down quite well with the audience, in which 'Danton's supporters were in the minority'; while the reviewer of *La Lanterne* noted the play's 'historical realism', as well as the authors' debt to 'the perspectives and opinions of Louis Blanc, Ernest Hamel and the learned Professeur Aulard'.[7]

However, the Robespierre play which stands out in the history of the last decade of the nineteenth century – for its political impact rather than for its artistic quality – is one whose author sought to redress the balance and to go against the revisionist tide of pro-Robespierre sentiment. This was Sardou's *Thermidor*, which after a successful première at the Comédie-Française in January 1891, was the occasion on its second performance of a serious riot, provoked by left-wing students who were outraged by the author's condemnation of the Terror. The Minister of the Interior banned further performances of the play, a ban which Clemenceau upheld with his famous phrase 'la Révolution est un bloc' – that is, a historical event which republican Frenchmen a hundred years later must accept in its totality. Though *Thermidor* may be viewed as 'a Robespierre play', it is also representative of a number of the more distinguished dramatic treatments of the Terror whose authors chose to focus their play's primary dramatic interest on the domestic fortunes of a private family, real or fictional, leaving Robespierre and the other revolutionary leaders in the background. The Goncourt brothers' *La patrie en danger* (1873) and Paul Meurice's dramatisation of Hugo's novel *Quatrevingt-treize* (1882) are notable examples of such an approach, as Bernanos's *Dialogues des Carmélites* was to be at a later date. The central figure of Sardou's *Thermidor* is Labussière, the ex-actor who made use of his clerical post in the public prosecutor's office in order to destroy dossiers and save from the guillotine as many victims of the Terror as he could; but when the play was revised for production at the Porte-Saint-Martin in 1896 – a production which there was no attempt to ban – Sardou added scenes in which Robespierre is introduced in person (he is accused in the Convention and sentenced to death). The balance of sympathy is not altered in the revised version, although this is

[7] *Le magasin théâtral*, 1892.

no longer the case in a play with which Sardou followed *Thermidor* a few years later. This was *Robespierre, pièce en cinq actes et sept tableaux*, which had its première in an English translation at the Lyceum Theatre in 1899, with Henry Irving in the title rôle. Here, we are less concerned with historical revisionism or a debate about political theory than with a sort of sentimental rehabilitation. Robespierre is still a Jacobin extremist, agent of the hated Terror; but we are asked to interest ourselves in his efforts to save Olivier, his illegitimate son by a daughter of the *notaire* to whom, as a young law student from Arras, he had been articled. In other words, this is historical melodrama such as Dumas *père* might have written; it can hardly be regarded as a serious contribution to Robespierre historiography.

At this same period, however, Sardou took part in an exchange of pamphlets with the historian Hamel about the documentary sources for Robespierre's biography, in the course of which he refers to his own meeting as a child with the elderly Elisabeth Lebas, née Duplay, who had been both daughter and wife of Robespierre's close associates:

> Which Robespierre had she known? The one who lived in the family home, happy to be fawned upon there, almost loving towards Léonore and her sisters, sober, austere and chaste, speaking only in elegant phrases and maxims! The one who, on winter evenings, recited scenes from Racine and hummed to the pieces played on the harpsicord by Buonarotti. The one who, on evenings in the summer, tossed coins to the little Savoyards or took his dog, Brount, to bathe in the Seine, or who on visits to Saint-Ouen or Montmorency picked cherries in the orchards for his young friends and gathered cornflowers from the fields!
>
> With time, the image of the great man had become so idealised that she even saw him as handsome! She forgot the cat-like head, the prominent cheek-bones, the pock-marked visage; the bilious complexion, the green eyes ringed with red beneath the blue spectacles, the shrill voice, the dry tone, pedantic, peevish and abrupt; the haughty carriage of his head and the convulsive twitches. All these characteristics were wiped away and transformed into the gentle features of an apostle, a martyr for his creed for the salvation of mankind!
>
> For, indeed, the monster had his creed! To begin with, belief in himself; then in the sublimity of his ideas, which were entirely those of a disciple of Rousseau: in civilisation as the corrupter of morals; in the return to the state of nature, where mankind is, of course, perfect; in an egalitarian régime, under which the citizens would none the less bow beneath the yoke of a kind of theocracy of which he, the Incorruptible, would naturally be the supreme pontiff! 'A Jesuit seminary from Latin America', as the scornful Danton put it. In short, the most loathsome of tyrannies; but, for this madman and the visionaries who surrounded him, the perfect republic, founded on virtue![8]

This paradox is one which Robespierre's dramatist biographers of the

[8] V. Sardou, *La maison de Robespierre, réponse à M. E. Hamel, sénateur* (Paris, 1895), pp. 74–6.

nineteenth century almost all preferred to ignore. Simplifying the character in the interests of partisan polemic or of dramatic effectiveness, they reproduced either the fanatical monster or the pure, incorruptible idealist, seldom acknowledging the reverse of the coin. This approach can be seen clearly in what must have been the first Robespierre play to have been written outside France: *The Fall of Robespierre*, composed jointly by Coleridge and Southey, and dated 1794. Even allowing for the tremendous disillusionment felt by young idealists, when Wordsworth's 'Bliss was it in that dawn . . .' had given way to the bloodbath of the Terror, this English representation of Robespierre must be accounted one of the least subtle – both in the portrait painted at second hand by the *Conventionnels* who seek his death, and in the melodramatic emphasis of his own self-portrait:

> He whose heart sickens at the blood of traitors
> Would be himself a traitor, were he not
> A coward! 'Tis congenial souls alone
> Shed tears of sorrow for each other's fate.
> O thou art brave, my brother! and thine eye
> Full firmly shines amid the groaning battle –
> Yet in thine heart the woman-form of pity
> Asserts too large a share, an ill-timed guest!
> There is unsoundness in the state – Tomorrow
> Shall see it cleansed by wholesome massacre![9]

However, in Büchner's *Dantons Tod*, by general agreement the most distinguished play on the French Revolution written during either the nineteenth or the twentieth century, the author's poetic intuition offers layers of imaginative understanding beneath the surface of what was already in 1835 the standard opposition between the 'appallingly righteous' Robespierre and a Danton who is sickened by the butchery, to the point that he can declare: 'I would rather be guillotined than guillotine.'[10] Still, Robespierre's assumption of Messianic status in the passage in which he compares himself to Christ hardly makes him more sympathetic in dramatic terms than the 'monster' or 'maniac' later described by Sardou.[11] To the extent that Büchner's play is structured to make us focus on Danton as a tragic hero, we are invited, one could

[9] Act I, scene i, lines 100–9: *The Poetical Works of S. T. Coleridge*, ed. J. D. Campbell (London, 1905), p. 213.

[10] Act II, scene i: Georg Büchner, *Danton's Death*, trans. Howard Brenton and Jane Fry, in Büchner, *The Complete Plays* (London, 1987), p. 34.

[11] *Ibid.*, Act I, scene ii: p. 32. 'Messiah of blood, who is not sacrificed but sacrifices. Yes. He redeemed them with his blood, I redeem them with their own. He made them sinners, I take the sin upon me. He had the ecstasy of pain. I have the torment of the executioner. Who denies himself the more, he or I?'

argue, to see Robespierre as a functional representative of the historical process rather than as a fully rounded figure in his own right. Even so, a recent article dealing with Büchner's interpretation of the historical Robespierre argues for the playwright's major interest in this character:

> Büchner's sympathy may have originated in the failure of his own revolutionary struggle in the duchy of Hessen. But in *Dantons Tod* this situation is heightened immeasurably in that Robespierre is here shown as caught in the agonizing dilemma of striving for the political liberation of humanity while being compelled to sanction the deaths of thousands ... While therefore Büchner's Robespierre, like the historical figure, must confront complex problems and struggle with them in the depths of his conscience, other dramatic and historical interpretations of ... Robespierre in the nineteenth century content themselves with a facile condemnation of the revolutionary dictator as a bloodthirsty tyrant.[12]

Despite this, Büchner's Robespierre seems to lack both the three-dimensional stature and the compelling psychological interest with which the playwright succeeded in endowing his eponymous central character.

If Büchner's play is generally recognised as surpassing all other treatments of the subject produced by the Romantic generation, in France or abroad, there was to be one French man of letters at the end of the century – Romain Rolland – who was capable of transcending his contemporaries' generally simplistic approach to historical biography, and who devoted more than forty years of his life to the search for a dramatic form in which to clothe his passionate interest in the Revolution as the most appropriate subject for what he called a 'theatre of the people'. Rolland's theoretical exposition of his ideas for a new kind of theatre with a socially and politically educative rôle found its fullest expression in *Le théâtre du peuple*, first published in 1903, while the practical illustration of this, his *Théâtre de la Révolution*, took the form of an epic cycle of eight plays, of very diverse style and scope, of which the first title was published in 1898 and the last as late as 1939. The two major contributions to the series are *Danton*, published in 1899 and performed in 1900, and *Robespierre*, which was published forty years later. That this latter play has remained unperformed is partly, no doubt, because of its own vast epic structure – over 300 pages of text, and a hypothetical playing-time of six hours or so – which leads one to believe that for all its author's theatrical ambitions, such a play is really a kind of vast closet drama, addressed to the reader rather than to the spectator. Indeed, a reviewer of a performance of *Le jeu de l'amour et de*

[12] R. Taylor, 'History and the transcendence of subjectivity in Büchner's Robespierre', *Neophilologus* 72 (1988), 83.

la mort, another play of the cycle, originally produced in 1928 and revived in 1939, claimed that Rolland's over-didactic approach would be more appropriate to an academic 'soutenance de thèse': 'One leaves full of admiration for M. Rolland's perspicacity and impartiality, but also full of rancour towards the playwright. A production should be banned when it is simply unable to bring the material to life.'[13] However, Robert Merle, in a perceptive if politically one-sided article on *Le théâtre de la Révolution*, suggested that another reason for the non-performance of Rolland's final play is to be seen in the bias and prejudice of the Paris theatre establishment, 'strictly controlled by the hidden censorship of the ruling classes'.[14] What is certain is that, over the forty years of the composition of his cycle of plays, Rolland never compromised his aim to 'rekindle the faith of the nation with flames from the republican epic, so that the work which was broken off in 1794 may be revived and carried through by a people both more mature and more conscious of its destiny'.[15] At the opposite pole from the concept of theatre as popular entertainment, *Le théâtre de la Révolution* is the dramatised version of a philosophy of history which sought to justify the Revolution, with all its cruelty, its self-defeating rivalries and its lack of a clear direction, as a necessary step in the evolution of a popular consciousness on a national level. In an important postface to his *Robespierre*, Rolland wrote:

I have been concerned in this play, as I have always been in my drama dealing with the Revolution, more with the characters' moral veracity than with factual accuracy. Nevertheless, I have pursued the latter much more closely here than in any other of my plays. I am hopeful that the true face of history is mirrored in *Robespierre* – more accurately than was the case with my *Danton*. That was written too early, before the fruitful research which has reconstructed the history of the Revolution.[16]

In Rolland's view, Thermidor brought the end of the Revolution: the Revolution dominated by Robespierre 'not only through the integrity of his character, but also through the clarity of his mind and his unswerving commitment to the popular cause'.[17] This integrity was acknowledged even by his enemies at the time, he continued:

Why, after such testimonies given by the very men who executed him, has it been necessary to wait for more than a century before finally reconsidering our verdict on Robespierre? It is not undertaken, despite the generous promptings of Lamartine, the idolatrous hero-worship of a Hamel, the committed archival

[13] *Mercure de France*, 15 August 1939.
[14] Robert Merle, 'Le théâtre de la Révolution', *Europe* 439–40 (1965), 26.
[15] Romain Rolland, *Le 14 juillet* (1902), foreword.
[16] Romain Rolland, *Robespierre* (Paris, 1939), p. 311. [17] *Ibid.*, p. 312.

research of Mathiez and his followers. The greatest figure of the Revolution still has no statue in France.[18]

But Rolland's portrait of Robespierre is no mere hagiographical exercise. He saw the key to his play as being the *sincerity* of the major protagonists, defeated by their own human weaknesses:

> All these men ... were sincere and passionate republicans ... And yet they became bent on destroying their own creation, the Republic. They were brought by their passions, their fury and their suspicions to a veritable frenzy which made them incapable of seeing where they were going and which even threw them into the arms of bitter enemies of the Revolution. Therein was a fate as inescapable as that which destroyed Oedipus.[19]

Whereas most of the nineteenth-century dramatists examined here regarded this paradox as the source of dramatic – or melodramatic – effect, Rolland saw it as the way into an impressively sympathetic psychological study of his hero.

The play opens with Robespierre and the Duplay family watching the tumbril pass by containing Danton and his associates. As other dramatists have done, Rolland explicitly framed the closing months of Robespierre's life between Danton's death and his own, as Danton calls out: 'Robespierre! I open the grave-pit. You will follow me there ... A bientôt!', to which Robespierre replies ('firmly'): 'A bientôt! So be it!' But such a quotation, taken out of context, would give a misleading view of the dramatic focus of this large-scale epic drama, which is loosely structured in a series of twenty-four tableaux, most of them filled out with supernumeraries to provide a lively, colourful background to the presentation of the principal characters. The presence of the dead Danton may brood over the play, but, in spite of the author's invocation of an ineluctable fate, the predominant impression left with the reader is one of characters controlled by a motivation that is all too human. Alongside the striking portrayal of simple friendship – that of Robespierre with the Duplay family, that between Saint-Just and Le Bas, for instance – we also see abundant evidence of selfishness, jealousy, treachery and the lust for power. One melodramatic motif – though given the play's diffuse structure, its impact lacks the crudity that is typical of melodrama – is perhaps to be seen in the rôle given to Fouché as a skilful manipulator, with the suggestion that Robespierre was the victim of unscrupulous intriguers, and that the crimes carried out in the Revolution's name were the work of cynical self-seekers rather than of the sincere idealists among the revolutionaries.

Altogether, this must rank as the most *nuancé* of all the more recent dramatic portraits of Robespierre. In Rolland's *Danton* of 1899, our

[18] *Ibid.*, p. 314. [19] *Ibid.*, pp. 7–8.

sympathy had certainly been enlisted for the 'Shakespearian glutton, jovial and larger-than-life', as the author calls the eponymous hero, who takes no pains to hide his scorn for Robespierre: 'So long as a man has a weak stomach and stunted senses, provided he lives off a morsel of cheese and sleeps in a single bed, you call him Incorruptible, and the word does away with courage and vitality. I despise such anaemic virtues.'[20] Forty years later, Rolland felt justified in presenting a Robespierre in his way more noble than the worldly, sensuous Danton. With his own belief in the permanent importance of the Revolution as a unique event in the evolution of humanity now underpinned by the academic research of Mathiez and others, he presented in his Robespierre an ascetic hero, saintly even, courageous in meeting his death and refusing to save himself by means in which he does not believe. As with Büchner's Robespierre, a parallel is suggested with the sufferings of Christ, but this analogy is merely hinted at by Rolland. Robespierre is taunted by the gendarmes, like Christ by the soldiers; and when he is arrested, a former associate twice denies knowing him:

> – I nevertheless heard that you were his friend.
> – Someone's been lying. I swear it's not true.
> – If you're telling the truth, spit!
> – I swear – and spit.[21]

This is a good deal more discreet, and much less offensive, than the comparison which Büchner's Robespierre himself makes – to his own advantage – between his self-sacrifice and that of Christ.

Romain Rolland's vast contribution to the dramatic treatment of the Robespierre theme spanned nearly half a century, and takes us to the threshold of the Second World War.[22] When we emerge into the post-war literary scene, we enter a period in which the 'straight' representation of history has most notably given way to two different approaches. There is, on the one hand, a more imaginative manipulation of historical material – often with a view to drawing suggestive parallels between the past and the present day – and, accordingly, such devices as the flashback, distortion of the time-scale or the play within the play are employed. On the other hand, there is an approach to historical material by means of improvised, collectivist spectacle, illustrated in Ariane Mnouchkine's *1789* (1970) and *1793* (1972). The latter play shows a

[20] Romain Rolland, *Danton*, Act III, in *Théâtre de la Révolution* (Paris, 1926), p. 98 (separate pagination).

[21] Rolland, *Robespierre*, pp. 293–4.

[22] For a recent assessment of Rolland's concept of a 'revolutionary theatre', see V. Battaglia, 'Romain Rolland et le Théâtre de la Révolution', *Revue de l'histoire du théâtre* 162 (1989), 178–95.

total rejection of 'event-based' history, and the events of 1793 are portrayed without showing Robespierre, or any other leading figure, as a participant at first hand.

There have, it is true, in this period, been treatments of the Robespierre theme that have remained faithful to the more conventional form of a historical chronicle. One such, premièred at the Barbican in London in 1986, is *The Danton Affair* by Pam Gems, a rewriting of a Polish original (itself inspired by Büchner's play) by Stanislawa Przybyszewska, staged in 1931. The Polish play set out to rehabilitate Robespierre, and to adjust the focus of Büchner's version; this produced a very striking play, particularly successful in Andrzej Wajda's production in 1975 (as well as in his subsequent film version). Gems's rewriting of this was motivated by a desire to remain independent, as regards point of view, of both Büchner and Przybyszewska. However, this resulted in a sadly reductive exercise, producing an atmosphere of strident vulgarity in which Danton, Robespierre and the other leading figures on the public stage are deprived of all nobility and dignity, and the undoubted idealism of the Revolution is replaced by the trivial squabbling of an unattractive pack of pygmies.

One of the criticisms usually levelled against Anouilh's *Pauvre Bitos, ou le dîner de têtes* of 1956 is that, despite its technical brilliance, it suffers from the lack of a sympathetic character. The author's point of view is evident enough: he makes a clear stand against political extremism, whether of the left or the right; and, by setting his play in the 1950s, he was able to present telling parallels between the events of the Revolution and those of his own day, particularly the savage purges of those suspected of wartime collaboration. The structure of *Pauvre Bitos* is quite masterly. Several wealthy right-wingers, representing the social élite of their provincial community, have come together for a 'dîner de têtes', whose guests are invited not only to present themselves made up to represent Danton, Camille Desmoulins or whoever it might be, but also to rehearse the career and personality of the historical figure allotted to them, so as to produce a spontaneous 'happening'. However, it soon becomes clear that the real purpose of the entertainment is the humiliation of Bitos, an ambitious young public prosecutor of humble origins, who is making a name for himself by his merciless vendetta against right-wing collaborators and profiteers. Bitos has been invited to come as Robespierre; and the theatricality of the occasion is strikingly enhanced when he makes a belated entrance not only with appropriate wig and make-up, but in full costume – the Incorruptible's famous sky-blue outfit. The baiting of the outsider develops with increasing dramatic tension, until the pistol-shot fired by the young man hired to impersonate the gendarme Merda brings the first act to an end. Act II takes place in the fevered imagination of Bitos, who has fainted at the sound of the shot: in this dream-sequence he becomes Robespierre, while the others also become the historical figures whose identity they have been assuming. A third act brings us back to reality, and a truce is patched up between Bitos and his tormentors.

Judged simply as historical drama, *Pauvre Bitos* would provide further evidence, like his plays on Joan of Arc, Becket and Napoleon, that history was for Anouilh the occasion for a fancy-dress charade. What this play sets out to do, however, is to use the past to offer a perspective on the present; and the switch between the present day and the events of the Revolution is the source of challenging parallels of attitude and motivation. The material of the dream-sequence has been well researched, and the balance of sympathy – or lack of sympathy – between Robespierre and his opponents carries dramatic conviction as an illustration at second hand of the lack of sympathetic appeal Anouilh found in the doctrinaire extremism of his own day. His Robespierre, like the twentieth-century Bitos who incarnates him in the 'dîner de têtes', is a far remove from the idealist portrayed by the historical revisionists: he is an ambitious upstart motivated by vindictiveness and fear. The character playing Danton says to Bitos-Robespierre in Act I:

> I loved eating, I loved women, I loved life. And that's the reason you had me killed, hypocrite! You believed you hated carelessness, disorder and dirt; it was the people that you hated! And you know why? Because they scared you, just as women did – hence your virtue – and life too. You killed us all because you didn't know how to live. We paid dearly for your complexes.[23]

One of the most recent Robespierre plays is *Le chant du retour* by Véra Feyder, performed in 1989 at Arras. It presents us with a miscellaneous collection of inhabitants of present-day Arras, who are all involved in some way in preparations for the celebrations of the bicentenary of the Revolution, and are waiting for the return from exile of Maxime, a political revolutionary who is due to take on the rôle of Robespierre. He arrives, bringing with him a motley group of revolutionary activists from all over the world; and the message of the play seems to be that two hundred years on from the events of 1789, the revolutionary crusade against the forces of authority and repression has taken on a world-wide dimension. This is put across suggestively rather than by more direct didactic means; and not only is the parallel between the historical Robespierre and his twentieth-century analogue much less forceful than

[23] Jean Anouilh, *Pauvre Bitos, ou le dîner de têtes*, ed. W. D. Howarth (London, 1958), p. 51; and see T. Malachy, '*Pauvre Bitos* d'Anouilh: l'éclatement théâtral d'un mythe', *Revue de l'histoire du théâtre* 162 (1989), 196–201.

in the case of *Pauvre Bitos*, but the message that the returning revolutionary embodies is too diffuse to carry conviction – at least to the reader of the play, if not to its spectators. It is interesting, however, to set *Le chant du retour* alongside *Pauvre Bitos* as examples of what may be said to have become the dominant attitude of our own day to the historical subject – seeing it as a pretext for the imaginative spectacle of metatheatre: an attitude most notably illustrated in Peter Weiss's *Marat/ Sade*.

It is worth closing with an anecdotal reference to a historical drama by Fritz Hochwälder, *The Public Prosecutor*, of 1948. *Der Öffentliche Ankläger* cannot be regarded as a Robespierre play: its action, taking place after Thermidor, focuses on the relationship between Fouquier-Tinville and the Talliens. However, when it was performed at the Oxford Playhouse in 1954, a programme-note included a reference to Robespierre, in which he was described as the 'pea-green Incorruptible'. One might suggest that this memorable misprint, for all its absurdity, does perhaps embody an unconscious lesson. For despite its highly ironical use by Carlyle, whose 'sea-green Incorruptible' really seems to have been intended as a forceful oxymoron, the epithet 'sea-green' retains certain noble associations of a literary character, and – taken out of context – inevitably conjures up a vision of the idealist hero of nineteenth-century revisionist historiography. No such ambivalence can possibly attach to the ignoble 'pea-green', which evokes unambiguously the physically unattractive Robespierre, with bilious countenance betraying his dyspepsia, and pebble glasses to correct his short sight. This is the Robespierre of Anouilh above all, much less convinced than some playwrights have been of the personal charisma of the deputy from Arras. The different portraits are no doubt selective, and each needs the other to restore the balance. But one may conclude by proposing, not wholly frivolously, that anyone who is tempted to interpret the portrait of the sea-green Incorruptible in too favourable a light might do well not to forget entirely his pea-green counterpart.

Part V

Conclusion

16 French historians and Robespierre

(Dedicated to the memory of François Furet)

François Crouzet

It is very clear that Robespierre played a key rôle in the French Revolution, and also that, two centuries after his death, he remains a controversial figure, whom many have hated, many have worshipped, and who still exerts a kind of fascination. A survey of the various views which historians have held of Robespierre, and of the controversies about him, can thus throw some light upon the development of the Revolution's historiography and its correlation with the vicissitudes of French political and intellectual life, into which the very bias and special pleadings of many historians can provide useful insights. As John McManners has rightly remarked: 'Party strife and inherited prejudices have branded their mark upon most French historians of the Revolution.'[1]

This is why this essay will only consider French historians, from Adolphe Thiers onwards, though the major contributions which British and American scholars have made to our knowledge of the French Revolution are of immense importance. But here we shall consider the debate on Robespierre – especially in relation to the Terror – as a political Franco-French debate, an aspect of the nation's permanent civil war (to the violence of which the Terror's legacy has greatly contributed).

Three main stages can be observed in French historians' perceptions of Robespierre, leaving aside the royalist ones.[2]

In the nineteenth century, when liberalism was dominant, most historians were critical of Robespierre, though a minority, with socialist leanings, held more favourable views.

[1] J. McManners, 'The historiography of the French Revolution', in G. R. Potter *et al.* (eds.), *The New Cambridge Modern History*, 14 vols. (Cambridge, 1968), vol. III, p. 618.

[2] To most of them, Robespierre was just the most monstrous of revolutionary criminals; but there were exceptions, especially some writers associated with Action française, or who had, in the 1930s, fascist leanings. They rejected 1789, but saw in the Terror some socialist and nationalist, i.e. proto-fascist, ideas, and they had 'a certain admiration for Robespierre': George L. Mosse, 'Fascism and the French Revolution', *Journal of Contemporary History* 24 (1989), 22–3. I am indebted to the late Denis Richet for this reference.

In the twentieth century, as socialism, and especially Marxism-Leninism, came to prevail, many historians became unconditional supporters of the Incorruptible, to the point of idolatry.

During the past thirty years, the tide has turned again; a more balanced view of Robespierre has been put forward; still the Robespierrists are fighting on.

I

In the nineteenth century, all leading historians of the French Revolution, but one, held unfavourable views of Robespierre, whatever their political convictions.[3] This was the case with Adolphe Thiers and Auguste Mignet, who were supporters of constitutional monarchy; with Alphonse de Lamartine, who was a moderate republican; and with Jules Michelet, who was a passionate populist and romantic republican, like his friend Edgar Quinet. Such views can also be found in the works of the positivist philosopher Auguste Comte, who admired the revolutionary government of 1793, or in those of Hippolyte Taine, who hated the French Revolution, lock, stock and barrel; and in the writings of Alphonse Aulard, who held the chair of the history of the French Revolution at the Sorbonne from its foundation in 1891 up to 1922 and who was the official historian in the heyday of the Third Republic.[4]

The range of views on Robespierre which historians put forward was wide; one can only stress some traits of his character which are the most frequently mentioned.

First, except with Taine, these traits were not all negative. Several historians acknowledged that Robespierre had all the virtues which earned him the nickname of the Incorruptible: he was honest, hard-working, poor, steadfast; he led a Spartan life; he sincerely wanted the reign of democracy and reason. They even praised his policies at some moments of his career.[5]

[3] Godechot was wrong to maintain that only men from the right or the centre have been hostile to Robespierre; Alice Gérard concedes that there were 'republican anti-Robespierrists'. Jacques Godechot, 'L'historiographie française de Robespierre', in *Actes du colloque Robespierre. XIIe congrès international des sciences historiques (Vienne, 3 septembre 1965). Avant-propos par Albert Soboul* (Paris, 1967), pp. 167–8; Alice Gérard, *La Révolution française, mythes et interprétation 1789–1970* (Paris, 1970), pp. 127–8.

[4] He had been teaching the history of the Revolution at the Sorbonne since 1886.
Tocqueville is not mentioned here, as his works contain hardly any references to Robespierre.

[5] See, e.g.: Adolphe Thiers, *Histoire de la Révolution française* (1823–7), quoted from the Furne edition, 2 vols. (Paris, n.d.), vol. I, pp. 587, 590, 707, vol. II, p. 92; Jules Michelet, *Histoire de la Révolution française* (1847–53), quoted from the 'Bouquins' edition, 2 vols. (Paris, 1987), vol. II, pp. 504, 543, 590, 592, 594, 672; Edgar Quinet,

However, negative aspects prevailed. Thiers and Michelet agreed that there was a dark side to Robespierre's mind and imagination, and most historians stressed how distrustful and suspicious he was. Michelet described him as 'the eternal denunciator', then 'the Republic's great prosecutor' and eventually a judge-cum-dictator, with a 'monomania of absolute purification'. Both Michelet and Quinet observed, like some recent historians, that the constant denunciation of traitors was a powerful political weapon in his hands.[6]

There was some doubt as to whether Robespierre had been a hypocrite. Michelet wrote first that he did not need to lie, as he believed everything he said; but he also described him as a perfect political Tartuffe. Taine had a good phrase about 'a hypocrite convinced that he is sincere'. There also was some doubt about his cruelty. Thiers and Lamartine saw Robespierre as pitiless and implacable. Quinet wrote that he had no scruples about felling the few heads which were obstacles to the advent of justice on earth; but he added that, possibly, his soul was not atrocious enough, so that he became tired of killing people – and it ruined him. According to Michelet, he was not born cruel, but his mind and heart were distorted by hatred, so that his impulses towards clemency evaporated.[7]

Despite such differences and qualifications, overall judgements on Robespierre were quite unfavourable.

To Thiers, he was 'one of the most hateful beings who ruled over men, one of the vilest, one would even say', but for his conviction and integrity. Mignet saw Robespierre as a man of ordinary talents, with an extreme ambition, and as a fanatic. Lamartine was more lenient to this 'Calvin of politics', as he called him; a tyrant, who became a victim, he was not a man of action. Quinet also wrote that Robespierre did not have the constitution of those men who conquer an empire.[8]

Michelet wrote a great deal about Robespierre and not without contradictions, but, in the new edition of his history of the French Revolution which was published in 1869, he added a preface to volume

La Révolution, 3 vols. (Paris, 1865), quoted from the 1876 edition, vol. II, p. 443; Alphonse Aulard, *Histoire politique de la Révolution française* (Paris, 1901), p. 422.

6 Thiers, *Histoire*, vol. I, pp. 456, 490–2, 587, 708, 752, 759, 771, vol. II, pp. 44–6, 48, 51 (he was the only writer to see pride and conceit as the leading traits of Robespierre); Michelet, *Histoire*, vol. II, pp. 370, 594, 651, 674, 704, 710, 804–5; Quinet, *Révolution*, vol. II, pp. 445–6.

7 Thiers, *Histoire*, vol. I, pp. 490, 492, 718, 722, 775; vol. II, p. 92; Michelet, *Histoire*, vol. II, pp. 354, 362–3, 595, 668, 672, 757; Quinet, *Révolution*, vol. II, pp. 448, 450; Hippolyte Taine, *Les origines de la France contemporaine*, 6 vols. (Paris, 1876–94), part II, vol. III, p. 215.

8 Thiers, *Histoire*, vol. II, p. 92; Godechot, 'L'historiographie', pp. 170–1, 176–7; Quinet, *Révolution*, vol. III, p. 99.

V, with the title 'The Tyrant', which was a diatribe against Robespierre.[9] Michelet saw him as a second-rate lawyer and man of letters, who was a true patriot and had some talents, with a strong will and great skill as a parliamentarian, but no original ideas – not enough to make a great man.[10] In other passages, Michelet was more scathing: 'Robespierre is certainly the most tragic subject which history offers, but also the most comic. Shakespeare has nothing like this.' Moreover, Robespierre was the man of the Great Terror, 'the dictator of the scaffold', 'the pontiff of the guillotine'. His soul was 'naturally tyrannical' and his dictatorship destroyed the Republic by depriving it of its vitality. Anticipating later writers, Michelet considered that the Revolution came to its end not in Thermidor, but in Germinal, when Robespierre had Hébert and Danton executed.[11]

As for Quinet, who saw the Terror as a revival of absolutism, Robespierre was to him a new Richelieu, a reincarnation of *raison d'Etat*. And he left a baneful inheritance: the idea, which prevailed among many French democrats, that dictatorship was necessary to establish a free society.[12]

Auguste Comte called Robespierre a 'sanguinary phrase-monger', an 'ambitious sophist', the self-proclaimed pontiff of 'deism by law'. Taine defined him as the typical *cuistre* (pedant), a mixture of stupidity, abstraction and quackery. He was the perfect end-product, stunted and sterile, of the French classical mind, which had been the progenitor of Jacobinism. He became as extremist as the madman Marat: in both cases, 'one sees ferocity piercing through philanthropy and the pedant become executioner'.[13]

Aulard, who disliked Taine very much, was, none the less, very harsh

[9] Modern Robespierrists have shown much self-delusion and/or bad faith, by trying to minimise the hostility to Robespierre of Michelet – who is dear to the left; see Gérard Walter, *Robespierre*, 4th edition (Paris, 1946), pp. 601, 605; Paul Viallaneix, 'La Révolution française. Histoire et idéologies', *Magazine littéraire* 258 (1988), 62–3. Godechot has just fourteen lines on Michelet and Robespierre. Actually Michelet's view partly resulted from his hatred of the Second Empire: 'The tyrant is born from the tyrant. The Jacobin, garrulous tyrant brings about the military tyrant' (*Histoire*, vol. II, p. 365).

Robespierrists tried also to transform Lamartine into a fascinated admirer of Robespierre; they overlooked (perhaps deliberately) some explicit condemnations of the latter. See Walter, *Robespierre*, pp. 601–4; Henri Guillemin, 'La Révolution française', *Magazine littéraire* 258 (1988), 51–3.

[10] Michelet, *Histoire*, vol. II, pp. 350, 474, 543, 547, 590, 592, 671–2, 704. However, on p. 365, Michelet conceded that Robespierre was a great man.

[11] *Ibid.*, vol. II, pp. 352–3, 362, 365, 672, 742–4, 756–7, 805.

[12] Quinet, *Révolution*, vol. II, pp. 464–6, vol. III, p. 102.

[13] Auguste Comte, *Cours de philosophie politique*, 6 vols. (Paris, 1830–42), vol. VI, pp. 310–11; Taine, *Origines*, part II, vol. III, pp. 190–2, 194, 202, 204–5, 208–212, 215, 217, 220; McManners, 'Historiography', pp. 640–1.

in 1885, in addressing the 'apologists of Robespierre': 'I maintain that Robespierre treacherously ... and in cold blood murdered his brother-at-arms, his magnanimous comrade, the good and great Danton. I refuse to personify the French Revolution in this pious slanderer and mystical murderer.' However, in his well-known textbook of 1901, on the political history of the Revolution, Aulard was less brutal: he recognised in Robespierre the usual virtues, but he condemned his opportunism and the policy of this 'dictator of truth', who liquidated anybody who disagreed with him. Still, Aulard admitted that responsibility for the Terror did not entirely lie with him and was shared by all members of the Committee of Public Safety.[14]

The condemnation of Robespierre by nineteenth-century historians was mainly on moral and humanitarian grounds: he had violated basic liberties and sent to their deaths many innocents – and many good revolutionaries too. However, the historians who have been mentioned, apart from Taine, approved of the French Revolution – even if they were divided between admirers of '89 and of '93 – and they did not completely repudiate the Terror. They accepted that, in 1793, strong government and drastic measures were indispensable to save the Republic and France herself.[15] Michelet wrote bluntly that 'a few very great culprits' had to be executed. None the less, historians were shocked by the prolongation of the Terror after the foreign invasion had been repelled, and by the Great Terror of Messidor, which was unleashed by the law of 22 Prairial (10 June 1794). Quinet described it as a system of barbarity and folly, a revival of the Middle Ages. Aulard wrote of a 'butchery of the guilty and the innocent, worthy of the old régime, worthy of the Inquisition', of 'judicial massacres', which were atrocious, awful and anachronistic.[16]

Many thought that Robespierre was responsible for the worst aspects of the Terror and that those awful events resulted from his intellectual and moral failings. Admittedly, this was not the view of Michelet or Taine, who did not see the individual as the *primum mobile* of history. Michelet wrote that the Terror must be explained, not by an individual's

14 Walter, *Robespierre*, p. 611; Aulard, *Histoire politique*, pp. 201–4, 235, 291, 339, 341, 422–4, 452, 500.

15 As McManners ('Historiography', p. 622) has seen, better than many Frenchmen, these historians were intensely patriotic and the policy of the Committee of Public Safety roused a mixture of admiration and awe (see, e.g., Thiers, *Histoire*, vol. I, pp. 612, 650, 770, vol. II, p. 91; Michelet, *Histoire*, vol. II, p. 744).

16 Michelet, *Histoire*, vol. II, pp. 359, 807–9; Quinet, *Révolution*, vol. II, pp. 451–2, 466, vol. III, p. 97; Taine, *Origines*, vol. III, p. 218; Aulard, *Histoire politique*, pp. 363, 366, 495; also Thiers, *Histoire*, vol. II, pp. 48–50, 52, 91–2; Comte, *Cours*, vol. VI, pp. 307–11; François Furet, 'Quinet', in François Furet and Mona Ozouf (eds.), *Dictionnaire critique de la Révolution française* (Paris, 1988), pp. 1048–52.

biography, but by 'the environment which was his own. Robespierre must be seen within the framework of the Jacobin inquisition.' He also wrote of 'this small lawyer who one morning was raised by some whirlwind', of the 'fatality' which carried him at the end of his life, when he was 'the serf of the Terror'.[17]

In some respects, anti-Robespierrism was a variant of the 'theory of circumstances' by which historians supporting the Revolution have explained and justified its radicalisation, and especially the bloody repression during the Jacobin period, which made them, as humanitarians, uneasy. This theory invokes the impact of circumstances which were external to the Revolution itself – resistance by the court and the privileged, aristocratic plots and, above all, the pressure of foreign and civil war. The Terror was the product of the tragic situation in which the Republic found itself in 1793; it was dictated by the necessities of national defence, even though it violated the principles of 1789. This view was convenient to supporters of both the liberal and the Jacobin traditions and it allowed a patriotic consensus. It was therefore widely adopted, from Thiers and Mignet, and Auguste Comte, to Aulard who brought it to its point of perfection.[18]

On the other hand, modern Robespierrists have exploited this stance to heap discredit on nineteenth-century liberal-minded historians, whose humanitarian feelings have moreover been dismissed as *petit-bourgeois* sentimentality. In their eyes, republican historians who attacked Robespierre were in fact trying to rally the middle classes to the republican cause. Public opinion associated republican government with the guillotine, and this made the bourgeoisie nervous. In order to dispel its fears, one had to dissociate the Republic from the Terror, and the easy way was to shift all the blame for the latter on to a scapegoat – the unfortunate Robespierre. Thus the Revolution and the Republic could be made respectable.[19]

In fact, it is unfair to explain the stand which those high-minded historians took by purely political and tactical motivations. Indeed, Michelet and Quinet wrote on the Terror after – and not before – the Second Republic, when Napoleon III was solidly in power. As for Lamartine, he had written in 1847 that he wanted to give to the people

[17] Michelet, *Histoire*, vol. II, pp. 349, 358, 758–9, 794–5, 804–5.

[18] Aulard, *Histoire politique*, pp. 357–9, 362–3, 366–8; Thiers, *Histoire*, vol. II, p. 91; Comte, *Cours*, vol. VI, pp. 304–6; McManners, 'Historiography', pp. 626–7, 644–5; François Furet, 'Terreur', in Furet and Ozouf, *Dictionnaire*, pp. 165–6.

[19] The anti-Robespierrism of Taine and Aulard has been explained by the necessity to comfort the bourgeois, who had been terrified by the Commune of 1871 (Godechot, 'L'historiographie', p. 181). Actually Taine's dim view of the Revolution antedates the Commune, which only gave to his *Origines* a sharper tone.

'a distaste for executions in order that the coming revolution may be exempt from the excesses of the first'.[20] It is also unfair to charge those talented historians with credulously swallowing the 'black legend' of Robespierre, which his enemies ('twice murderers', as they are called by some writers) had fabricated after his fall.

One reason, however, why some republican historians were hostile to Robespierre was their anti-clericalism. First, they saw his dictatorship as a kind of papacy: 'he had the heart of a priest, rather than of a king', wrote Michelet. His constant denunciation of conspirators and traitors was all too like the methods of the Inquisition – a grave reproach in the nineteenth century. However, the chief grievance was Robespierre's religious policy. Michelet blamed him for preventing the development of the worship of reason and for stopping the campaign of dechristianisation; this 'crossed out the eighteenth century' and was 'a dangerous return to the past'. And of course, Michelet condemned the establishment of the cult of the Supreme Being, 'a weak and pallid bastard of Rousseau'. Aulard, who was a freethinker, also censured Robespierre as a 'reactionary', for promoting the 'neo-christianity of Rousseau'.[21]

On the other hand, Danton had been an atheist, who, according to Aulard, wanted a secular and not a 'theocratic' policy. This is one of the reasons why Aulard made Danton an anti-Robespierre, the true incarnation of the Revolution and the hero of the Third Republic.

There was nothing new in this preference.[22] Thiers had written that Danton had much more genius and energy than Robespierre; Michelet had celebrated Danton's patriotic leadership in 1792 and strongly condemned the Dantonists' execution as 'an incurable wound' to 'all friends of liberty'. As for Auguste Comte, who was in favour of a temporary dictatorship, he had praised Danton for having exercised it and for having organised national defence; he also belonged to the materialist school of Diderot, the only eighteenth-century philosopher

[20] Quoted in McManners, 'Historiography', p. 629. Lamartine also refused 'to atone later for what is never atoned for, to redeem actual crimes by the holiness of future institutions' (quoted in Godechot, 'L'historiographie', p. 177).

One can add that, during the first half of the nineteenth century, many people still living had had relatives and/or friends executed, or at least gaoled, during the Terror. Praising Robespierre or Saint-Just was as shocking as would be nowadays a eulogy of Himmler or Eichmann.

[21] Gérard, *Révolution*, p. 128; Michelet, *Histoire*, vol. II, pp. 352, 355, 357, 644, 672, 674, 729, 758, 794; Quinet, *Révolution*, vol. II, p. 451; Aulard, *Histoire politique*, p. 424.

[22] Contrary to the view of Walter (*Robespierre*, p. 612) and others that 'Dantonism' was created by Aulard (with some borrowing from Comte). See Mona Ozouf, 'Danton', in Furet and Ozouf, *Dictionnaire*, pp. 248–9. Walter (*Robespierre*, p. 611) also saw 'Dantonism' as a bourgeois plot (to which Aulard was an accomplice!) to obscure the truly revolutionary aspects of the Revolution as its centenary was approaching.

of whom Comte approved. Comte therefore made Danton the hero who best represented the republican ideal.[23]

Besides, Aulard extolled Danton as a pragmatist and a precursor of the Third Republic. He typically wrote: 'Danton proceeds from Mirabeau, as Gambetta will proceed from Danton.' Above all, he had been 'for a time the man of the nation ... the leader of defence, the herald of patriotism'.[24] Later historians have rightly linked Aulard's views to the consolidation of the Third Republic. In the 1880s, the Revolution was at last in power, it had become a national institution: the time had come for republican historians to present an ecumenical picture of it, which would be acceptable to most French people. By condemning Robespierre and celebrating Danton, historians could solve the dilemma of '89 or '93, which had divided republicans. Dantonism was a 'historical compromise', a syncretic cult, which cleared away the most unsavoury episodes of the Revolution while extolling its policy of national defence and its victories in battle – a useful comfort for the national ego after the shock of 1870.[25]

During the centenary in 1889, Danton was the man: he had saved France and fallen a victim to the Terror for trying to stop it. His statue was erected in the heart of the Latin Quarter. However, his cult reached its official peak in 1909, with the launching of the battleship *Danton*, the first of a class of six, the others being named *Voltaire*, *Diderot*, *Mirabeau*, *Condorcet* and *Vergniaud* (the last two men had been, like Danton, victims of the Robespierrist Terror).[26] Except for Carnot, in 1894, no Montagnard has given his name to a French warship; the Soviets renamed an ex-tsarist battleship *Marat*, but Robespierre did not share this honour and was only commemorated in an embankment on the Neva, in Leningrad. *Danton* was sunk by a German U-boat in 1917.

The *Dantons* – strange-looking ships with five funnels – were obsolete from the start, both technically and ideologically. First, they were outclassed by the *dreadnought* battleships which the Royal Navy produced from 1906. Secondly, Aulard wrongly believed that he had closed the

23 Thiers, *Histoire*, vol. II, p. 92; Comte, *Cours*, vol. VI, pp. 308–10 and *Système de politique positive*, 4 vols. (Paris, 1851–4), vol. I, p. 116; Michelet, *Histoire*, vol. II, pp. 710, 726, 736, 742; McManners, 'Historiography', p. 628; Godechot, 'L'historiographie', pp. 168, 174.

24 Aulard, *Histoire politique*, pp. 424–5.

25 François Furet, 'Histoire universitaire de la Révolution', in Furet and Ozouf, *Dictionnaire*, pp. 979–80, 986–7; Godechot, 'L'historiographie', pp. 182–3.

26 And two armoured cruisers were named *Jules Michelet* and *Edgar Quinet*, after two historians who had been hostile to Robespierre! Those ships' names are, of course, typical of the radical and anti-clerical climate of the 1900s: they were partly chosen to annoy naval officers, who were often Catholics and royalists. See *Almanach de Gotha* (1913), p. 881.

debate on the Revolution. However, Robespierrism raised its head again and embarked on an offensive which was to end in total victory.

II

Although the mainstream of nineteenth-century historians had been hostile to Robespierre, a minority group had supported him. And modern Robespierrists have painstakingly uncovered a number of obscure writers who had worked for the rehabilitation of the Incorruptible. This line started with Paganel (1810), a former member of the Convention, Guillaume Lallement (1820) and Laurent de l'Ardèche (1827). Then came Buonarroti and his book on Babeuf (1828); the latter had censured 'Maximilien le Cruel' but, under the Directory, he had tried to revive Robespierrist ideals and proclaimed 'Robespierrism is democracy' – which was to be the motto of the school of historians now under consideration. Buonarroti was important as the link between the last of the *sans-culottes*, on one hand, and the left-wing republicans and early socialists of the second quarter of the nineteenth century, on the other, to whom he transmitted the cult of Robespierre and the belief that the latter's ideas had inspired Babeuf's communism.[27]

In the view of socialists, the French Revolution was only a first, imperfect, unfinished episode, which would be followed by a second, socialist revolution. This led them to focus on the most radical and least bourgeois period of the French Revolution, to extol Robespierre as the apostle and martyr of democratic and social progress – because socialism was anticipated in some of his policies – and, of course, to deplore the untimely cessation of such progress at Thermidor. Indeed, almost all historians who have been sympathetic to Robespierre were socialists or at least had socialist leanings.

Such were, in the 1830s, Albert Laponneraye, who befriended Charlotte Robespierre in her last years, and Philippe Buchez, a Christian socialist. Buchez was hostile to the bourgeois and individualist revolution of 1789, but he extolled the Terror, particularly because it was akin to the massacres of St Bartholomew. Robespierre, in his view, had only one shortcoming – he was not a Roman Catholic – but he had left the promise of a new and brotherly society. In the 1840s, Tissot, Cabet and Esquiros, who wrote laudatory lives of Robespierre, were also socialists.

[27] This paragraph is derived from: Godechot, 'L'historiographie', pp. 171–8; Walter, *Robespierre*, pp. 586–92, 598, 601; Gérard, *Révolution*, pp. 127–8; McManners, 'Historiography', pp. 627–9.

There was a good deal of special pleading by Walter and Godechot, as some of the writers they have exhumed, while rectifying the very negative image of Robespierre which prevailed in their time, were not unconditional admirers of him.

However, Ernest Hamel was only a failed republican politician; in 1865, he published a life of Robespierre in three volumes of over 2,000 pages. Even ardent Robespierrists disapproved of this large but 'grotesque piece of idolatry' in which Robespierre was several times compared to Christ.[28]

A few years earlier, Louis Blanc had published his history of the French Revolution; it was the only major work of the nineteenth century which was favourable to Robespierre.

Even so, Louis Blanc's stand for Robespierre and for the Terror was a defensive one. He firmly believed in the theory of circumstances: the Terror was awful, but counter-revolutionary plots were responsible for it. Moreover, Blanc dissociated Robespierre from the Terror: he had wanted to stop it at the end of 1793 and again in the spring of 1794 (after the death of Danton, which Blanc strongly deplored and attributed to a 'blameworthy weakness' on Robespierre's part). Still, he was powerless to do so, lacking a majority in the Committees and he had nothing to do with the law of 22 Prairial. Blanc stressed the *grandeur* and moderation of Robespierre. He was the head of the 'parti des honnêtes gens'; he stood for strong government in the service of the poor and weak; and he left the great legacy of the constitution of 1793, which was never implemented, but was inspired by liberty and justice.[29]

It is significant that this defence of Robespierre has been criticised as too soft by later Robespierrists like Gérard Walter. The horror at the shedding of blood, which Blanc several times expressed, is dismissed as the 'purely physiological reaction' of a sentimentalist *petit-bourgeois*. Walter added that Robespierre could rather be blamed for not being rigorous enough.[30] This is unsurprising: twentieth-century apologists of the Terror of the Year II have actually been justifying terror in their own times. Yet, Blanc had written about the terrorists: 'Their violence has bequeathed a peaceful destiny to us ... the Terror by its very excesses has forever become impossible.'[31] This optimism, typical of a man of 1848, was given the lie in the next century.

[28] Godechot, 'L'historiographie', pp. 174–5, 178–80; Walter, *Robespierre*, pp. 609–10; Michelet, *Histoire*, vol. II, p. 361: 'Buchez ... sanctifying pell-mell 2 September and St Bartholomew'.

[29] Louis Blanc, *Histoire de la Révolution française* (1847–62), quoted from the Docks de la Librairie edition, 2 vols. (Paris, n.d.), vol. II, pp. 375, 423, 428, 432, 458–9, 475, 480–2, 527–8, 538; François Furet, 'Louis Blanc', in Furet and Ozouf, *Dictionnaire*, pp. 930–2.

[30] Walter, *Robespierre*, p. 608.

[31] Quoted in McManners, 'Historiography', p. 629.

III

The twentieth century has been the age of mass murder and extermination on a scale which reduces the Terror of the Year II to child's play (though the verb 'exterminer' was not rare in the discourse of Robespierre and his friends). No surprise therefore that historians, being more accustomed to violence, more hardened, have been more indulgent than their predecessors towards the Terror and the man who incarnated it. This indulgence has indeed turned into praise, under the influence of socialism, especially in its Marxist-Leninist form.

A decisive step in the rehabilitation of Robespierre was the publication by Jean Jaurès, between 1900 and 1904, of his *Socialist History of the French Revolution.*[32] Jaurès was not an unconditional admirer of Robespierre. He appreciated, of course, his campaign for peace in 1792, but he saw his temper as jealous and his thinking as narrow, especially in the matter of economics, where Robespierre kept to archaic and pessimistic views. Although he had been wise to restrain dechristianisation, the celebration of the Supreme Being was 'unfortunate'.[33]

Nevertheless, Jaurès has nothing but praise for the wise and firm policy of Robespierre during the summer of 1793, and it was with regard to this period that Jaurès wrote a passage which is often quoted, though often out of context: 'Here, under this sun of June 1793, which warms up your bitter struggle, – I am with Robespierre and go to sit next to him at the Jacobins.'[34] Actually this was an answer to left-wing socialists who preferred extremists, like Jacques Roux or Hébert, to Robespierre. Jaurès's approach was to elucidate, at each stage of the Revolution, the policy most useful to the Revolution as a whole and to democracy. And during that summer of 1793, that was the policy of Robespierre, who tried to unite the revolutionary forces, both bourgeois and popular, in order to crush the enemies of the Revolution without falling into excesses, at a time when there was no socialist alternative. Obviously these views were closely related to the politics of Jaurès's time, to his support of the *Bloc des gauches*, to his fight against extreme socialists, who advocated violent revolution. By praising Robespierre,

[32] Jean Jaurès, *Histoire socialiste de la Révolution française*, published between 1900 and 1904, had new editions in 1922–4 (8 vols., edited by A. Mathiez), 1968–73 (7 vols., edited by A. Soboul) and 1983–6 (4 vols.). In all three cases, the publishing houses (Librairie de l'Humanité, Editions Sociales and Editions Messidor) were communist. This shows the work's acceptability in those quarters, but also an effort to annex Jaurès. Quotations are from the edition produced by Soboul.

[33] Madeleine Rebérioux, 'Jaurès et Robespierre', in *Actes du colloque Robespierre*, pp. 192–5, 199; Godechot, 'L'historiographie', pp. 168, 184–5.

[34] Jaurès, *Histoire socialiste*, vol. VI, pp. 171–2, 201–4.

Jaurès wanted to promote the thesis that the way to socialism was through democracy, which the Incorruptible incarnated.[35]

With regard to the Terror, Jaurès was sometimes uneasy. He accepted that it was necessary for the defence of the Revolution and that 'some terrible examples' had to be made. Even so, he maintained that Robespierre tried to moderate repression, but had to proceed carefully, in order not to weaken the revolutionary movement. As for the law of 22 Prairial, Jaurès called it 'atrocious', 'a stupid engine of useless slaughter', 'an instrument of murder', but he maintained that Robespierre had wanted to concentrate this intensification of terrorism within a few awful weeks, in order to have the justification and the means to stop it for good. This was 'an insane dream' and, moreover, the Convention distorted the bill, which became 'a law of mechanical murder'. Like Louis Blanc, Jaurès was pleading for Robespierre's 'limited responsibility' for the Terror and deplored the excesses of the latter.[36] Still, his final judgement was not unqualified. 'I have told how immense . . . were Robespierre's services', organising the revolutionary government, 'rescuing France from civil war, anarchy and defeat'. But he conceded that, in his last months, he was 'struck by doubt, blindness and giddiness'; he lost his grip and his fall became inevitable. None the less, 9 Thermidor was a 'fatal moment'.[37]

Such nuances were to be swept away by Albert Mathiez. From his break with Aulard in 1908 up to his tragic death in 1932, he worked unceasingly 'to do justice to Robespierre', and also to destroy Danton's reputation. He maintained that his objectives were purely scholarly, but Gérard Walter, one of his followers, has written of Mathiez's 'fervent historical apostolate' – a good expression, as it has a religious component, and it led to a kind of worship of Robespierre.[38]

Mathiez produced a flow of articles, which were gathered in book form under the title *Etudes robespierristes*, but, owing to his early death, he did not write the biography of Robespierre which was expected. Still,

35 Rebérioux, 'Jaurès et Robespierre', pp. 196–8; Mona Ozouf, 'Jaurès', in Furet and Ozouf, *Dictionnaire*, p. 1005; McManners, 'Historiography', p. 645.

36 Jaurès, *Histoire socialiste*, vol. VI, pp. 300–1, 367–9, 498–9, 501–4; Rebérioux, 'Jaurès et Robespierre', p. 195.

In their respective editions of the *Histoire socialiste*, Mathiez (vol. VIII, p. 503) and Soboul (vol. VI, p. 499, n.19) both 'corrected' Jaurès on this point.

37 Jaurès, *Histoire socialiste*, vol. VI, p. 516.

According to the interpretation of Jaurès by Rebérioux, a former communist activist, the constant melancholy of Robespierre resulted from the contradictions of the bourgeois and democratic revolution. He cruelly felt its imperfections, but was unable to have an anticipatory vision of socialism. ('Jaurès et Robespierre', pp. 202–4.)

38 Walter, *Robespierre*, p. 612; Godechot, 'L'historiographie', p. 185; McManners, 'Historiography', pp. 646–7; also Furet, 'Histoire universitaire', pp. 988–90; M. Vovelle, 'La Révolution française', *Magazine littéraire* 258 (1988), 76–7.

his textbook on the French Revolution down to Thermidor was a bible for history students over several decades.[39] A lecture he gave at the end of his life, but which was published only in 1977, is a good summary of his views.[40] It is called 'Robespierre: History and Legend'; in it, Mathiez refuted one by one the charges which had been made against his hero, of whom he painted an idealised, heart-rending portrait.

It is untrue that Robespierre was callous; he had a delicate sensibility; 'he loved but once and his love was pure'. He was a born orator, who could rise to sublime, 'lyrical and already romantic' accents. He had a talent for administration and was an efficient head of government. He was neither ambitious, nor jealous, nor Machiavellian; he was right in fighting the Hébertists and Dantonists. 'Ah!', wrote Mathiez, 'if I had something with which to reproach Robespierre, it might be that he waited too long before abandoning Danton', 'this corrupt tribune'. It is also untrue that he favoured Roman Catholicism; his deism was purely social.

Robespierre was the founder of democracy in France, but he also loved the poor and had a social programme. Mathiez maintained that, by the decrees of Ventôse, he launched a grand policy of wealth redistribution and social justice.[41] As Alfred Cobban wrote, Robespierre was thus 'canonised . . . as the saint of social democracy'.[42]

How could such a man have been cruel and the feeder of the guillotine? He was 'meek and loving. The suffering of others was painful to him.' Of course, there was the Revolutionary Tribunal, but this was just like the courts martial during the First World War, and Robespierre did his best to keep repression to its necessary minimum. As for the law of 22 Prairial, Mathiez wrote: 'I do not intend to defend this law', which was 'atrocious'. None the less, he then commenced an embarrassed and intricate reasoning, to minimise the part Robespierre had in it (the whole Committee of Public Safety was responsible), to show that it was connected with the generous decrees of Ventôse, and to prove that it resulted in 'butcheries' only because of sabotage by Robespierre's enemies.[43]

Years before, Quinet had written: 'One idea at least had never occurred to Robespierre's contemporaries – to suppose that he had no part in the Terror.' Recently, Furet wrote of a 'hagiography where a

[39] A. Mathiez, *La Révolution française*, 3 vols. (Paris, 1922–4); repr., 1 vol. , 1960, 1985, 1989.

[40] Albert Mathiez, 'Robespierre. L'histoire et la légende', *AHRF* 49 (1977), 5–31.

[41] *Ibid.*, 10–24.

[42] Alfred Cobban, *The Social Interpretation of the French Revolution* (Cambridge, 1964), p. 121; see also Furet, 'Histoire universitaire', pp. 990–1.

[43] Mathiez, 'Robespierre', 25–9.

moralising naïveté mixes with partisan fanaticism, to present the ghastly spring of 1794 as the passing triumph of fraternity'.[44]

Mathiez's apostolate had started before the First World War, but the Russian Revolution of 1917 gave it a new significance, and to Robespierrism a lasting success.

Mathiez had been a socialist from his youth, but, in 1920, alarmed by the success of the right at the French general election of 1919, he joined the communist party, and published two articles, 'Bolshevism and Jacobinism' and 'Lenin and Robespierre'. A short extract gives the gist of them: 'Between the methods of the Bolsheviks and those of the French Montagnards . . . there is a close relationship and a sort of logical kinship. Jacobinism and Bolshevism are . . . two dictatorships, which use the same means – terror, requisition, taxes – and which have the same aim – the transformation of society.' Then came a detailed demonstration, which brought together quotations from Robespierre, Saint-Just and Lenin.[45]

As a matter of fact, Mathiez left the communist party in 1922, but without breaking with the intellectual system which had first led him there. François Furet rightly wrote that 'since Mathiez, the ghost of the Russian Revolution haunts the history of the French Revolution'. Historians of the latter have projected on to the past their feelings and views for or against the Bolshevik revolution and the Soviet régime; debates on the two revolutions cannot be disentangled. To many writers, 1793 was a prelude to 1917, the Bolsheviks were the heirs to the Jacobins, whose final aims they were able to achieve, and the Montagnards anticipated the Soviet system: historians therefore searched the French Revolution to find precedents which would justify what had happened and was happening in the USSR.[46] There was also, undoubtedly, on the part of some writers, the idea of justifying in advance a new terror, when, in France or elsewhere, communism would take over.

The best example of these links concerned purges in leadership. The Moscow trials of the Bukharino-Trotskyites in 1936–7 were assimilated to the 'fall of factions',[47] the fate of the Dantonists and Hébertists in 1794: the corruption of Danton, which Mathiez had demonstrated, was

[44] Quinet, *Révolution*, vol. III, p. 101; Furet, 'Histoire universitaire', pp. 990–1.

[45] Albert Mathiez, 'Le Bolchévisme et le Jacobinisme', *Scientia* 27 (1920), 3–16 (the quotation is from page 3).

Mathiez stressed that the Bolsheviks 'voluntarily and knowingly imitate the French revolutionaries'. (This was true: they were obsessed by the French Revolution and particularly its Jacobin period.) However, he had to concede that they had 'improved the Jacobin methods'.

[46] Furet, 'Histoire universitaire', pp. 983, 988–90; François Furet, *Penser la Révolution française* (Paris, 1978), pp. 19–20, 22, 140–2.

[47] This expression, which means the execution of the Hébertists and Dantonists, is a good

used to make respectable the liquidation by Stalin of his old comrades. Moreover, as Stalin could do no wrong, the executions of Danton and Hébert were endowed by the Moscow trials with more legitimacy; as Furet put it, 'the Soviet experience illustrated in its turn the necessity of dictatorship and terror' in revolutionary France.[48] The present author was brought up by his father on the view that Thermidor would not have happened if Robespierre had been as ruthless as Stalin. So there was justification both of the present by the past, and of the past by the present. The French and Russian revolutions were like two facing mirrors, in which images multiply indefinitely.

Needless to say, Robespierre was many times compared to Lenin and later to Stalin. Recently, some left-wing writers have complained about such assimilations, but this kind of nonsense had been started by Mathiez,[49] and the left kept it alive up to the 1950s at least.

Such were the origins of what is often called *la Vulgate*, that is a Jacobin-Marxist or Leninist-Populist interpretation of the French Revolution. The power of this 'strange intellectual product', created by the extreme left wing of French academic historians, and its influence, which was almost inverse to its intellectual mediocrity, have been remarkable.[50]

There was a naïve and meek version of the *Vulgate* respecting Robespierre. He was the man who had tried to keep peace and then to introduce in France a truly democratic régime, a social democracy (the term was used), by achieving equality not only in the political sphere, but also in the social one.[51]

There was also, however, a less bland view – that a major merit of Robespierre was to have experimented, for the first time in history, with a system of revolutionary dictatorship, and to have started 'the revolution of the poor' against the rich. The necessity of dictatorship and terror, to save the Republic and France, was first postulated, and then a transfer was achieved, from necessity to admiration, to the idea that 'popular' dictatorship and terror against the bourgeoisie are good things

example of the *langue de bois* (newspeak), which has spread into writings on the French Revolution under Marxist influence.

48 Furet, 'Histoire universitaire', p. 983; also Furet, *Penser la Révolution française*, p. 142.

49 Mathiez ('Robespierre', 9) complained that Robespierre had been made by some writers to look like Lenin. It 'was convenient and it was profitable', he wrote, forgetting that he had made this comparison in 1920 – as Soboul ironically recalled in a footnote!

50 Furet, *Penser la Révolution française*, pp. 30, 144, 206; Furet, 'Histoire universitaire', pp. 983, 990, 996–7.

51 Godechot, 'L'historiographie', p. 167; Marc Bouloiseau, *Robespierre* (Paris, 1961), pp. 124–5.

per se.[52] This was an obvious case of teleology, which valued the Year II for its annunciatory value and as a justification of Stalinism.[53]

The *Vulgate* also tried to promote the strategy of the Popular Front, which was followed by the communist party for most of the time from the 1930s onwards. Robespierre was extolled for preaching and incarnating the union between the *sans-culottes* and the progressive, Montagnard bourgeoisie. Both Georges Lefebvre and Jean Massin explicitly wrote that this union amounted to what is called nowadays a popular front. Jean Bruhat praised Robespierre for having organised and directed the popular forces, in order to force the bourgeoisie's hand.[54]

The *Vulgate* led, quite naturally, to a cult of Robespierre. In a lecture of 1920, Mathiez repeatedly stated, as in a litany, 'We love Robespierre, because . . .' Jean Massin wrote at the beginning of his biography:

> I am not trying to hide how much affection I have for him [Robespierre]. Or that his existence is linked to my pride to be French . . . I have to relate the epic of a hero . . . more than anybody, he was the strength of the Revolution, the very march of our new-born nation was incarnated in him . . . When everything seemed lost, Robespierre appeared like the face of hope.

And he went on: this 'giant', this 'man with a burning heart . . . a lion and not a fox . . . gave up his private life to devote himself entirely to the happiness of France and the world'. The only reservation Massin suggested was that Robespierre was not a Marxist and cared too much about morals. To Marc Bouloiseau, he was 'the saint of democracy', an 'expiatory victim', who 'remains alive in the hearts of humble people'.[55]

As good Stalinists, many *Vulgate* writers were less embarrassed and fussy about the Terror than their predecessors had been.[56] It was no longer justified as defensive – an answer to the counter-revolution – but

52 Albert Soboul, *Précis d'histoire de la Révolution française* (Paris, 1975), pp. 290–4; Jean Massin, *Robespierre* (Paris, 1955), p. 191; see also Furet, 'Histoire universitaire', p. 990.

53 This is especially clear in Labrousse's writings. 'The ephemeral Year II left upon the future an imposing reflection which illuminated the nineteenth century': Ernest Labrousse and Roland Mousnier, *Le XVIIIe siècle* (Paris, 1953), p. 427. He dealt with the Terror rather cryptically, using euphemisms, but there is no doubt that it appealed to his romantic side. There is also this obscure sentence: 'The blood of the Great Terror, which can appear gratuitous to many malcontents, creates disgust in the public' (*ibid.*, p. 419). See also *ibid.*, pp. 405, 408, 415–16, 420.

54 Georges Lefebvre, *La Révolution française* (Paris, 1930), quoted from the revised 1951 edition, p. 397; Massin, *Robespierre*, p. 190; Jean Bruhat, *De Maximilien Robespierre et du Robespierrisme* (Paris, 1958), p. 28. Bruhat was a history lecturer and a communist activist.

55 Massin, *Robespierre*, pp. 6–7, 226; Bouloiseau, *Robespierre*, p. 122.

56 Lefebvre, who had a dry personality, did not show much sympathy for victims. He described the drownings at Nantes as a means to empty 'without formality' the prisons, which were dangerous sources of contagious diseases. To him, there were all sorts of good reasons for the Terror, including one, *a posteriori*, that it helped to run a command

as an offensive instrument to regenerate man. The warmest apology for the Terror was written by Massin. He quoted Robespierre: 'One leads the people by reason and the people's enemies by terror.' This maxim 'answered in advance all those who believe they dishonour the Revolution by making it ashamed for the blood it was forced to shed. They are the same people who gloss modestly over the white terror.' This is a key argument for Massin – and for many left-wing historians:[57] they juxtapose the revolutionary killings (of which they stress there were not so many) with the far more numerous victims of counter-revolutionary repression, for instance in 1848 and 1871. Massin even mentioned the French soldiers who were shot after the mutinies of 1917: 2,700 of them at least were later rehabilitated – that is just the number of persons who were guillotined in Paris in 1793–4. So, why so much fuss? Possibly, wrote Massin, because the latter included royalty, prelates, bankers and landowners, and he suggested that they more or less got what they deserved: as Barnave had said in 1789, 'was this blood so pure?' This is typical of the double-standard, which is frequent on the left: repression is praised or censured according to whether its victims were 'reactionaries' or 'progressive'. Consequently Massin wrote that Robespierre would not have accepted the efforts by some of his posthumous supporters to declare him 'not guilty' of the Terror.[58] But this does not mean he accepted that the Terror, which was to him 'an emanation of virtue', became 'a system of murders'. Actually Massin did not go the whole hog; even he found the law of 22 Prairial too hard to swallow. He approved of Georges Lefebvre who declared it unnecessary, and, like several other historians, maintained that Robespierre could not be held responsible for the barbarous way in which it was enforced.[59] Eventually, Albert Soboul was the only one who had nothing to say against the Great Terror. He justified it by the continuance of aristocratic plotting and, in typical newspeak, concluded that it excised ('retrancha') from the nation some elements which could not be assimilated.[60]

The most talented and scholarly historian of the Jacobin school was Georges Lefebvre, though he also suffered from bias and narrowness. His 'synthetical view' of the Revolution was, in Furet's words, that of 'a

economy. Still he wrote that national defence did not demand such a 'repressive passion' as the law of 22 Prairial. (*Révolution française*, pp. 371, 400–3, 407–8.)

[57] E.g., Mathiez, 'Robespierre', 6. This argument had been used by Clemenceau in his famous speech of 29 January 1891, on the Revolution as a block: '"You well know that the white terror has made more victims than the other" (triple round of applause on the left).'

[58] Massin, *Robespierre*, pp. 224–7. However, those mistaken supporters of Robespierre included Louis Blanc, Jaurès and Mathiez, as we have seen.

[59] *Ibid.*, pp. 257–9, 262–5; Lefebvre, *Révolution française*, p. 408.

[60] Soboul, *Précis d'histoire*, pp. 320–2.

militant of the cartel of the left or of the Popular Front'.[61] He felt a personal devotion towards Robespierre: when he accepted the presidency of the Société des Etudes robespierristes and the editorship of its journal, it was 'out of fidelity to the memory of Maximilien Robespierre'.

Yet his view of the Incorruptible was less sentimental and sugary than Mathiez's portrait. Robespierre was cold and distant, except among close friends; his natural suspiciousness made him see all opponents as traitors; he was pitiless, touchy and did not forgive easily.

To Lefebvre, Robespierre was the historical leader of French democracy, a wise statesman, prudent and moderate. But he did not conceive of the idea of a selective and disciplined party – on the lines of communist parties – as the fulcrum of revolutionary dictatorship. He was an intellectual and a parliamentarian, who never had direct contact with the people, even though he was attentive to the claims of the *sans-culottes* and careful to adapt his conduct to circumstances.

Robespierre thought it the duty of the Republic to care for the poor, to procure them education, to improve their condition; he was hostile to an excessive concentration of wealth. He therefore left an interventionist tradition of social democracy. However, Lefebvre refuted Mathiez's thesis on the socialist elements in the decrees of Ventôse. His disciple, Albert Soboul, went further and considered them as only a tactical manoeuvre in the fight against extremists.

To Lefebvre, Robespierre was 'the resolute and faithful representative of the revolutionary mentality' and 'the intrepid defender of the Revolution of 1789 . . . the immovable and incorruptible head of revolutionary Resistance'. The reversal of rôles – from 'terrorist' to 'defender' – is interesting, as is the use of the word 'Resistance' – Lefebvre's brother, a professor of geography, had been beheaded by the Nazis during the Occupation. None the less, this portrait of Robespierre is obviously less flattering than the one by Mathiez.[62]

The retreat went on with Albert Soboul, though he was the perfect representative of the Jacobin-Bolshevik interpretation at its most reductionist level. However, his research on the *sans-culottes* of Paris had demonstrated to him the basic contradiction between their social aims and political methods, on the one hand, and the views of the revolutionary government, including Robespierre, on the other. There had been a tactical *rapprochement* between the two, but the execution of

[61] Furet, 'Histoire universitaire', pp. 992, 995, 997; Furet, *Penser la Révolution française*, p. 24.

[62] See particularly Georges Lefebvre, 'Remarks on Robespierre', *French Historical Studies* 1 (1958), 7–10 and *Révolution française*, pp. 416–18.

Hébert and his friends left the *sans-culottes* bewildered and they became disaffected and hostile to the government.

Moreover, Soboul, as a Marxist, did not approve of Robespierre's spiritual outlook, which prevented him from understanding economic and social realities. He was supported by socially heterogeneous elements, without any class consciousness. Indeed, he was a prisoner of contradictions which could not be solved and his fall was thus inevitable.[63]

There is an irony, which Alfred Cobban noted,[64] in the fact that these orthodox Marxist historians were influenced by a writer whom they strongly criticised. Daniel Guérin was the only dissenting voice from the left during the long period when the *Vulgate* was dominant. Guérin was a Trotskyite who had been disappointed both by the Popular Front's failure to revolutionise France and by the bureaucratic Soviet system: he saw Robespierre as a mixture of Léon Blum and Stalin. In his book of 1946 on the class struggle during the French Revolution, he maintained that Robespierre had manoeuvred to defend the interests of the bourgeoisie and to deceive the people, breaking the back of the popular movement and liquidating its leaders. For the Revolution, this was the beginning of the end.[65]

A last question about the *Vulgate*: how should one explain its influence? Among academic historians, from the 1930s to the 1960s, the *Vulgate* was generally accepted. Mathiez had indeed defeated Aulard, and the Jacobin-Marxist interpretation was supreme in most general works and textbooks on the Revolution, as well as in biographies of Robespierre by writers such as Gérard Walter, Jean Massin, Marc Bouloiseau and others. It also percolated into school textbooks, so that millions of French people were brought up in the worship of Robespierre.

The talent, the passion and the perseverance of Georges Lefebvre and Albert Soboul, the successors of Mathiez as leaders of this school, must be first mentioned, as well as the support they received from Ernest Labrousse. They were indefatigable and pugnacious fighters, men with a mission, who felt responsible for the posthumous fate of the French Revolution and of its leaders. And they had strong political commitments. Lefebvre had been a socialist up to 1940; after 1945, he became

63 Soboul, *Précis d'histoire*, pp. 268, 307, 311, 313, 336, 338–40, 343–6; Furet, *Penser la Révolution française*, p. 145.

64 Cobban, *Social Interpretation*, p. 121.

65 Daniel Guérin, *La lutte des classes sous la Première République 1793–1797* (Paris, 1946). The Vulgatists answered, not unreasonably, that there was no proletariat in France in the 1790s and that the only issue was the struggle of the bourgeoisie against feudalism.

a fellow-traveller of the communist party. Soboul was a member of the communist party all his life. So were lesser men.[66]

A 'Marxist' explanation of this commitment can be suggested:[67] the leaders of the Jacobin school were all born in 'humble circumstances', in the kind of lower middle class which had supplied the *sans-culotterie* with its cadres.[68] On the other hand, Aulard had belonged to a rather bourgeois family, and the leaders of revisionism (about whom more later) mostly have an upper middle-class background.[69] Moreover, Mathiez, Lefebvre and Soboul did not have easy careers: they taught in *lycées* for years and were appointed to the Sorbonne rather late in life.

Lefebvre wrote that the revolutionary *petite bourgeoisie* identified with Robespierre, who, like them, was poor and led an austere life.[70] It may well be that the Robespierrist historians had the same feelings, and also that they were bitter men, full of social resentment and hatred for the upper classes, both in the present and in the past. They did not mind – to say the least – if members of those classes were liquidated. Indeed, some historians of this school had such a terrorist's view of history that they must be considered as terrorists who did not get their chance: had they had the opportunity, they would have sent thousands of class enemies to their deaths, and one can even imagine that they would have enjoyed giving the *coup de grâce*![71]

This very bloody-mindedness was a force for success among the *lumpen-intelligentsia* of French academics and teachers, inasmuch as many of the latter had the same background as the Robespierrist historians, the same bitterness and class hatred, the same passion for equality. They were ready for the *Vulgate*.

A last – but decisive – factor was the growing influence of the communist party on intellectuals and teachers. The hegemony of the *Vulgate* coincided with the period when this influence was very strong – though the *Vulgate* spread well beyond the range of the latter. Having made a successful take-over of the history of the French Revolution, the

66 Vovelle, 'La Révolution française', *Magazine littéraire*, 76.

67 Marxist is in inverted commas! In a review of an earlier version of this essay, M. Vovelle did not like my views, but did not realise that I had been joking and denounced my approach for its vulgarity: *AHRF* 62 (1990), 506–7.

68 E.g., Mathiez came from a peasant family of Franche-Comté. Cf. Furet, 'Histoire universitaire', p. 988; Vovelle, 'La Révolution française', *Magazine littéraire*, 78; *Who's Who in France 1985–1986*, p. 1470.

69 Furet was the son of a banker. D. Richet came from a family of eminent doctors; his grandfather won a Nobel Prize. *Who's Who in France 1985–1986*, p. 593.

70 Lefebvre, *Révolution française*, p. 417. It was impossible not to think of the Duplay household when visiting Lefebvre in his small house at Boulogne-Billancourt.

71 See Michelet, *Histoire*, vol. II, p. 354, on the 'ferocity of scholars' who wrote on the French Revolution.

communists carefully protected their conquests. The *Vulgate* gave a legal value to the idea that the followers of Lenin and Stalin were the rightful heirs to the Jacobin patrimony, and this legitimation was useful in defending the image of the Soviet Union.[72]

IV

In 1965, Jacques Godechot rejoiced that French historians were united and unanimous on Robespierre. The reactionary enemies of the latter were becoming extinct, the supporters of Danton were gone. All historians were following the trail which Hamel and Louis Blanc had blazed and which Mathiez had 'finally and definitively laid out'.[73]

This was naïve – nothing is definitive in historiography. Indeed, in the same year, a fire-ship was launched, which was to do serious damage to the *Vulgate*: *La Révolution française* by François Furet and Denis Richet.[74] This was the birth of the 'revisionist school', which now requires investigation.

The two authors had been for a time members of the communist party, but they were disappointed by 'Soviet totalitarianism' and 'all kinds of power which are based on Marxism'. This influenced their view of history and led to criticism of the *Vulgate*. Subsequently, with much of the French left-wing intelligentsia, they became increasingly aware of the disastrous character of the communist experiences in the twentieth century. So, the Soviet example came back, boomerang-like, to strike its French 'origins': the Gulag obliged one to think again about the Jacobin Terror. Having earlier been absolved from any crime, the two revolutions now came to be considered as synonymous with coercion and repression. This growing aversion to Marxism is one of the reasons why revisionist thinking has evolved over the years.[75]

At the start, we have the book of 1965, in which the chapters on the period 1792–5 were written by Denis Richet. At their heart was the concept of *dérapage* (skidding) of the French Revolution in 1791–2. Unlike the *Vulgate*, this view reduced the significance of the Terror, which became a brief parenthesis, set against the broad stream of liberalism which has dominated French history from the mid-eighteenth century. It also encouraged a critical approach to historians who high-

[72] Furet, *Penser la Révolution française*, p. 145; Furet, 'Terreur', p. 165; Furet, 'Histoire universitaire', pp. 996–7.

[73] Godechot, 'L'historiographie', p. 189.

[74] François Furet and Denis Richet, *La Révolution française*, 2 vols. (Paris, 1965–6). References are to the second edition, 1973.

[75] Furet, *Penser la Révolution française*, pp. 27–9; also his interview in 'La Révolution française', *Magazine littéraire* 258 (1988), 18–20.

lighted its 'anticipations', the aspects which 'announced' the Russian Revolution. As for the idea that it was necessary for the victory of the liberal revolution, that belongs to teleological metaphysics.[76]

Robespierre inevitably suffered from such cutting down to size of the period during which he ruled,[77] though his portrait by Richet was by no means a hostile one. Robespierre appeared as a competent and skilful politician, a great parliamentary leader, a brilliant tactician, who created – in France – the technique of managing assemblies. For a year, he successfully defended before the Convention, which did not like him, a government which often was divided.[78]

On the other hand, Richet argued that the mean traits of his character were factors aiding his success and popularity: he was prone to personal attacks, to suspicion, to denunciation, to low intrigues. And eventually, in the spring of 1794, Robespierre, like Saint-Just, was carried away towards Utopia. Having to face economic realities and the materialism of the bourgeoisie, which they hated, they resorted to *fuite en avant*, to bloody and utopian solutions: dictatorship, the Great Terror, the cult of the Supreme Being. Consequently, Thermidor was only a return to reality, or, as Furet wrote later, the victory of civil society over a political mirage – judgements which provoked loud protests, like the conclusion that Robespierre had 'dishonoured terror and virtue together'.[79]

Years elapsed and, in 1978, François Furet produced a new Robespierre – quite different from the one by Richet. First, he laid down that the psychology of Robespierre had nothing to do with his historical rôle and does not explain anything. His private virtues, his spartan life, his loving – or cruel – temper were of no importance. Furthermore, unlike Mirabeau, whose career was not worthy of his genius, Robespierre had a fate which was disproportionate to his talents: he had the strange privilege to incarnate the Revolution, to be the Revolution in power. He was the only leader to voice the pure revolutionary ideology, and to use his mastery of communication as an instrument to conquer and retain power. The revolutionary discourse was a Manichaean discourse of plot and suspicion, of aristocrats and people, of traitors and patriots; and

[76] Furet and Richet, *Révolution française*, pp. 10, 203–5, 233. The dictatorship of the Year II was not a model for all revolutions, but the contingent and exceptional product of 'circumstances'; organised terror was an expedient to prevent the new massacres of which the *sans-culottes* dreamed. So, at this stage, revisionism adopted the 'theory of circumstances', which Furet subsequently repudiated.

[77] On the earlier period, it is said that the significance of Robespierre's opposition to war in 1792 has been much overestimated. *Ibid.*, pp. 129, 150.

[78] *Ibid.*, pp. 208, 221–3.

[79] *Ibid.*, pp. 222, 247–8, 254, 453; Furet, *Penser la Révolution française*, pp. 98, 116–18, 123; Bronislaw Baczko, 'Robespierre-roi ou comment sortir de la Terreur', *Le Débat* 39 (1986), 115–16 (on the pathology of terrorist imagination).

Robespierre, who believed everything he said and whose genius was Manichaean, spoke it better than anyone else. That is why he rose to supreme power: to him people were either good or wicked, patriots or traitors.[80]

While recognising that the Manichaean preaching of Robespierre filled up the prisons and fed the guillotine, Furet concluded that he was an immortal figure, because the Revolution spoke through his mouth its most tragic and its purest discourse.[81]

Furet thus stressed the connection between the Terror and revolutionary ideology; this ran counter to the 'theory of circumstances', which he vigorously criticised in his later work. 'The truth is that the Terror is part and parcel of revolutionary ideology' and that it largely created the so-called circumstances (especially foreign war). As a dialectical mechanism of people and plot, the Terror was in position in the early summer of 1789, and the first terrorist acts took place at that time. 'There is no difference of nature', wrote Furet, '... between the murders of Foulon and Bertier and the massacres of September 1792.' Moreover, the terrorist mentality was not confined to the *sans-culottes*: by 1793, 'the discourse of the Terror was on the lips of almost all revolutionary leaders' and, by the end of the year, it gave up the argument of circumstances and of the war for something deeper. Terror became an instrument of regeneration and Robespierre theorised it into the government of virtue and identified it with the Revolution.[82]

From this point of view, the Robespierrist Terror was much more than a parenthesis in the history of the French Revolution. In fact, Furet stressed the unity of the Revolution, rather than the contrast between the two revolutions, of '89 and of '92–3. 'It is correct that there is no break between the two revolutions ... From the meeting of the Estates General to the dictatorship of the Committee of Public Safety, the same dynamics are at work. They are in position as early as '89, though not yet dominating.' That '93 logically derived from '89 had hitherto only been maintained by counter-revolutionaries. This was revisionism indeed. On the other hand, Furet denied that the French Revolution was the progenitor of modern totalitarianism, and he did not see much in common between the French and the Russian revolutions – except some similarity between the Jacobin and the Bolshevik terrors.[83]

80 Furet, *Penser la Révolution française*, pp. 94–6, 98–102, 109–15, 264, 279.

81 *Ibid.*, pp. 101–14.

82 *Ibid.*, pp. 90–1, 103–7, 113–15, 202; Furet, 'Terreur', pp. 156, 165–9.
The thinking of Furet on these matters did not change significantly between 1978 and 1988. See also his article in *L'Express*, 7–13 July 1989, pp. 57–64, and his interview, 'Après Robespierre, Staline ...', *L'Histoire* 177 (1994), 50–3.

83 Furet, *Penser la Révolution française*, p. 94; Furet, 'Terreur', p. 169. However, Furet

In the *Dictionnaire* of the Revolution, which was published in 1988 and edited by François Furet and Mona Ozouf, the essay on Robespierre was by Patrice Gueniffey; it fits with Furet's view of the Terror.[84]

There was in Robespierre a complete absence of private passions and of private life; he was a 'pure' citizen, who devoted all of himself to the Revolution. Though he brought the revolutionary ideological discourse to its perfection, he had no coherent or original ideology, especially on social questions (and he did not know the real people). His only aim was the conquest of power and ideas had to yield to tactical imperatives. He was an opportunist of genius and most skilful in parliamentary tactics – as Michelet and Richet had observed – and manipulation.

Robespierre had early understood – and it was a natural intuition – that the dynamics of the Revolution could not be stopped. He turned therefore to the people and gained political weight by becoming judge, censor, watchful sentinel. Speaking a discourse of sermonising inquisition, of systematic, permanent, universal suspicion and denunciation, he reigned by the spoken word and terrorised his opponents, well before terror had become the order of the day.

In power, Robespierre succeeded where his predecessors had failed: he stabilised the Revolution, but not to terminate it, as he wanted to regenerate the people, which meant more and more proscriptions. Gueniffey stated that Robespierre played a crucial rôle in the Terror, even though at the end he had lost control over it. He also stressed the close connection between the feast of the Supreme Being and the law of 22 Prairial: the new religion gave the Terror a moral foundation and an additional legitimacy. In a later article (1994), Gueniffey developed these views, under the title 'The itinerary of a tyrant'. The secret of Robespierre's ascendancy lay not in his character, but in his complete personal investment in politics, in his understanding that the way to power was to let himself be carried away by the revolutionary torrent. His fall meant the resurrection of *la société réelle*.[85]

In such portraits, Robespierre appears as soulless, ambitious, Machiavellian, suspicious and blood-stained – a return to the view of most nineteenth-century historians. Moreover, in a recent synthesis on the

conceded that the Terror had some of its roots 'in an egalitarian fanaticism, born from an unegalitarian pathology of the old society ... In the genesis of the bloody dictatorship of the Year II, the ancien régime and the Revolution had cumulative effects.'

[84] Patrice Gueniffey, 'Robespierre', in Furet and Ozouf, *Dictionnaire*, pp. 318–33. See also Ran Halévi, 'Feuillants', in *ibid.*, pp. 366–8, on Robespierre's skill in manipulation in 1791.

[85] P. Gueniffey, 'Itinéraire d'un tyran', *L'Histoire* 177 (1994), 36–47.

Revolution, Jean Meyer has stressed that, although the personality of Robespierre remains mysterious, mistrust was its basic trait. The more cruelly the Revolution behaved, the sooner virtue would triumph, and the nearer a radiant future for the people would be. Indeed, Meyer considers that Robespierre appealed to murder, to massacre, to genocide, 'in the strictest meaning that the Nuremberg trials gave to the ... [last] word'.[86]

The revisionist school has won a wide audience, thanks to the talent of its leaders, to friendly coverage by the media and to favourable circumstances, such as the collapse of the Soviet Union and the decline of communism in France. And, of course, it offered something new and stimulating in lieu of an old and worn-out refrain.

However, the Jacobin-Marxists have not given up. The work of Furet and Richet has been fiercely attacked by Claude Mazauric, who is both a history professor and a member of the central committee of the communist party. His was a typically Stalinist performance, which accused the two authors, *inter alia*, of having betrayed their country.[87]

Later on, Michel Vovelle, Soboul's successor at the Sorbonne, returned to the fray, taking advantage of the task the socialist government had given him – responsibility for the bicentenary from the *scientifique* point of view.[88] His aim has been to isolate Furet's group, and to reconstruct a sort of Popular Front of left-wing historians (he went as far as pretending that Aulard and the Jacobin school had been in broad agreement!). His tactic was to attack violently the 'counter-revolutionary historians', and notably Pierre Chaunu, who had passionately condemned the atrocities which were perpetrated by republican troops during the repression in the Vendée. Then, Vovelle accused Furet of having opened the breach into which extreme right-wing writers, such as Chaunu, who hate the Revolution, rushed.[89]

86 A. Corvisier, J. Meyer and J.-P. Poussou, *La Révolution française*, 2 vols. (Paris, 1991), vol. II, pp. 827–33.

87 See Claude Mazauric, *Sur la Révolution française* (Paris, 1970), which developed a review of Furet and Richet, *Révolution française*, 'Réflexions sur une nouvelle conception de la Révolution française', *AHRF* 39 (1967), 339–60. Response in Furet, *Penser la Révolution française*, pp. 123, 153–4. The Jacobin cause then suffered a blow, when Soboul was caught red-handed plagiarising the very people – Furet and Richet – he was abusing. See Denis Richet and Albert Soboul, 'Correspondance', *Annales ESC* 25 (1970), 1494–6; anon., 'Comment Albert Soboul écrit l'histoire', *Contrepoint* 5 (1971), 105–18.

88 Remark made by Marcel Gauchet (who is the editor of *Le Débat*) at the colloquium *Actualité de la Révolution française*, Débat du samedi 5 décembre 1987, sous la présidence de Laurent Fabius, former Socialist Prime Minister (Paris, n.d.), p. 5.

89 Michel Vovelle, 'L'historiographie de la Révolution française à la veille du bicentenaire', *Estudos Avançados* 1 (1987), 60–72, especially 62–6, 71–2, and 'Un siècle d'historiographie révolutionnaire (1880–1887)', in Michel Vovelle (ed.), *L'état de la France*

As for Robespierre, Vovelle continues to see him as the representative of the Montagnard bourgeoisie, who understood that only union with the popular forces would make the Revolution victorious. Hence, the basically bourgeois revolution reached a democratic and anticipatory peak during the Year II, because of the Terror, for which Vovelle is an ardent apologist.[90]

In any case, the *Vulgate* remains influential, partly through sheer *vis inertiae*. Many university and school teachers have been brought up on it and they go on teaching it. Most textbooks – especially those for schools – remain permeated with it.[91]

It also was the official doctrine of the French Socialist régime. During a ceremony at the Sorbonne in January 1988 to honour the *regretté* Robert Maxwell, President Mitterrand stated that he inclined towards Clemenceau's idea of the Revolution as a block, and that, anyhow, those who had criticised the Revolution had proved to be enemies of democracy and should be treated as such. Jean Poperen, who was in turn a communist students' leader, a history teacher and lecturer, and eventually a Socialist minister, is the author of writings on Robespierre which are ultra-Stalinist.[92] In 1986, Max Gallo, historian, novelist and politician – he had been a minister at the beginning of Mitterrand's rule – published an 'Open letter to Maximilien Robespierre'. This is a repulsive tract, because it insults several scholars, but it is revealing of recent attitudes on the left.[93]

Gallo says little about Robespierre: chiefly that, despite his shortcomings, his meanness and his crimes (*sic*), Gallo, like Jaurès, would go and sit beside him at the Jacobins. Most of the pamphlet is made up of attacks on Furet – in a rather covert way – and on Chaunu and others on

pendant la Révolution 1789–1799 (Paris, 1988), pp. 543–7. See also 'La Révolution française', *Magazine littéraire*, p. 75, and *Actualité de la Révolution française*, pp. 1–4. Vovelle maintains that the revisionist school has now lost its *élan*, while the Jacobin school (as he calls it) is thriving again.

90 See, e.g., 'La Révolution française', *Magazine littéraire*, p. 77.

91 The lasting survival of Robespierrism in the French teaching profession was confirmed by an opinion poll of 300 secondary school teachers (*L'Express*, 7–13 July 1989, pp. 68–70): 68 per cent of them said that they felt sympathy for Robespierre (admittedly, Sieyès and Danton achieved 72 per cent) and 64 per cent considered that his rôle during the Revolution had been positive. Moreover, 61 per cent of those polled thought that the Terror was the consequence of attacks on the Revolution by its foreign and domestic enemies – i.e. they accepted the 'theory of circumstances'. Soboul appeared to them the greatest historian of the Revolution.

92 Jean Poperen, *Robespierre. Textes choisis* (Paris, 1958); see pp. 22, 24–6, 32–3, 39–40, 42–4.

93 Max Gallo, *Lettre ouverte à Maximilien Robespierre sur les nouveaux muscadins* (Paris, 1986), p. 11–3, 24–6, 85.

the right – with undiluted venom.[94] However, Gallo recognises that the mediocre Jacobin-Bolshevik *Vulgate* has collapsed.[95] Moreover – and this is the most important – he disclaims any nostalgia for a return to the guillotine, to the Terror or to any kind of massacres. He proclaims that civil peace must be preserved at any cost, that human life is sacred, that any death for which men are responsible is a scandal.[96] This is very illuminating about the climate of cold civil war which prevailed in France in the 1980s: was there any other Western democracy in which a politician would have felt that such disclaimers were necessary?[97] But this pamphlet probably also bears testimony to the demise of the cult of Robespierre among the French left (communists excepted). One might also mention that Régis Debray, a former companion of Che Guevara, and later a close friend and adviser of Mitterrand, has praised Gallo's work as tonic and regretted that Robespierre was too much seen, by a masochist left, through the eyes of Solzhenitsyn. He concluded, none the less, that he did not want to 'excuse what is inexcusable, the infernal columns [in the Vendée], the *septembriseurs*'.[98]

The eschatological dream of purificatory massacre, which, for a long time, had made many on the French left into potential *septembriseurs*, has evaporated (after all, none of the historians mentioned, but one, had been pleased with the 'Grande Terreur de Messidor'). The emphasis, during the bicentenary, was more on the Declaration of the Rights of Man than on the guillotine, and Robespierre was not much mentioned. A boiled-down, sanitised view of the Revolution prevailed.

As for the impression which the debates among historians and politicians have made upon the French public, one can use some opinion polls which were carried out in 1989 to estimate it. One of them had a question about the revolutionary leaders, asking whether they were 'sympathiques' or 'antipathiques'. Opinions on Robespierre were

94 *Ibid.*, pp. 18–9, 23, 34–5, 41, 49, 58, 67, 83, 92, 139. Gallo demanded that anti-revolutionary historians be expelled from French universities.

95 At times, however, Gallo regrets and defends it, as preferable to the revisionist neo-*Vulgate*: *ibid.*, pp. 32, 43, 74, 78.

96 *Ibid.*, pp. 14, 109, 138, 165–6.

97 In October 1981, during the conference of the socialist party in Valence (after Mitterrand's election), Paul Quilès (who later became a minister) asked for more heads to roll and argued for not repeating Robespierre's mistake on 8 Thermidor – being too lenient to, and vague about, his enemies. This statement caused some emotion; the official explanation was that it was not to be taken literally and that Quilès had demanded only the dismissal of top civil servants who had right-wing opinions. This incident is proof of the power which the Robespierrist myth had retained.

98 *Actualité de la Révolution française*, pp. 13–16, 18.

split: 32 per cent found him 'sympathique', 34 per cent 'antipathique', 34 per cent had no opinion. Of communist supporters, 58 per cent were pro-Robespierre, but only 35 per cent of socialist supporters were. Mirabeau, Danton and Carnot obtained almost the same percentage of favourable votes as Robespierre; only Lafayette and Bonaparte received over 50 per cent.[99]

So Robespierre cannot be considered a popular figure. Unlike Danton, he has neither a street named after him nor a monument in Paris, only a Métro station in the suburb of Montreuil since 1936, thanks to its communist city council.[100] As Gallo and Alice Gérard recognise, his name continues to frighten and he remains associated with the Terror and the guillotine (both in France and abroad). An opinion poll of January 1988 showed that 68 per cent of the persons questioned thought that the executions during the French Revolution were 'an abomination', only 19 per cent saw them as necessary, and 13 per cent had no opinion. However, 41 per cent of communists were in favour of the executions and 46 per cent were against – as were 66 per cent of socialists.[101] The French people may actually be less violent and fond of massacres than is often thought.

V

This essay may be judged as too harsh on the Jacobin school of historians, but the author's grievance against them is that they blackened the French Revolution by assimilating it to the Bolshevik revolution. Fortunately, their view was destroyed by the collapse of communism and of the Soviet Union. Indeed, the revolutions of 1989 gave a new legitimacy to that of 1789 – and in the very year of the bicentenary! The French Revolution again appears as a revolution of liberty. It is also remarkable that, in 1994, one could celebrate the two liberations France has enjoyed: the liberation *tout court*, fifty years ago, in June–August 1944, thanks to Britain and the USA, and also the forgotten liberation

[99] *Figaro-Magazine*, 23 January 1988, pp. 63–4. See also *ibid.*, 10 December 1988, for another poll which demonstrated the ignorance of French people: 25 per cent of persons polled thought that Robespierre was a Girondin, only 21 per cent knew him to be a Montagnard, and 45 per cent had no opinion.

[100] It is, however, significant that the class of 1968 of the Ecole Nationale d'Administration took the name of 'Robespierre'. In fact, many top French civil servants support the socialist party. See Gérard, *Révolution*, pp. 129–31.

[101] *Figaro-Magazine*, 23 January 1988, p. 63. This magazine is very right-wing, but the poll was done by a serious institute, SOFRES.

of Thermidor Year II, two hundred years earlier.[102] It is a pity that the latter was not properly commemorated.[103]

102 In one of the last chats I had with the late Richard Cobb, I asked him about the reactions to the fall of Robespierre in the provinces and the armies. 'Mais c'était une libération . . .', was his immediate answer.

103 Actually, there was a commemoration on 28 July 1994, but by a group of Robespierrists, under the leadership of one Maximilien Cuttoli, who gathered on the site of Robespierre's execution. *L'Humanité*, the communist party daily, hailed Robespierre as a great figure in the 'progressive history of France'. Cf. the article by Charles Bremner in *The Times*, 29 July 1994, p. 10.

Index